Why Americans Don't Join the Party

Why Americans Don't
Join the Party

RACE, IMMIGRATION, AND THE FAILURE (OF POLITICAL PARTIES) TO ENGAGE THE ELECTORATE

Zoltan L. Hajnal
Taeku Lee

PRINCETON UNIVERSITY PRESS
PRINCETON AND OXFORD

Published by Princeton University Press, 41 William Street, Princeton, New Jersey 08540
In the United Kingdom: Princeton University Press, 6 Oxford Street, Woodstock,
Oxfordshire OX20 1TW

press.princeton.edu

Jacket art: *We March Today We Vote Tomorrow.* Photograph by Alex Thamer

Library of Congress Cataloging-in-Publication Data

Hajnal, Zoltan, 1968–
    Why Americans don't join the party : race, immigration, and the failure (of political
parties) to engage the electorate / Zoltan L. Hajnal, Taeku Lee.
        p. cm.
    Includes bibliographical references and index.
    ISBN 978-0-691-14878-6 (hardcover : alk. paper) — ISBN 978-0-691-14879-3 (pbk. :
alk. paper)   1. Identity politics—United States.   2. Allegiance—United States.
3. Political alienation—United States.   4. Democratic Party (U.S.)—Membership.
5. Republican Party (U.S. : 1854–)—Membership.   6. African Americans—
Politics and government.   7. United States—Emigration and immigration—Political
aspects.   I. Lee, Taeku.   II. Title.
    JK1764.H34 2011
    324.273011—dc22   2010029112

British Library Cataloging-in-Publication Data is available

This book has been composed in Sabon

Printed on acid-free paper. ∞

Printed in the United States of America

10 9 8 7 6 5 4 3 2 1

Contents

Figures and Tables

Acknowledgments

THIS IS A book about relationships. It is about the ties that Americans of diverse racial and ethnic colors have, or fail to have, to the Democratic Party and the Republican Party. For some, the relationship is a lifelong bond, an arranged political marriage forged out of the class position or ascriptive identities one is born into and the formative experiences of preadult socialization. For others, it is a relationship of abnegation and alienation, a bittersweet solitude rendered by disenchantment, frustration, and iconoclasm. And for yet others, the relationship is embryonic, a liminal state that passes through stages of uncertainty, belonging, and neglect. These divergent attachments are moored by our sense of who we are (identity), what believe in (ideology), and how we know (information).

The book is also about the relationship that the two of us have had with each other and with this project. That relationship began with an animated conversation over breakfast at the Omni Shoreham Hotel in Washington, DC, at the annual meeting of the American Political Science Association many, many moons ago (which, in frightfully clear terms, translates to 10 years, or 121 moons). Between gulps of hot coffee and noshes of toast and jam, we agreed that this project was inherently interesting and potentially important. In passing, we probably also noted the many theoretical roadblocks and empirical thickets that stood between our fledgling ideas and a completed and compelling book. Judging by the number of years it took to complete, it is clear that we underestimated the level of hoe work and sheer lunacy required to get this far. Along the way, however, we occasionally found time to set our shovels aside, savor moments of discovery, and delight in our deepening friendship.

No relationship (no matter how soaring or sordid) survives without sustaining social and pecuniary resources. Ours is no exception. Our family, friends, colleagues, and supporting institutions have contributed enormously to this undertaking. We benefited from conversations (real and virtual) with colleagues around the country who gave generously of their time while asking for nothing in return. In particular, we are grateful to (in alphabetical order) Larry Bobo, Cathy Cohen, Michael Dawson, Paul Frymer, Claudine Gay, Donald Green, Susan Herbst, Vincent Hutchings, Michael Jones-Correa, Jane Junn, Don Kinder, Eric Oliver, Christopher Parker, Karthick Ramakrishnan, Ricardo Ramírez, Mark Sawyer, David Sears, Jessica Trounstine, Nicholas Valentino, and Janelle Wong, as well as anonymous reviewers for Princeton University Press and the University of Chicago Press, for their insightful comments, sage advice, and timely nudges.

We also had the privilege of presenting this project to audiences at several of the nation's best universities. Feedback (negative and positive) from participants at the Nation of Immigrants conference at the University of California, Berkeley, and the Third Minnesota Symposium on Political Psychology were instrumental in the early stages of this project. Our ideas and arguments got much needed spit and polish from conference, colloquium, and seminar participants at the University of Chicago, UCLA, UCSD, and the audience members and fellow panelists at several annual meetings of the Midwest Political Science Association and the American Political Science Association. There is, without question, a degree of pomp and circumstance involved in these public forums for the presentation of scholarly work, but in our case at least, also a measure of genuine interchange and illumination.

Equally critical to a long-lived project such as this one are relationships built on monetary sustenance and institutional support. We benefited from the generosity of the Russell Sage Foundation; the Center for the Study of Democratic Politics at Princeton University; the Center for Comparative Immigration Studies at the University of California, San Diego; and the Institute for Governmental Studies and the Earl Warren Institute on Race, Ethnicity, and Diversity at the University of California, Berkeley. We thank Aixa Cintron-Velez at the Russell Sage Foundation for support that sustained our efforts through most of one critical summer of this project. Larry Bartels's center at Princeton provided Hajnal with a one-year fellowship, an unparalleled intellectual environment, time off from teaching, and friendly support. Wayne Cornelius and the Center for Comparative Immigration Studies provided Hajnal with another great home and more helpful comments from smart colleagues. Bruce Cain and Jack Citrin, at the Institute for Government Studies, and Maria Blanco and Christopher Edley, at the Warren Institute, were instrumental in providing research support and in creating a thriving scholarly community for research on race and immigration at Berkeley for Taeku Lee.

The University of California, Berkeley, and the University of California, San Diego, also provided nurturing, sustaining professional homes for this project. At UCSD, Marisa Abrajano, Amy Bridges, Gary Jacobson, Thad Kousser, and Jessica Trounstine all offered wise counsel and, even more important, their friendship. At Berkeley, Wendy Brown, Pradeep Chhibber, Jack Citrin, Lisa García Bedolla, Laura Stoker, and Rob van Houweling were especially pivotal in their support and persuasive in their inputs on the project; Nicole Fox, Loan Le, Ayn Lowry, Michael Murakami, Tatishe Nteta, and Chip Reese gave the project a hand up through their expert research and editorial assistance. A special shout-out goes to Pepper Culpepper, Archon Fung, and Sanjeev Khagram, Taeku's band of brothers from his previous home base at Harvard's Kennedy School of Government. We would also be remiss not to note that both Berkeley and UCSD had the foresight (read: guilelessness) to offer us gainful employment (eventually, with tenure, even!), entrust us with the paramount work of teaching California's future leaders and training its future scholars, and secure for us unmatched amenities for free and critical inquiry. These institutions are capstones in California's public education system, a national treasure that is imperiled by current political and economic circumstances. They demand our gratitude, pride, and collective struggle for their continued flourishing.

Princeton University Press has been a joy to work with. We owe a special debt to Chuck Myers, who steered this hulking manuscript through with a skillful and steady hand. His dexterous guidance ultimately enabled us to craft a much finer product than would otherwise have been possible. Our efficient, capable, and friendly production editor, Sara Lerner, made sure that the final months of our work on this book progressed far more expeditiously than the first nine and a half years.

The relationships that matter vitally to us and to our work extend far and beyond the ivied walls (or, in the case of Berkeley and UCSD, the eucalyptus shades) of academia. Our progress in this project and our overall well-being were aided in no small part by close friends who provided critical moral support and helped us navigate the tricky (sometimes treacherous) tides of academia with integrity and a twinkle. Zoli thanks Amy, Paul, Chris, Donn, Tim, and Ethan. Taeku thanks Dong, Ed, Fred, John, and Lawland. True friends and companions, all.

We reserve our final words and deepest gratitude for the most cherished relationships in our lives. Our families truly give us purpose. This book is dedicated to them, especially to the three sprouts who carry on our family traditions: Lina Hajnal, Ella Lee, and Linus Lee.

To Catherine, my role model and big sister extraordinaire: I hope one day to have your courage and your noble convictions. To my parents, Vivian and Zoltan: You have given more than a child could ever hope for. Your love, patience, encouragement, and friendship have been omnipresent and have provided a foundation of happiness and morality that will forever guide my life. To my wife, Barbara Walter: You mean everything to me. You are my best friend. You are my soul mate. You are the love of my life. Your smile is infectious, your jokes are mischievous, and your presence is exhilarating. Without you, life would be dull gray. Finally, to my daughter, Lina: I am not sure how or if you helped me write this book. Typically, you pulled me away from work. But less work has meant more joy. It has been an incredible thrill to be a part of your life and to watch you grow up into the amazing person that you are. You are kind, you are cool, you are fun, you are beautiful, and you are giving. I am incredibly proud to call you my daughter.

To my parents, Dong Mock and June Oak: You are my roots and my trunk, grown from loam filled with duty, decency, and determination and watered with love, immeasurable and unconditional. I owe a life's debt and pledge to repay it forward in a thousand and one ways, big and small. To my siblings, Jungku and Jinku: Thanks for putting up with my fumbling, bumbling salad days; for leading by example; for pressuring me (gently, firmly) to follow and keep reaching just beyond my grasp; for the shoulder to lean on when I needed it. To my life force, better whole, and partner in crime, Shirley: You are the air I breathe, the water I drink, and spirit I inhabit. Life with you is ever sweet, savory, and spicy. I am still, and will always be, smitten. Finally, to my two spunky wizards and BFFs, Ella Jaeyoung and Linus Jaejun Lee: You have taught me to love, learn, and laugh in wholly unexpected, delightful ways. May the Force be with you both. Always.

Why Americans Don't Join the Party

CHAPTER 1

Introduction

Tweedledum and Tweedledee
Agreed to have a battle;
For Tweedledum said Tweedledee
Had spoiled his nice new rattle.

Just then flew down a monstrous crow,
As black as a tar-barrel!
Which frightened both the heroes so,
They quite forgot their quarrel.

—Lewis Carroll

TUESDAY, NOVEMBER 4, 2008: millions of Americans participate in the quadrennial political ritual of electing a president. The day was, in the elements, unexceptional. The Northwest endured wet and windy weather, a hard rain fell over Southern California, and light precipitation descended on the Northeast. Yet the sun shone in the heart of the country, with record-warm fall temperatures in the seventies, as Chicagoans reveled boisterously on a historic day. The estimated 131 million voters who constituted the American electorate that day had elected the first American of African heritage to the highest office in the land. A body politic that had, at the nation's founding, consented to counting African Americans in fractions for purposes of allocating political offices without any rights of representation; that had witnessed the effective dismantlement of the African American franchise in the Jim Crow South, following the hard-earned progress of Reconstruction and the Fourteenth and Fifteenth Amendments; that had subsequently gloried in the effective reinstatement of the African American franchise, only to suffer through the continued deployment of the "race card" in electioneering, had done what few would have thought imaginable even a year earlier.

Spokespersons across many divides—partisan, ideological, racial—came together to commemorate and cherish the moment. President-elect Obama noted in his acceptance speech, "It's been a long time coming, but tonight, because of what we did on this date in this election at this defining moment, change has come to America." His foe during the election, Republican Senator John McCain, also recognized that "this is a historic election . . . we have come a long way from the injustices that once stained our nation's reputation." Similarly, in the editorial pages of the *Los Angeles Times* the following Wednesday, two African Americans who were usually at ideological loggerheads came to a rapprochement on the significance of the 2008 election. The progressive Michael Eric Dyson declared Obama's ascendancy a "quantum leap of racial progress. . . . Today is a benchmark that helps to fulfill—and rescue—America's democratic reputation" (Dyson 2008). Even the conservative Shelby Steele, while registering a decidedly more sober and skeptical tone, asked aloud, "Does his victory mean that America is now officially beyond racism? . . . Doesn't a black in the Oval Office put the lie to both black inferiority and white racism?"

This rosy blush of "postracial" expectations quickly wilted under the glare of finer facts about of the 2008 election. Pollsters and the punditry alike were initially flush with predictions of a record turnout, bolstered by a mobilized youth vote and a decided willingness on the part of white voters to defy the "Bradley effect" and aver their support for a black president. Yet a deeper dig into the data reveals a decidedly racial cast to the 2008 election outcome. Of the 5 million new voters in 2008 (compared with the election tallies of 2004), an estimated 2 million were African American voters, another 2 million Latino ones, and 600,000 Asian American. According to the Current Population Survey, the number of non-Hispanic white voters remained unchanged between 2004 and 2008 (U.S. Census Bureau, July 20, 2009). Moreover, while the voting rate of eighteen- to twenty-four-year-olds increased from 47 percent in 2004 to 49 percent in 2008, this increase was highest among African American youth.

Perhaps more pointedly, Obama did not emerge victorious because he won over white America. In the end, a clear majority—57 percent—of all white voters opposed his candidacy. To put a finer point on it, the first ripples of the flood of scholarly studies on the 2008 election have emphatically found continued evidence of racial bias in whites' electoral preferences (see, e.g., Jackman and Vavreck 2009; Pasek et al. 2009; Tesler and Sears 2010). Rather, Obama won in large part because the African Americans, Latinos, and Asian Americans who had expanded the voter rolls had supported his candidacy in overwhelming numbers. Quite apart from symbolizing our collective journey into a postracial era, the 2008 election appears to reinforce the realpolitik of the twin influences of an increasingly diverse electorate and a persistent racial divide in the hearts and minds of American voters.

The growing clout of racial-minority voters is indeed impressive. Less than fifty years ago, white voters made up 95 percent of the active electorate.[1] One could argue that white voters operatively controlled the outcome of any national context and that in these electoral contexts, it mattered little, practically, whom minorities favored. By the time of the Obama-McCain contest, the population of whites had declined to 74 percent of the electorate. Thus, while whites may still constitute an imposing majority of voting Americans, their dominance has greatly diminished. Ever-larger numbers of black, Hispanic, and Asian American voters are filling the void and promise to continue doing so into the future.

The racial divide in the 2008 vote is equally impressive. Setting aside both public and privately viewed sentiments that Obama enjoyed his electoral success because, as Senate Majority Leader Harry Reid indiscreetly put it, he was a "light-skinned" candidate of African American descent with "no Negro dialect," the evidence of racial dissensus even in these allegedly best of circumstances is widespread. On one side, voters from the three largest racial and ethnic minority groups strongly favored Obama. He won 95 percent of the black vote, 67 percent of the Latino vote, and 62 percent of the Asian American vote.[2] On the other side, the clear majority of white voters favored McCain. Only 43 percent of white voters chose to support the Democratic nominee. Moreover, the first wave of studies on the 2008 election find little change in whites' racial-policy preferences compared with the 1988 election, when the Reverend Jesse Jackson made an unsuccessful but legitimate run for the Democratic nomination for president and little change in the role of racial resentment in whites' vote choices between 1988 and 2008 (Tesler and Sears, 2010). Despite talk of a postracial politics, the 2008 contest was as racially divided as any election in American presidential history.

To boot, there is little chance that this decidedly racial cast to American electoral politics will diminish in future contests. If anything, the continued change in the demographics of the U.S. voting population suggests that the significance of racial diversity and division will become only more important in the future. With whites predicted to lose their majority status in this nation somewhere near the middle part of this century, the balance of racial power will continue to shift and the outcomes of American democracy will increasingly hinge on the preferences and actions of racial minorities.

This has tremendous implications for anyone involved or interested in American politics, and it has more than obvious import for the nation's two major political parties, the Democrats and the Republicans. Put sim-

---

[1] This is the proportion of all voters in the 1960 presidential election who identified as white (based on the American National Election Studies).

[2] All figures are derived from CNN exit polls.

ply, the future success of both parties depends in no small measure on winning over this relatively new racial and ethnic minority electorate. The burden on the Republican Party is clearly more onerous at this point. With McCain garnering almost all of his support from white Americans—90 percent of all his votes in the general election came from white voters—and with the proportion of white Americans dwindling, the Republican Party will have to try to make inroads into the minority population. An electoral renaissance of the Republican Party is unlikely to present itself without a successful shift in the partisan proclivities of minority voters and without motivating greater participation among those voters of color who are already sympathetic to the Republican cause.

This may seem like a tall order. Decades of initiatives by the Democratic Party in support of the civil rights movement and other causes that are important to the African American community have created a widely held perception that the Democratic Party is the party of minority interests (Carmines and Stimson 1989). Obama's ascendancy to the presidency and his tacit role as leader of the Democratic Party could serve to further solidify a Democratic majority among the minority electorate.[3] Despite the gesture of nominating Michael Steele as the chair of the Republican National Committee in 2009, recent immigrant bashing by certain segments of the Republican leadership and past efforts by Republican strategists to use racialized campaigns to generate a winning white majority also do little to portend large-scale minority gains for the Republican Party in the near future (Edsall and Edsall 1992).

But one of the main storylines of this book is that the role of African Americans, Latinos, and Asian Americans in this partisan competition is far from predetermined. Despite the fact that these communities of color voted overwhelmingly for Obama in the 2008 presidential contest, the single most important finding in our research is that the bulk of this segment of the electorate remains uncertain about its place in the partisan landscape of the nation. The best data we have indicate that the clear majority of immigrant-based groups such as Latinos and Asian Americans are not affiliated with either of the two major parties. Among Latinos in the 2006 Latino National Survey, only 44 percent of respondents identified as either Republican or Democratic. In the 2008 National Asian American survey, that figure was an almost identical 46 percent. Even among the most steadfastly Democratic electorate in America—the African American community—the 2004 American National Election Studies (ANES) found that 38 percent chose not to identify with a major

---

[3] It is, however, important to note that there are already signs of discontent because of the reluctance of President Obama and the Democratic Party to pursue comprehensive immigration reform or to address racial inequality in a significant way.

party, and about 40 percent will not label themselves as Democrats (even if they vote for a Democratic candidate for political office).[4] In fact, even among whites in the 2004 ANES, fully 39 percent chose not to identify as either Republican or Democrat.

Critically, among Latinos and Asian Americans, the bulk of those who reject partisan affiliation do not label themselves as Independents—a population that can, at times, conceal significant partisan ties. Instead, for both the Latino and Asian American population, the single largest group is what we call *nonidentifiers*, individuals who refuse to place themselves on the party-identification scale and who instead offer responses such as "don't know," "no preference," or "none of the above." These previously unrecognized nonidentifiers represent some 38 percent of the Latino population and another 36 percent of the Asian American population. Moreover, while the lack of a partisan affiliation is most pronounced within immigrant-based groups, it occurs within almost all segments of the public.

Another important plotline in this racial and partisan equation is that there is every reason to believe that this diverse, unaligned population can be mobilized and integrated into one of the two major parties. The racial and ethnic minority population, as we will see, is far from homogeneous in its political interests, social identities, and life experiences. Accompanying the nation's demographic diversity is a multiplicity of core issue concerns and ideological orientations, a bricolage of salient social identities, and a wide range of experience with and knowledge about American democracy. This will make targeting this diverse population complex and will probably require a multipronged approach. But it will also create openings for both parties. Republicans, for example, can point to the moral conservatism of many Latinos and Asian Americans as an avenue for partisan incorporation. Likewise, Democrats can point to minorities' widespread experiences with racial discrimination as an issue to exploit. Moreover, the evidence suggests that once a party touches on the right message, mobilization becomes possible. Experimental research indicates that contact to encourage voter participation does work and that it can be effective with members of the minority population (Ramírez and Wong 2006). Broader historical patterns also imply that if the motivation is strong enough, members of the minority population will become energized and involved in the partisan fray. In response to Proposition 187, an anti–illegal immigrant initiative that was pushed by a Republican gover-

---

[4] The reasons for equating African Americans with Democratic Party identification are clearer when partisanship is limited to the choice between identifying as a Democrat or a Republican. In the 2004 ANES, the proportion of African American Democrats exceeds that of African American Republicans by a ratio of roughly 38 to 1 (60 percent to 1.6 percent).

nor in the 1990s, naturalization rates, voter turnout, and identification with the Democratic Party increased substantially among Latinos in California (Bowler et al. 2006; Pantoja et al. 2001). The spontaneous mobilization of over three million immigrants in Los Angeles and other cities in support of immigrants' rights during the 2007 congressional debates on comprehensive immigration reform further attests to the potential of minority mobilization (Bada, Fox, and Selee 2006). The bottom line is that there is a real opportunity for both major parties. Party leaders and advocates need only act, and in response the growing number of unaligned immigrants and minorities could offer a critical electoral edge.

The focus of this book is this linkage of racial and partisan considerations that we have just outlined. Our main goal is to offer a more encompassing model of partisan choice, one that incorporates the diverse range of people and perspectives found in America today. We seek to explain why—precisely for reasons of racial and ethnic definition and immigrant experience—the pathways to partisanship or nonpartisanship vary among whites, African Americans, and immigration-based groups such as Latinos and Asian Americans. In the ensuing pages, we explain why an account of the attachments (or lack thereof) of racial and ethnic minorities and immigrants to the present-day political parties is important, why increased attention to nonpartisanship is warranted, and how the two are linked.

Is there a need for a new theory of partisanship? We maintain that the two dominant theories of partisanship—the Michigan School and the Downsian approach—do an excellent job of accounting for the partisan choices of the bulk of Americans whose views and experiences allow them to fit neatly along the spectrum of partisanship that defines the nation's politics. But we also believe that these two theories often fail to consider the unique experiences and concerns of different segments of our increasingly diverse public. The Michigan School, for example, contends that party identification is a strong psychological attachment that is developed early in life and largely inherited from one's parents through preadult socialization. But how can parental partisanship explain the party identification of immigrants whose parents have no obvious partisan connections in the American domain? The Downsian approach also neglects to incorporate some of the distinctive aspects of America's diverse democracy. According to the Downsian model, individuals attach to the party whose publicly declared positions on the main issues of the day come closest to their ideal point on a liberal-conservative scale. But what happens if one has little knowledge of those issues or if your core issue concerns are ignored by both parties? What are the likely partisan attachments of the Filipino who is altogether unfamiliar with the issue stances of either party? What of the African American whose main ideological motivation involves the debate between integration and black autonomy? What of the Puerto Rican who is committed to Puerto Rican statehood?

In providing a comprehensive theory of party identification, we seek to understand not only how Americans who fit neatly into the partisan structure choose an affiliation but also how other Americans whose interests, ideologies, and identities fit less well choose to align or not align with one of the two major parties. That is, we offer an encompassing account of the partisan attachments that Americans have (or lack) and show how the pathways and patterns of partisanship vary crucially by groups defined by race and immigrant origins.

In our theoretical account, we contend that the partisan significance of America's growing demographic diversity can be accounted for largely by three factors that have generally been overlooked in accounts of party identification: (1) disparity in levels of information across the electorate, (2) the salience of distinct social identities, and (3) divergence in core issue concerns and ideological orientations. Thus, our story, which we detail in the coming pages, is one of the central role of information, identity, and ideology in shaping party identification, and the variation in the dynamic interplay of these three factors between whites, African Americans, and immigration-based groups such as Latinos and Asian Americans. We hope that our account will not only provide a greater understanding of the large numbers of unaligned partisan misfits who characterize America's increasingly diverse electorate but also offer both incentives and strategies to incorporate this population.

America's Racial Transformation

To stress the importance of understanding how patterns of partisanship vary by race and immigrant origins, we need to go back roughly four decades in time. The year 1965 is often thought of as a defining moment in our nation's history of racial politics. What defines this moment for many is the juxtaposition of two formative events—the passage of the landmark Voting Rights Act of 1965 and, less than a week after President Lyndon Baines Johnson's official signing ceremony, the explosion of the Los Angeles community of Watts into a racially motivated riot and conflagration.

More often overlooked—until recently—was the passage of the Immigration Act of 1965. Commonly referred to as the Hart-Celler Act, the Immigration Act of 1965 passed amendments that aimed to undo the restrictive quotas of the Johnson-Reed Immigration Act of 1924 and the McCarran-Walter Immigration and Naturalization Act of 1952. Hart-Celler was spurred by the same impulse that drove the successful passage of the Civil Rights Act of 1964 and Voting Rights Act of 1965: an urgent quest to rid the United States of any appearance of unequal political standing. Vice President Hubert Humphrey drew this linkage explicitly when he declared: "We must in 1965 remove all elements in our immigration law which suggest that there are second-class people. . . . We want to bring our immigration law into line with the spirit of the Civil Rights Act of 1964" (quoted in Tichenor 2002, 215). Upon signing the Hart-Celler Act, President Johnson declared that it would "repair a deep and painful flaw in the fabric of American justice. It corrects a cruel and enduring wrong in the conduct of the American nation" (Public Papers of the Presidents of the United States 1965, 1038).

The historical significance of the Hart-Celler Act was initially somewhat understated because its legislative impact was widely viewed as anodyne. The terms of the bill were rather modest. U.S. immigration policy would no longer set quotas based on national origin; it would allow for preferences to be given to relatives of persons already in the United States and for preferences by labor skills and professional training. Eastern and southern Europeans were expected to be the chief beneficiaries of these amendments, but in relatively limited numbers. The Immigration Act of 1965 received its support largely as an important symbolic gesture in the Cold War.

In the bill-signing ceremony, President Johnson took a moment to remark that "this bill we sign today is not a revolutionary bill. It does not affect the lives of millions. It will not reshape the structure of our daily lives, or really add importantly to either our wealth or our power" (Public Papers of the Presidents of the United States 1965, 1038). Johnson was not alone in this expectation. Attorney General Robert F. Kennedy, in his 1964 testimony to Congress, remarked: "I would say for the Asia-Pacific Triangle . . . 5,000 immigrants would come the first year, but we do not expect that there would be any great influx after that." Senator Edward Kennedy, in subcommittee hearings, said, "The bill will not flood our cities with immigrants. It will not upset the ethnic mix of our society."[5]

Today these conservative expectations of the Hart-Celler Act, with the full benefit of hindsight, seem almost comically off the mark. As many scholars have observed, the provisions of the Hart-Celler Act sparked a sweeping transformation in the nation's demographic composition (e.g., Portes and Zhou 1993; Tienda 2002; Hirschman, Alba, Farley 2000; Lee and Bean 2004; Segura and Rodrigues 2006). In terms of sheer volume, we are witnessing the largest influx of immigrants since the early twenti-

[5] For more details on the historical background, legislative dynamics, and ideological currents leading to the passage of the Immigration Act of 1965, see, e.g., Reimers (1992), Tichenor (2002), and Ngai (2004).

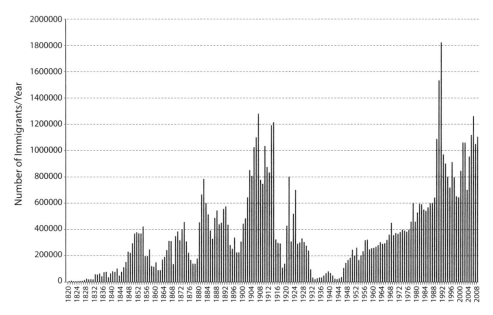

Figure 1.1. Trends in immigration, 1821–2008

eth century (see figure 1.1). In the period from 1995 to 2000, a net of more than 1.2 million people flowed into the United States per year (in-migration less out-migration). To give some comparative scale to the phenomenon, we compare migration flows into the United States with those of other nations in the Group of Eight (Japan, Canada, the United Kingdom, France, Germany, Italy, and the Russian Federation). In this comparison, Russia appears as the next closest in net gains at roughly 300,000 persons per year (Gans 2006). According to Census Bureau statistics, immigrants and their children comprise close to one in four Americans today, with more than 34 million foreign-born and more than 30 million second-generation immigrants in the United States in 2004 (U.S. Census Bureau 2005).

In addition to the upsurge in the foreign-born, this wave of immigration has produced a sea change in the racial and ethnic composition of this nation. Contemporary immigrants come from different shores than the earlier immigrants from Europe, arriving instead from Asia, the Caribbean, and Latin America. As figure 1.2 shows, until the first decade of the twentieth century, about 90 percent of new migrants to the United States set sail from European shores. By the 1980s, this proportion had dwindled to about 12 percent, with about 80 percent of new migrants coming from Asia and the Americas (U.S. Department of Homeland Se-

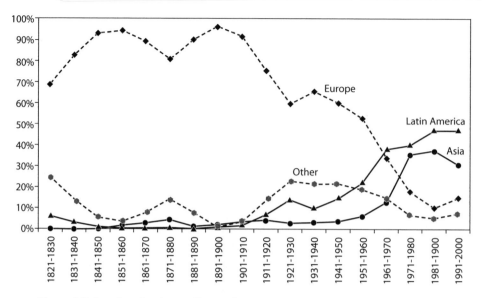

Figure 1.2. Immigration by sending region

curity 2006). The impact of this change in global emigration rates on the nation's racial/ethnic composition cannot be understated. In the 1960 census, African Americans constituted 92 percent of the nonwhite population of the United States. By the time of the 2000 census, African Americans made up only about 50 percent of the nonwhite population.[6] Many social and political observers tout the fact that African Americans are now no longer the largest nonwhite population in the United States.

These demographic shifts, moreover, are likely to continue in the foreseeable future, as we show in figure 1.3. According to Census Bureau projections, the U.S. Latino population will grow from 36 million today to more than 100 million by 2050; the Asian American population will grow from 11 million today to more than 33 million by 2050. Sometime in the middle of this century, African Americans will comprise only one of every three nonwhites, and white Americans will no longer be a numerical ma-

---

[6] Given the introduction of a separate Hispanic "ethnicity" question and the introduction of a multiracial identifier labeled "mark one or more" in 2000, there is no single correct representation of the proportion of African Americans in the nonwhite population. The lower bound is 48.5 percent (where the population count for African Americans excludes black Hispanics and excludes individuals who mark "African American" in combination with another racial category); the upper bound is 52.1 percent (where the population of African Americans includes both excluded groups); a middle-ground estimate is 49.5 percent (where the population of African Americans includes black Hispanics but excludes individuals who are black in combination with another racial category).

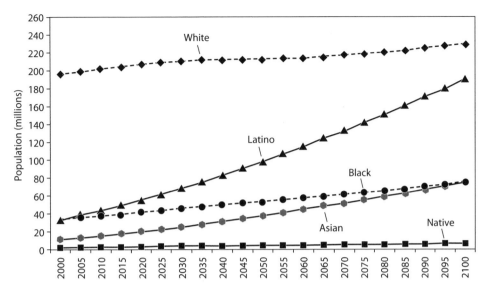

Figure 1.3. Census population projections, 2000–2100

jority in the nation. America, in short, will become a "majority-minority," a composition that already describes the populations of New Mexico, Hawaii, and California, as well as three of the four most populous cities in the nation—New York, Los Angeles, and Houston. These wide-reaching changes tell us emphatically that a clear understanding of politics in America increasingly requires a better understanding of the attitudes, attachments, and actions of racial and ethnic minorities.

THE CENTRALITY OF PARTISAN ATTACHMENTS

In this book we endeavor to explain how America's growing diversity finds its way into the nation's partisan politics. How does the American body politic—taken as a racially and ethnically heterogeneous corpus—choose to align itself with a particular party or, as is all too often the case, fail to so align? These questions are worth asking because an individual's relationship to parties, commonly referred to by the terms "partisanship" and "party identification," is one of the most elemental features of American political life.

For better or for worse, the American people have hung their most deeply held political convictions and sentiments, anxieties and aspirations, with a political party for about as long as they have existed. Martin van Buren, founder of the first political machine in New York and principal architect of the first national political party (the Jacksonian Democrats), writes of "an unbroken succession. . . . Neither the influences of marriage connections, nor of sectarian prejudices, nor any of the strong motives which often determine the ordinary actions of men, have . . . been sufficient to override the bias of party organization and sympathy, devotion to which has, on both sides, as a rule, been a master-passion of their members" (Martin van Buren 1867, 7). Today, our understanding of this "master-passion" has come principally to rest on one point: the concept of party identification. Virtually every published work in political science on public opinion, voting behavior, and political participation using survey data includes some version of the party-identification scale. As Alan Gerber and Donald Green put it, "In the field of public opinion and electoral behavior, no explanatory variable is more pervasive than party identification" (Gerber and Green 1998, 794). Given this seeming ubiquity, it is also not very surprising to find that "the psychological attachment of individuals to one or the other of the major parties . . . reveals more about their political attitudes and behaviors than any other single opinion" (Keefe and Hetherington 2003, 169).

As we shall describe in more detail in chapter 2, the reasons that party identification is so central to the way Americans think and act on politics are clear. Partisan habits are something that Americans are born into, starting with the partisanship of their parents and sustained through pre-adult and early adult socialization (Campbell et al. 1960). For adults, it is a psychological attachment that serves as a critical means of navigating a political information environment that is often saturated with complex details and hortatory messages (Fiorina 1981, Popkin 1991). Voters can do without encyclopedic knowledge about each candidate's issue positions and can navigate strategic communications by simply knowing which party and politicians they trust (and which they do not) and then using partisan cues to figure out "who is for what" (Lupia and McCubbins 1998). In effect, in the United States, "Democrat," "Republican," and "Independent" are the defining identities in the political realm (Green et al. 2002).

Growing Doubts about the Parties of Today

Two recent developments have, however, left some doubt about the ongoing effectiveness of parties in engaging different segments of the public. One potentially important limitation of the American party system is that is has remained remarkably stable in the face of the nation's rapidly diversifying electorate. Party politics, of course, has not remained the same in the last few decades. Parties today are more national and candidate-centered in their focus, and there has also been a growing ideological polarization between elites in the Democratic and Republican parties (Wattenberg 1996; Aldrich 1995; Hetherington 2001; Green and Herrnson 2002; McCarty et al. 2006).[7] Yet at the same time, at the most basic level of the number of firms in a competitive market for party organizations, the total has remained constant at two for a remarkably long period of time. Since the onset of the post-1965 wave of immigration, there have been only nominal third-party challenges, such as George Wallace's American Independent Party in 1968 and H. Ross Perot's United We Stand and Reform parties in 1992 and 1996. As one recent comparative study of party systems in the United States, Great Britain, and India notes, "Since the early twentieth century, the United States has displayed a pattern of virtually complete two-partism—that is, two national parties compete and win seats in every major region in the nation" (Chibber and Kollman 2004).[8]

Thus, while the polity has grown increasingly diverse and complex, the marketplace of political ideas, ideologies, and institutions in America remains a partisan duopoly. The period prior to the civil rights movement and the Immigration Act of 1965—characterized by highly restrictionist immigration laws and highly segregationist social mores and political rights—perhaps represents the kind of stable equilibrium under which a partisan duopoly might capably canvass and coalesce the interests of the polity and serve as institutional intermediaries between the public and government. Our current era, however, begs key questions about how well Americans fit into and are represented by the party system. How can only two major parties speak to an American electorate characterized by a dizzying array of experiences, motivations, and worldviews? How well do the two parties succeed at attracting those who are in various aspects "different"? Where do Americans whose interests, identities, and ideological beliefs are not recognized and represented by the two major parties go?

The other development that has led some to question the current relevance of parties is the seeming reluctance or inability of the Democratic and Republican parties to mobilize America's newcomers. The classic view of political parties is of institutional umbrellas that capture and consolidate a diverse coalition of interests (see, e.g., Key 1964, Sorauf 1964, Eldersveld 1964; cf. Aldrich 1995). In this classic view, parties are the pivotal organizational brokers between ordinary individuals in civil

---

[7] There is an open debate as to whether this elite-level polarization has been accompanied by a similar polarization in the mass public (Abramowitz and Saunders 1998; Fiorina et al. 2005; Ansolabehere et al. 2006).

[8] See also Rosenstone, Behr, and Lazarus (1984), Gillespie (1993), Sifry (2003), Hirano and Synder (2007).

society and government. Thus, scholars write that "political parties created democracy" (Schattschneider 1942, 1) and that "political parties lie at the heart of American politics" (Aldrich 1995, 3). And as goes the ability of parties to accommodate the diversity of interests, identities, and ideological beliefs of ordinary Americans, so does America's aspiration for a vigorous pluralist democracy.

Viewed through the focal lens we wear in this book—race and immigration—parties are the key institutional mechanisms for leveling the political playing field because they "enable the many to pool their resources to offset the advantages of the few" (Dahl 1961a, 245). Certainly, we hold dear cherished notions of the traditional role that parties played as a portal to civic engagement and the democratic inclusion of strangers to America's shores. By these mythologized accounts, machine ward bosses met immigrants at the docks, secured for them hearth and home, and shepherded them through the trials and tribulations of acquiring citizenship (Dahl 1961a, Wolfinger 1965). Such a view, of course, overstates the fervor of old-style parties to actively incorporate the entire range of immigrant Americans. More recent scholarship suggests that the willingness of parties to incorporate new citizens was not equal across all immigrant groups (Ignatiev 1995, Jacobson 1998), all historical contexts (Mayhew 1986), or all electoral circumstances (Erie 1990). The important point, however, is that local parties more often than not incorporated immigrants out of political expediency and necessity, not out of a sense of party responsibility or civic duty.

The warrants of expediency and need in electoral competition hold today as well, as political parties are pushed to target minorities and immigrant communities in campaigns. Campaign spending on Spanish-language advertisements, for example, has grown dramatically. Between 2000 and 2008, spending on Spanish-language ads in the presidential campaigns increased from $3 million to close to $50 million (Segal 2006, Shoer 2008). More and more candidates are using Spanish in their speeches and creating Spanish-language Web sites. Barack Obama—taking a page from President Lyndon Johnson's famous co-optation of the civil rights movement's rallying cry "We shall overcome"—used, as a core theme of his campaign, the motto of the United Farm Workers and the rallying cry of the spring 2006 immigrant protest marches: "¡Sí se puede!" (Yes we can!). To foray from the sublime to the ridiculous in this regard, our current political era is one in which former president Bill Clinton touts Toni Morrison's declaration that Clinton is the first "black President" in U.S. history and in which another former president, George W. Bush, touts his own place in history as the first and only bilingual (English and Spanish) president of the United States. Credible or credulous, these white politicians claim credit and electoral capital for their ability to "authentically" represent the interests of minority electorates.

Yet the brunt of the evidence from carefully considered scholarship finds that parties no longer function as the institutional keys to democratic inclusion for racial minorities and immigrant-based electorates. For immigrants, the balance of the scholarship on how today's political parties compare with those of yesteryear finds for the most part that today's parties lack the organizational capacity, the political incentives, the cultural literacy, and perhaps even the democratic resolve to guide new immigrants into the political process and secure their loyalties to a particular party (see, e.g., Jones-Correa 1998; Gerstle and Mollenkopf 2001; Ramírez 2002; Wong 2006). Similarly, while the origins of our party system can be attributed in no small measure to the need to create an institutional form that would subsume factional and regional conflicts (Aldrich 1995; read here: the "peculiar" institution of slavery), it has become all too easy for both political parties to ignore the interests and hopes of an "electorally captured" group such as African Americans and relegate issues of race to the periphery of their partisan policy agenda (see, e.g., Walton 1972; Walters 1988; Frymer 1999). Simply in terms of the number of partisan contacts, there is clear evidence that the parties are much less active in trying to mobilize voters today than they were in earlier periods—and even more so when these voters are racial and ethnic minorities (Rosenstone and Hansen 1993; Ramírez and Wong 2006).[9] Moreover, in the most prominent recent instance in which immigrants were politically engaged and mobilized—the protest marches that occurred across the nation from late March to early May 2006 and rallied somewhere between 3.6 million to over 5 million individuals (Bada, Fox, and Selee 2006)—both Democratic and Republican party elites, far from being at the vanguard, were clearly caught off guard. Thus, in the end, neither the Democratic nor the Republican Party has been so eager as to alter its core agenda and its party platform to actively recruit new electorates—at least, those segments of the electorate defined by race, ethnicity, and immigration.

CONCERNS ABOUT INCORPORATION AND REPRESENTATION

This apparent lack of effort on the part of America's partisan duopoly to engage the nation's increasingly diverse electorate raises real concerns about the political incorporation and meaningful representation of different minority communities. We have already seen that the majority of

[9] It is, however, important to note that even today the two major parties are the primary gateway through which Americans are mobilized to act in the political arena (Rosenstone and Hansen 1993). Parties may be much less active in voter mobilization than they were in the past, but they still constitute a potentially critical actor in any expansion of the mobilization process.

the Latino and Asian American population and large numbers of African Americans claim to have no allegiance to either of America's major parties. We have also revealed that the plurality of both immigrant-based communities (38 percent of Latinos and 36 percent of Asian Americans) are nonidentifiers who are not even willing to place themselves at any point along the partisan spectrum and instead proffer responses such as "not sure" or "'no preference."[10] If parties are the main institutional force driving the political incorporation of the minority community, the widespread disconnect with today's parties implies that America's newcomers and its other minorities could be falling through the cracks.

One of the putative results of this underwhelming partisan presence in the everyday lives of America's minorities is equally disappointing rates of political participation. According to the 2004 American Community Survey, only 28 percent of Latino adults and 30 percent of Asian American adults vote. That pales in comparison with the 66 percent participation rate among whites. African Americans fall somewhere in the middle, at a participation rate of 56 percent. Much of the gap is due to a lack of citizenship among a large portion of the minority population. But even among citizens, there are clear disparities in political participation. Voter registration rates, for example, even when confined to the citizen population, reveal substantial racial inequities. Fully 75 of white adult citizens are registered. That compares with a rate of only 52 percent among Asian Americans, 58 percent among Latinos, and 69 percent among African Americans. On almost every measurable aspect of political incorporation, racial minorities trail the white majority.

This underparticipation is also reflected in gross underrepresentation among the nation's elected officials. Despite the nation's vast demographic transformation, the political leadership of the United States remains overwhelmingly white. Although the national population is now roughly 13 percent African American, blacks hold only 1.8 percent of all elected offices nationwide (JCPS 2003). Latinos are even worse off, occupying less than 1 percent of the nation's elected offices, even though they account for 15 percent of the nation's population (or 8 percent of all

---

[10] Uncertainty about the value of the two parties is not only evident in basic measures of party identification. Among Latinos, surveys also regularly reveal a prevalent sense that neither party is a clear advocate for Latino group interests. In the 2006 Latino National Politics Survey, for example, only 1 percent of Latino respondents agreed that political parties in America look out for their concerns. As one recent report on the Latino population indicated: "If anything, the survey shows that a growing number of Latinos are dissatisfied with both of the major parties" (Suro and Escobar 2006). African Americans too express this sense of political marginality. About a quarter of all African Americans, according to our analysis of recent surveys, believe that neither the Democratic nor the Republican Party works hard for black interests, and some 38 percent favor the creation of a black political party (data from the National Black Election Studies of 1996, 1992, and 1984).

adult citizens) (NALEO 2008). And Asian Americans hold a negligible fraction of all offices, despite representing about 4 percent of the national population (or 3 percent of adult citizens) (APALC 2007). The consequences of all of this could be severe. Inequities in all aspects of political incorporation are more than likely to be associated with imbalances in democratic responsiveness. American democracy may speak more to the interests of the established white majority than to the concerns of the growing and increasingly diverse minority population.

OUR PROJECT

Fostering greater partisan mobilization and stronger ties to the two parties is not going to solve all of the problems of inequality in American democracy, but it could be an important first step. Thus, our primary goal in addressing these disparities is to develop a more comprehensive theory of partisan choice, one that identifies and highlights the general reasons why such a large group of Americans remains largely unattached to the two major parties. By offering a partisan model that explicitly considers and incorporates the diverse range of people and perspectives found in America today, we hope to provide both parties and other interested observers with the means and the motivation to more fully incorporate this currently unaligned and often unengaged population.

EXISTING THEORIES

How then do people choose parties? As we shall see in the ensuing chapter, two accounts currently dominate our understanding of party identification. The first is a social-psychological view developed in the 1940s and 1950s by Angus Campbell and his colleagues at the University of Michigan. This Michigan School of thought, as we refer to it in this book, posits that party identification is a strong psychological attachment that is developed early in life and is either inherited from one's parents or absorbed in other arenas of preadult socialization (see, e.g., Campbell et al. 1960; Beck and Jennings 1991; Niemi and Jennings 1991). Much like our religion and religiosity, our attachments to a party and the party system are something we grow up with. The key implications of this account, in its classical rendition in *The American Voter* (Campbell et al. 1960), are that partisanship is very stable over time; partisanship better predicts vote choice than one's positions on issues or one's views of the candidates running for office; partisanship is an expressive act and "extensions of the self" (Miller and Shanks 1996, 122); and partisanship is the "unmoved mover" that puts an indelible imprint on one's political attitudes and actions.

The main alternative to this Michigan School of thought is what we call the Downsian school of thought, following its lineal descent from Anthony Downs's *An Economic Theory of Democracy* (1957). This more economistic account views party identification as a rational choice defined by information, instrumental reasoning, and self-understood interests (see, e.g., Fiorina 1981; Franklin and Jackson 1983; Achen 1992, 2001; Erikson et al. 2002). In contrast to the Michigan model, here not only do issues and candidates matter, but the stability of partisanship varies as a function of where voters and candidates stand on the issues. The first clear elaboration of this Downsian model is most often attributed to Morris Fiorina's view of party identification as "a running tally of retrospective evaluations of party promises and performance" (1981, 84), with more recent elaborations giving formal representation to this retrospective process through Bayesian learning models (Achen 1992, 2001; Green and Gerber 1998; Grynaviski 2006). Importantly, the self-understood interests that underlie this Downsian choice are typically viewed as fitting a continuum of political preference orderings—from extremely liberal to extremely conservative. In the hurly-burly of American politics, self-proclaimed liberals, more often than not, identify as Democrats, self-proclaimed conservatives ally with the Republican Party, and those with more middle-of-the-road views tend to end up as Independents.

We review both the Michigan and the Downsian model of party identification in greater, gorier detail in chapters 2 and 3. There, our focus is on how well both accounts explain nonpartisanship and the varying patterns of partisanship (and nonpartisanship) by race/ethnic group. Here our chief aim is a more general synthetic introduction. As one scholar of parties describes the difference between these two accounts, the individual under the Michigan model is "more of a *rationalizing* voter than a rational one" (Wattenberg 1996, 13). One is thus a story of psychological foundations; the other is a story in which one's political "master-passion" is, at least in principle, constantly open to revision and updating.

Despite these major differences, both accounts share an approach to measurement. In both cases, partisanship is typically measured as a simple, linear scale, with Democrats and Republicans on the poles and Independents or nonpartisans placed squarely in the middle. The Downsian and Michigan accounts of partisan choices and this linear model of partisanship have proven to be remarkably resistant to modification. Despite a range of conceptual critiques and a host of measurement issues that we outline later in the book, virtually every work that uses or studies partisanship in America utilizes this linear scale and employs one or both of these theoretical perspectives. This basic linear scale, in particular, remains almost universal in its use and dominant in its sway over how we believe Americans think and act in the political sphere.

Our own view is not that these traditional theoretical accounts or the standard linear measurement models of party identification are wrong. In highlighting the fact that the political views and orientations of a growing number of Americans do not fit comfortably with the fixed choice of identifying as a Democrat or a Republican, we do not seek to refute the reality that a lion's share of Americans continue to hold unrelenting attachments to the Democratic and Republican parties. These attachments remain the single best predictor of whether one votes, how one votes, and what political preferences underlie one's vote choice. Furthermore, the evidence is quite clear that most Americans can quite capably place themselves along the linear partisan scale highlighted in so many studies of American political behavior. In short, existing theories and measurement approaches tell us a lot about how Americans choose parties.

LIMITATIONS TO EXISTING THEORIES

At the same time, however, these theories and approaches do not tell us everything. A number of concerns and criticisms have been raised against these conventional accounts, which we review and discuss in some detail in the coming chapters. For the present, we note that one issue that has not drawn much attention is the relative absence of any consideration of race or immigration in the general literature on political parties and party identification. Paul Frymer, one of the few exceptions to this general rule, observes that the ability of parties to successfully include and incorporate a diversity of groups and interests is typically taken as a presumption, rather than as a topic worthy of empirical scrutiny; he notes that "scholars of African American politics make dramatically different arguments about the two-party system's impact for democratic inclusion, emphasizing its limits and exclusionary nature" (2005, 122). Many studies simply drop respondents of color from the analysis, and thus general accounts incorporate little of our understanding of how race works in America or how the immigrant experience differentiates segments of the population. This absence is understandable, given that accounts were by and large developed when America was a much less diverse place than it is today. In the mid-twentieth-century milieu out of which the study of party identification was born—a time when 90 percent of the U.S. population was white and all but a tiny fraction was native-born—ignoring or relegating to a footnote the centrality of race and the immigrant experience may have seemed analytically expedient. In today's politics, we ignore race and immigration at our peril.

We are, of course, not the first scholars to observe that the world around us has become more diverse. More recent scholarship has, accordingly, begun to try to rectify this omission. There is a welter of recent works that have focused specifically on the political choices of African Americans, Asian Americans, and Latinos and on the political incorporation of immigrants, expanding our understanding of each individual group. This literature has also been extremely important in shifting the focus of attention away from the white majority and in beginning to identify the ways in which minorities and immigrants might be different.

Nevertheless, in our view, our understanding of the relationship between race, immigration, and partisanship remains incomplete. With a few exceptions, studies of party identification in communities of color simply reapply some version of the Michigan or Downsian model to these new groups. In so doing, such works assume that the influence of information uncertainty, a liberal-conservative ideology, and one's racial/ethnic identity is no different for Latinos, Asian Americans, and African Americans from what it is for whites. The converse of this last point is also a limitation of much of the existing work: most studies focus on explaining the party identification of a single group, albeit a panethnic group in the case of Latinos and Asian Americans. In so doing, they neglect to compare the underlying basis of party identification both *across* groups and *within* groups. Thus, we are left with a series of ethnically separate literatures that focus on the peculiarities of each group in isolation.

Alternate Pathways to (Non)Partisanship: Information, Ideology, and Identity

This book thus offers an account of race and partisanship that unifies and expands upon these multiple, ethnic-specific literatures. But are racial and ethnic minorities really different? And do any of these differences alter the ways in which individuals choose parties? The nub of our story is that the partisan choices of all racial and ethnic groups share three key factors—the primary social *identities* and the *ideological* commitments that individuals bring and the *information* environments that individuals negotiate in deciding whether to affiliate with a party and which party to affiliate with—but that the particular ways in which information, ideology, and identity matter to our partisan choices varies across racial/ethnic groups. Our proposed framework of information, ideology, and identity is less an attempt to challenge and replace the existing Downsian and Michigan schools of thought than an effort to synthesize and adapt both frameworks to build a coherent and comparative explanation of party

Figure 1.4. Identity, ideology, information, and party identification

identification among whites, African Americans, Latinos, and Asian Americans. In doing this, we hope to complement existing accounts with key alternate dimensions of partisan choice that engage and address some of the aforementioned limitations of conventional theories of party identification.

Figure 1.4 schematically presents one synthesized representation of how the Michigan and Downsian schools of thought fit with one another and with the role of information, ideology, and identity that we propound in this book. We follow Achen's effort to synthesize insights from both models by distinguishing "long-term party identification" from shorter-term factors (1992, 2001). Long-term considerations (e.g., one's prior political socialization or one's central political predispositions) are both logically and, based on the weight of the evidence, empirically prior to shorter-term considerations (e.g., one's "running tally" of retrospective evaluations or Bayesian learning). This distinction also parallels political science's prevailing view of the nature of public opinion, John Zaller and Stanley Feldman's "receive-accept-sample" model, in which opinion is an averaging function of short-term "top-of-the-head" considerations that are defined by one's level of political awareness and longer-term "core political predispositions" such as ideology, partisanship, and, we submit, race (see Zaller and Feldman 1992, Zaller 1992; on race as a core predisposition, see Lee 2002).

Both short-term and long-term factors contribute to one's partisanship, with the crux of the dispute between the Michigan and Downsian schools being which is foreground and which is background. To this core set of relationships, we layer in our emphasis on ideology, identity, and information as variants on long-term and short-term influences. As we discuss later, we expect ideology and identity to be longer-term influences on partisanship because prior political socialization is not always equal across publics defined by race/ethnicity and immigrant status. Similarly, while retrospective and Bayesian evaluations are information-based accounts of short(er)-term influences on partisanship, we argue for a more complex consideration of the role of information in which not all observations or messages are equally transmitted or similarly influential on one's partisan evaluations and partisanship across publics defined by race/ethnicity and immigrant status.

Information

Our argument for adapting and refining our specification of the long-term and short-term influences on (non)partisanship across the contexts of race and immigration begins with the easy and readily apparent insight that not all newcomers to the United States arrive with fully formed and well-acculturated views on politics. Sociologists (and some historians and political scientists) debate whether the process of coming to terms with a new society (and, by corollary, its social, economic, and political institutions) follows a linear, sequential process of assimilation (Gordon 1964, Alba and Nee 2003), results from forming a sense of racial identity and disadvantage (Glazer and Moynihan 1963), or develops in an uneven, segmented trajectory, where some groups are seamlessly integrated into the main lines of American life and other groups find those main lines only selectively open to them or blocked altogether (Portes and Zhou 1993). Yet by all accounts, immigrants do not come fully versant in politics, American-style.

The point about incomplete socialization and unequal information environments does not apply only to first-generation immigrants. The offspring of immigrants often continue to reside in ethnic enclaves, retain the language of their parents, rely principally on ethnic media for their political information, and otherwise face continued hardship and barriers to full inclusion that leave them socially isolated. Similarly, the everyday lives and information environments of many African Americans continue to be isolated by forces within and external to the community—from a "counterpublic" sphere of "barbershops, bibles, and BET," to borrow from a recent title (Harris-Lacewell 2004; see also Dawson 2001), to the persistent hypersegregation of residential neighborhoods, the resegregation of public schools, the disproportionate sequestering of African American men in prisons, detention centers, and other penal institutions, and so on (Wilson 1987, Massey and Denton 1993, Boger and Orfield 2005, J. Miller 1996).

Such circumstances have, we argue, important consequences for one's politics and one's relationship to political parties. The choice not to identify with either of the two major parties, for instance, may not be the result of a lack of interest in politics or a sense of political alienation. Rather, under conditions of uncertainty and low information about the party system and each party individually, nonpartisanship may simply be a rationally adaptive strategy. Instead of choosing between two parties that one may be unfamiliar with or express allegiance to a party that one does not yet trust, a more reasoned option is to opt out altogether by professing nonpartisanship.

Ideology

Another readily identifiable feature of both the immigrant and racial minority communities pertinent to party identification is that attention to the liberal-conservative ideological dimension that divides the two parties and that purportedly drives partisanship is decidedly uneven. Immigrants and racial and ethnic minorities are certainly not immune to a single-minded focus on the core debates that separate Democrats from Republicans. At the same time, however, they are especially likely to have concerns that are peripheral to the national partisan discussion. For immigrants, prolonged exposure to and prior socialization in a range of different political belief systems—from communist or former communist societies such as Cuba, Russia, and Vietnam to authoritarian or former authoritarian states like Peru, Pakistan, and Nigeria to mature democracies such as India, South Korea, and Costa Rica—should bring alternate issue concerns and ideological commitments to the fore. In particular, these alternate ideological orientations that immigrants bring may cut orthogonally to the liberal-to-conservative continuum that separates the two parties. For racial and ethnic groups, there are group-specific ideologies—like the nation-building ideologies of *mestizaje* among Latinos (Anzaldúa 1987) or the multiple ideological traditions in the history of African American political thought (McCartney 1991, Dawson 2001).

The consequence, once again, is diminished attachment to both parties. For any individual, the less that her core issue concerns are addressed by the parties and the more orthogonal her ideological predispositions are to the liberal-conservative scale that divides the two parties, the greater the ambiguity that partisan choices are likely to present. Latino immigrants, for example, who wish to see more open borders may have no clearly attractive partisan option. Similarly, the 40 percent of the African American population that favors black separatist institutions may see no point in declaring allegiance to white-dominated institutions such as the Democratic and Republican parties. With little motivation for choosing either party, many of these individuals will remain nonpartisan or Independent. Once again, nonpartisanship becomes a rationally adaptive strategy for those who do not "fit."

The potential orthogonality of ideological views is not the only way we expect our existing views of party identification to be complicated vis-à-vis ideology. For most Americans, the typical spectrum of ideology from very liberal to very conservative views is sufficiently capacious to capture both their individual orientation and their perceptions of where political parties and their candidates stand. Some, however, may have intensely held nonnegotiable positions on issues that the two major parties and their candidates either choose to avoid taking positions on if possible (e.g., Puerto Rican statehood, environmental rights, reparations for descendants of slaves forcibly brought from Africa) or choose positions that are so ambiguous and similar to the other party/candidate that for someone with intense preferences on the matter, the two parties look no different. Others may hold crosscutting ideological views (i.e., conservative on social/moral issues but a liberal on economic policy) that make it difficult for them to comfortably ally with a major party. By mapping partisanship on a linear scale with Democrats on the liberal Left, Republicans on the conservative Right, and nonpartisans in the moderate middle, we are, in fact, presuming that the standard set of liberal-conservative ideological concerns is the only kind of ideological predisposition that matters to one's partisan identification.

Identity

A final insight that is visible through the twin lenses of race and immigration is that one's primary political identity is often intimately linked to one's primary social group identity. Here there is a spectrum across racial and ethnic groups in America in the salience of identities and their significance for defining a group politics. At one end of the spectrum are African Americans, for whom blackness is so distinct and defining an identity that for many African Americans, a "black utility heuristic" (where an African American divines what is in her best interest by first considering what is in the best interest of African Americans as a group) governs one's political calculus (Dawson 1994). At the other end of the spectrum are whites, for whom whiteness is a taken-for-granted privilege that is perceived to be synonymous with "free" and "independent" and invisible as an identity to whites themselves (Roediger 1991, Feagin and Vera 1995, Lipsitz 1998). Between these antipodes are immigrant-based groups such as Latinos and Asian Americans, who vary in their paths toward assimilation and in their patterns of racialization (compare, e.g., Telles and Ortiz 2008; Jiménez 2008). Even for Latinos and Asian Americans—groups that are notable for the juxtaposition and paradox of externally perceived homogeneity and internally experienced heterogeneity as panethnic groups—racial and ethnic identity can be a script that, when activated, powerfully motivated their political engagement and partisanship (Padilla 1984; Lopez and Espiritu 1990; Espiritu 1992; Pantoja et al. 2001; Barreto 2007).

Racial/ethnic group identity thus represents a third key dimension in partisan choice. For some members of these communities of color, group identity will replace liberal-conservative ideology as the core dimension of their political calculus. If the major political parties downplay their appeals to racial/ethnic minority groups or present appeals that run counter to the perceived interests of such groups, then a group-based political calculus may push one toward nonpartisanship rather than identification with a major party. The key is how neatly a group identity coexists with the political identity of Democratic or Republican partisanship. For all groups and individuals, the more their primary group identity matters and the less one of the two parties is clearly aligned with that identity, the greater the tendency to identify as Independent or nonpartisan.

These three dimensions—information uncertainty, ideological heterogeneity, and identity formation—form the foundation stones of our account of party identification. Importantly, all three dimensions have similar implications for partisan choices. In each case, immigrants, racial minorities, and whites with distinct ideological profiles will be motivated to remain neutral between the two major parties. When the choices the Democratic and Republican parties present to the American public do not match our available stock of political knowledge (information), our deeply held political beliefs (ideology), or how we think of ourselves (identity), nonpartisanship becomes a rationally adaptive strategy.

The Structure of Partisan Choice

This elaboration of three alternative pathways to partisanship and non-partisanship has a perhaps even more important implication. The fact that multiple, orthogonal dimensions affect party choice implies that partisan choices at the beginning of the twenty-first century may no longer be so neatly ordered along a single dimension with Democrats on the left, Republicans on the right, and Independents in the middle. Diversity may affect not only the degree of attachment to the parties but also how many Americans think about parties in the first place. Many Americans whom scholars might place in the middle of a party-identification continuum from strong Republicans to strong Democrats may have political commitments and hold views that are far from middling. The wide-ranging motivations that we identified in these pages imply that nonpartisans will be a heterogeneous group with potentially extreme views along some ideological dimension, deep concerns on issues not raised by the two parties, or strong identities that are poorly served by either party. In effect, many nonpartisans may be far removed from our traditional impressions of Independents, namely ideologically middle-of-the-road, apathetic, alienated, or otherwise apolitical.

Diversity, Broken Down

In the main empirical body of this book, we offer support for our empirical account of partisanship by focusing on three distinct sets of Americans: (1) African Americans, (2) Latinos and Asian Americans, two key immigrant-based groups, and (3) white Americans. This grouping of the U.S. population will strike some as excessively reductionist, flattening the rich diversity within each subpopulation. Others will object that focusing the looking glass in this way reifies groups and falls prey to a "groupist" logic that assumes these subpopulations are fundamental social units of analysis. Still others will add to this groupist objection the further protestation that there is only a single model of political reasoning and human psychology, not multiple models for each arbitrarily defined, historically contingent group.

We are quite sympathetic to each of these concerns and have written about them elsewhere (Lee 2008). In the present case, our choice of grouping the U.S. population in this way is analytically motivated. Specifically, our central claims are that (a) partisanship is defined by one's information, ideology, and identity and that (b) these three factors interact in distinct ways for African Americans, immigration-based groups such as Latinos and Asian Americans, and white Americans. To put it one way, the modal nonpartisan in each of these groups arrives at her nonpartisanship via a distinct trajectory, which we summarize below. For the present, while the following pages will liberally refer to racial and ethnic groups in global and homogenizing terms, the analyses and interpretations should be read with the complexity of actual group experiences and opinions in mind. Where possible and where warranted by theoretical imperatives, we endeavor to bring a finer level of granularity to our discussion of each aggregate group.

We begin with African Americans, who, we argue, represent the archetype of a subpopulation for whom racial group identity plays a central, defining role in shaping partisan choice. If party identification is shaped by racial identity for any group, we should find it within the African American community. The long history and continued presence of racial domination and antiblack discrimination in the United States too should be a factor in bringing nonliberal/conservative ideological orientation and nonmainstream issue concerns to the fore for African Americans. In particular, adherence to black nationalism and its variants has deep roots in the African American community, and we find evidence that this specific ideological orientation has consequences for African American nonpartisanship.

Our next grouping, Latinos and Asian Americans, represents new and growing entrants to a political system. As a consequence of their recency and dynamism, these groups offer an opportunity to critically examine how partisanship is acquired when preadult political socialization into the American two-party system cannot be assumed. Here there are two key dimensions to partisanship acquisition: (1) what newcomers to the United States bring with them in terms of political information, ideology, identity, experiences, and the like; and (2) what newcomers learn about political and social relations upon coming to the United States. Thus we are both interested in knowing whether newcomers' prior socialization and continued ties to their home country shape patterns of (non)partisanship and whether and how they learn and navigate the terrain of politics and race in the United States. Underlying these dimensions, furthermore, is the central question of how immigrants adapt and become incorporated into a new political society. To the extent that our party system is fully inclusive, we might expect to find evidence of a classic process of assimilation, where Latinos and Asian Americans are more likely to be partisans the longer they are rooted in the United States and more likely to identify with a party based on their left-right ideological commitments and their parents' partisan habits. If, on the other hand, the party system is less than fully open to the interests and demands of Latinos and Asian Americans, we might find a more ethnically particularistic or segmented account of partisanship.

We end our analysis of groups with white Americans. Whites are typically, in the language of the social sciences, taken to be the "null group" against which other groups are compared. Here we want to know if the lessons that we have learned from considering race and immigration seriously shed any light on the partisan dynamics of the majority white population. We believe, as W.E.B. DuBois noted long ago, that by studying groups such as African Americans who have been marginalized by the larger society, we learn not only about the marginalized group but also about the interests and actions of a larger community that has actively sought to keep minorities on the outside. As we noted earlier, we expect a more capacious view of ideology and interests to generate some new insights into white nonpartisanship. Beyond scholarly treatises that exhort us to examine multiple ideological traditions (e.g., Hochschild 1981, Smith 1993), we can simply look on the ground to find a diverse range of issues (globalization, urban sprawl, environmentalism, women's rights, perhaps even immigration) that are central to the political worldview of many whites but that are not yet well represented by either major party. Moreover, in the post–civil rights era, the ideological beliefs of a growing proportion of whites put them at the crosshairs of traditional New Deal

partisan cleavages—for example, economically liberal but racially conservative, advocates of full civil liberties but also weak, minimal government to protect those liberties, and so on.

A Few Words on Terminology

In the ensuing chapter, we give some thought to the proposition that to
understand a theory we must first understand the conditions in which
that theory originated. So we endeavor to situate the ontology of the
concept of party identification in currents of political science as a discipline in the middle of the twentieth century. Here we give a moment to
another important proposition: namely that irrespective of the conditions in which a theory originated, we must at least understand the
words that are being used. Giovanni Sartori once observed that "as we
are . . . prisoners of the words we pick, we had better pick them well"
(1984, 60; quoted in Gerring 1999, 357). We use many words in this
book and hope to be clear about why we pick them and how we use
them. In particular, there are two clusters of terms that we use repeatedly and that require mention.

First are terms used to describe the relationship that ordinary individuals have or fail to have to a political party or to our party system. In most
of the scholarship we have encountered on parties (and, importantly, in
everyday use), the terms "party identification" and "partisanship" are
used interchangeably (W. E. Miller 1991, Miller and Shanks 1996).[11] Our
text mirrors this approach.

Second are categories employed to delineate the options that individuals choose within the realm of party identification. These options are il-
lustrated in figure 1.5. The first major distinction we make along the
partisanship scale is between "partisans"—those who profess some allegiance to either of the main parties in American politics—and "nonpartisans"—those who, at least at first blush, claim no ties to either of these
partisan institutions. Within the category of nonpartisans, we further distinguish between "Independents" and "nonidentifiers." The Independents
group consists simply of individuals who when asked initially about their
partisanship, claim to be Independents or profess allegiance to another
party. Nonidentifiers are, by contrast, individuals who claim no place on
the partisanship scale. They offer any number of uncommitted responses

---

[11] We do the same here, noting the exception of no less a scholar of partisanship than
Warren Miller, who remained steadfast to the conceptual difference between one's first-
order identification with a party (i.e., simply agreeing to the root question, "Do you usually
think of yourself as a Republican [or] a Democrat?") and the secondary relationship to
parties among Independents.

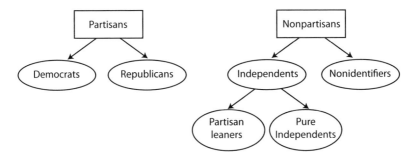

Figure 1.5. Partisanship categories

such as "don't know," "none of the above," "not sure," or "refuse." Or they simply protest against the irrelevance or incomprehensibility of the choices (Democrat, Republican, and Independent) before them.

We believe that one of the main contributions of this book is recognizing and attempting to understand this group. Nonidentifiers have typically been viewed as a residual category that has been ignored and deleted from any ensuing academic analysis. Dropping nonidentifiers as "missing data" is, as we will see, often a reasonable approach for whites and African Americans. It is a major omission for Latinos and Asian Americans. We will demonstrate that nonidentifiers are both numerous among the Latino and Asian American populations—making up the plurality of both groups—and readily explicable. Finally, within the category of Independents, like others before us, we also consider the distinction between "Independent leaners," who when pressed a second time, do admit some sort of leaning or attachment to one of the nation's two major parties, and "pure Independents," who refuse to indicate a preference for either party. In line with existing scholarship, we believe that this distinction is important and that there is sometimes a real danger in lumping Independent leaners with other nonpartisans. It is clear, as Keith and his colleagues (1992) have ably demonstrated, that large segments of the "leaning" population are, in fact, closet partisans. However, we also hope to show that the importance of the pure-versus-leaner distinction varies considerably across racial and ethnic groups. Thus, in the analysis that follows, we typically repeat our analysis in two ways. We first show our results with leaners included as nonpartisans but then replicate the analysis with leaners excluded, detailing any notable differences that emerge.

A second cluster of terms that require some choice and clarity at the outset concern the definition of populations by race, ethnicity, and national origin. First, we often use the terms "race" and "ethnicity" interchangeably, as well as their hybridized variants, "ethnoracial" and "race/ethnicity." We recognize, of course, that these terms define interrelated and overlapping, but not equivalent, concepts. The similarities and dissimilarities between these terms have been well covered elsewhere (see, e.g., Omi and Winant 1994; Cornell and Hartman 1998; Hattam 2007). The most widely applied difference between the two terms is that race marks processes of external ascription and internal identification by putatively indelible (often biologically based) traits such as skin color and phenotype. Ethnicity, however, is commonly used to identify the ostensibly nonbiological processes of ascription and identification by traits such as one's language and dialect, religion, culture, national origin, and the like. Where the terms are employed selectively to distinguish between minority groups in America, we follow a common convention of referring to African Americans as a racial group and to Latinos and Asian Americans as panethnic groups. The latter term denotes the prevailing practice of glomming multiple, heterogeneous ethnic/national origin groups under the umbrella categories of Latino and Asian American.

With the terms used to denote the specific groups we analyze in this book, we too are quite specific. We use "white" to refer, in the first instance, to survey respondents who self-identify with that racial/ethnic category and, more generally, to refer to individuals to whom the category of white is ascribed by virtue of their phenotypic appearance or European descent. Using similar criteria—self-identification in the first instance and general boundary conditions—we use both "black" and "African American" in this book. We favor the use of "Latino" over "Hispanic" for two important reasons: (1) the latter term is sometimes used to describe a language-based identity of all Spanish-speaking people, which would include individuals we do not intend to encompass, such as Americans from Spain and the Philippines; (2) the former term more precisely and exclusively refers to individuals of Latin American origin. In our data analysis (i.e., given the data sets we analyze), "Latino" denotes primarily Americans of Mexican, Puerto Rican, and Cuban origin.[12] Finally, we opt for the term "Asian American" rather than its alternatives "Asian Pacific American," "Asian Pacific Islander American," and "Asian Americans and Pacific Islanders" for the very practical reason that none of our data include Pacific Islanders. In our data analysis, "Asian American" denotes primarily Americans of Chinese, Filipino, Indian, Japanese, Korean, and Vietnamese origin.

---

[12] One other point on terms here is that we follow common convention by using the masculine form of "Latino" (cf. "Latina") in reference to both sexes of the population of Americans of Latin American origin.

OUTLINE OF THE REMAINING CHAPTERS

Chapter 2 traces the origins of the study of party identification. We start with the midcentury debate over "responsible" party politics and show how, through the development of the Michigan and Downsian models of partisanship, the study of the "party in the electorate" has come to take a singular form. Today the concept of party identification is viewed in psychological terms and operationalized in almost every instance as a linear scale—measured in opinion surveys—of self-identification from strong Republicans on the far political right to strong Democrats on the far political left and Independents at the midpoint. While there have been ample criticisms of this linear view, they have been largely treated as technical footnotes, rather than concerns at the core of either school of thought on party identification.

In chapter 3 we reinvigorate the force behind these methodological criticisms by considering political Independents anew, through the lens of racial identity and immigrant assimilation. The chapter begins by tracing the historical evolution of Independents in the study of party identification. We theorize nonpartisanship as a multidimensional identity that interacts in important ways with one's primary social group identities, ideological predispositions, and information constraints. The chapter concludes with our expectations for the distinct pathways toward nonpartisanship for African Americans, whites, and immigrant-based groups such as Asians and Latinos.

We begin our empirical analysis in chapter 4 with the case of African American party identification. While black partisanship is distinctive for the predominant role of a racially defined group calculus, we argue that the link between individual choice, group interests, and the coordination of collective choice in favor of the Democratic Party is neither automatic nor simple. We demonstrate that exit from the Democratic Party occurs under three conditions: when the sense of group identity is attenuated, when commitments to black autonomy are intensified, and when evaluations change as to which party best serves the interests of African Americans.

We continue to test our account of race, immigration, and nonpartisanship in chapters 5 and 6 with an examination of immigration-based groups such as Latinos and Asian Americans. Unlike thearchetypal identity-based dynamics of African Americans, the partisan choices of Latinos and Asian Americans are mediated by a more pronounced ambivalence and proliferation of identities that are in formation. We argue that for Latinos and Asian Americans, partisanship should be conceived of and tested as a sequential choice: in the first instance, partisan thinking is either meaningful or irrelevant; in the second step, if partisan thinking has import and pertinence, then one chooses to call oneself a Democrat, a Republican, or an Independent. The first step is one in which uncertainty and ambivalence about politics for immigrants and their offspring are dominant; in the second step, ideological orientation and identity formation become more important to choice. In chapters 5 and 6 we show important commonalities between Latinos and Asian Americans, but perhaps more striking and signal differences.

The strong test of our alternate account of partisan choice is its ability to shed new light on white Americans, the almost exclusive province of previous research. In chapter 7, we show evidence for two as-yet-unconsidered routes to Independence for whites: policy extremism (being so far to the right or left as to be at odds with both parties) and partisan ambivalence (holding irreconcilably conflicting views—e.g., racial conservatism and policy liberalism). In both cases, those who are far from the middle ideologically end up violating the assumptions of a linear model of partisanship by identifying as Independent.

Much of the focus on political Independents in the extant literature centers on whether identifying as a nonpartisan has any bearing on partisan behavior, with the best evidence weighing against the behavioral distinctiveness of Independents. In chapter 8, we argue that the lack of behavioral distinctiveness results less from the irrelevance of Independence as a political alternative and more from the lack of tangible choices in a given election and an unwavering focus on white Independents. In elections where a viable third-party option exists, Independent voters are more than willing to abandon the two major parties. Similarly, measures of a willingness to abandon weak partisan allegiances in favor of the other party, a third party, or nonparticipation vary dramatically across racial and ethnic groups. By better understanding *why* individuals identify as Independents, we argue, we can better understand *when* that nonpartisan identification will lead to nonpartisan behavior.

In the conclusion, we review the book, recasting its theoretical contribution and empirical findings vis-à-vis the history of the scholarly study of parties and their historical role in incorporating racial/ethnic minorities. We also situate our theses and findings within current debates on ideological polarization, identity politics, and the putative decline of parties. We close with some thoughts in the normative and prescriptive realms: what our findings tell us about the vigor of American democracy, viewed through the lens of partisanship and nonpartisanship, and what they suggest for party organizations that wish to bring more otherwise nonpartisan voters into their fold.

CHAPTER 2

Party Identification: The Historical and Ontological Origins of a Concept

> The political parties that I style great are those which cling to principles rather than to their consequences; to general and not to special cases; to ideas and not to men. These parties are usually distinguished by nobler features, more generous passions, more genuine convictions, and a more bold and open conduct than the others. . . . America has had great parties, but has them no longer; and if her happiness is thereby considerably increased, her morality has suffered.
> —Alexis de Tocqueville

> All I know is we're not Republicans. My father isn't.—Judith, age 10
> —Fred Greenstein

IN THIS OPENING chapter, we trace the historical and ontological origins of what we now call party identification. We situate the origins of our current linear measurement model of party identification within three broad intellectual shifts of the last half century: the decline of a more praxis-oriented, normative advocacy of "responsible" party politics and the roughly contemporaneous rise of the two most prominent developments in recent political science scholarship—the survey-based, cognitively oriented study of political behavior and the game theoretic, mathematically oriented analyses of electoral competition. These latter two frameworks motivate the leading present-day accounts of the party in the electorate, the enduring psychological attachments associated with Angus Campbell and his colleagues at the University of Michigan, and the more positivist, rational, and ideological model derived from Anthony Downs's rediscovery of the median voter theorem. The rest of the chapter describes these two frameworks and the principal concerns and criticisms raised against both schools of thought—focusing on the particular way in which the concept is defined and operationalized as a linear measure of individual-level attributes. Although our historical account will recognize the three different views of parties (as physical organizations, as organs of governance, and as collectives of voters), our focus in subsequent chapters will fall squarely on the party in the electorate and will delve into the attachments (or lack thereof) of ordinary citizens.

The goal of the chapter is to lay the foundations for a modified account of party identification. In chapter 3 we link the methodological concerns raised here with two important omissions in the foundation work on party identification (inattention to racial and ethnic heterogeneity in the electorate and limited concern for the role of nonpartisanship) to propose a more contingent but also more robust model of party (non)identification.

THE EARLY STUDIES OF PARTY SYSTEMS

In *Party Government,* E. E. Schattschneider famously declared that "modern democracy is unthinkable save in terms of the political parties" (1942, 1). Some sixty years hence, one might equally forcefully claim that modern parties are unthinkable save in terms of their constituent electorates. Today, we mostly take for granted that there are three chief components to thinking about political parties: their structure as organizations, their function in governance, and their basis in the citizenry of a polity. This central place of partisans in the electorate in our very conception of political parties, however, is a relatively recent phenomenon. The concepts and categories with which we are all too familiar today—partisanship acquisition and party identification as Democrats, Republicans, and Independents—have emerged in the main over the latter half of the twentieth century. As we shall see, the 1950s mark a turning point in how political scientists have come to study political parties.

The first critical backdrop to the emergence of our current view of party identification is the landmark effort by the Committee on Political Parties of the American Political Science Association (APSA) from 1946 to 1950 to consider, as systematically as it could, given the science of the day, how the work of political parties might be improved to better the governance of the United States.[1] Culminating in the publication of "Toward a More Responsible Two-Party System" by the *American Political Science Review* in 1950, the report of the APSA committee was sweeping in scope and ambition. Theodore Lowi would proclaim it as "second only to the 1937 President's Committee on Administrative Management as a contribution by academics to public discourse on the fundamentals of American democracy" (1985, 68). In particular, it represented a mile-

---

[1] Much of this discussion of the 1950 report by the APSA Committee on Political Parties is based on discussions in Kirkpatrick (1971), Pomper (1971), David (1992), White (1992), and Green and Herrnson (2002).

stone in the organized effort of political scientists to marshal the prevailing research on what parties actually do to reflect upon what parties *should* do.

The committee had sixteen members: Schattschneider as its chair, some well-known scholars of parties such as Clarence Berdahl, Hugh Bone, Louise Overacker, and Howard Penniman, and others, like Merle Fainsod and Fritz Morstein Marx, who were not among the leading "stasiologists" of the day. The basic diagnosis of the Committee Report was that the U.S. party system functioned "as two loose associations of state and local organizations, with very little national machinery and very little national cohesion," with the result that "either party, when in power, is ill-equipped to organize its members in the legislature and the executive branches into a government held together and guided by a party program. . . . This is a very serious matter, for it affects the very heartbeat of American democracy" (American Political Science Association 1950, v). This diagnosis serves as a point of departure for a long and detailed set of proposals to better organize a more "responsible" two-party system in the United States.

From the very start, this effort to meaningfully engage the doggedly messy world of politics met with substantial skepticism. The report is perhaps as notable for the breadth and depth of the criticisms it sparked as it is for its historical place in political science scholarship on political parties. The objections ranged from differences on how "responsibility" ought to be defined (Ranney 1951, 1954), to challenges to its diagnosis about what ails the American two-party system (J. Turner 1951), to quarrels about the report's sympathies toward majoritarian, parliamentarian, and Westminsterian party systems (Pennock 1952, Epstein 1956), to condemnation of the policy prescriptions themselves and, especially, their lack of foundation in careful political analysis (J. Turner 1951, Kirkpatrick 1971). One of the report's sharpest critics was a former committee member and signatory on the report, Evron Kirkpatrick. On the occasion of the twentieth anniversary of the Committee Report, Kirkpatrick surveyed the litany of criticisms brought against the work and drew the unsparing conclusion that "collectively, these criticisms amount to an indictment of the Report's analysis and recommendations as ill-conceived, ill-formulated, and, most often, simply mistaken about parties, about people and about political systems" (1971, 968–69).

The authors of the report at least partly anticipated such a response. They took pains to circulate an initial draft and canvass critical views of their analyses and recommendations before publishing their work for the general public. They also noted in the report that "the Committee on Political Parties is impressed with its own limitations, with the areas that have remained inadequately illuminated, and with the rich opportunities for research that challenge the imagination of the students of political parties" (American Political Science Association 1950, ix). Some fifty years hence, these words are powerful not only for their verisimilitude but also for their irony. As a recent retrospective on the state of responsible partisanship notes, the current status of political parties has moved both closer to the report's goals in terms of the growing national focus of U.S. politics *and* further from these goals in terms of the ascendancy of a candidate-centered focus of U.S. politics (Green and Herrnson 2002). Moreover, the decades following the 1950 report have, as the committee openly hoped, given rise to an upsurge of research into political parties. But little of it, however, turned on the questions that took center stage in the Committee Report.

Rather, one of the most substantial and significant topics germane to the study of political parties in the last half century has been the focus on the interests, intentions, and actions of rank-and-file party identifiers. The report itself gives conspicuously little attention to what V. O. Key termed "the party in the electorate" (1942). There is a minimal and highly speculative discussion of what role the electorate might play in achieving party responsibility in which the boundaries of party membership are left undefined (Ranney 1951), and the discussion is organized around the familiar tripartite division of the electorate into nonvoters, "standpatters," and "switchers" (American Political Science Association 1950, 90).[2] The report does consider the underlying motivations of these segments of the electorate, albeit briefly and crudely. Nonvoters are presumed to be motivated by their perception that elections do not matter and that the candidates are insufficiently distinct. Much like Ray Kinsella's fabled aphorism in *Field of Dreams,* the presumption is that if a responsible two-party system is built, these nonparticipants will come to the electoral process. Party regulars, by contrast, are viewed as principally motivated by an interest in seeing their views "respected and carried out."

Importantly, vote switchers are clearly perceived as the most influential and prized electorate. This more rational, issue-based, and *independent* group of "active but less than wholly committed voters" is described as the "keepers of the public conscience" and the critical segment in deciding whether a more responsible party system can be achieved. As the committee puts it, "It is this group that is willing to make an electoral choice and wants a choice to make; that wants to vote for a program and resents not having it carried out" (American Political Science Association 1950, 91). We can strain to see a thin theory of how the electorate matters to the viability of a party system, but to the extent that the APSA

---

[2] The terms "standpatters" and "switchers," used to describe voting patterns, are usually attributed to Key (1942).

Committee Report intended to set the agenda for future research on political parties, partisanship as we know it today is wholly absent.

To a degree, this absence is unsurprising, given E. E. Schattschneider's
reputedly pivotal influence on the committee's deliberations and its final
report. Less than a decade earlier, Schattschneider, in *Party Government,*
made clear that "whatever else the parties may be, they are not associations of the voters who support the party candidates" (1942, 52) and that
"the concept of the parties as a mass association of partisans has no historical basis" (54).[3] The absence of a conception of the party in the electorate, however, is somewhat ironic, given Schattschneider's later articulation in *The Semisovereign People* of the critical role that mass audiences
play in determining the outcome of contentious pluralist politics (1960).[4]
What applied to political competition generally—whether responsible or
not—was not seen by the APSA Committee on Political Parties in 1950 to
apply to partisan and electoral competition. As Herbert Weisberg (2002)
and Pomper and Weiner (2002) argue, in retrospect it is this latter incarnation of Schattschneider that has won the day, as the dynamic role of the
party in the electorate has shown itself to be an important impetus toward greater party responsibility.

PARTISANSHIP AND PARADIGM SHIFT IN POLITICAL SCIENCE

To properly situate the evolution of a place for ordinary people in party
politics, we need to understand the vestigial links between the APSA
committee's views on party responsibility and the previously dominant
state-centered paradigm of politics. The committee and its chair, Schattschneider, are caught in the crosscurrents of a paradigm shift. The very
notion of political parties as organized factions vying against each other
in the competitive marketplace of political ideas and institutions for the
hearts and minds of ordinary Americans embodies the core aims of a
pluralist paradigm of political science research. Yet the Committee Report also reflects a longing for more normative ends such as "national
cohesion" through party responsibility.

---

[3] Not all members of the APSA Committee had so clearly ignored the role of party activism and attachment. See, for example, Berdahl (1942).

[4] As Schattschneider would put it, "Every fight consists of two parts: (1) the few individuals who are actively engaged at the center and (2) the audience that is irresistibly attracted
to the scene. The spectators are as much a part of the overall situation as are the overt combatants ... for, likely as not, the *audience* determines the outcomes of the fight. . . . To understand any conflict it is necessary therefore to keep constantly in mind the relations between the combatants and the audience. . . . *This is the basic pattern of all politics*" (1960,
2, italics in original).

This state-centered paradigm dates back to the origins of political science in the late nineteenth century as an organized social science discipline. The discipline's founders, Francis Lieber (Columbia), Theodore Dwight Woolsey (Yale), John Burgess (Columbia), W. W. Willoughby (Johns Hopkins), and others, clearly derogated the idea that the core foundation of politics on American soil should be about what our founding fathers directed their focus to—the "consent of the governed," rooted in the "inalienable rights of men." Rather, the founders were all deeply influenced by the German tradition of scholarship on the politics of the time, in which the "state" was an organic entity and the center of a disciplinary focus. Lieber, commonly acknowledged as the first scholar to advocate the scientific study of politics as an academic discipline in America, describes the state as "the greatest institution on earth" (1838, 78) and a "sacred institution . . . [that] elevates everything that appertains to it" (180).

For Lieber, Woolsey, and others, the rights of persons did not exist outside the state. Rather, natural rights made sense only within the context of the state and society. No one is more direct about this than Burgess, who described the state as "the source of individual liberty" (1890, 89) and who remarked that although "the revolutionists of the 18th century said that individual liberty was a natural right; that it belonged to the individual as a human being, without regard to the state or society in which or the government under which, he lived . . . it is easy to see that this view is utterly impracticable and barren. There never was, and there never can be, any liberty on this earth among human beings outside of state organization" (175). Burgess went on to describe the state as "the most perfect organ which has as yet been attained in the civilization of the world for the interpretation of the human consciousness of right. It furnishes the best vantage-ground as yet reached for the contemplation of the purpose of the sojourn of mankind upon earth" (85).

Furthermore, these founders propounded a teleological view of the relationship of persons, society, and the state. The term "government" was explicitly distinguished from "state," with government representing the mechanical means of executing the will of the state. Sovereignty that obtained to the state was described by Burgess as "original, absolute, unlimited universal power over the individual subject and over all associations of subjects" (1890, 53). Burgess, however, takes a moment to note: "Of course the State may abuse its unlimited power over the individual, but this is never to be presumed. It is the human organ least likely to be wrong, and therefore, we must hold to the principle that the State can do no wrong" (56).

Such a state-centered, normatively laden stasiology as found in the

APSA Committee Report in 1950 may strike readers of today's parties literature as peculiar, if not disingenuous or otherwise off base. The shift from the approach to the study of parties in the APSA Committee Report to that which emerged in the 1940s and 1950s and prevails to the present day closely parallels what scholars of the history of ideas have described as a "paradigm shift" in political science as a discipline. There is some contention as to whether political science has undergone one or multiple paradigm shifts, but the practice of viewing politics through a panoptic state was replaced by a shift toward pluralism and behavioralism sometime between World War I and the mid-1950s (Dahl 1961a, Farr 1995, Gunnell 1995, Dryzek 2006).[5] The impulse behind the move to pluralism as an empirical and normative framework was a rejection of the statist's predilection for viewing America's diversity as a "problem," rather than a defining feature of its polity. This plea for a pluralist conception of liberalism joined well with the behavioralist spur to (1) study politics using scientific methods and (2) study politics by observing, systematically, how people behave (Farr 1995). As we shall see in the coming sections, the emergence of the study of party identification powerfully embodies both core aims of behavioralism and pluralism—political parties were the obvious institutional form for examining how individuals acted in groups to pursue collective goals, and the "party in the electorate" would be best researched by using the most scientific method of the day to discern voter intentions, the public opinion survey.

This turn to the historiography of the discipline's approach to parties serves to foreground two critical points that we return to at this chapter's end. The first of these is that the methods and frameworks we bring to our analysis are not prefigured by some essential nature of the phenomenon we seek to study and explain. Second, following Kuhn's thoughts on scientific revolutions, paradigms not only capture prevailing social conventions for capturing reality but can sometimes also be constitutive of that reality (Kuhn 1962). Thus, as the normative framework of plural liberalism and the empirical framework of political behavioralism come to the foreground, so too does a conception of political parties in which parties are valued normatively as an institutional intermediary between

---

[5] The bones of contention here on the singularity or multiplicity of paradigm shifts revolve around several issues: (1) whether the rise of behavioralism really counts as a structural revolution; (2) similarly for pluralism; (3) whether pluralism and behavioralism are separate or conjoined transformations in the discipline; (4) whether the "postbehavioralist" and "postpluralist" shifts over the last few decades—principally in the direction of formal models premised on rational choice, the direction of historical institutionalism, or perhaps even the most recent Perestroika revolt—count as yet another kind (or kinds) of paradigm shift (see J. B. Cohen 1985, Ball 1993, Farr 1995, Laitin 1995, Gunnell 2007, Dryzek 2006).

the people and their government and viewed empirically through the subjective lens of the people, as they affiliate, or fail to affiliate, with these institutional intermediaries.

THE PARTY IN THE ELECTORATE

The movement, if not revolution, toward pluralism after World War I and toward behavioralism after World War II marked the end of what one midcentury scholar termed the "political-biography-cum-political-ideology" phase of stasiology (Diamant 1954, 377). In its place, we find a more prominent place for nonelites and party identifiers in the research agendas of political scientists that emerge roughly contemporaneously with the APSA report of the Committee on Political Parties. In fact, even as early as 1924, we find a pretty sound repudiation of Burke's classic definition of parties and an affirmation of a more pluralist and electorally centered view: "What we seem to have in the United States is a division of the electorate into two great groups, neither of which is a political party in the sense of a band of men bound together by a common doctrine or a specific program . . . but only in the sense that each constitutes a great body of voters that have been in the habit of acting together on election day for the purpose of accomplishing certain tangible and immediate results" (E. E. Robinson 1924, 7).

In 1949, Dayton David McKean wrote that political parties exist "because of widely held opinions of two kinds, those approving of parties in general, and those approving of a particular party program, platform, or combination of party opinions and interests" (111). McKean made his case in substantial measure with a secondary analysis of Gallup (or the American Institute of Public Opinion, AIPO, as it was known at the time) poll data on self-identification with a party label. These Gallup polls represent the earliest incarnation of the survey measurement of the party in the electorate. The Gallup party-identification measure was first asked in March 1937: "Do you regard yourself as a Republican, a Democrat, or a Socialist?" By November 1939, the AIPO asked a variant of the now more familiar version of its party-identification question: "In politics, do you consider yourself a Republican, a Democrat . . . or an Independent?" And this party-identification question came to be a regular component of Gallup polls by the mid-1940s, when it began to be included among their standard battery of demographic items at the end of their questionnaire. In this initial conception, however, there is little indication that the attachment of ordinary individuals to party labels is a *defining* characteristic of political parties, not to mention little evidence that this attachment might act as a force that would impel the two-party system toward greater party responsibility.

The foundation for this stronger case is made several years later with the third, fourth, and fifth editions of V. O. Key.'s *Politics, Parties, and Pressure Groups* (1964), out of which the term "the party in the electorate" came to be a fixture in the lexicon of party scholars.[6] Key propounded a distinction between three different conceptions of political parties: the party as an organization, those members of political parties who hold government offices, and those ordinary individuals who identify with and support political parties through their vote and their active political participation. As Key argues, the "inner circle" of party leaders and activists "would amount to nothing without its following of faithful partisans" (1958, 232). Key describes partisanship among ordinary citizens as a "psychological attachment" of "remarkable durability" such that "even if the party member is an unfaithful attendant at party functions and an infrequent contributor to its finances, he is likely to have a strong attachment to the heroes of the party, to its principles as he interprets them, and to its candidates on election day" (233). This attachment, however, is further described as varying in intensity, "from the most unquestioning loyalty to the most casual sense of affiliation" (233).[7]

MEASURING PARTY IDENTIFICATION

Following closely on Key's heels are the efforts of social scientists at the University of Michigan's Survey Research Center to develop new methods to measure this psychological attachment. In a national survey of the American public fielded in June 1951, George Belknap and Angus Campbell sought to establish the influence of party identification on one's foreign policy views by asking respondents, "If a presidential election were held today, do you think you would vote for the Democratic, Republican, or for some other party?" (Belknap and Campbell 1952). The core expectation was that party identification mattered because "individual perceptions, evaluations, and behavior are determined in large part by the standards and values of the groups with which the person identifies" (601). This initial assessment of identification with political parties, however, was measured by one's likely vote intention. By the authors' own admis-

[6] As Weisberg (2002) notes, Key is careful to attribute the phrase "the party in the electorate" to Ralph Goldman's doctoral dissertation (1951).

[7] Interestingly, rather than describe this variance in party identification as a linear continuum, Key uses the metaphor of concentric circles, from a "small hard core of leaders and workers" to successively distal circles of people with diminishing loyalty to the party.

sion, the question wording "obviously represents a minimal expression of identification with a political party," and care is taken to note that "additional research is planned to explore this concept more fully and to develop a measure of degree of party identification" (601).

The political context of this need to develop a firmer foundation for the relationship between party identification and voting behavior was the electoral ascendance of Dwight David Eisenhower, the first Republican elected to the White House after twenty years of Democratic dominance. Clearly, vote intention alone is insufficiently discriminating in explaining Eisenhower's victory, since the Democrats retained a substantial majority of both houses of Congress. To preview, the enduring contribution of the Michigan approach to party identification would be to distinguish between long-term factors (party identification) that explained the continued Democratic control of Congress and short-term factors (candidate and issue-based considerations) that explained the ability of a popular Republican war hero to carry the day in 1952 and 1956.

The development of a more precise and probing measure of party identification would come in a 1951 pilot study of political attitudes in Ann Arbor, Michigan, by Warren Miller (Weisberg 2002). Then in the following year, the Michigan party-identification measure was fully launched in the 1952 American National Election Studies (ANES), and it is this multiple-item format that has been asked in every ANES since (Campbell, Gurin, and Miller 1954). Respondents are asked two of the following three items about their party identification. All respondents are first asked, "Generally speaking, do you usually think of yourself as a Republican, a Democrat, an Independent, or what?" Those who self-identify with a party are then asked, "Would you call yourself a strong [Republican/Democrat] or not a very strong [Republican/Democrat]?" And those who self-identify as an Independent are asked, "Do you think of yourself as closer to the Republican or Democratic Party?"

As we noted earlier vis-à-vis the initial Gallup polls, Campbell and his colleagues did not break entirely new ground in asking individuals to self-identify with a political party. What was groundbreaking, however, was the staunch effort made to develop and test a coherent account of a person's attachment to a political party and the implications this holds for her politics. On this point, there are two revealing differences between the question wording the Gallup poll used and that designed for the ANES. First, the ANES frames the consideration of its question with the phrase "generally speaking" and the word "usually." There is no such prompt with the Gallup poll. The underlying motivation behind the Michigan version of the question is the desire to tap into a stable predisposition and an enduring attachment to a political party. This contrast is even more prominent in the more recent modification of the Gallup ques-

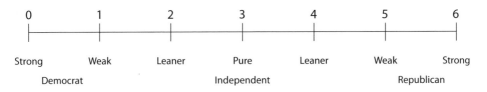

Figure 2.1. Party identification as a linear unidimensional scale

tion wording: "In politics, *as of today*, do you consider yourself a Republican, a Democrat, or an Independent?" (italics inserted). Note that the question cannot discriminate between, on the one hand, the stable partisan for whom "today" is no different from yesterday or tomorrow vis-à-vis his self-identification as a Republican or Democrat from, on the other hand, the more capricious citizen whose relationship to political parties is inconstant from one day to the next.

The second key difference is the use of follow-up questions in the ANES to distinguish between shades of attachments. As Campbell and his colleagues describe it, "The partisan self-image of all but the few individuals who disclaim any involvement in politics permits us to place each person in these samples on a continuum of partisanship extending from strong Republican to strongly Democratic. We use the word 'continuum' because we suppose that party identification is not simply a dichotomy but has a wide range of intensities in each partisan direction" (Campbell et al. 1960, 122). Most often, the sequence of questions in the ANES is used to construct a unidimensional variable composed of seven ordered categories, such as the one shown in figure 2.1.

By this coding, "weak" Democrats and Republicans are those who identify with these corresponding parties but whose identification is not strong. "Leaner" Democrats and Republicans are those who choose to identify as Independents in answer to the initial question but are willing to acknowledge a partisan bent, with the term "pure Independents" reserved for those who identify as Independents in answer to the initial question but reject any partisan inclinations in answer to the follow-up question. Pure Independents are placed squarely in the middle of the scale. In most uses of this party-identification scale today, the seven ordered categories are coded into an interval scale such as the zero- to six-point figure above, where the difference in strength of partisanship between a strong and a weak Democrat is assumed to be identical to, say, the difference between a pure Independent and a Democratic leaner.

Beyond this pointed comparison with the Gallup poll, the approach to studying the party in the electorate by asking randomly selected adults in opinion polls to self-identify with a political party or as an Independent also marks a turning point in the modern study of political behavior. The use of survey data garnered great favor for several reasons. First, it promised to move the prevailing scholarship beyond what Campbell and his colleagues described as "tendentious" journalistic and historical accounts that "rest on anecdotal material or on impressionistic judgments" (1960, 12). The use of randomly sampled survey data and statistical inference enabled a rigorous means of adjudicating between these anecdotes and impressions. Survey data also promised to hone in on the underlying relationships motivating voting behavior. Prior political science research (e.g., Eldersveld 1951; Lipset et al. 1954) focused on the analysis of aggregate election statistics of states, counties, wards, and precincts that allowed, at best, fragile inferences on individual-level vote choices.[8] Moreover, the other favored conceptualization of party identification—one's intention to vote for a party (Belknap and Campbell 1952; Berelson et al. 1954)—was tautological, unfalsifiable, and generally of little use in drawing causal inferences about voting behavior.

This empirical articulation of party identification is also noteworthy in defining what party identification is not. Party identification has to cover more than those formally affiliated and active members of a political party, since this leaves the vote choice of too many unaffiliated and inactive citizens unexplained. Party identification also has to be more than just one's vote intention or past voting record, since, in the first case, the relationship of vote intention to vote choice is practically tautological and, in the second case, the fact that voters switch parties across election cycles goes unexplained. As Campbell and his colleagues contend, what better explains the variations in individual vote choice is one's identification with political parties, conceived of as "a psychological attachment, which can persist without legal recognition or evidence of formal membership and even without a consistent record of party support" (1960, 121)?

It turns out that this scale of party identification fares extraordinarily well in explaining how we vote (Campbell and Stokes 1959; Campbell et al. 1960; Miller and Shanks 1996). Party identification was able to account for more of the variation in vote choice than any competing explanation of the day. Specifically, the Michigan School's measure better explained a wide range of outcomes than the influence of social groupings such as union membership, urban-rural residence, and religion. Lazarsfeld and his colleagues at Columbia's Bureau of Applied Social Research drew their inferences about voting behavior based on an "Index of Politi-

---

[8] The fragility here is due to the "ecological inference problem" (G. King 1997)—individual-level patterns cannot be reliably inferred from aggregate-level data. The concern with ecological correlations was roughly concurrent with the work of Campbell et al. (see Robinson 1950 and L. Goodman 1953).

cal Predispositions" studied in two separate contexts—Erie County, Ohio (Lazarsfeld et al. 1944) and Elmira, New York (Berelson et al. 1954). Campbell and his colleagues countered, seemingly definitively and with a broader inferential reach, that social groupings mattered less when political predispositions were properly conceived of as party identification and survey data were properly collected from a random sample of the population of adults in the United States writ large.[9]

MEASUREMENT ISSUES IN PARTY IDENTIFICATION

It should be clear from our discussion thus far that how we have come to study and think about party identification today was far from preordained a half century ago. It was by no means certain to Angus Campbell and his young trio of collaborators in the 1940s that "the party in the electorate" would be so critical to our understanding of party politics and, even more so, that it would take the particularly behavioral and, subsequent to that, cognitive form that it takes today. Having noted this, it is fair to say that today this measure of party identification is seemingly ubiquitous in its use, uniform in its operationalization, and universal in its sway over how we think and act in the political sphere. As Alan Gerber and Donald Green put it, "In the field of public opinion and electoral behavior, no explanatory variable is more pervasive than party identification" (1998, 794). Everett Carll Ladd of the Roper Institute notes that "no other measure of voters' partisan preferences and the parties' strength has been deemed nearly so telling a political statistic, or used as widely as party identification" (1991, 17). And Donald Kinder and David Sears declare that "party identification remains the single most important determinant of individual voting decisions" (1985, 686). Despite this seemingly overwhelming consensus, few measures in political science have been as closely and critically scrutinized as party identification. There have been several forceful analyses on how we currently measure party identification and a vigorous debate over why people come to identify with a political party.

On measurement, there have been numerous studies of alternate question wordings from the standard ANES multi-item measure. Gallup and NBC polls, for instance, use the lead-in "In politics today / as of today"; Harris and Roper polls prompt respondents with "Regardless of how you voted / may have voted"; Associated Press polls ask the unadorned ver-

[9] There were several randomly sampled national opinion surveys of political opinion prior to the 1952 ANES: a 1944 poll by the National Opinion Research Center and the 1948 ANES by the Survey Research Center of the University of Michigan. These surveys, however, did not ask respondents to self-identify with a political party.

sion: "Are you a Democrat, Republican, or what"; and so on with other variants. These differences, it turns out, can be consequential. Party identification is no different from any other attitude item in its vulnerability to survey context. Yet the full force of a particular question wording ultimately depends on the underlying conceptions of party identification at stake. The comparison between the ANES wording and the Gallup wording, for instance, rests principally on the conceptual distinction between partisanship as a long-term predisposition and partisanship as a potentially short-term attachment. Viewed thus, it is not surprising that the Gallup version leads to greater variance across surveys in the distribution of party identification (Abramson and Ostrom 1991) and a greater tendency to self-identify with the party that is leading in preelection polls (Borrelli, Lockerbie, and Niemi 1987).

A second concern about the proper measurement of party identification is how the multiple-item ANES party-identification measure should be scaled. As we noted earlier, the most common practice is to use all the available variation in a 7-point (0 to 6) integer scale, where the measurement approach assumes that the difference between a "0" (strong Democrats in figure 2.1) and a "1" (weak Democrats) vis-à-vis one's partisanship is identical to the difference between a "2" (Democratic leaners) and a "3" (pure Independents) or between a "3" (pure Independents) and a "4" (Republican leaners), and so on. As Keith et al. (1992) and others (Lodge and Tursky 1979, Weisberg 1980, Miller and Wattenberg 1983) have shown, the differences between these categories are not always equal, especially in the virtually indistinguishable behavioral differences between weak partisans and Independent leaners. William Jacoby (1982) argues that the standard 7-point scale systematically shrinks the intervals between the Republican categories of the scale. In the extreme, John Petrocik (1974) finds that the standard party-identification scale violates the basic axiom of transitivity in its relationship to key behavioral indicators of partisanship—put plainly, Independent leaners appear at times more partisan in their behavior than do weak Republicans or weak Democrats.

Based on these studies, several alternatives to the standard 7-point scale have been advocated. One proposal is to combine weak partisans and Independent leaners and measure party identification as a 5-point scale, but this does not take full account of the potentially errant assumption of equal intervals between categories of partisanship. Thus Morris Fiorina (1981) proposes discarding the idea of party identification as an interval-level variable and measuring it instead categorically, with the use of polychotomous dependent variable estimators when party identification is the dependent variable and, presumably, dichotomous "dummy" variables for each category when party identification is an explanatory variable (see also Franklin and Jackson 1983). Warren Miller himself has advocated

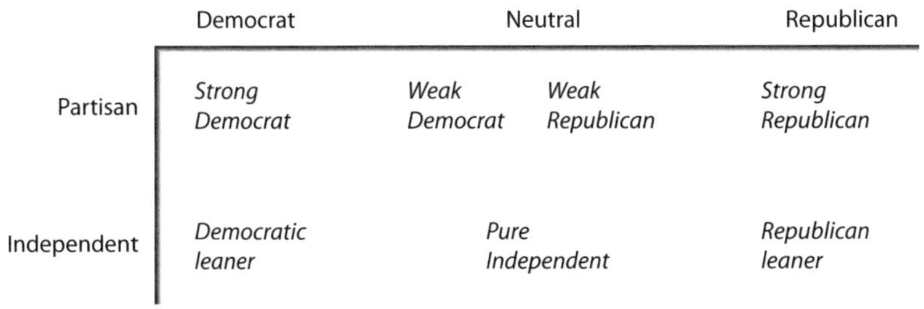

	Democrat	Neutral		Republican
Partisan	*Strong Democrat*	*Weak Democrat*	*Weak Republican*	*Strong Republican*
Independent	*Democratic leaner*	*Pure Independent*		*Republican leaner*

Figure 2.2. Party identification in two dimensions

the use of only the first item in the ANES multi-item measure, in which respondents are simply asked to self-identify with the labels "Democrat," "Republican," and "Independent" (W. E. Miller 1991, Miller and Shanks 1996). These are compelling alternatives to minimize error in our measurement and strengthen the inferences we draw about party identification, but they fail to deliver an account of why the intervals between categories are unequal or their behavioral effects intransitive.

One influential and controversial account of these patterns is that party identification is multidimensional. That is, contrary to the Michigan party-identification scale's assumption that there is a single linear continuum from strong Republicans to strong Democrats, Herbert Weisberg (1980, 1983) and others (see especially Katz 1979; Howell 1980; Valentine and Van Wingen 1980; Jacoby 1982; Kamieniecki 1985, 1988) contend that this standard measure conflates an individual's attitudes toward several distinct objects—one's general views of political parties, one's specific view of the Republican and Democratic parties, and one's political independence. As Weisberg (1980) notes, the ANES measure and its accompanying seven-point scale make several potentially errant assumptions about the concept of party identification. First, they assume that Independence is either the absence of strong partisanship or neutrality with respect to both parties. At least two potentially distinct and empirically testable dimensions emerge from this assumption: one continuum in which the midpoint of one's identification as a Republican or Democrat is neutrality, another continuum from strong partisanship to Independence. Each of the seven ANES categories would then fit into these two dimensions, as shown in figure 2.2.

This argument for party identification as a two-dimensional concept is roughly analogous to Claggett's (1981) and Shively's (1979) proposals to separate out party acquisition from partisan intensity. In addition to the assumption about Independence, the standard ANES measure assumes singularity and equality: that is, each individual identifies with one and only one political party, and this attachment is equally strong

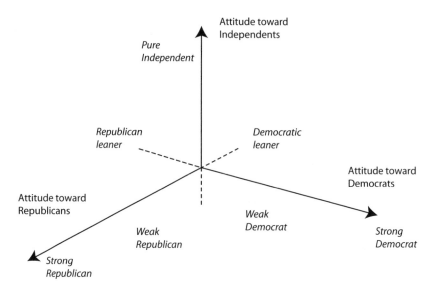

Figure 2.3. Party identification in three dimensions

and salient across individuals. More specifically, on the assumption of singularity, the tacit assumption in the standard ANES measure is that a positive valence toward the Democratic Party implies a negative valence toward the Republican Party. In principle, one might be positive toward both or negative toward both but willing to choose one as a predominant self-identification if constrained to do so. The consequence of these assumptions is that party identification might be better measured in three dimensions, with each of the seven ANES categories potentially mapped onto the three-dimensional space, as shown in figure 2.3 (also adapted from Weisberg 1980).

Figures 2.2 and 2.3 make the graphic case for what a more multidimensional conception of party identification might look like. The empirical case favoring party identification as a multidimensional construct is based principally on studies that show the inconsistent ordering across the seven partisan categories and the poor convergent validity with feeling thermometer scores on political parties and Independents, a reasonable alternative to the ANES linear self-identification measure. Jacoby (1982) finds that only two in three college undergraduates order their identification with party labels in a manner consistent with the standard linear ANES scale. Weisberg (1980) shows that only one in two respondents gave ANES feeling thermometer scores to political parties and Independents that were compatible with their party identification on the standard linear ANES scale. Weisberg also shows that the correlations between feeling thermometer scores for the Republican and Democratic parties are not highly negative (as the idea of party identification as a linear continuum presumes) but range from zero to only somewhat negative. Alvarez (1990) found that slightly more than one in three respondents to the ANES revealed a transitive correspondence between his party identification and his feeling thermometer rating. Somewhat against the weight of these findings, Donald Green (1988) argues that a substantial measure of the seeming inconsistency between one's affect toward the Democratic and Republican parties results from measurement error—specifically, the upward bias in thermometer ratings. Once this measurement error is explicitly modeled with confirmatory factor analysis, the correlation between Green's latent party factors turns out to be very strongly negative.

These measurement issues—wording, scaling, and dimensionality—do not exhaust the concerns that have been raised against the ANES party-identification items.[10] Yet they are, in large measure, politely ignored, with their critical force often in lieu of practical considerations. For example, a typical response to the issue of dimensionality is John Kessel's view that "some citizens have multiple (partisan and Independent) reference groups, some citizens have only one such reference group, and some citizens have no such reference group. No one-dimensional taxonomy is going to capture all of this, but the traditional classification is a good first approximation" (1984, 529 [from Weisberg 1993, 723–74]). Morris Fiorina even goes so far as to defend a unidimensional scale on the grounds that a multidimensional scale would "let methodology run away with the substance" (1981, 105). Explicit in Fiorina's provocation and implicit in Kessel's pragmatism is the shared feature of most methodological critiques of party identification: namely, that they capably demonstrate anomalous, contradictory empirical patterns without using these critiques as a foundation for a more substantive challenge to our existing theoretical accounts of what party identification is and why people come to have it.

CONCEPTUAL ISSUES IN PARTY IDENTIFICATION

Methodological concerns notwithstanding, the genie of party identification is out of the bottle, and there is no putting it back in again. Yet there is ample debate among capable judges over just who this genie is and where her powers come from. In this section we sketch, in critical relief, the two leading theoretical accounts of party identification. We describe

[10] For a detailed inventory of these concerns, see Weisberg (1993).

the more social-psychological account first articulated by scholars at the University of Michigan and the subsequent emergence of a more information-based and ideology-rooted Downsian view. We next identify some limitations common to each account. To preview, both accounts fall shy of the mark in explaining why we self-identify as political Independents and how this self-identification varies across racial and ethnic groups. In chapter 3 we argue that these two relatively neglected facets of party identification—political Independents and racial/ethnic group differences—offer critical leverage to our modified, more general account of party identification. This modified account, importantly, stakes its ground on theoretical foundations, not methodological considerations or empirical consequences.

The Michigan School

The story of party identification, in its debut by Campbell, Converse, Miller, and Stokes (1960), is simple and straightforward enough. Party identification is, in the first instance, the psychological attachment of an individual to an institution—specifically, a political party. As Warren Miller describes it, this "sense of belonging to the political group" constitutes "an important part of the individual's self-identity as a political actor . . . our individual sense of *personal identity* is derived from groups to which we belong" (1991, 22; italics in original). According to the authors of *The American Voter*, "Most Americans have this sense of attachment with one party or the other. And for the individual who does, the strength and direction of party identification are facts of central importance in accounting for attitude and behavior" (Campbell et al. 1960, 121).

The claim in *The American Voter* is that this psychological attachment to party is the most primitive element in a "funnel of causality" explaining vote choice, with other factors such as attitudes about the Democratic and Republican candidates, about foreign and domestic issues, and about the groups involved in the election as the more immediate, proximate elements. By defining and measuring party identification as an enduring psychological attachment in this chain of relationships, Campbell and his colleagues propounded the insightful and influential distinction between short-term considerations (e.g., issues and candidates specific to a campaign) and long-term predispositions such as party identification (Campbell and Stokes 1959; Campbell et al. 1960).[11]

Beyond this linkage of political institutions to personal identity, Camp-

---

[11] This basic framework is predominant even today, in models of public opinion and political behavior such as John Zaller's "receive-accept-sample" theory (1992).

bell and his colleagues described three defining characteristics of party identification. Partisanship, as a habit of the heart and mind, is acquired very early in one's life, with few exceptions corresponding to the partisan habits of one's parents. About three out of four individuals with parents of the same party would self-identify with that party (Campbell et al. 1960, 147). This habit, moreover, persists over the course of an individual's life. More than 90 percent of self-identified Democrats reported never having identified as Republicans, and about 80 percent of self-identified Republicans reported never having identified as Democrats (148). Third, almost all Americans could locate themselves somewhere on the ANES continuum of party identification. Across seven initial Michigan studies from October 1952 through October 1958, just about 95 percent of respondents were able to locate themselves somewhere on the party-identification scale (124).[12]

Each of these defining characteristics has been challenged in the half century since the first Michigan surveys. On the ubiquity of self-placement on the party-identification scale, subsequent studies have found a substantially greater proportion of "partisan misfits," ranging from 10 percent (Miller and Wattenberg 1983) to almost 30 percent (Weisberg 1980; Dennis 1988a; Niemi et al. 1991). On durability and stability, subsequent studies describe significant movement in party identification over time with evidence based on panel studies (Allsop and Weisberg 1988; Brody and Rothenberg 1988) and the unmistakable surge in Americans who identified as Independents during the 1970s and 1980s (Wattenberg 1996). Perhaps more devastating than this apparent instability over time were studies that suggested that party identification may not be the underlying predisposition in a funnel of causality leading to one's vote decision. Rather, short-term considerations that led individuals to vote against their long-term party identification appeared to influence their identification (Jackson 1975; Page and Jones 1979).[13] More recently, however, Donald Green and his colleagues have generated renewed vigor for the thesis that party identification is a remarkably durable and potent attribute, especially once the exigencies of measurement error are taken into account (Green and Palmquist 1990, 1994; Green et al. 1998, 2002).

Perhaps the most forceful and sustained attack against the Michigan school of thought, however, is reserved for the view that party identification is principally the product of one's preadult socialization. It may yet

---

[12] Arguably, a fourth defining characteristic is that party identification—to the extent that cognition and affect were sharply differentiated at the time—is a distinctly "affective orientation to an important group-object in his environment" (121).

[13] There is also a lively debate over whether changes in presidential approval and economic evaluations at the aggregate level shift the distribution of "macropartisanship" (MacKuen et al. 1989; cf. Abramson and Ostrom 1991; Green et al. 1998).

be the case that the single strongest predictor of an individual's party identification is the partisanship of that person's parents, but the strength of this relationship still leaves unanswered questions about the theoretical foundation of that relationship and empirical anomalies in that relationship. Data on parental partisanship are at best an indirect instrument of the actual socialization process that generates partisan loyalties. In more precise studies of childhood socialization conducted by Kent Jennings and his colleagues using a three-wave panel study of parents and their children in 1965, 1973, and 1982, fully 40 percent of children whose parents shared the same party loyalties defected from that partisan attachment (Jennings and Niemi 1974, 1981; Jennings and Markus 1984; Niemi and Jennings 1991).

THE DOWNSIAN MODEL

The result that familial socialization could not account for the party identification of a significant portion of Americans opened the door for what has become the leading alternative to the Michigan school of thought. If it is not the case that we always mimic the partisan habits of our parents, then—so the argument goes—our party identification is probably the reflection of our judgments about each political party, given our general ideological preferences over alternate states of the political world. Alternatively put, in this account, party identification is the manifestation of the perceived affinity between a person's political wants and needs and the publicly stated positions of the two parties on those issues. It is worth noting that this view of the party in the electorate too has its origins in the tumultuous sea changes in the intellectual currents of the mid-twentieth century. Earlier we noted the shift—viewed through the change in focus from the 1950 APSA Committee on Parties report to the 1960 publication of *The American Voter*—from a research agenda wrought out of normative, praxis-oriented concerns about how parties as organizations might be changed to one based in empirical tests of competing causal claims about how parties are situated in the electorate. This shift well exemplifies the behavioral revolution (Ross 1991), and its subsequent cognitive turn, in political science.

A shift in the research agenda of political scientists of comparable significance has been the move to ply the tools of the microeconomic trade—of especial note, axioms of instrumental rationality and market competition—to construct a "positive theory" of individuals and institutions in the political realm. With respect to the party in the electorate, this economistic turn is most often attributed to the formal derivation of the median voter theorem in Anthony Downs's (1957) and Duncan Black's roughly contemporaneous works (1948, 1958). Both scholars draw from Hotelling's (1929) initial insights on economic competition under duopolies, and the most commonly known result of the median voter theorem is perhaps still best stated by Hotelling, who observes that the "competition for votes between the Republican and Democratic parties does not lead to a clear drawing of issues, and adoption of two strongly contrasted positions between which the voter may choose. Instead, each party strives to make its platform as much like the others as possible" (1929, 54).

This articulation of the centripetal force of electoral competition is often taken as damning refutation of the APSA Committee on Parties' advocacy of party responsibility. The assumption (or perhaps aspiration) of the committee members was that if parties offered voters clear choices with well-defined differences, voters would make responsible electoral decisions that would hold parties accountable for their platforms. Given a bare-bones account of individual rationality, voter motivation, and candidates' strategic response, however, the median voter theorem shows that parties have no incentives to offer clear and distinct electoral choices.

To an extent, this seemingly devastating implication should have come as no surprise to the APSA Committee on Parties, as the central insights of the median voter theorem were hardly earth-shattering for the leading political scientists of Downs's or Hotelling's day. Observations of ideological convergence and the reluctance of parties to take on consequential issues date at least as far back as the end of the nineteenth century. Thus James Bryce observes that "the great parties were like two bottles. Each bore a label denoting the kind of liquor it contained, but each was empty" (1888, 3), and A. Lawrence Lowell claims that in two-party systems, the parties tend to move toward one another at the "political center of gravity" (1898). Among Downs's and Black's contemporaries, Schattschneider notes that "the most common criticism made of the American parties is not that they have been tyrannical but that they have been indistinguishable" (1942, 85); Key observes that the act of juggling different forces within the party in the electorate tends "to pull the party leaderships from their contrasting anchorages toward the center ... party appeals often sound much alike and thereby contribute to the bewilderment of observers of American politics" (1964, 220).[14]

What was novel and made a lasting impact was the carefully constructed logic underlying this centripetal result, wrought from arguments about competition in the duopolistic marketplace of ideas on the institutional side and arguments about rational ignorance, information costs, and the optimal use of partisan heuristics on the individual side. The keystone is the idea of "proximity voting": that individuals have

[14] See also Sait (1942, 190) and W. Goodman (1956, 45–46).

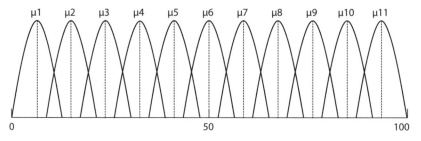

μ1   μ2   μ3   μ4   μ5   μ6   μ7   μ8   μ9   μ10   μ11

0   50   100

Figure 2.4. Mapping policy preferences on a single dimension

distinct preferences over the universe of possible political outcomes (with an optimal outcome and monotonically diminishing utilities as we move away from that "ideal point") and that each individual will vote for the party or candidate whose publicly declared position on a given issue comes the closest to her ideal point. Figure 2.4 shows a typical spatial representation of voter preferences over a single unidimensional continuum, from extremely liberal outcomes on one end to extremely conservative ones on the other. Where a person sits on this continuum depends on the pleasure or pain she derives from the range of possible states of the political world, represented by a utility function with a maximum at a person's "ideal point" (represented as $\mu1$, $\mu2$, $\mu3$, ... $\mu11$) and monotonically diminishing levels of pleasure as we move away from that ideal point along the continuum. Set proximity voting into motion, and the median voter theorem obtains: when parties, or candidates, are motivated to win a majority share (50 percent plus 1) of the electoral vote, they will move inexorably toward one another until they converge at the ideal point of the median voter in the electorate (in figure 2.4, at the ideal point of voter 6, or $\mu6$).[15]

Building on this foundation—and following in similar footsteps taken by Jackson (1975) and Page and Jones (1979)—Morris Fiorina redefined "party identification" as "the difference between an individual's past political experiences with the two parties, perturbed by a factor ... that represents effects not included directly in an individual's political experiences" (e.g., parents' party identification) (1981, 89). Party identification is thus reconceptualized as the "running-tally of retrospective evalua-

[15] Some additional technical details are necessary for the theorem to hold. First, the choice set for a given election is between two (and only two) candidates, representing two (and only two) major political parties. Second, elections are decided by majority rule. Third, the principal means for candidates to win or lose is by positioning themselves along the continuum. Finally, there needs to be an odd number of voters in every election, although the basic intuition of the theorem is intact even when this condition is not met.

tions" of both parties or, in Achen's (1992, 2001) rendition, the Bayesian process of updating one's long-term predisposition to identify with a party with shorter-term considerations (see also Gerber and Green 1998). Party identification, from this standpoint, is also an efficient heuristic to use low-information opinion cues to deduce more complete information about an issue or candidate (Popkin 1991, Lupia and McCubbins 1998).

This Downsian account presents a tidy alternative explanation for the bedrock empirical relationship between party identification and voting behavior. The direction and strength of voters' partisanship predict their likely vote choice, presumably because the match between voters' and candidates' parties reflects a match between voters' and candidates' ideological preference orderings. That is, underlying this view of party identification is the presumption that a continuum of political preference orderings—from extremely liberal to extremely conservative— undergirds voters' party identification (Jackson 1975, Franklin and Jackson 1983, D. Green 1988, Abramowitz and Saunders 1998). The presumed empirical relationship that results is between a linear continuum of partisanship and a linear continuum of ideology: strong liberals are the most likely group to identify as strong Democrats, strong conservatives are the most likely group to identify as strong Republicans, and staunch moderates are the most likely group to identify as pure Independents. Party identification, from this Downsian view, is the heuristic that enables us to most efficiently decode which candidate's or party's declared positions best approximate our ideal point.

This relationship is seemingly at odds with the thrust of *The American Voter*'s (1960) finding that policy preferences and ideological consistency appear to pale in comparison with party identification as an antecedent of individual vote choice. As the authors put it, "Forces not based on party loyalty that influence the decisions of the American electorate appear almost wholly free of ideological correlation" (Campbell et al. 1960).[16] Philip Converse's subsequent "The Nature of Belief Systems in Mass Publics" (1964) presents the most exacting and devastating refutation of the idea of ideology as a constraint on our political preferences. The publicly stated opinions of ordinary individuals—asked of the same people on the same set of policy items over different points in time—hang together so loosely and with no visible common thread of liberal or conservative ideological thinking that Converse deemed these responses "non-attitudes" (1964, 1970). Donald Stokes (1963) further contested Downs's idea that political preferences mapped easily onto a single ideo-

[16] At roughly the same time, Herbert McCloskey and his coauthors began to suggest the irrelevance of liberalism and conservatism to one's party identification and political orientation (McCloskey 1958; McCloskey et al. 1960; McCloskey 1964).

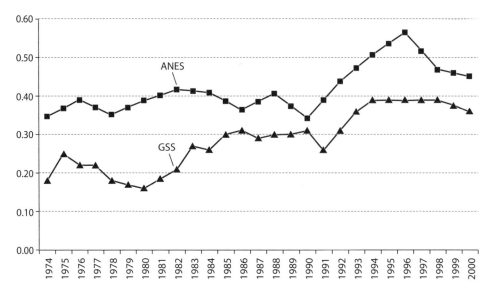

Figure 2.5. Correlation of party identification and ideology, 1974–2000

logical dimension, a critique that would later be formalized by McKelvey (1976), Enelow and Hinich (1984), and others.[17]

The first attempt to reestablish a more coherent, constrained basis for Americans' public policy views foundered on the rough current of question wording (Nie et al. 1979; cf. Bishop, Oldendick, and Tuchfarber 1978; Bishop, Tuchfarber, and Oldendick 1978; Sullivan et al. 1978). In fact, efforts to adjudicate the seeming potency of party identification and the seeming impotence of ideology as a constraint, and the relationship between the two, continue to focus on methodological issues such as measurement error and the commensurability of survey items (Achen 1975; D. Green 1988; Krosnick and Berent 1993). More recently, however, the evidence favoring a more intimate relationship between partisanship and ideology is gaining force, and it is doing so as a result of substantive shifts in the nature of partisan politics in the United States. Specifically, the evidence of the increasing coherence of ideology as a primary political predisposition coincides with the evidence of a rise in the ideological polarization of elites and masses (Dionne 1991; Fiorina et al. 2005). Numerous studies suggest a resurgence of sharp partisan differences in congressional roll-call voting and primaries (e.g., Poole and Rosenthal 1984, 1997; Ansolabehere et al. 2001; Burden 2001; McCarty et al. 2006).

[17] See also Duverger (1954, 231–33) and Sartori (1976, 335–36).

To the extent that public opinion responds to elite cues (Carmines and Stimson 1989; Brody 1991; Zaller 1992), this increasing elite ideological polarization may result in the greater clarity of partisan cues at the mass level (Hetherington 2001). The upshot here is that Americans are increasingly able to find decisive differences between the two parties and correctly place the Democrats and Republicans ideologically. Figure 2.5 presents simple bivariate correlations over time (1974 to 2000) between two similarly scaled (seven-point) measures of party identification and liberal-conservative ideology from two separate sources—the American National Election Studies and the General Social Survey (GSS). The positive relationship between party identification and left-right ideology is consistently higher in ANES surveys than in GSS surveys, but the principal point here is that the relationship is strongly and increasingly positive, growing more than twofold, from 1980 to the mid-1990s, according to the GSS.[18] Thus, as Donald Green suggests, "The mass public draws evaluative connections *across* ideological and partisan groups in relative coherent ways" (1988, 772).

Yet, this growing linkage between partisanship and ideological self-placement does not necessarily imply that party polarization among elite politicians has brought on ideological and partisan polarization among ordinary Americans. It simply means that the two scales are increasing in their correspondence. The nation as a whole may be growing more moderate ideologically, and more Independent in partisan terms, and the pattern over time that we see in figure 2.5 would hold. As Fiorina and his colleagues argue, "Americans are closely divided, but we are not deeply divided, and we are closely divided because many of us are ambivalent and uncertain, and consequently reluctant to make firm commitments to parties, politicians, or policies" (2005, ix). Even Fiorina's critics in the debate on whether the masses are following elites in being divided acknowledge that Americans, for the most part, are ideological moderates (Abramowitz and Saunders 2008).

Moreover, as we shall see in chapter 3, one striking feature of the growing linkage of party identification and ideological self-placement is that it has occurred at roughly the same time that the proportion of nonpartisans in America has grown. Thus, while it may no longer be accurate to portray America's two major parties as Tweedledum and Tweedledee, many Americans may still view them as insufficiently distinct to matter to *them*. Voters (and nonvoters) in America continue to face a very limited menu of partisan choices. Furthermore, by comparison with the ideological spectrum of major parties in European nations,

---

[18] In the most recent 2008 ANES data, this relationship continues to hold strong, with a correlation coefficient of 0.52.

American party choices come with a limited and mostly centrist range of ideological views and policy positions (Castles and Mair 1984). Thus, despite assertions that parties play the functional role of collecting and representing the diverse interests of a plural electorate—and, as a result, enable a working democracy—there are reasons to worry that America's major parties and its two-party system remain alienating, unrepresentative, uninformative, and offscreen to many. Party identification, the once regnant force on mass beliefs during the midcentury era in which Converse and his colleagues at Michigan did much of their research, may no longer govern supremely or singularly.

The Michigan and Downsian Approaches in Historical Context

In this chapter, we have started our journey toward a fuller account of race, immigration, and political Independents by mapping the historical and ontological origins of the political-scientific study of party identification. Our narrative starts in the middle decades of the twentieth century, a critical juncture in these origins. Prior to this period, the political science scholarship on parties (as exemplified by the 1950 APSA Committee on Parties report) vigorously engaged real-world consequences and normative controversies but neglected, in the main, to consider the "party in the electorate" as a topic of inquiry. In the ensuing decades, the attachments of ordinary individuals to political parties not only began to take center stage but also came to be embodied in a distinct and, for the most part, invariant form.

This distinct and invariant embodiment of what party identification is and how we study it, moreover, comes to light from the inspiration to develop a cumulative science of politics and governance (Ross 1979; Lowi 1992; Farr and Seidelman 1993; Farr 1995). In the process, the focus of this science vis-à-vis the party in the electorate has primarily been shaped by the way in which political action has come to be conceptualized and party identification has come to be operationalized. Viewed as a linear continuum from strong ties to the Democratic Party to strong ties to the Republican Party, party identification takes on a form that fits comfortably with both the Michigan and the Downsian account—in the first case, vis-à-vis the varying intensities of social group identification, and in the second case, vis-à-vis the underlying dimension of left-right ideological preferences. The upshot, as Keith and others put it, is that "in its modern meaning, 'party identification' is a product of survey research" (1992, 3). To most scholars in this field today, party identification, ontologically, does not exist outside of how we measure it in social surveys. As we have seen in this chapter, one effect is that much of the critical debate about party identification is focused on competing claims over the appropriate methodology (how to define, operationalize, and scale party identification) and the better explanatory model (whether party identification is better viewed as a product of long-term considerations, such as one's socialization and social group identity, or shorter-term considerations, like running tallies of parties and their candidates).

Rather than focus on adjudicating whether we are bound by the ties of habit and history *or* by the ties of information and interest, our standpoint is that the explanatory fit of this positivist, measurement-based study of partisanship depends on the historical contexts and relevant groups and the substance of party competition. One key point of this chapter is that *how* we choose to study political phenomena depends in no small measure on *when* we choose to study them. The transformation in how we study political parties and the relationship of ordinary individuals to them over the last half century or more have been nothing short of sweeping. Not coincidentally, the post–World War II milieu out of which the APSA committee report beckoned the end of one era of stasiology and *The American Voter* heralded the onset of another is markedly different from our present-day era. Beyond the general observation that political science research is probably better characterized today as postbehavioralist and postpluralist and the more specific impression that the study of parties and political behavior too has changed with it (Reiter 2006), we call attention in chapter 3 to two other important changes: the nature of pluralism vis-à-vis racial/ethnic diversity and, with it, the growing importance and multidimensional determinants of nonpartisanship.

To underscore the importance of properly situating the study of party identification in historical context, we turn to the 1952 election, which was the origin of the ANES root-party identification question—a conceptualization in which party identification is explicit prior to partisan voting behavior. It is no surprise that this root question arises out of the seemingly contradictory circumstances of the 1952 election, in which a Republican candidate, General Dwight D. Eisenhower, successfully gained the presidency despite the overwhelmingly Democratic "partisanship" of the country. Similarly, it is no surprise that the empirical evidence favoring a more ideology- and information-based Downsian view of party identification coincides with the growing polarization of party elites and the politics of divided government. Thus, the seeming conceptual rift between the Michigan and Downsian schools of party identification is ultimately a not-so-useful and a not-so-oppositional dichotomy. Like many other competing theoretical frameworks in the social sciences, it is less a case of which is right than it is a case of properly specifying the contexts in which *both* the Michigan *and* the Downsian views add to our understanding of the relationship that the mass electorate has (or fails to develop) with the party system in the United States.

Recognizing the contingent contributions of each account, however, is not equivalent to conceptual carelessness, theoretical agnosticism, or a radical form of contextual relativism. To avoid these pitfalls, we animate the broader directive to understand the party in the electorate by considering what has actually changed since *The American Voter* vis-à-vis the relationship that mass electorates have with the political parties that purport to represent them. In the chapter that follows, we present the case that both the Michigan and the Downsian schools of thought have yet to fully take account of two major transformations of the last half century—one in the actual distribution of party identification and the other in the individuals comprising the mass electorate. We argue that these foundational changes give new force to the methodological criticisms and conceptual limitations we have discussed in this chapter and, as a result, critical leverage into what a more capacious theory of party identification might look like. Thus, in chapter 3 we make the case for focusing analytically and substantively on the choice not to self-identify with either the Democratic or the Republican Party and on the racially and ethnically group-specific pathways to that (non)partisan identification.

Identity, Ideology, Information, and the Dimensionality of Nonpartisanship

> No party holds the privilege of dictating to me how I shall vote. If loyalty to party is a form of patriotism, I am no patriot. If there is any valuable difference between a monarchist and an American, it lies in the theory that the American can decide for himself what is patriotic and what isn't.
>
> —Mark Twain

> I'm *nothing*. Don't holler about it.
>
> —Anonymous survey respondent
> on her party identification

NONPARTISANS TODAY ARE one of the most interesting and influential voting groups in the nation. With roughly a third of the population identifying as Independent, the fate of elections and the balance of power between Democrats and Republicans are often defined by the will and whimsy of nonpartisans. As such, every election cycle is saturated with intense scrutiny of Independents by candidates, their consultants, and media commentators alike. Yet despite all of this attention, our understanding of why individuals identify as nonpartisan is in many ways limited. With the exception of a few studies that we will discuss in detail, the literature on nonpartisans seeks more than anything else to understand the behavioral implications of Independence. The core debate has been whether most Independents, by nature of their voting preferences, should be viewed as closet partisans rather than as Independent. Most studies ignore the prior and potentially critical question of why people identify as nonpartisan in the first place. As Jack Dennis, one of the foremost scholars of Independents, laments, "At a time when a very large proportion of Americans is embracing more non-party forms of political identity, it is hard to understand either what such emerging identities consist of, where they come from, or how they are most apt to be expressed in politics . . . the basis for a theory of political independence and/or nonpartisanship [cannot be] found in the political science literature" (1988b, 198).

Our pitch for a revised account of party identification is thrown

straight down the middle of the ANES scale and takes aim at its categorization of nonpartisans. Specifically, in this chapter we follow the lead of
other scholars discussed in chapter 2 in questioning the logic of this linear, unidimensional scale, which presumes that nonpartisans fall squarely
between strong Democrats and strong Republicans and, often by corollary, between extreme liberals and extreme conservatives. We begin with
a historical overview of the oft-normative accounts with which scholars
of American politics have portrayed Independents. We revisit the Michigan and Downsian schools of thought on partisanship and then question
the basic premises behind a linear, unidimensional scale. We further articulate the limited purview of both accounts of party identification in
explaining why members of different racial and ethnic communities come
to self-identify as nonpartisan. We then focus on three distinct motivations of the minority and immigrant population—informational uncertainty, ideological ambivalence, and identity formation—to build a larger
framework for understanding the multiple pathways to nonpartisanship
that are progressively more important in America's increasingly diverse
population.

A History of the Study of Independents: From Privileged Status to Misfits

Attention to Independents and other nonpartisans among scholars of political parties, as Samuel Eldersveld (1952) notes, has been one of "fits
and starts," dating at least as far back as A. Lawrence Lowell's 1898 essay
on "oscillations in vote choice." Through these fits, starts, and oscillations, the status of political Independents has shifted from a positive conception to a negative one—both normatively and empirically. Normatively, there has been a decided shift in the way we think about political
Independents—from Independents as virtuous citizens to Independents
as fickle and feeble voters who threaten democratic stability, a shift that
shades the background of our empirical analysis in this book. This change
is most visible in the contrast between the rise of Mugwump Independents in the last decades of the nineteenth century and the emergence of
third-party presidential candidates in the latter half of the twentieth century. As Charles Merriam (1922) and others described it, the rise of Independents occured following the Civil War and the widespread perception
that corruption within the parties in the name of patriotism was ram-
pant.[1] It is in this era that James Bryce writes, "Neither party has as a

---

[1] By one account, the origin of Independents is dated to the 1854 election, under the influence of a "secret political society, guided by a few men and with wide ramifications,

party any clean-cut principles, any distinctive tenets . . . [b]oth have certainly war cries, organizations, interests, enlisted in their support. But those interests are in the main the interests of getting or keeping the patronage of the government" (1888, 3). James Russell Lowell takes a more acid pen to the point and declares, "Parties refuse to see, or, if they see, to look into, vicious methods which help them to a majority, and each is thus estopped from sincere protest against the same methods when employed by the other. . . . But the practices of which I have been speaking are slowly and surely filching from us the whole of our country—all, at least, that made it the best to live in and the easiest to die for" (1888, 305–6).

In this milieu, the growing view among many was that "it was the right and duty of intelligent men to leave the party in a crisis" (Merriam 1922, 89). Merriam defines Independence as "a movement in the direction of a new attitude toward the sacredness of party allegiance. It was a protest against blind adherence to a political party, against the persistence of party habits after their period of usefulness or reason for existence had gone by" (1922, 89–90). Merriam and Harold Gosnell hailed as "one of the triumphs of the independent voter" (1949, 196) the Mugwumps, who were widely seen as playing a decisive role in Grover Cleveland's successful bid for the presidency, the first Democrat to be so elected in twenty-four years. This sense that Independents were critical patriots on a mission to fight for all that is right and good in American political life was often grandiloquently defended by the leading intellectuals of the day, such as Mark Twain, the reformer Carl Schurz, and the poet James Russell Lowell. In Lowell's essay "The Place of Independents in Politics," Independents were defined by referring to the following poem, in which nonpartisanship is unambiguously identified with liberty itself.

> I honor the man who is ready to sink
> Half his present repute for the freedom to think,
> And when he has thought, be his cause strong or weak,
> Will risk t'other half for the freedom to speak,
> Caring naught for what vengeance the mob has in store,
> Let that mob be the upper ten thousand or lower. (1888, 299)

This generally positive accounting of political Independents is even present as late as the middle of the twentieth century. In "The Independent Vote," Samuel Eldersveld interprets as political Independents that third grouping of the electorate defined by the APSA Committee on Political Parties as those individuals who "base their electoral choice upon

---

pledged to the exclusion from office of all except the native-born, and those friendly to such exclusion" (E. E. Robinson 1924, 146).

the political performance of the two parties" (1952, 90). If this reading is correct, we have already seen that the committee members view this as the most critical element of the electorate in reinforcing party responsibility and democratic accountability. Independents, at least from the mid-centuryweltanschauung of the APSA Committee on Political Parties, are the equivalent of Fiorina's retrospectively rational actors.

At roughly the same juncture in the twentieth century, at the leading edge of the behavioral revolution, the conception of Independents shifted discernibly. Eldersveld's classic study of political Independents is notable for placing—even before Eldersveld's colleagues at the University of Michigan began to measure party identification as a psychological attachment—Independents at the midpoint of a continuum between loyal Republicans and staunch Democrats (1952, 739). Moreover, as the leading texts on political parties of the day evince, Independents came to be defined in behavioral terms. To put a finer point on it, Independents were viewed as those voters who acted *independently from* either political party—either by making choices without party allegiances or by periodically switching their allegiances. Thus, Eldersveld notes that Independents can be defined by self-identification in social surveys, but "self-perceptions may be completely erroneous" (1952, 737). Presaging more recent debates, Eldersveld's point is that a person who calls herself an Independent but consistently votes for the issues and candidates of just one party is no Independent at all.

This shift, importantly, entails an epistemological makeover in how we think about Independents. Political Independents are no longer viewed as the vanguard of political reform, the darling of the cognoscenti or, for that matter, an entity with any positive normative bearing. Rather, Independence is defined either as the absence of a presence (the presence being partisanship) or as an artifact of social measurement (i.e., the midpoint of a continuum). In Eldersveld's oft-quoted observation, for example, the stance is decidedly a more neutral one: "Independents may be many or few; they may be increasing or not; a real pattern may or may not exist; independents may be of many undetermined types; they may be intelligent or fickle; and the effects of independent voting on the political system may be beneficent or dangerous" (1952, 735).[2] Each of these possibilities begs questions that demand a discrimi-

---

[2] Similarly, an issue of the *New York Times Magazine* from 1952 defines the Independent as "a statistical rather than a mortal entity. He doesn't fit into any neat categories of wealth, social position or intellectual outlook. He's as likely to be a farmer as a small business man or a wage-earner. He has no particular habitat, has no special religious preoccupations nor any marked regional or tribal prejudices to be exploited. Nor is his independence always a matter of will and principles to be melted down by sound logic" (July 13, p. 8, quoted in W. Goodman 1956).

nating empirical inquiry, an inquiry based more on the "objective" operationalization of Independents than on any normative aspirations for enlightened democratic citizenship.

Where opinions about Independents are expressed beyond the neutral confines of social scientific measurement, the evaluative standpoint turns distinctly negative. Thus, implicit in Philip Converse's (1966) notion of a "normal vote" lurks the idea that voting that is not patterned by one's enduring psychological attachments to a political party is *ab*normal.[3] V. O. Key more explicitly describes Independents as "an ignorant and uninformed sector of the electorate highly susceptible to influence by factors irrelevant to the solemn performance of its civic duties" (1966, 92). Similarly, more recent scholars such as William Crotty increasingly decry Independents as "an unstable vote" that "introduces into elections an increased volatility that today's fluid politics do not need. . . . Its volatility and malleability does little to ease the concern of those who value stability and order in American politics" (1984, 37). Among public intellectuals, Hedrick Smith goes so far as to blame Independents for triggering "the individualism of a new breed of politicians" with "highly independent campaign styles" (1988, 685–86) that effectively short-circuit the power of political parties to act responsibly. The change over the course of a few short decades could not be starker, with Independents shifting from consideration as the stewards of responsible parties in the electorate to its vandals.[4]

Growing Nonpartisanship

This epistemological and evaluative move, perhaps ironically, perhaps revealingly, occured in the midst of a remarkable rise in the proportion of Americans who chose to identify as Independents over the second half of

[3] Converse, of course, intends the concept of a "normal" vote to be purely descriptive and without normative content. Thus, it is used to distinguish the regular partisan division of the electorate over long periods of time from deviations from such a division in any given election.

[4] Apropos of the focus in this book on political Independents and immigrant groups, there is a fascinating parallel shift in the positioning of immigrants relative to this shift in meaning conferred on Independents. In short, in the fin-de-siècle valorization of Independents by the Mugwumps, there is often, interwoven into criticisms of party corruption and irresponsibility, colorful and derisive mention of the political incorporation of immigrants by urban machines as proof of this corruption and irresponsibility. By contrast, in the post-1965 era of new immigrants from Asia and Latin America, the associations have been inverted. Now Independents are no longer valorized, but immigrants are also no longer as zealously mobilized into active partisanship. Although an enticing parallel, a more thorough consideration of this shift is beyond the scope of this chapter.

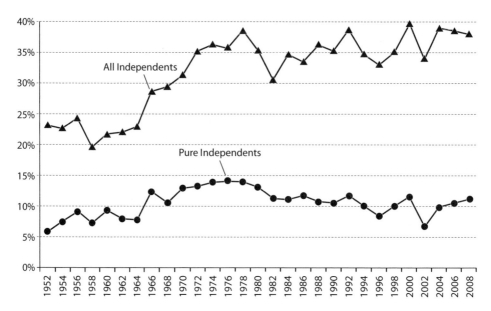

Figure 3.1. Proportion of Independents in America, 1952–2008

the twentieth century. Figure 3.1 shows data from the ANES from 1952 through 2008. We present both the proportion of individuals who self-identify as Independents in answer to the root question in the ANES ("Independent Total") and the proportion of pure Independents who do so without also indicating an inclination for either the Democratic or the Republican Party in the follow-up question ("Independent Only"). The most striking change over time is an upsurge starting with the 1958 ANES, where just under 20 percent of respondents identified as Independent, to the 1978 ANES, where this percentage nearly doubled to just below 40.[5] By the 1980s, this increase resulted in the self-identification of more Americans as Independent than those who self-identified with either party.

Preelection surveys are not the only data sources that reveal a substantial increase in nonpartisanship. Data on party registration closely parallel the trend in figure 3.1. Between 1960 and 2004, the percentage of all

[5] As Green, Gerber, and de Boef (1999) note, with such trend analysis it is often critical to distinguish random sampling errors from real trends in public opinion. Doing so with the Kalman filter algorithm (Green's "Samplemeiser" software at http://vote.research.yale.edu/samplemiser.html) does not appreciably change our substantive interpretation about changes in self-identification as Independent over time. It does, however, somewhat shrink the "doubling" effect from the late 1950s to the late 1970s and flatten the year-to-year variance from 1980 on.

eligible adults who registered as Independent or some other third-party option grew from 1.6 to 21.7 (Committee on the American Electorate 2006). Exit poll data also reveal a growing trend in nonpartisanship over a several-decades-long time span. Although we know that these figures overstate the trend, since many who identify or register as Independent can and often do act like their partisan brethren come Election Day, the rise still seems remarkable (Keith et al. 1992).

CURRENT THEORIES OF INDEPENDENTS

To be fair, most current theories of Independence and nonpartisanship avoid much of the normative language of earlier scholars. Yet the background assumption that nonpartisans are somehow "misfits" and out of the norm remains. In this section, we outline the two main theoretical accounts of nonpartisans as well as the principal critique of these conventional accounts. The most enduring view of nonpartisans follows from *The American Voter*. Party identification and thus Independence are here less a function of one's ideological predispositions, attentiveness, and perceptions than an outcome of one's initial political footprints from childhood and early adulthood (Campbell et al. 1960; Converse and Markus 1979). Although several variants of this model have been put forward, all maintain that partisanship is acquired early in life and remains with us throughout our remaining years (Beck and Jennings 1991, Niemi and Jennings 1991). In most cases, we simply assume the partisan choices of our parents. Independents are then more than likely to be the children of Independent parents.

A more negative view of Independents also emerges in the Michigan School's accounts of nonpartisans. This version sees Independents not just as the offspring of Independents but also as nonideologues who are unattached to any party because they are uninvolved, uninformed, and uninterested in the world of politics (Miller and Wattenberg 1983; Campbell et al. 1960). In this view, nonpartisanship is a default mode for those who pay little attention to politics and have little to say about the issues, candidates, and parties.[6] This account strongly challenges the idealized view of the Independent as a virtuous citizen who is "attentive to politics, concerned with the course of government, who weighs the rival appeals of a campaign and reaches a judgment that is unswayed by partisan prejudice" Campbell et al. 1960, 143). It turns out, at least on the basis of the

---

[6] By this account, one's degree of *politicization* is the parallel continuum that underlies party identification. Strong partisans are apt not only to be more intense about their party identification but also more interested, informed, and active as citizens.

1952–56 Center for Political Studies (CPS) Panel Study data analyzed by Campbell and his colleagues, that this view of political Independents is a popular myth. Rather, this normative ideal

> fits poorly the characteristics of the Independents in our samples. Far from being more attentive, interested, and informed, Independents tend as a group to be somewhat less involved in politics. They have somewhat poorer knowledge of the issues, their image of the candidates is fainter, their interest in the campaign is less, their concern over the outcome is relatively slight, and their choice between competing candidates . . . seems much less to spring from discoverable evaluations of the elements of national politics. (143)

From this perspective, nonpartisans represent the absence of anything concrete or meaningful. They remain detached from partisan politics because they are apolitical animals.

The main alternative to this view of nonpartisans emerges out of the rationalist, ideologically centered accounts that Downs and others put forward. In this alternate view, individuals end up identifying as nonpartisan because their ideological ideal point lies somewhere in the middle between left-leaning Democrats and more conservative Republicans. Although few explicitly make the claim that Independence equals ideological moderation, the sense of Independents as being in the ideological center with views somewhere between the two parties is implicit in most studies of partisanship and is a clear outgrowth of the linear scale of partisanship (Carmines and Stimson 1989; Layman and Carmines 1997; Abramowitz 1994; Alvarez and Nagler 1998; Abramowitz and Saunders 1998).[7] When almost every study of American voting behavior incorporates this scale of party identification, it puts Independents in the middle. Whether the effort is conscious or not, Independents are presumed to hold few, if any, strong views about politics, and what opinions they do hold are "middle of the road."

There are a couple of common elements to both of these conventional views of nonpartisanship. First, both accounts place Independents squarely in the middle of a linear partisan scale. Whether by virtue of moderate views, disinterest in the political sphere, or long-term predispositions that can be traced to one's parents, individuals who identify as Independent can be reasonably and logically situated between Democrats and Republicans. If Independence is measured as an ordinal scale (cf. a categorical, unordered scale) with an assumed monotonicity and equidis-

---

[7] To state this point more emphatically, whenever scholars attempt to explain party identification in any of its linear forms (e.g., a 3-, 5-, and 7-point categorical scale) with a scale made up either of general ideological leaning or more specific policy questions, there is an underlying assumption that Independents fall near the middle of both the ideological and partisan scales.

tance from both extremes of the scale, a person who self-classifies as Independent is thus as unlikely to convert to a strong Democrat as she is to convert to a strong Republican." Importantly, while this view of Independents is widely employed, it has rarely been tested (but see Keith et al. 1992 and Rosenstone et al. 1984). Rather, most studies just simply assume that Independence fits into a neatly ordered, linear "continuum of partisanship" (Campbell et al. 1960, 122–23).

The principal alternative to these conventional accounts emerges from a third strand of work that focuses on the dimensionality of party identification. As we noted in the previous chapter, there are compelling arguments for the view that the standard seven-point ANES scale conflates at least two empirically distinct dimensions of party identification. Following Weisberg (1980), we described in chapter 2 how the standard linear scale of party identification might instead be reconfigured as a two-dimensional space of attitudes toward political parties on one axis and attitudes toward political independence on the other (see also Dennis 1988a, 1988b; Valentine and Van Wingen 1980; Alvarez 1990).

This line of research has led to several alternate dimensions of Independence. In particular, Jack Dennis, in his Political Independence in America series (1998a, 1998b, 1992), identifies four different sources of Independence. The first and, for many, the defining feature of Independence is neutrality or indifference to the two parties. Put plainly, we identify as Independents when we observe no distinctions between the two parties. A second reason for Independence, according to Dennis, is self-perceived variability in voting behavior. I am Independent because I sometimes vote for Democrats and sometimes vote for Republicans. Although these two dimensions certainly offer potentially important insights into Independence, neither account strongly refutes the Independents-in-the-middle modeling approach. Indeed, it seems reasonable to place those who are indifferent to the parties and those who vote regularly for both parties somewhere near the middle of the partisan spectrum.[8] Thus, once again, Independents fall neatly between partisans of the two parties.

The two other dimensions that Dennis exposes are harder to fit within the confines of a linear partisan scale. Both are related to a rejection of the party system and the idea of political parties as a basis for democratic decision making. This rejection can be manifest directly as positive views of Independence (i.e., in-group affinity) or alternatively as negative views of both parties (i.e., out-group derogation). In the former version—which Dennis calls "political autonomy"—attachment to the ideals of Independence is rooted most prominently in the Lockean ideal of individualism

---

[8] Indifference could, however, as we will note in more detail, also be the result of extreme views. Thus, it is not always appropriate to place those with indifferent partisan views in the middle between Democrats and Republicans.

and echoes earlier, more normatively positive accounts of Independents as virtuous. In the latter version—which Dennis calls "antipartyism"— Independents are disaffected, disgruntled former partisans (Rosenstone et al. 1984; Collett 1996). As Rosenstone and his colleagues put it, "Only when voters feel estranged from the major party candidates will they seek out information on other alternatives" (128). Being Independent is thus explicitly defined as being opposed to the two major parties.[9]

Concerns about Existing Accounts

Raising questions about the dimensionality of partisanship is an important task, and in our own theory of nonpartisanship we draw heavily from the work of Dennis, Weisberg, and others. Nevertheless, it is important to highlight two critical failings of this dimensionality literature. The first and most obvious is the relatively thin theoretical basis for the work. Weisberg, Dennis, Greene, and others provide compelling evidence that whether one identifies with the two-party system and which party one chooses to identify with are distinct elements of an individual's party identification. Yet, none of these scholars offers much in the way of a full-fledged theory of nonpartisanship. Each of the proposed new dimensions of partisanship describes only proximate causes of Independence. None offers a sense of the underlying motivations for these attitudes. Put another way, none really tells us why people have a particular set of attitudes toward the parties or Independence in the first place.[10] Why, for example, do some Americans feel indifferent toward or even dislike the two parties? What is it about their lives or their policy views that leads them to have these impressions of the parties or to vote in the ways they do? To really understand why people end up as nonpartisans as , we need to answer these deeper questions.[11] Developing a more general, unified

[9] Weisberg (1980) suggests a similarly complex model in which Independence is not only a function of views of the two major parties but also of political Independence and political parties in general.

[10] Admittedly, this is not their primary goal. Steven Greene, for example, is principally interested in bringing a more recent theory of intergroup dynamics to add support to the original foundation of party identification in *The American Voter* with newer social psychological scaffolding. Dennis is principally interested in testing some unexamined speculations in Campbell et al. about self-identification as an Independent (1988b, 200) and using appropriate, more recent statistical methods to do so.

[11] What is also missing in these studies is a more capacious account of the distinct categories of nonpartisanship. Steven Greene, for instance, focuses the analysis chiefly on comparing Independent leaners with weak and strong partisans to the first-stage question, with a clear eye toward those who underscore the behavioral similarities between these two party-identification categories. In doing so, Greene falls short of considering how the categories of nonpartisanship—partisan leaners, pure Independents, and those who refuse to place themselves anywhere on the standard linear continuum—might differ. A person's ambiva-

account of the multiple pathways to nonpartisanship is imperative because it is substantively and, ultimately, normatively consequential for how we think about who identifies as a nonpartisan, why she does so so, and the import the answers to these questions hold for electoral competition under party politics in the United States.

The other problem with this literature—one that is probably a direct outgrowth of its limited theoretical grounding—is its relatively meager impact on how we think about and measure party identification. As Johnston's authoritative review of the party-identification literature concludes, this "initiative seems to have gained more ritual genuflection than widespread acceptance" (2006, 334). Despite the efforts of Weisberg, Dennis, and others to highlight the multidimensional nature of partisanship, the linear scale anchored by a single liberal-conservative ideological dimension remains the standard employed in almost all studies of American political behavior. As Petrocik notes, "The index of party identification is so universally accepted as the variable around which to organize a discussion of political behavior in the United States that it is difficult to find a monograph or research article which does not introduce [the linear party index] as a consideration in the analysis" (1974, 31). Despite decades of revision, Keith and his colleagues' exhaustive study of partisanship concludes, "We see no problems with the traditional measure" (1992, 196).

The bottom line is that while we know there are imperfections linked to the measurement of party identification as a linear scale, we know little about the substantive sources of any alternate dimensions of partisan choices. The end result is that we tend to ignore these irregularities and instead fall back on more simplistic modeling choices.

RACE, IDENTITY, AND (NON)PARTISANSHIP

We have reviewed several extant accounts of (non)partisanship, each with its insights and short sights. In this section, we take account of both the strengths and limitations to develop our own story about partisan choices. We start with the core proposition—that the social groups (from

---

lence (i.e., answering "not sure" to the typical question), detachment (i.e., stating that the person does not think in partisan terms), or noncompliance (i.e., refusing to answer the question) might, for example, tells us a great deal about her sense of political identity and attachment to political institutions. Dennis, likewise, focuses on showing what is distinct about each of the four types of political Independents he presents, confirmed by principal components analysis, to the exclusion of any account of whether and, if so, how these dimensions of Independence are conceptually linked. However, as we have already implied, even a casual consideration suggests probable relationships between what Dennis calls "antipartyism" and political autonomy and probable relationships between partisan neutrality and partisan variability from the standpoint of the Downsian view of party identification.

the Michigan School's standpoint) and the ideological predispositions (from the Downsian view's standpoint) that define one's partisan or non-partisan self-identification are multiple and interactive. To make this point, we start with the observation that scholars who take seriously party identification as a social identity do so in isolation, without regard to other primary social identities that might inform and influence a person's political orientation. This exclusiveness stems, perhaps, from the historical origins of party identification that we have discussed—specifically, the manner in which *The American Voter* controverted the claims of Paul Lazarsfeld and his colleagues in *The People's Choice*: "A person thinks politically, as he is socially. Social characteristics determine political preference" (1944, 27). What Campbell and his colleagues showed, rather decisively, was that the key factors in their "funnel of causality"—party identification, evaluations of candidates, and evaluations of the relevant political issues—trumped any patterned influence of social groups in defining our electoral choices.

Yet there is wisdom lost in inferring from this impressive empirical result that nonpartisan social groups are irrelevant, of secondary import, or ultimately reducible in their influence on partisan considerations. *Partisan Hearts and Minds* (Green et al. 2002), perhaps the most forceful restatement of the power and persistence of party identification in which partisanship is viewed as a social identity, is illustrative of this exclusion of nonpartisan social identities. *Ab initio*, Donald Green and his colleagues acknowledge that "identification with political parties is a minor part of the typical American's self-conception. Race, sex, ethnicity, religion, region, and social class come immediately to mind as core social identities; political party does not" (2002, 2). Yet they note that "when our attention turns to politics, however, partisan attachments become highly influential, whereas more fundamental social identities . . . tend to have less predictive power."

Partisan Hearts and Minds does acknowledge one exception to this rule. Race, too, is a powerful predictor of one's vote choice, the authors note. Yet Green and his colleagues assert that this power stems principally from the predominant alignment of African Americans as staunch Democrats. The political proclivities of other racial and ethnic groups, they suggest, are not so distinctively organized by their nonpartisan identities. The implication they draw is "not that race is unimportant but rather that its influence on electoral choice is mediated largely by partisan affiliation" (3). In affirming the Michigan School's "funnel of causality," however, Green and his colleagues proffer a somewhat uncomfortable juxtaposition of claims: race is a "fundamental social identity," yet one with foundations that are permeable enough for partisan identity to absorb it. Moreover, after the authors make the claim that race (qua African Americans) is distinctive and important but refereed by partisanship, African Americans are to be found virtually nowhere in any of the tables, figures, or other empirical analyses in the book. Where racial/ethnic groups are again considered at all, it is only to make the case that party identification is akin in its stability over time to racial/ethnic identification—falling somewhere between the nigh-on invariant identification as Italian Americans and the more fickle identification as English Americans (75–78).

This absence of race and ethnicity from a consideration of party identification, moreover, is not unique to *Partisan Hearts and Minds*. In many instances, such as *The Myth of the Independent Voter*, African Americans, Latinos, and Asian Americans are simply excluded from the analysis. Keith and his collaborators justify this exclusion on the grounds that Independence is chiefly a white phenomenon, and that since "the increase in Independents was confined to the white population . . . most of our analysis in subsequent chapters excludes blacks" (1992, 26). These authors further argue that including African Americans would only confuse the analysis; "because blacks are the most disaffected of any major population group, omitting them also avoids complications if one examines relationships between alienation and independence" (Keith et al. 1992, 32). Likewise, in the landmark book *Dynamics of the Party System*, James Sundquist readily admits that his analysis of Independents "disregards blacks" (1983, 403). Perhaps even more egregiously, in trying to determine whether or not racial concerns affect partisanship, Abramowitz (1994) takes the questionable and all-too-determining step of dropping all African Americans from the analysis. In yet other cases, such as Jack Dennis's series of articles on political Independents, there is no mention of race/ethnicity whatsoever.

Recusing race in this manner is, unfortunately, all too commonplace in political science research (Dawson and Wilson 1991; Lee 2002; Dawson and Cohen 2002). We argue that racial and ethnic identities, as an influence on one's politics, are not too insignificant in number, too invariant in their influence on one's politics, or too readily reducible to partisan considerations. Rather than ignore race as a consideration, we expect the distinctive political characteristics of African Americans, Asian Americans, Latinos, and white Americans to give us critical variation and insight into whether we identify with a party and, if so, which one. As something of a face validity consideration that "race matters" to our understanding of partisanship patterns writ large, figure 3.2 shows the change over time in the self-categorization of Independents disaggregated by racial/ethnic group.[12]

The main observation to take note of is that what we make of politi-

---

[12] There are too few Asian Americans in the ANES samples to include them in the analysis.

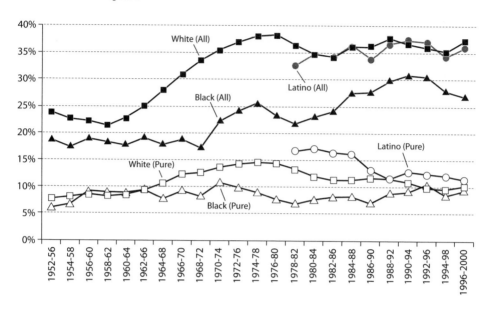

Figure 3.2. Proportion of Independents by race/ethnicity, 1952–2000

cal Independents over the last half century depends largely on which group and which category of Independents we examine. If we focus on those who self-identify as Independent in answer to the root ANES question ("All"), we find that the notable racial difference is the relatively lower proportion of African Americans who identify as Independents, with Latinos and whites seemingly tracking together over time. Based just on this analysis, one might concur with Donald Green and his colleagues and draw the inference that what is distinctive about race is the partisanship patterns of African Americans, and these patterns are driven by their disproportionate allegiance to the Democratic Party. If we focus on those Independents who indicate no partisan leanings ("Pure"), we find that each group differs in its allegiances over time from the other groups. The proportion of white pure Independents appears to roughly have doubled from the 1950s to the mid-1970s, then has crept down in the last two decades; the proportion of Latino pure Independents, from the time such analysis became possible (1978), appears to have declined steadily and at a faster clip than for white Americans; the proportion of African American pure Independents appears to have increased slowly over time. Notably, these racially/ethnically distinct trends have, more or less, converged in the last decade of the ANES on the same point, with roughly 10 percent of survey respondents identifying themselves as pure Independents in all groups. One inference to

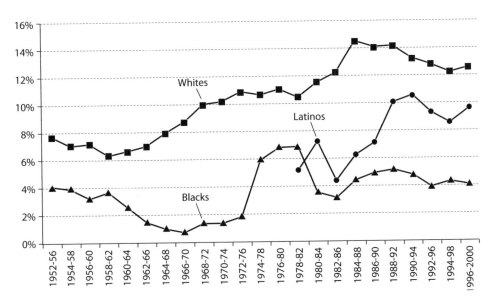

Figure 3.3. Independents leaning Republican, by race/ethnicity

draw from this comparison might be that patterns of partisanship are racially distinct; an alternative might be a story of the gradual diminishment of racial and ethnic differences over time.

Similarly divergent inferences become accessible when examining both Republican leaners (figure 3.3) and Democratic leaners (not shown). With Republican leaners, there are again racial and ethnic differences and commonalities over time. Whites are noticeably more likely than are African Americans to self-identify as Independent, with a partial eye toward the Republican Party, showing a steady increase from the late 1950s to the late 1980s. African Americans, however, have not remained constant; there is a clear upsurge in black Republican leaners from the late 1960s up through the present day. And with Latinos, there is an even more dramatic increase in self-identification as Republican leaners, the net effect of which is that Latinos are similar to African Americans in their base rates of identification in the late 1970s and much closer to white Americans by the 1990s.[13] These figures suggest, with compelling visual effect, that there are racially and ethnically distinct patterns of party identification.

[13] Among Democratic leaners, the most conspicuous result is the lack of any differences. Similar percentages in each group identify as leaners, and this proportion changes over time similarly for each group.

Testing Conventional Accounts of (Non)Partisanship

To give a more empirical bite to this suggestion, we demonstrate that the two principal theories of party identification—the Michigan and Downsian accounts—offer a far from complete explanation of the self-identification of African American and Latino Independents. The chief expectation of the Michigan School is that Independents so identify as a result of their preadult socialization or their political apathy and indifference. The chief expectation of the Downsian view is that Independents so identify as a result of their ideological moderation. In table 3.1, we test these hypotheses with a logit analysis, using data from the ANES from 1978 to 2000. Preadult socialization is measured by the party identification of one's parents (specifically, whether they were Independents). We test for the effects of ideological self-placement by comparing moderates (the base category) with conservatives and liberals (strong and weak). The degree of political engagement is measured by respondents' level of political knowledge, their self-reported political-interest levels, their personal political efficacy, their trust in government, and their self-reported voting or political participation. Asian Americans are not included in the analysis due to their small numbers in the ANES sample.

The effect of ideology is tested by comparing self-described moderates (the three middle categories of the seven-point ideological self-placement scale) with strong and weak conservatives and liberals. To further assess the level of indifference to the parties, we include a dummy measure indicating whether or not the respondent indicated that she saw "important differences in what the Republican and Democrats stand for." Finally, to see if Dennis's principled Independents account fits different racial/ethnic groups, we incorporate in our test a measure of affect toward the two major parties—a count of how many more "dislikes" than "likes" each respondent can name about the parties. Details on question wording and coding for each of these variables, as well as descriptive statistics for each racial group, are included in the online appendix (http://press.princeton .edu/titles/9468.html).

The basic conclusion of this test is that although conventional accounts fare reasonably well in accounting for the partisan decision making of white Americans, their ability to explain the partisan choices of racial and ethnic minorities is more mixed.[14] For whites, both the Downsian and the Michigan accounts seem to fit the partisan proclivities of most of the population.[15] Ideological moderation and partisan indifference

---

[14] When we repeat the analysis focusing on pure Independents (including Independent leaners as partisans), we reach the same conclusion.

[15] One interesting anomaly among white Americans is that many strong liberals appear

TABLE 3.1
Testing Conventional Models of Independence

	Whites	Blacks	Latinos
The Downsian ideology model			
Independents as moderates			
Strong liberal	−.00 (.20)	−.09 (.34)	.27 (.59)
Liberal	−.15 (.09)^	−.14 (.23)	−.57 (.41)
Conservative	−.48 (.07)**	.15 (.29)	−.26 (.29)
Strong conservative	−.59 (.15)**	1.1 (.39)**	−1.9 (1.1)^
Independents as indifferent			
Recognize party differences	−.04 (.01)*	.01 (.05)	.03 (.05)
The Michigan School			
Childhood socialization			
Parents Independent	.83 (.06)**	.98 (.19)**	1.0 (.32)**
Apolitical			
Political knowledge	−.19 (.06)**	.11 (.17)	−.05 (.23)
Political interest	−.18 (.04)**	−.54 (.12)**	−.18 (.16)
Political efficacy	−.02 (.00)**	−.01 (.02)	−.00 (.02)
Political participation	−.14 (.03)**	.04 (.09)	−.21 (.14)
Antiparty Independents			
Dislike parties	.12 (.01)**	.03 (.05)	.19 (.06)**

Note: This table is based on an analysis of 8,030 whites, 850 African Americans, and 443 Latinos in the ANES, 1978–2000. Significance levels: **p < .01 *p < .05 ^ p < .10.

strongly and significantly predict the rate of Independence among the white population.[16] So too does childhood socialization and political apathy. Having one or more parents who identified as Independents appreciably increases one's odds of identifying as a nonpartisan. Also, those

---

to resist identification with the Democratic Party in favor of Independence. As we will see, this attenuated relationship between ideology and partisanship is neither a statistical artifact nor irrational and unexplainable behavior. Rather, as we show, many extreme liberals feel that they are not well represented by a Democratic Party that is near the center on the issues they care about and as a result opt for Independence.

[16] It is not just a basic liberal-conservative orientation that tends to separate out white moderates. In alternate tests, we included measures of policy preferences on a variety of issues central to the partisan debate in American national elections. Those who tended to hold moderate or middle-of-the-road views across a range of basic policy questions were significantly more likely to identify as Independents. Thus, the "Independents as moderates" claim seems to fairly accurately depict the partisan choices of at least some white Americans. The issues we tested were the overall level of government spending, government's role in health insurance, financial aid to blacks, the merits of guaranteeing full employment, busing to achieve integration, defense spending, and strategies to deal with urban unrest.

who feel that government is too complicated and those who are less interested and less active in politics are significantly more likely to be non-partisan or Independent.[17] Dennis's claims about principled Independents are also borne out for whites. Those who have more negative views of the two major parties are significantly more likely to identify as Independent.[18] Although the entire model does not explain a lot of the variation in white partisanship, it is still fair to say that for many white Americans Independence is fairly accurately portrayed by the range of theoretical accounts that exist in the literature.[19]

The decision-making processes of African Americans and Latinos, however, seem to be less closely tied to the basic dimensions portrayed in the literature. Judging simply by the number of significant variables, existing theories are less relevant to either group. The Downsian ideological model, in particular, fails to help us place blacks and Latinos on the partisan scale.[20] For Latinos, strong conservatism is the only ideological self-placement that predicts a lesser likelihood of identifying as an Independent. For African Americans, the one category of ideological self-placement that is significant is signed in the wrong direction—strong conservatives are more apt than moderates to choose to identify as Independent. Within the African American community, Independents are less likely to come from the center of the ideological spectrum than they are from the conservative extreme. In short, there is little support for an Independents-as-moderates view of party choice among minorities.

Although some of the reduced significance in the Latino and African American models is surely due to the smaller sample size, much of it is

[17] In subsequent chapters, we explore our disagreement with the authors of *The American Voter* over the precise meaning of this tie between political engagement and partisanship. Specifically, we believe that for many individuals a lack of political engagement and nonpartisanship result from a rational skepticism.

[18] Dennis's political-autonomy dimension also garners support. In alternate tests, we find that those with more positive views of political Independence (as measured by a feeling thermometer toward "political independence") were significantly more likely to identify as Independents. Since this measure is available in only a few ANES years, it is not included in the final model. Its inclusion has no noticeable effect on the other relationships in table 3.1.

[19] Only a small fraction of the variation in whites' party choice is explained by the model (pseudo R-squared = .05). Moreover, the magnitude of the effects we see in table 3.1 are not particularly large. When we calculated the probability that any given individual would identify as Independent under different scenarios, we found that variations along each of the three dimensions did not greatly increase the odds of identifying as nonpartisan. This suggests that conventional accounts represent a far from complete understanding of Independence among whites and white partisanship more generally. Undoubtedly, other dimensions and other factors also come into play.

[20] We tend to reach the same conclusion when we replace the self-perceived liberal-conservative ideology scale with each respondent's policy preferences on a variety of issues central to the partisan debate in American national elections.

not. Not only are most of the relationships insignificant, but many are signed in the wrong direction or of tiny magnitude. To help ensure that the differences between whites and nonwhites are not an artifact of the larger sample of whites, we undertook three additional tests. First, we analyzed repeated iterations of the regression in table 3.1 with a reduced sample of whites. Second, we repeated—as closely as possible—the analysis of blacks and Latinos in table 3.1 using larger samples from single-year studies of those two communities (the 1996 National Black Election Survey and the 2006 Latino National Politics Survey). Finally, we added interactions between race and each of the conventional accounts. In each, there was clear evidence that some factors mattered less for minorities. In particular, liberal-conservative ideology was the factor that consistently mattered less to blacks and Latinos.

The other two conventional perspectives do, however, get support from our analysis. Parental socialization appears to work for all three racial groups. It is, however, worth noting that many first- and second-generation immigrants—a majority of the Latino and Asian American populations—will probably not have much of a parental partisan cue to follow. A lack of political engagement appears to be relevant for one of the two minority groups.[21] For African Americans, there is some sign of a link between political apathy and Independence. Similarly, principled Independence or the model of generally negative views of political parties applies to one minority group. Among Latinos, those with more critical views of the parties are more likely to identify as nonpartisans.

The Continued Partisan Significance of Race

All of this is perhaps not surprising, given that these models were designed to help us understand mainstream American politics. In their formation, the choices and experiences of racial and ethnic minorities and immigrants were largely ignored. Yet these preliminary findings clearly point to some notable differences in party identification by race/ethnic group. At root, the reason that we expect a more explicit consideration of race and ethnicity to shed such light is that party identification as a social identity is not likely to be singular or exclusive in its influence on our political bearing. We take our personal identity to be the resul of the multiple, crosscutting group identities that define us. When applied to the study of the party in the electorate, this insight is voiced even in the gen-

---

[21] Even the effects for blacks, however, are much less clear than the effects for whites. For African Americans, only one of the measures of politicization significantly predicts political Independence, whereas for whites, all five of our measures reach a statistically significant relationship.

eration before the behavioral revolution by Charles Merriam, who describes the social group bases of party identification by noting:

> It is also possible to make a study of the party system by viewing the various social forces and elements out of which the party is made, and by showing how these factors are combined to produce the Republican or Democratic or other party result. We may look at the various groupings, of class, race, religion, section, in their relation to parties. . . . We may see how the party becomes a going concern, an institution, an attitude; how party allegiance becomes part of the political heritage of many persons. . . . We may, in short begin the analysis of the party by examining its composition in terms of political and social forces. (1922, 1–2).

While our attachment to one of the two principal political parties in the United States is apt to define political identity and orientation for many of us, not all of us identify so exclusively or forcefully with a political party, and many of us define ourselves politically through nonpartisan social group identities. Viewed thus, the central question is not whether party identification precedes racial-group identification or vice versa, but rather how both enduring attachments interact to define our relationship to political parties.

Thus, these findings raise important questions about how and why minorities and immigrants are different and what these differences can tell us about the process of choosing to identify or to not identify with a particular party. The answers are, we contend, not that difficult to find. By focusing on basic characteristics of the immigrant and minority communities, we can quickly expose a series of problematic assumptions that undergird conventional models of partisanship. Then, building on each of these unique characteristics, we can identify distinct new dimensions of partisan choice. Finally, by considering how these factors work together to affect all segments of the population, we can develop a more encompassing theory of partisanship.

WHY RACE MATTERS: INFORMATION, IDEOLOGY, AND IDENTITY

So what is it that is different about racial and ethnic minorities and immigrant groups? In the introduction we noted three defining characteristics of the immigrant and minority communities—information uncertainty, ideological ambivalence, and identity formation. In this chapter, we show that by ignoring these characteristics, conventional accounts of partisanship make problematic assumptions about partisan choice. Further, we delineate how each of these three factors should influence the partisan choices of different groups and explain how, for a range of Americans, they should lead to Independence or nonpartisanship.

A vital but largely unexamined assumption undergirding conventional accounts of party identification is that individuals have enough information to make decisions about partisanship. Conventional models, in fact, assume a fairly intimate, lifelong relationship with party politics. Take the example of identifying as an Independent. Individuals who end up identifying as Independents because they are ideological moderates have surveyed the partisan debate and found that they are indifferent to the parties and thus fit most accurately in the middle. Similarly, for the offspring of Independents who follow the partisanship of their parents, partisanship is acquired only after a lengthy socialization process that depends on generations of knowledge of the American party system. Finally, Americans who end up as Independent because they are apolitical have at least had the opportunity to be involved in partisan politics and have ultimately discarded that world as uninteresting or unimportant.

However, none of these accounts fits well immigrant ethnic groups who often have only a limited familiarity with politics and the partisan choices that they face here. That is, Asians and Latinos are not likely, either as immigrants or as second- or third-generation tenderfoots treading on terra incognita, to be fully "assimilated," with a strong sense of personal political efficacy or trust in political institutions or a deep understanding of left-right ideology, characteristics that are expected of more seasoned democratic citizens in America (cf. de la Garza et al. 1996; Parker 2003).[22] In particular, the foreign-born and their offspring—a group that constitutes a majority of the Latino and Asian American population—simply have fewer chances to learn basic facts about American politics and to understand the core concepts that flow through America's partisan discourse. Socialization in another political system, less time spent in the United States, and a host of other barriers suggest that many members of these communities will not know enough or be comfortable enough with the partisan options in America to make straightforward decisions about partisanship.

This insight can also be applied more broadly. Although African Americans and white Americans generally do not suffer from the kinds of informational barriers that immigrants face, there are members in both communities who stand apart from mainstream America and its politics. Some whites, and a greater number of African Americans, live in ex-

---

[22] We share Brubaker's view that it is possible to distinguish between assimilation as a normative goal and assimilation as a social process that merits empirical study. Also, we share Brubaker's dictum to move beyond the question of "how much assimilation" to the questions "assimilation in what respect, over what period of time, and to what reference population?" (2001, 544).

tremely poor, socially isolated communities where their ability to interact with and learn about mainstream political institutions is severely curtailed (Wilson 1987). For this group, as well as for the larger immigrant community, the act of identifying with a party may involve considerable uncertainty.

Our first proposed modification to the Michigan and Downsian accounts of party identification, then, is to suggest that uncertainty represents a distinctive path to self-identification as a nonpartisan—notably different from ideological moderation or nonpartisan socialization. Ultimately, rather than support a system that they do not yet fully trust and make a choice between parties that they know little about, individual Americans are likely to end up with the default choice—Independence. For many, then, choosing Independence is an affirmation of rational skepticism.

A second important concept underlying conventional models of partisanship is pluralism—namely that the policy agenda resulting from the two-party system faithfully represents the needs and interests of the polity—and, by analogy, that individuals can place their own political needs and interests comfortably within the liberal-conservative continuum that divides the two parties. This one-dimensional view of partisanship, however, is likely to run afoul of the range of political views and issue concerns that animate the politics of America's increasingly diverse population. A brief overview of the politics of minority and immigrant communities and—once our interest in alternate dimensions has been sparked—a more in-depth accounting of the ideological structure of the white population show that the Democratic-Republican divide does not dependably incorporate the views of all individuals and groups.

For Latinos and Asian Americans, for example, concerns about the role of immigrants in American society and core issues related to politics in their home country often prove difficult to place on a left-right partisan scale. Likewise, for African Americans debates between those who support black autonomy and those who favor racial integration may not map easily onto a liberal-conservative ideological dimension. And this may not solely be a minority or immigrant phenomenon. Whites, too, are diverse, and for those members of the white population whose views are mixed in a way that does not fit neatly along the liberal-conservative partisan divide or who care deeply about an issue that both parties have only minimally addressed, the positions of either party may not represent their interests very well. More broadly, across America's diverse population there are likely to be a range of core concerns and ideological debates that do not accord well with a partisanship scale that is measured along a single dimension.

For those with core political beliefs and issue concerns that are inadequately represented by either party, there is little motivation to choose a party. Instead, a reasonable and, we argue, rational alternative is to choose neither and to remain nonpartisan. Thus, in this view nonpartisanship is not merely the midpoint on a continuum but also the default result for those motivated by a range of distinct orthogonal ideological dimensions and issue concerns that do not mesh well with a left-right partisanship divide.

Our third concern with both the Michigan School and the Downsian "running tally" view of partisanship is inattention to the complex ways in which social identities might influence partisanship. If race matters in these models, it is largely because of an attachment to a party that presents a policy platform that favors the liberal or conservative position of members of a particular racial group. Thus, the Democratic Party's clear association with what is widely perceived to be a racially liberal policy agenda attracts blacks (and some whites) who favor that agenda (Carmines and Stimson 1989).

We contend, however, that beyond this policy dimension are a range of social identities that can be salient enough to influence partisan patterns in a variety of complex ways. For African Americans, in particular, racial group identity is so encompassing that any shift in the political calculus is likely to be the consequence of a prior shift in their sense of a racially "linked fate" (Dawson 1994). Exit from the Democratic Party may, thus, signify less a change in policy positions and than a diminishing racial group identity or an unhinging of the link between partisan and racial group identities.

For immigrant-based groups such as Latinos and Asian Americans, we expect racially and ethnically defined "groupness" to be a shifting entity—more of a formation than a result. Thus, partisanship choice is likely, at least in part, to reflect knowledge about how race and ethnicity are lived in the United States. For those whose experiences with discrimination are more limited and whose identities as minorities are more tenuous—an outlook held by many Latinos and Asian Americans—an identity characterized by uncertainty is unlikely to offer much assistance in the choice of parties. Uncertainty surrounding one's identity may in turn lead to a similar uncertainty surrounding partisanship choices—a situation that, more than anything else, is likely to lead to nonpartisanship.

For individuals from any group, we also expect racial identities and other political predispositions to clash in ways that occasionally lead to nonpartisanship. For example, for individuals who have a set of issue concerns and ideological positions that consistently push them toward the Republican Party—Cuban Americans come to mind—a stronger minority identity should serve to muddy the waters and encourage abstention in the form of nonpartisanship. In all of these cases, party choice will be related to group loyalty, and nonpartisanship will represent more than ideological moderation.

AFRICAN AMERICANS: EXIT FROM THE DEMOCRATIC PARTY

These three dimensions, information, ideology, and identity, form the core of our theoretical account of partisanship. In the following sections, we show how these dimensions help to delineate the distinct pathways to party identification or nonidentification for blacks, immigrant-based groups such as Latinos and Asian Americans, and ultimately whites as well. In the case of African American partisanship, Dawson (1994), Tate (1994), and others have shown personal identity and group identity are mutually constitutive in the notion of a "black utility heuristic"—namely, what benefits my group benefits me. Yet this linkage implies neither stasis nor isomorphism. Although Dawson notes that "the relative homogeneity of black public opinion has been generally considered one of the few certainties of modern American politics" (2001, 44), it is important to remember that African Americans have not always so univocally identified with the Democratic Party. Prior to the Great Depression and the New Deal era, it was more commonplace to think of African Americans as identifying with the party of Lincoln (Weiss 1983, Marable 1990, Frymer 1999). Similarly, the linkage of racial group identity to political party identification alone would not explain the twofold increase in African Americans who self-identify as political Independents, as shown in figure 3.2. Equally important, race is not such a totalizing force in African American politics that black political thought is homogeneous (Dawson 2001) or exclusive of other salient primary social identities. Some of the most important recent work on racial politics and race relations engages the intersections of race with class (Gilliam 1986, Welch and Foster 1987; Wilson 1987), gender (Morrison 1992; Gay and Tate 1998), sexuality (C. J. Cohen 1999), and national identity (Parker 2003; Citrin and Sears 2005; Sawyer 2005).

The upshot of our discussion in this section is that race is a sufficiently pervasive and far-reaching organizing influence on American social, economic, and political life that we expect it to have an important and independent influence on our party identification for many Americans. We do not, however, expect race to vanquish, or be vanquished by, other salient group identities. Dawson's claim that "belief in the importance of black interests translates into preference for the Democratic Party" (Dawson 1994, 113) is a bit too deterministic.

More specifically, a sense of linked fate may not automatically translate into support for the Democratic Party without the two key steps necessary to link black interests with identification with the Democratic Party. First, African Americans must believe that black interests are best served through mainstream political institutions such as parties. This is an especially critical step because of the strong sense of mistrust toward mainstream white institutions within the African American community and strong sentiment in favor of autonomous and counterpublic black institutions. For instance, Dawson notes substantial increases over time in support for a black political party, with almost 40 percent of African Americans currently championing a black nationalist agenda (Dawson 2001, 83). To the extent that African Americans think of the Democratic Party as a mainstream white institution, support for black autonomy could severely undercut the link between black group interests and the Democratic Party. Importantly, this dimension—autonomy versus integration—has been largely ignored in previous accounts of black partisanship.

Second, even if individual African Americans conclude that blacks' interests are best served through mainstream political institutions, they must still decide which institution best serves these. Although this choice may seem obvious to many (perhaps most) African Americans, it may not be so obvious to everyone. Specifically, the group calculus must be linked to the social act of coordinating the decision on which party to throw one's support behind. Although Barack Obama's rise to the presidency and his presumed role as leader of the Democratic Party may make the link between a party and black interests temporarily clearer, emerging signs of discontent suggest that any gains the Democrats make may not last. Given the increasing prominence of black Republicans and conservatives such as Clarence Thomas, Alan Keyes, Condoleezza Rice, and Colin Powell, expanding support for black nationalism (Dawson 2001, Brown and Shaw 2002, Davis and Brown 2002), and what many perceive to be efforts by the Democratic Party and even Obama to downplay race and ignore a racially progressive agenda (Frymer 1999), genuine skepticism about the Democratic Party is conceivable.

To put a sharper point on how this matters to an explanation of non-partisanship, we add that if race were simply reducible to partisanship considerations, as Green and his colleagues suggest, we would have no explanation for the substantial (and growing) portion of African Americans who identify as political Independents. Similarly, if partisanship considerations were simply reducible to a linked-fate heuristic, as implied in Dawson's and Tate's accounts of African American party identification, we would have no explanation for the calculus of black political Independents. As we shall see in chapter 4, it is also not the case that the racial foundation of black party identification has been trumped by changing ideological and economic considerations. Against these explanations, we shall show that black nonpartisanship is best explained by the factors that contribute to the decoupling of racial group identity from partisan political identity.

A further implication of our argument is that while race is likely to remain a central factor in black partisan decision making, racial identity can cut both ways, and occasionally a black identity will lead to distance from both the Democratic and the Republican parties. The other implication is that African Americans may differ from other groups not simply in terms of which factors determine party identification but also in the structure of choice. For African Americans a multidimensional, unordered model is likely to more accurately depict their partisan decision-making process than is a simple, linear scale.

In chapter 4 we juxtapose these arguments about the distinct steps that are required to translate linked fate into Democratic partisanship and the importance of black separatism in determining black partisan choices against three popular but as-yet-untested alternate explanations for the movement of African Americans away from the Democratic Party. Specifically, we assess the impact of the declining significance of race (Wilson 1978), the growing black middle class (Thernstrom and Thernstrom 1997; Hutchinson 1999), and an increase in black conservatism (Sowell 1981, Hamilton 1982) on the partisan locations of individual African Americans. As we shall see, it is not the case that the racial foundation of black party identification has been trumped by the declining significance of race, a rightward shift in ideology, or changing economic considerations. Against these reductionist explanations, we shall show that black nonpartisanship is best explained by the factors that contribute to the decoupling of racial group identity from partisan political identity.

IMMIGRANTS: UNCERTAINTY, AMBIVALENCE, IDENTITY,
    AND NONPARTISANSHIP

An important corollary to our claim that race matters to our understanding of party identification is the point that race as a consideration is not exclusive to African Americans. Even in texts on party identification that do give some consideration to race (e.g., Campbell et al. 1960; Nie et al. 1976; Kaminiecki 1985; Miller and Shanks 1996), the not-too-subtle implication is that race is consequential only to the extent that African Americans are different from white Americans. Absent from these comparisons is a consideration of any other racial/ethnic group—most conspicuously, the distinctive political characteristics of Asian Americans and Latino Americans. This absence is especially notable given the profound transformation in the demographic landscape of the United States since the Hart-Celler amendments to the Immigration and Nationality Act of 1965 that we noted in the first pages of this book.

So how do immigrants and their offspring make decisions about the American party system? As we have noted, despite the enormous attention given by political scientists to the question of party identification in America, little of it has focused on racial and ethnic minorities or new immigrants to the United States. Moreover, the handful of studies that do exist (e.g., Abrajano and Alvarez 2010; Nicholson and Segura 2005; Wong et al. 2009; Uhlaner and Garcia 2005; Lien et al. 2004; Cain et al. 1991; Uhlaner et al. 2000; Wong 2001; Alvarez and García Bedolla 2003), by and large, face several limitations. First, their principal substantive focus is on explaining the partisanship patterns of particular groups, rather than endeavoring to draw from these patterns some new insights into the nature and dynamics of party identification writ large (but see Bowler et al. 2006).[23] Second, their principal concern, operationally, is explaining the variation in how these emerging groups fix their loyalties given the pairwise choice between the Democratic and Republican parties. Third, with a few important exceptions, the research into the partisanship of these groups has simply adopted a conventional understanding of party identification. The predominant assumption is that Latinos, Asian Americans, and others distinguish parties along the same single, linear liberal-conservative dimension. Finally, much of this work is incomplete and insufficiently discriminating. Take, for instance, the finding that immigrants' partisanship is defined by time spent in the United States (Cain et al. 1991; Wong 2000). While valid, the measure of lived years is too rough to enable one to distinguish between the different facets that might vary with tenure (experiences in one's workplace and neighborhood, citizenship status, civic engagement, familiarization with political parties and left-right ideology, and the like); nor does it specify the underlying mechanisms by which time matters (e.g., information uncertainty, ideological ambivalence, and identity formation).

This focus on explaining the party identification of Latinos and Asians is important in its own right. For all the reasons we have just described, it is of great political consequence whether Latinos and Asians choose to coordinate their political attachments around one particular party, as African Americans have done over many decades, or whether race/ethnicity recedes to relative insignificance when they choose between the two parties. Important or not, this focus on predicting whether Latinos and Asians will line up as Democrats or Republicans misses what is perhaps

---

[23] There are also several recent works on the role of partisan mobilization in Asian and Latino participation, with a focus on voter registration and voter turnout (Pantoja et al. 2001; Ramírez 2002; Wong 2002; Barreto et al. 2003).

most distinctive about the party identification of immigrant-based groups, namely, the relative absence of any relationship to parties. A disproportionate number of Latinos and Asian Americans (relative to whites and African Americans) reject the pairwise choice between the Democrats and the Republicans, or even the tripartite choice between Democrats, Republicans, and Independents.

The Widespread Nonpartisanship of Latinos and Asian Americans

Table 3.2 shows the responses of Asian Americans and Latinos to the standard party-identification question in several recent surveys: the 1993–94 Multi-city Survey of Urban Inequality (MCSUI), the 2001 Pilot National Asian American Politics Survey, the 2002 and 2004 Kaiser Family Foundation/Pew Hispanic Center National Survey of Latinos, the 2006 Latino National Survey (LNS), and the 2008 National Asian American Survey. Not all of these surveys are representative of the national population of these groups, but to the extent that they diverge from the national population, they focus on the groups we are most interested in—immigrants and their offspring.[24]

Fully 61 percent of Asian American respondents and 47 percent of Latino respondents in the MCSUI noted no partisan preferences, refused to answer, indicated uncertainty, or answered "don't know." Among Asian Americans in the MCSUI, only 28 percent identified either as Democrats or as Republicans; among Latinos, only 39 percent located themselves on this continuum. Even in the more nationally representative 2006 Latino National Survey and the 2008 National Asian American Politics Survey, only a minority (44 percent in both surveys) of all respondents affiliated themselves with a major party. This distinct lack of enthusiasm for the major parties is evident in every one of the surveys listed in table 3.2. This reluctance stands in marked contrast to the emphatic conclusion of the authors of *The American Voter*: "The partisan self-image of *all but the few* individuals who disclaim any involvement in politics per-

[24] The two Pew surveys and the LNS survey are designed to be representative of the national Hispanic population. Importantly, this includes noncitizens, a group that is omitted in studies such as the ANES. The MCSUI survey oversamples minorities in major urban centers and seeks to obtain stratification that includes poor, immigrant neighborhoods. The PNAAPS surveys respondents from the five major urban centers of Asian Americans—New York, Chicago, Los Angeles, San Francisco, and Honolulu. The 2008 NAAS is drawn from an extensive ethnic name list that oversamples respondents from California, the New York/New Jersey metro area, and other metro areas that represent new destinations for Asian American immigrants (see Wong et al. 2009 for more information on the survey).

TABLE 3.2.
Asian Americans, Latinos, and Nonpartisanship

	Democrat/ Republican	Independent	Not sure/ Don't know/ Refused	Something else /No pref./ Do not think in these terms
Asian Americans				
1993–94 MCSUI (LA)	28	11	6	55
2001 PNAAPS (5 cities)	50	13	18	20
2008 NAAS	44	20	10	26
Hispanics/Latinos				
1993–94 MCSUI (4 cities)	39	14	4	43
2002 PEW	51	28	11	10
2004 PEW	49	26	14	12
2006 LNS	44	17	20	16

mits us to place each person in these samples on a continuum of partisanship extending from strong Republican to strongly Democratic" (Campbell et al. 1960, 122; our emphasis).

This finding of nonpartisanship among Asian Americans and Latinos is a strong validation of our earlier expectation that party identification is not likely to be fully represented by a standard, linear, unidimensional continuum. As we shall further argue, neither is it likely to be completely explained by the Michigan School or the Downsian view of party identification. Asian Americans and Latinos are more of a moving target than the "unmoved mover" of Campbell and his colleagues. Similarly, unlike Downsian voters who consume information shortcuts in the duopolistic competition between the Republican and Democratic parties, most Asians and Latinos simply have no preferences regarding these goods and are unable to place themselves on a Downsian ideological continuum.

The reason for this poor theoretical fit, we assert, is that the partisanship patterns of immigrant-based groups are characterized by the processes of immigrant acculturation and political incorporation—the degree to which new entrants come to understand the rules of social, political, and economic engagement in the United States. To be more specific, we maintain that the unique context of immigration implicates three distinct factors: information uncertainty, ideological ambivalence, and identity formation. These three factors, which form the core of our more general account of party identification and political independence, are, we argue, particularly critical in the party identification of Latinos and Asian Americans.

INFORMATION UNCERTAINTY

The first dimension, information uncertainty, shapes the partisan choices of immigrants and their children because these relative newcomers often do not know enough about American politics and American parties to know where they fit in. Conventional accounts of party identification assume a fairly intimate, lifelong relationship with party politics. Let us take the example of identifying as an Independent. According to the Michigan School, Independents are the offspring of parents who are Independents or grew up in a climate of political socialization that led them to identify as political Independents. In a modified account of party identification as a social identity, the corollary would be that Independents so identify because this accords with their sense of a political group identity. According to the Downsian view, Independents so identify either due to their steadfast ideological moderation or due to their inability to see meaningful differences between the two parties.

Both the Michigan and the Downsian accounts, in short, presume fully assimilated and well-socialized citizens. With immigration-based groups, none of the preconditions for these pathways to Independence applies: there is no familiarity with the U.S.-centric left-right ideological continuum, no knowledge of issue differences between Democrats and Republicans, and no sufficiently habituated loyalties to the two-party system in the United States. Rather than make a choice between parties that they know little about or support a party or political system that they do not yet trust, many Latinos and Asians identify as nonpartisans, a rationally skeptical response to this uncertain and unfamiliar political environment. To put a finer point on it, two distinct and sequential choices undergird the relationship of Latinos and Asian Americans to political parties. As newcomers to the United States, Asians and Latinos first have to decide whether they have a sufficient feel for the game and adequate knowledge of its rules of engagement to play. If not, they are likely (as many do) to indicate no preference or give one of the noncompliant responses (refusal or answering "not sure" or "don't know"). If they choose to play, then they must decide which team—Democrats, Republicans, or Independents—to join.

IDEOLOGICAL AMBIVALENCE

Second, we argue that political predispositions, the anchors that typically steady us in uncertain and unfamiliar environments, also have shaky moorings for immigrant-based racial/ethnic groups. Specifically, two cen-

tral predispositions, immigrants' ideological roots and their sense of ra-
cial/ethnic group identity, are more moving targets than they are unmoved
movers. Regarding ideological roots, we posit that the partisan choices
are shaped by ambivalence and that ambivalence works in two distinct
ways. First, we expect Asians and Latinos to be ambivalent about their
party identification because they have yet to "own" the terms of ideological discourse used in the United States. That is, Asians and Latinos are not
likely, either as immigrants or as second- or third-generation tenderfoots,
to have assimilated a strong sense of personal political efficacy or trust in
political institutions or a deep understanding of left-right ideology, which
is expected of more seasoned democratic citizens in America (cf. de la
Garza et al. 1996; Parker 2003). Rather, these new Americans are more
likely, at least initially, to try to adapt the cultural values, religious mores,
and terms of ideological discourse from their homeland context to the
United States.

Ambivalence can also shape partisanship a second way. Many immigrant-based groups might well be described as what Philip Converse
called "issue publics." That is, their politics is in large measure defined by
very specific issue concerns—such as the concerns of Cubans, Vietnamese, and Koreans with U.S. post–Cold War foreign policy; the concern of
Puerto Ricans and Pacific Islanders with statehood and sovereignty; and
the concerns of Arabs and Muslims with civil liberties in a post-911 era.
While the major parties often stake well-defined positions on these issues,
these concerns are seldom central to either party's platform. Thus, establishing durable party allegiances on the basis of such issues may leave
these groups vulnerable either to shifting political tides or to discord after
new issues arise from their immigrant experiences in the United States
(e.g., Vietnamese Americans may like the Republican Party's more hawk-
ish foreign policy but also like the Democratic Party's more liberal social
welfare and civil rights policies).

IDENTITY FORMATION

Finally, we expect that for Asian Americans and Latinos, racially and
ethnically defined "groupness" will be a shifting entity—more a formation than a result. That is, this process of identity formation is also likely
to be characterized by uncertainty and ambivalence. Much of the debate
over Latinos and Asian Americans as social group identities is whether
there is any "there there." Although many scholars have ably demonstrated that the political orientation of Asian Americans and Latinos can
be shaped by their ethnic and panethnic identity, this influence is often
quite contingent (Padilla 1984; Espiritu 1992; Pachon and DeSipio 1994;

Jones-Correa and Leal 1996; Jones-Correa 1998; Bobo and Johnson 2000; Lee 2004). As Lee (2004) shows, when Asian Americans strongly believe that their lot in life is adjoined to the fate of other Asian Americans, this has a significant effect on their likelihood of having a party that they identify with. And that party is generally the Democratic Party. But only a small fraction of all Asian Americans hold this belief. Thus, we expect the political and social group identities of Asians and Latinos to interact in often complex ways to influence how different immigrants and their children think about the major parties, the American political process, and the utility of civic and political engagement.[25]

Extremism, Ambivalence, and White Nonpartisans

In this penultimate section of this chapter, we turn to our third and final case: the self-identification of white Americans as political Independents. As we noted earlier, the lion's share of political science scholarship on party identification (and more pointedly, political Independents) ignores or brackets nonwhite racial and ethnic groups, focusing principally on the enduring attachments of white Americans. One key objective of our book is to articulate a theoretical framework that is able to explain the unique features of party identification among African Americans, Latinos, and Asian Americans. The greater ambition, however, is to exploit some enduring methodological tensions and theoretical debates on party identification to develop a more general framework for party identification writ large. The crucial test of this aspiration is whether our account adds to our existing explanations of the party identification of all groups. Specifically, we do not argue against the applicability of existing accounts of political Independents to whites, since they are developed to explain the partisan choices of whites. But our framework should tell us something these conventional accounts do not about white Independents.

Recall that we started this chapter by taking aim at the unidimensional view of party identification, where Independents are assumed to be in the middle of a linear continuum and, in the Downsian view, where this linear continuum is anchored by a unidimensional scale of ideological beliefs ranging from liberal to conservative. We argue that even among

---

[25] For example, a stronger belief in the importance of race and a clearer recognition of one's status as a racial minority should affect party choice in different ways for different national origin groups. For Mexicans who already lean toward the Democratic Party, racial consciousness should reinforce existing partisanship cues and lead to strong Democratic Party preferences. For Cubans, the opposite should happen: Racial consciousness should cut against the community's traditional allegiance to the Republican Party and potentially result in greater numbers of Independents.

whites, many individuals do not fit so neatly into conventional partisan or ideological spaces. Moreover, we posit two distinct pathways to Independence among white Americans, avenues that hitherto have been missing from existing explanations of political Independents. The first among these builds on a neglected (yet central) claim in Downs's *An Economic Theory of Democracy;* the second borrows from critiques of Downs.

First, much of the focus on Downs's work has been on the expectation of an ideological convergence at the preferred policies of the median voter. Often neglected from Downs's initial formulation, however, is his companion expectation that parties would avoid controversial issues or take deliberately ambiguous positions on them. The premise behind Downs's expectation is that some issues are so salient for particular constituencies that it behooves strategic parties to avoid offering clear positions on them. The corresponding premise, from the standpoint of mass publics, is that there are clusters of individuals analogous to Converse's "issue publics." We posit that these individuals are unified by such intense and extreme positions on an issue that they are especially prone to agreeing with George C. Wallace's infamous dictum that "there's not a dime's worth of difference" between the Democrats and Republicans.[26] The relevant difference here, however, is that these voters fail to see a difference between the two parties *not* because they are so similar *to one another* vis-à-vis convergence to the median voter, but because they are both so far removed from the voters' preferences. Gerald Garvey (1966) notes that political parties may have strategic incentives to diverge from the median voter to ensure that their extreme liberal and conservative wings do not flee the party altogether and abstain from the political process. John Petrocik (1996) further notes that political parties sometimes "capture" such constituencies by credibly claiming "ownership" of their issues. In cases where both parties fail to do this, however, individuals should self-identify as nonpartisans rather than choose between Tweedledum and Tweedledee. Thus, in direct opposition to conventional accounts, we posit that it is sometimes ideological *extremism* (i.e., ideological distance from *both* parties) and not ideological moderation or a lack of differentiation between convergent parties that predicts whether voters identify as Independents.

The second, yet relatively unexamined, pathway to nonpartisanship for whites emerges out of the recognition that there is little empirical support for Downs's assumption that ideological beliefs can be mapped onto a single, unidimensional continuum. As Donald Stokes first put the case,

---

[26] This notion of issue publics might also be thought of in terms of Austen-Smith's (1984) consideration of "multiple constituencies," where the central dilemma facing both parties is the difficulty in finding a resultant median voter vector across the multiple constituencies.

"When our respondents are asked directly to describe the parties in terms of the liberal-conservative distinction, nearly half confess that the terms are unfamiliar. And the bizarre meanings given the terms by many of those who do attempt to use them suggest that we are eliciting artificial answers that have little to do with the public's everyday perceptions of the parties" (1963, 370). The multidimensionality of ideological beliefs is a point also echoed by some of Stokes's contemporaries, who comment on the bases of multiparty systems in Europe (Duverger 1954, Sartori 1976), and serves as the stimulus for much formal work on whether the centripetal median voter result would hold under multidimensional issue spaces (McKelvey 1976; McKelvey and Ordeshook 1976; Enelow and Hinich 1984; cf. Ferejohn 1993).

For our purposes, the fact of multiple ideological issue dimensions harks back to our earlier discussion of multiple identities. Ideologies, like identities, need not be reducible to one another or subsumed by one another. Sometimes what is distinctive about a person's political profile is that there is conflict and dissonance between ideological dimensions.[27] A person who is generally liberal, for example, may hold antiblack or anti-immigrant views, which make simple party identification by ideological placement difficult. Similarly, there may be a breach between a person's fiscal liberalism (or conservatism) and his or her moral conservatism (or liberalism). As these two examples suggest, we think that this kind of "ideological ambivalence" is especially likely when one of the ideological strands evokes a salient social identity (e.g., race or religion, in the two examples above). Here, too, nonpartisanship is not the result of ideological moderation. Rather, for individuals who hold strongly liberal views on some issues and strongly conservative views on others, nonpartisanship is largely a function of ambivalence.

IMPLICATIONS

This multidimensional view of party choice and nonpartisanship has important implications for scholars and practitioners of American politics. For political practitioners, there are important lessons about who nonpartisans are and what role they could play in shaping the balance of power in future electoral contests. In particular, our account of nonparti-

---

[27] Dissonance and ambiguity are regularly invoked in discussions of public opinion. Layman and Carmines (1997) and Alvarez and Brehm (1993) are among a lengthy list of authors who highlight the importance that ambiguity can play in opinion formation. Others have even noted how ambivalence about parties can affect voter choice (Basinger and Lavine 2005, S. Greene 2005) and how ambivalence destabilizes party identification (Keele and Wolak 2006).

sans leads to a different normative view of nonpartisans. Nonpartisans should not simply be dismissed as nonideologues prone to apathy and inactivity. Rather, as we indicate, there are multiple routes to nonpartisanship, many of which suggest that Independents are anything but apolitical. On certain issues, nonpartisans are the most engaged and most interested members of the American public. In turn, this more positive view of nonpartisans leads to a different conclusion about the possibility that nonpartisans will be important political actors. If nonpartisans are seen as apolitical nonideologues, there is little reason to try to mobilize them. Everything we know about political participation suggests that such efforts will be futile. However, if we see nonpartisans as simply lacking in experience with American politics or as caring about issues that are not yet on the parties' agendas, then there is every reason to believe that they can be integrated and mobilized. It seems clear that unaligned, uninvolved minorities and others can and will become actively involved in party politics if the right issues come along and enter the arena of party politics. Given the growing number of unaligned citizens, the party that can more successfully navigate these issues could have a critical electoral edge.

This account also suggests that parties and practitioners ignore race and ethnicity at their own peril. If our understanding of the unique circumstances and considerations of each is accurate, then a race to the median-voter approach is unlikely to work, as there is unlikely to be one median voter. Rather, members of different racial and ethnic groups will have divergent core concerns that motivate their decisions. Without a multipronged approach that seeks in some way to speak to each of these different perspectives, parties will have a difficult time acquiring a working majority.

For scholars of American politics, there are also important lessons. The alternative dimensions of nonpartisanship that we highlight in this chapter not only inform us about the partisan choices of individual members of these groups but also help us to understand the broader workings of party identification in America. The first key lesson explored here is that America's two-party system is unlikely to be able to incorporate effectively the views of an increasingly diverse public. Put succinctly, there will be a lot of misfits who, for a range of reasons, end up as nonpartisans. In highlighting the diverse set of knowledge levels, ideological concerns, and identities that members of different groups have, we are essentially emphasizing all of the reasons why two parties who locate themselves at two points along a liberal-conservative ideological continuum will be unable to attract broad swaths of the American public. There is, to put it mildly, a disjuncture between the concerns of the American public in the twenty-first century and the structure of the American party system.

The other vital lesson for scholars who wish to examine partisanship in an empirical fashion is that a simple, linear scale of partisanship is no longer adequate to explain the range of dimensions in partisan choice across the American population. The multiple pathways to partisanship that we put forward in this book have implications not only for *which* party Americans ultimately choose to align with but also for *how* they go about choosing between the three options of Democrat, Independent, and Republican. For many Americans, the choice, as conventional accounts maintain, should be one of simply deciding where to place themselves along a linear continuum ranging from strongly Democratic on the left to Independent in the middle and finally to strongly Republican on the right. But for others, the structure of party choice is more complex than this simple linear continuum suggests. Indeed, the three choices may not be ordered at all, but different dimensions may come into play at different points in the decision-making process. This means that we should expect that the factors separating Democrats from nonpartisans will differ from the factors separating Democrats from Republicans, and for anyone interested in modeling partisan choices empirically, this means that we will have to use a different set of statistical tools.

Another lesson for scholars is that our analysis has ignored an important segment of the population that is particularly likely to be confused about partisanship and particularly unlikely to follow conventional models of partisan decision making. Typically, individuals who offer somewhat unclear responses such as "not sure" or "none of the above" or who refuse to answer the question altogether are viewed as apolitical and dropped from the analysis (Campbell et al. 1960). Empirically speaking, these kinds of responses are inconsequential when we consider the white population. Only about 2 percent of whites fit into these categories. But when we move on to the Latino and Asian American communities, the consequences of ignoring this population are much more severe. As we have seen earlier in this chapter, large segments of these communities choose not to place themselves in any of the three traditional categories of Democrat, Independent, or Republican. Among immigrants, these kinds of "noncodable" responses can, in fact, make up the majority of responses.

In our view, categorizing this population as apolitical or ignoring it altogether is inappropriate. Rather than dismiss these problematic responses, a more fruitful approach is to begin to think about why many Americans choose to offer these ambiguous responses. People's ambivalence (i.e., answering "no preference"), detachment (i.e., stating that they do not think in partisan terms), or noncompliance (i.e., refusing to answer the question) may tell us a great deal about their sense of political identity and attachment to political institutions.

Thus, in the analysis that follows, we will often make a distinction between Independents who willingly and clearly place themselves in the category Independent and nonpartisans who offer responses showing they do not choose Democrat, Independent, or Republican. Our view is that more conventional accounts of nonpartisanship—including holding middle-of-the-road political views, being socialized as Independent by one's parents, and feeling principally attached to the ideal of Independence—will help explain the choices of those who explicitly label themselves as Independent. By contrast, these conventional models will fare less well with nonidentifiers. We suspect that these nonidentifiers, by offering responses that do not clearly fit one of the three main categories, are, in fact, often indicating a lack of fit with the partisan scale itself. Further, we claim that many of the underlying factors affecting partisanship that we highlight in our model—including information uncertainty, ideological ambivalence, and doubts about social identity—are especially likely to lead to these kinds of ambiguous responses. Americans who have little information about the American party system, individuals whose core ideological concerns are orthogonal to the partisan divide, and people whose identities push them in different partisan directions will have reason to try to opt out of the partisan scale by giving unclear responses.

To see if these patterns hold, we repeat many of our empirical tests in two ways. In most of the analyses we present, we incorporate nonidentifiers in our larger category of nonpartisans. However, when there are large numbers of nonconformist responses, we attempt to analyze this group separately and in particular try to determine what kinds of factors lead individuals to offer less clear responses to the party-identification question.

REJOINDERS

Beyond these implications, there is at least one important concern in our focus on Independents. One issue, touched upon briefly already, is whether most Independents are, in fact, Independent at all. It turns out that in at least certain types of electoral contests and for certain types of Independents, the majority of Independents behave like closet partisans—that is, they consistently support the party they lean toward. The question then becomes, does it matter if people who identify as Independent vote like dyed-in-the-wool partisans on Election Day?

The evidence marshaled in favor of this view of Independents as closet partisans is impressive. Table 3.3 replicates the core analysis of *The Myth of the Independent Voter*, the seminal work on the partisan proclivities of

TABLE 3.3
The Vote for Democratic Candidates among White Americans, 1948–2000

	President	House	Senate
Strong Democrats	87%	90%	89%
Weak Democrats	64	77	76
Democratic leaners	69	73	71
Pure Independents	31	52	50
Republican leaners	11	30	27
Weak Republicans	13	25	25
Strong Republicans	3	11	9

Note: Adapted and updated from Keith et al. 1992.
Source: NES Cumulative File, 1948–2000.

nonpartisan voters (Keith et al. 1992). The table details the voting tendencies of different kinds of partisans and nonpartisans in congressional and presidential contests over the last half century. Judging from the behavior of the roughly 60 to 70 percent of Independents who are leaners—individuals who identify as Independent but who then reveal a preference for one of the two major parties when asked—partisan voting among Independents is widespread. The table shows quite clearly that in terms of their voting patterns in these national partisan contests, white Independent leaners are only marginally less partisan—and sometimes even more partisan—than weak partisans. In each type of election, a clear majority of all Independent leaners voted according to their partisan leanings. Based on similar results, Keith et al. unequivocally concluded that most Independents "*are largely closet Democrats and Republicans*" (Keith et al. 1992, 4 [italics in original]).

These findings, however, are limited in a number of important respects. First, and most obviously, they apply only to white Americans. It should be clear that just because white Independent leaners, "display an impressive tendency to vote for the candidate of the party they feel closer to," this does not tell us a lot about the partisan proclivities of Latino, African American, or Asian American Independents (1992, 65). If we are right, and the factors that drive party identification do differ across groups, this is a glaring omission.

Second, the analysis presented in *The Myth of the Independent Voter* and other accounts of Independents often fails to consider the full range of options available to nonpartisans in any given electoral contest. If, as we have suggested, neither party represents the interests of the multitude of Americans whose views do not fit neatly along the partisanship divide, then logically we might expect many nonpartisan voters to be searching for an alternative course of action (or inaction). Following the logic of Albert Hirschman (1970), we argue that assessments of the behavior of nonpartisans need to examine all of the options available, including exit, voice, and loyalty. As we will see, under the right circumstances, Independent leaners are especially apt to not remain loyal and to choose either exit or voice. We will show that in presidential contests, for example, white Independent leaners are more than twice as likely as weak partisans to choose to vote for a third party. Similarly, since nonpartisans who are ambivalent and uncertain about partisan options have much less reason to go to the polls in the first place, it is not surprising that we find that leaners and other types of nonpartisans are quite likely to abstain from voting altogether.

Third, these findings tend to ignore the possibility that the reason Independent leaners appear to vote consistently as partisans is that they lean toward the party that they just voted for in the current election. Keith and his colleagues own data show that from just one presidential contest to the next, a surprisingly large percentage of leaners—30 percent—switched their votes and vote for the other party. Moreover, of these vote switchers a third altered their partisan leanings to match their vote change. Using a range of panel data, our analysis will show that much of the perceived loyalty of leaners to one party is illusory.

Finally, and perhaps most important, all of this ignores context. How often nonpartisans express active support for candidates from one of the two major parties will vary significantly with the options that voters are afforded. Keith and his colleagues and others who examine the partisan proclivities of Independents focus exclusively on cases where partisan defections are highly unlikely—elections where the two parties are dominant and where there is little incentive or opportunity to choose an alternative candidate or party. Thus, partisan voting among leaners may be less the result of affinity for a particular party and more the result of a lack of a viable alternative. The importance of context is evident even in presidential elections, as we will see in chapter 8. In most presidential elections, no third-party candidate is even listed on the ballot across most states. In these elections, it is not surprising to find that few leaners defect to a third party. It is also not surprising to find that defections among leaners jump in presidential elections that do have third-party candidates on the ballot across most states. Even though these third-party candidates do not have a real chance of winning, roughly a quarter of all Independent leaners voted for the third-party candidate in recent decades. In elections involving viable candidates who do not represent the two parties, we find markedly higher partisan defections among Independents of all stripes.

None of these criticisms refutes the fact that most Independent leaners in most elections will probably vote for the party they lean toward, but they do raise important questions about just what Independence means across different groups and different contexts. They also suggest that it may be too early to categorize all Independent leaners as partisans and thus too problematic to simply lump leaners with other partisans when analyzing party identification.

To address our suspicions about the partisanship of Independents, we undertake two important tests in subsequent chapters. First, we repeat our analysis including or excluding different categories of Independents. Our primary analysis focuses on an inclusive category of nonpartisans that includes leaners and all others who do not identify as Democrats or Republicans. However, we also repeat all of the tests that are presented in the chapters that follow, grouping leaners with partisans and thus singling out pure Independents. To preview, when we repeat our analysis dropping Independent leaners from the nonpartisan category and focusing on pure Independents only, we find few striking differences in our account of party identification. Any substantial differences are noted. Second, we examine the voting behavior of pure Indepedents, leaners, and partisans across a range of electoral contexts. This analysis is presented primarily in chapter 6, but some discussion of the results is located in earlier chapters.

Toward a Theory: Information, Identity, and Ideology

In these first three chapters, we have taken a long and deliberate journey through our empirical analysis of the distinct pathways to nonpartisanship for blacks, Latinos, Asians, and whites. The backdrop to this sojourn has been the changing centrality of the role of political parties in the electorate and, with it, the coordination around a fixed conceptualization and operationalization of party identification. The particular vehicle of choice for political scientists, as we saw in chapter 2, is somewhat of a jalopy. It has suffered many nicks and dents over the years, but none so damaging that we are tempted to disembark and venture off on our own. Moreover, we have seen that two kinds of passengers use this vehicle. One kind thinks that party identification is the expression of our habits and history; the other thinks that party identification is an instrument with which to match our interests with the information necessary to act upon them. These passengers, by and by, get to their desired destinations in this vehicle.

In this chapter—to abuse the vehicular metaphor a final time—we remind our readers that party identification, like all jalopies, has a middle seat that nobody wants to sit on. Both the Michigan and the Downsian accounts give us an incomplete story of party identification, especially when held up against the distinctly bumpy, itchy characteristics of non-partisans in the middle. What is more, racially and ethnically defined electorates are often excluded from this seat in the jalopy. Our overarching argument in this chapter is that we can upgrade this vehicle to study the party in the electorate (and dress up its passengers) by taking this middle seat out—that is, by focusing on nonpartisans in their own right—and rebuilding it to comfortably fit the attributes of racially and ethnically defined electorates.

We close, then, by summarizing the main elements of this reconstruction vis-à-vis existing theories of party identification. The Michigan School, we have argued, offers an incomplete account for three principal reasons. First, party identification is not always best represented on a unidimensional scale. Nonpartisanship is not merely the absence of a social identification or the midpoint on a continuum. Second, not all individuals and groups are fully socialized into the two-party system in the United States. Immigrant-based groups such as Latinos and Asian Americans are especially apt to find shaky moorings as they strive to get a better fix on what parties and partisan choices mean in America. Third, party identification may not be exclusive of other salient social identities that matter to our political orientation. In the case of African Americans, racial group identity is often inextricable from partisan political identity, and what is distinctive is the severing of this linkage. In the case of whites, these other salient social identities (especially race and religion) may square poorly with their general ideological orientation. The end result is that for many Americans who find themselves lumped together in the catchall category of nonpartisan, partisanship choice is not merely the absence of a social identification or the midpoint on a continuum.

The Downsian, "running tally" view of partisanship too is incomplete for two reasons. First, not all individuals are equally familiar with the two-party system. With Asians and Latinos, in particular, we expect substantially greater uncertainty in establishing ideological proximity to the Democratic and Republican parties or the ability to take meaningful running tallies of each party's past performance. Second, not all issues and ideological beliefs fit comfortably on the liberal-conservative continuum. In the case of whites, ideological extremism and ambivalence (rather than moderation) may predict who identifies as Independent. With African Americans, ideological separatism (rather than moderation) may better predict nonpartisanship. With Asians and Latinos, ideological beliefs may be salient and durable, but serve only as useful anchors to fix partisan cues in the political context of one's home country.

To counteract these limitations, we build a more expanded account out of the following propositions. First, whether we identify with a political party and, if so, which party we identify with is a function of our prior political predispositions—specifically, our primary social group identities and ideological orientations. Second, these political predispositions may be multiple and interactive. Contra the Michigan School, we note that party identification is not always the sole identity that defines our relationship to political parties. Contra the Downsian view, we state that a unidimensional ideological continuum misses several ideologically based pathways to identification as nonpartisan. The ideological beliefs that define our (non)partisanship too may be multiple and interactive. Third, these predispositions may not be equally constant and durable across groups and circumstances. For many, they are prefigured in their preadult socialization à la Michigan School, but for others, party identification is a process of decision making under conditions of information uncertainty and a prior socialization outside the United States that is balanced against one's acculturation in political life in America. Our fourth and final proposition is that the distinctive features of three cases—African American, Asian American and Latino, and white American party identification— give us critical variation and analytic leverage in discovering which predispositions matter, how they interact, and whether they wield their influence with certainty. We now turn to a more careful consideration of each of the three distinctive pathways to nonpartisanship.

CHAPTER 4

Leaving the Mule Behind: Independents and African American Partisanship

> In this country, it's impossible for you to be aligned—with either party. Either party that you align yourself with is suicide . . . once you are aligning, you have no bargaining power—none whatsoever.
>
> —Malcolm X

> We must reject separatism from whatever source. We must reject white separatism. We must reject black separatism. We must hold true to the course on which we have embarked, the course which leads to an integrated society of magnificent pluralism.
>
> —Massachusetts Senator Edward Brooke

IN CHAPTERS 1 and 3, we noted that within the mainstream political science scholarship on party identification, race is often invisible. When race does come into view, moreover, we often see it through the prism of black-white relations in the United States. African American party identification is famously distinctive (and, by implication, anomalous) for being so disproportionately Democratic. In some versions of this story, the demographic status of being "black" is simply equated with the partisan identification as "Democrat," with all the inevitability and inflexibility of a stereotype that is resistant to counterevidence. In more sophisticated versions, demography is mediated by racial solidarity and group interests that govern the political opinions and behavior of African Americans. In terms of the linkage of racial group identity and political institutional identity, African Americans, to play on a coinage usually applied to Asian Americans, are the "model minority"—they demonstrate a strong and politically decisive sense of in-group solidarity. The coherence of defining a group basis to the politics of other emerging minority groups such as Asian and Latino Americans is generally held up to this standard.

In this sense, if race and partisan identities interact and intersect in illuminating and consequential ways, we should see it in bold relief with African Americans. Thus, in this opening empirical chapter, we reconsider the contemporary relationship of African Americans to political parties. We first sketch the history of party identification among African Americans, a history that underscores two important points. First, African Americans have not always been so overwhelmingly Democratic in their party identification. Second, in the last few decades—at least until the successful candidacy of Barack Obama—African Americans have been slowly but surely moving away from an exclusive relationship with the Democratic Party. These patterns frame our consideration of how African Americans come to identify (or choose not to identify) with a political party. We articulate several popular views on upward class mobility, rightward ideological drift, and downward significance of race as the engines of change in the contemporary African American political landscape.

We build an alternative account to these explanations out of the logical steps that link one's self-identification as an African American to one's partisan identification as a Democrat. This specification of how identity is linked to politics generates three expectations about African American party identification. Consistent with existing studies, the presence of a "linked-fate heuristic" is likely to be a key factor in defining black partisanship. In addition, we argue for the influence of two other factors: the perceived legitimacy of mainstream electoral politics as a venue for the pursuit of collective interests and the rational evaluation of the Democratic and Republican parties' efforts on behalf of these collective interests. In the main, we find that the exodus of some African Americans from the Democratic Party is the result of not solely upward class mobility or growing ideological conservatism but also a break in the links of their identity-to-politics chain—that is, a decoupling of their individual well-being from their collective welfare, their adhering to black separatist beliefs, and their assessment of the relative influence of the Democratic Party and the Republican Party as advocates for their political interests. We close by considering the impact of having a black Democratic president on future patterns in blacks' partisanship.

HISTORICAL TRENDS IN PARTISANSHIP

The history of African American partisanship is well known and well explained. The narrative usually begins with the Civil War, the manumission of black slaves, and Reconstruction. The secession of Southern states from the Union in 1861 created a political space for Abraham Lincoln's Republican Party to abolish racist laws, enlist African American troops in the fight, and pass the Thirteenth Amendment, which ultimately brought slavery to an end. For the newly enfranchised African Americans, the partisan cues could not have been clearer in the subsequent struggle between Southern Democrats, led by Andrew Johnson, and the Northern

Republicans over the legitimacy of Southern "Black Codes" (which stripped the newly emancipated African Americans of de jure political rights and de facto economic and social rights), the mandate of the Freedman's Bureau (to help with the social, legal, and economic transition of blacks out of slavery), and, ultimately, the Fourteenth and Fifteenth Amendments. Although the Republican Party was never able to make good on General William T. Sherman's Field Order No. 15 for "40 acres and a mule" and the radical rebuilding of the South ultimately gave way to the Compromise of 1877, in the interim some twenty black Republicans served in the U.S. House of Representatives and two in the Senate during Reconstruction, and African Americans came overwhelmingly to champion the Republican Party (van Woodward 1974, E. Foner 1988, Jaynes 1989). In fact, the allegiance of African Americans to the Republican Party was so dominant that, as Elsa Barkley Brown notes, black Democrats during early Reconstruction "were subject to the severest exclusion: disciplined within or quite often expelled from their churches, kicked out of mutual benefit societies; not allowed to work alongside others in the fields nor accepted in leadership positions at work or in the community" (E. B. Brown 1994, 124). Over the next century, disaffection with the Republican Party grew, but few blacks went so far as to support the Democratic Party (Walton 1972). Not until the Great Depression did the black community's almost unanimous support for the Republican Party begin to wane. Dire economic circumstances and the governmentally activist, economically redistributive, and politically egalitarian New Deal policies of Franklin D. Roosevelt created the pivotal conditions for a reconsideration of party allegiances to the Democratic Party (Sitkoff 1978, Weiss 1983). As figure 4.1 shows, this shift began with a change in the partisan voting behavior of African Americans and was followed by a change in their party identification. During Roosevelt's presidency, African Americans who identified with the Democratic Party were still in the minority, yet almost 70 percent of the black vote went to Roosevelt.[1]

In the ensuing decades, there was a discernible split between how African Americans voted and which party they identified with (Jaynes and Williams 1989, Walters 1988). But as figure 4.1 shows, there is a convergence of both dimensions of partisanship as large majorities of the black electorate began to support the Democratic Party and its candidates. In 1948 Harry Truman became the first person to win the U.S. presidency with only a minority of the white vote, a result that is attributed largely to Truman's various initiatives on behalf of African Americans, such as the issuance of Executive Order 9981 (effectively desegregating the armed

---

[1] The data for figure 4.1 come from Bositis (2004). The figure categorizes Independents who lean toward Democrats as Democrats.

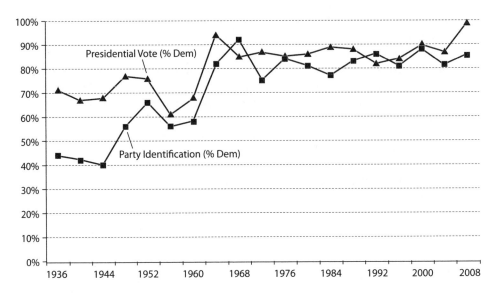

Figure 4.1. African American voting and party identification, 1936–2000

forces) and the establishment of the Civil Rights Commission (against the vociferous objections of the Southern "Dixiecrats," who bolted from party ranks to form the States' Rights Democratic Party). These events were paralleled over time by a vast migration of blacks from the rural South into Democratically controlled urban areas in the Northeast and Midwest. The 1954 congressional elections represented a milestone for many African Americans, with the successful candidaciesof Augustus Hawkins (D-CA), Adam Clayton Powell Jr. (D-NY), and William Dawson (D-IL) to the House of Representatives.

By the mid-1960s, there was an unmistakable shift in blacks' party support from the Republican to the Democratic Party, following a long decade of organized black insurgency in the South and the subsequent divergence of both parties on the politics of desegregation and equal rights for African Americans (Carmines and Stimson 1989; Lee 2002). According to some historical accounts, the pivotal moment in this upsurge of Democratic partisanship among black Americans occured in the 1960 presidential contest between John F. Kennedy and Richard M. Nixon, with Kennedy making a strategically timed and well-publicized phone call to Coretta Scott King (and his brother, who was working behind the scenes) after her husband, the Reverend Martin Luther King Jr., was jailed in Georgia (Garrow 1986, Marable 1991, Stern 1992). By 1964, the partisan signposts on racial equality and civil rights were unmistakable. After Arizona Senator Barry Goldwater—who infamously declared in his acceptance speech that "extremism in defense of liberty is no vice"—and Alabama Governor George Wallace—who equally infamously declared in his gubernatorial inauguration speech, "I draw the line in the dust and toss the gauntlet before the feet of tyranny and I say, segregation today, segregation tomorrow, segregation forever!"—it took little to convince most African Americans that the Democratic Party, under whose aegis the 1964 Civil Rights Act and the 1965 Voting Rights Act were successfully passed through legislation, would better serve their political interests. With over 90 percent of black voters supporting Lyndon B. Johnson in the 1964 presidential election, blacks' shift to Democratic partisanship was nearly complete. The subsequent defection of large numbers of white Americans to the Republican Party served only to solidify African American support for the Democratic Party, and by the early 1970s, blacks, by all accounts, had become "steadfast in their preference for the Democratic Party" (Tate 1994, 62). As the tail end of figure 4.1 shows, in the most recent 2008 presidential contest between Barack Obama and John McCain, the voting of African Americans reached an upper bound of sorts, with 99 percent of African American ANES respondents reporting choosing to vote for Obama.

Importantly, quite unlike the Downsian model of party identification described in chapter 2, most scholars of black politics do not explain this shifting group calculus in terms of the parallel liberal-to-conservative ideological alignment of African Americans. Instead, changes in black partisanship are explained by pointing to racial group interests. Scholars of black politics claim that movement into and out of the Republican Party was based almost exclusively on African Americans' assessment of which party would better serve black interests (Jones 1987, Walton 1972).[2] According to Pinderhughes, "Loyalty occurs among black voters because they consistently, almost uniformly, commit themselves to the party, faction or individual candidate that is most supportive of racial reform . . . studies have shown that this pattern repeats itself in the north and the south, in urban and rural areas, before and after the transition to the Democratic Party" (1987, 113).

The logic underlying this group-based voting is what Michael Dawson (1994) calls the "black utility heuristic" or the "linked fate heuristic" (see also Gurin, Hatchett, and Jackson 1989; Tate 1994). Each African American's *individual* utility function over a particular political choice is defined by a *group* calculus—racially defined group interests, benefits, and costs—because race has been "the decisive factor in determining the op-

[2] Weiss (1983) is one of the few who claim that economic and class interests played a more prominent role in black political choices over this period.

portunities and life chances available to virtually all African Americans" (Dawson 1994, 10). The effect of believing that one's individual fate is defined by the collective fate of all others in one's group, racially defined, is an efficient and effective heuristic for navigating the hurly-burly of politics. African Americans need only to decide if party platforms, presidential administrations, and governmental policies differ in their consequences for African Americans and choose accordingly. The upshot for African Americans since the mid-twentieth century has been that the "belief in the importance of black interests translates into preference for the Democratic Party" (Dawson 1994, 113). For most African Americans, one's primary social group identity (as black) determines one's primary political identity (as Democrat).

Recent Developments in Black Partisanship

This overwhelmingly Democratic alignment of African American partisanship has come at a cost, however. In Paul Frymer's (1999) turn of the phrase, African American political interests have become subject to "electoral capture"—by which a group's political interests ally so closely with one party that the party can essentially take the vote "for granted" and the opposing party has no strategic incentives to appeal to that group's interests. Kevin Phillips is often credited with making the case for the Republican Party's "Southern strategy"—to forge an electorally competitive coalition of traditional northern Republicans and racially conservative southern whites who would "desert their party in droves" if the Democratic Party could be portrayed as a "black party" (Frymer 1999, 101). For its part, the countermove of "Third Way" Democrats—often credited with playing a prominent role in Bill Clinton's 1992 presidential campaign—has been to leave race off the center stage, if not engage in a two-pronged machination that Michael Dawson terms "demonization and silence" (1993).[3]

Regardless of whether they are responding to this electoral catch-22, trends in African American party identification over the last four decades indicate that African Americans are, with increasing frequency, choosing not to identify as Democrats. Figure 4.2 shows the distribution of party identification for African Americans to the root American National Election Studies question from 1968 to 2004. Since the late 1960s, there has been a gradual but significant shift away from the Democratic Party. Al-

---

[3] Frymer, of course, is not the first person to note this electorally compromised position in which African Americans appear to find themselves and the explicit strategy of both parties that has put African Americans in such a position (see also Edsall and Edsall 1992; Huckfeldt and Kohfeld 1989; R. W. Walters 1988).

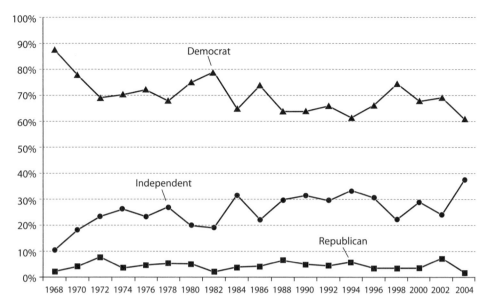

Figure 4.2. African American party identification, 1952–2002

though, a large majority of African Americans still choose to identify with the Democratic Party, the proportion of African Americans allied with the party has declined by roughly 20 percentage points during this period.[4] Among those who opt out of the Democratic Party, by far the vast majority leaves to become Independents.[5] According to the ANES, some 38 percent of all blacks in 2004 identified as Independents.[6]

Moreover, as figure 4.3 shows, there is a distinct pattern to those who identify as Independents. In the figure, Independents are disaggregated by the follow-up question in the ANES, where some Independents indicate a preference for the Democratic Party, others indicate a preference for the Republican Party, and still others indicate no preference at all. As the figure shows, the proportion of Republican leaners and pure Independents changed very little over time, whereas the proportion of Democratic leaners almost tripled from a low of about 8 percent in 1968 to roughly 20 percent by 2004.[7] In short, the proportion of African Ameri-

[4] This trend is mirrored in a range of surveys (see Luks and Elms 2003).

[5] Since so few African Americans are categorized as uncommitted nonpartisans, in this chapter we focus specifically on those respondents who label themselves Independent.

[6] These results are consistent with the three other surveys we examine. Republicans in the NES and other surveys represent about 5 percent of the black population.

[7] The trends are smoothed using the Kalman filter algorithm (see Green et al. 1999 and Donald Green's "Samplemeiser" software at http://vote.research.yale.edu/samplemiser.html).

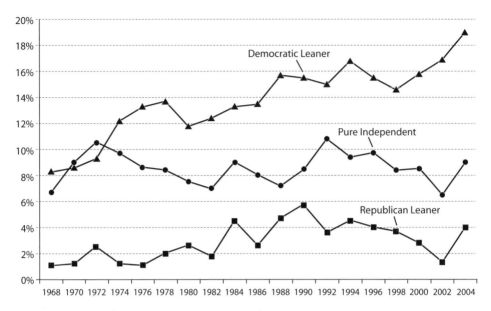

Figure 4.3. African American nonpartisanship, 1952–2002

can pure Independents and Republican leaners has remained relatively stable over time, and the most significant source of the rise of Independents is those African Americans who "exit" from their identification with the Democratic Party but retain their partisan habits as Democratic leaners. Black Americans may still vote overwhelmingly for the Democratic candidate in these elections, but it is clear from figure 4.3 that a substantial proportion of African Americans do not identify with the party.[8] How much Barack Obama's presidency has altered these patterns is something we return to at the end of the chapter.

UNDERSTANDING EXIT FROM THE DEMOCRATIC PARTY:
    EXISTING ACCOUNTS

These trends and puzzles set the backdrop of our foray into explaining African American party identification. The remainder of the chapter is pitched at two levels. First, what explains this recent shift in black partisanship? Second, what general account of party identification explains

---

The actual point estimate for 2004 is above 21 percent, but due to the smoothing, it appears below 20 percent in figure 4.3.

    [8] Later we detail what all of this means for the voting behavior of African Americans.

the political Independence of African Americans? We offer a more specu-lative, exploratory discussion of the first question as a means of generat-ing several more discriminating, testable hypotheses on the second ques-tion. We start with two commonly discussed trends in African American socioeconomic and political life—the rise of a black middle class and the upsurge of black conservatism—and consider how they might explain the rise in the proportion of black Independents. In the ensuing section, we present our own framework of African American political choice—an account that explicitly links the steps from a demographic identity as an African American to a political party identity—and consider the explana-tions for the findings of a decline in Democratic partisanship in this framework. This consideration leads us to three other factors that are likely to move African Americans away from identifying with the Demo-cratic Party—a decline in racial solidarity, an increase in support for ra-cial separatism, and a shift in the pairwise evaluation of political parties. We then put this range of explanations to an empirical test.

A Growing Economic Diversity

One of the most controversial and commonly examined changes in the status of African Americans since the civil rights era has been the alleged class bifurcation of the black community (Wilson 1978, Landry 1987). Over the last half century, a wide economic gulf has emerged within the African American community. On one end, the proportion of blacks in the middle class has grown dramatically. In terms of educational out-comes, occupational status, income, and wealth, there has been marked growth in the number of African Americans who have attained middle-class status (Blank 2001 and Bobo 2001). In fact, the percentage of Afri-can Americans calling themselves middle-class grew from only 12 percent in 1949 to 41 percent in the mid-1990s (Farley 1996).

At the other end of the spectrum, poor blacks have experienced eco-nomic stagnation and declining incomes. Almost a third of the African American population is still poor (Blank 2001). The number of blacks who are not only poor but also living in extremely poor inner-city neigh-borhoods has doubled (Jargowsky 1997).[9] As a consequence, blacks are in many ways more divided than are whites. The disparity between the top and bottom fifth of the black population in terms of income, educa-tion, victimization by violence, and job status is now greater than the disparity between the top and bottom fifth of the white population (Hochschild and Rodgers 1999).

---

[9] This trend halted in the late 1990s but appears to have resumed in the last few years (Jargowsky 2003, Wilson 2002, Pearlstein 2002).

This economic disparity and diversity, according to several scholars, is a potential source of political division as the interests of the black middle class diverge from the interests of less-advantaged members of the community (Wilson 1978, 1987; Sowell 1981; Thernstrom and Thernstrom 1997; Hutchinson 1999). Dawson concludes that "virtually all social science theories of race and class ... predict that black political diversity will follow black economic diversity" (1994, 45). The logic of why political diversity might follow from economic diversity is fairly straightforward. As one moves up the economic ladder, one's material interests change, and one becomes more interested in maintaining the status quo and less interested in the redistribution of resources. [10] Especially in the case of African Americans, the new ideological trappings of middle-class status should clash with the traditionally liberal core of the black political agenda, and political unity should decline (Hamilton 1982). Extended debates have been waged over whether this class effect really applies to blacks, but to the extent that it does, the following hypothesis should be true:

Hypothesis 1: The higher a person's socioeconomic status, the greater the likelihood of not identifying with the Democratic Party.

A Growing Conservatism

A variant on this argument about the material basis of changes in black political solidarity is that partisan choice is mediated by one's liberal-conservative ideology. As we noted in chapter 1, one of the two principal accounts of party identification is that it is rooted in a person's liberal-to-conservative ideological orientation (Green et al. 2002, D. Green 1988, Campbell et al. 1960, Franklin 1992, Franklin and Jackson 1983). If one's political ideology does anchor one's allegiance to political parties, then defection from the Democratic Party is likely to result from one change: increasing conservatism among blacks.[11]

This claim about the declining liberal politics of African Americans is

[10] For accounts of the decline of class politics, see Clark (1996). Evans (1999) and Manza and Brooks (1999) argue that class remains central. Dawson (1994) argues that class alone is insufficient. Many of these scholars make a sharp distinction between economic conservatism vis-à-vis rising class status and social conservatism vis-à-vis lower-class status (Lipset 1960).

[11] Obviously, this ideologically based account could be closely linked to a class-based model, since the most commonly hypothesized reason for the growing conservatism of African Americans is the economic gains made by middle-class blacks—with the presumption that concomitant with rising socioeconomic status come more conservative principles of limited government and economic individualism (Wilson 1987, Sowell 1981, Hamilton 1982). These two theories could be linked to a racial account as well. The declining significance of race could lead to class bifurcation and then middle-class conservatism among blacks.

admittedly controversial. Many scholars argue that African Americans remain resolutely liberal (Gilliam 1986, Hamilton 1982, Welch and Foster 1987). Some further suggest that, if anything, many blacks are too liberal for the Democratic Party and would prefer to have an option to the left of the mainstream Democratic Party (Pinderhughes 1986, Walters 1988, Reed 1995, Dawson 2001), although in these cases ideology is conceived of in more multidimensional and racially embedded ways than the unidimensional ANES self-placement scale. In any case, the increasing prominence of conservative black elites such as Clarence Thomas and Condoleezza Rice, the symbolic efforts of the Republican Party to woo black voters, and increased frustration with affirmative action and other elements of a traditional civil rights agenda all lead to our second hypothesis:

Hypothesis 2: The more conservative a person's ideological views, the greater the likelihood of not identifying with the Democratic Party.

DECLINING SIGNIFICANCE OF RACE?

A central claim of our book is that conventional accounts of party identification—that it is principally rooted in an individual's socioeconomic interests or ideological predispositions—are insufficient, especially as an explanation of the party choices of nonwhites. Given the strong communitarian, group basis of African American political thought, the effect of a person's newfound status among the middle class is unlikely to be filtered through the meritocratic lens of economic individualism alone. Nor, for that matter, are ideological shifts likely to be linearly related to partisanship shifts. Rather, as we noted earlier, much of black politics is more fully explained by theorizing the role of racial group identity as a mediating and independent factor. If black politics does, in fact, derive from group identity and a general characteristic of black politics is a decades-long shift away from identification with the Democratic Party, a plausible third conclusion to draw is that this change must be occurring as a result of a "declining significance of race."

This controversial thesis (see, e.g., Wilson 1978), related to speculations about the upward economic mobility and the rightward ideological shift of African Americans, is worth examining at some length. Declines in overt acts of discrimination, the codification of much of the civil rights agenda into law, and a softening of whites' views toward blacks all suggest that race may be less of a unifying force for African Americans (Schuman et al. 1997; Thernstrom and Thernstrom 1997). Similarly, declines in residential segregation, an increase in interracial contact in the workforce, and an increase in social interaction and intermarriage rates could also mean that racial barriers are falling and that the interests of individual blacks are less linked to race (Thernstrom and Thernstrom 1997; Sigelman et al. 1996).

The thesis of declining significance, much like the arguments about the rise of a black middle class and the growth of black conservatism, is, however, hotly contested. There is a wealth of compelling research arguing for the persistence of racism and unequal life chances. African Americans still lag far behind whites on most measures of socioeconomic well-being (Blank 2001). Most important, there are clear signs that prejudice persists (Kinder and Sanders 1996; Bobo 2001; Bonilla-Silva 2003), that racial discrimination in labor and housing markets is not amenable to legislative remedies (Kirschenman and Neckerman 1991; Massey and Denton 1993; Pager 2003; Bertrand and Mullainathan 2004), and that race remains an obdurate organizing principle in American social, economic, and political life (Brown et al. 2003).

From Identity to Politics

Ignoring for the moment the merits of the claim that race is declining in significance, it is instructive to consider how it is that structural changes in the life opportunities of African Americans (if such changes indeed have taken place) might affect the political calculus of African Americans vis-à-vis party identification. A typical view, as we described in chapter 3, is simply to equate the demographic classification "African American" with the political identification "Democrat." This view is both totalizing—and ignoring the substantial portion of African Americans who currently do not identify as Democrats—and inadequate as an explanatory account of historical trends in African American partisanship. Conceptually, there are at least five distinct logical steps linking a demographic classification to a collective political choice, such as which party to identify with.

The rationale for trying to treat the nexus between "identity" and "politics" in an almost surgically precise manner is that there has been an outbreak of intellectual production that claims a central role of "identity" as a key explanatory variable that explains a remarkable range of political phenomena. This upsurge of research has not been altogether well received. One review of this literature declares that studies of identity face "a crisis of overproduction and consequent devaluation of meaning" (Brubaker and Cooper 2000, 3). Another review finds that "there is not much consensus on how to define "identity"; nor is there consistency in the procedures used for determining the content and scope of identity, agreement on where to look for evidence that identity indeed affects knowledge, interpretations, beliefs, preferences, and strategies, and agreement on how identity affects these components of action" (Abdelal et al.

2001, 1). A clear implication of these reviews is that discussions of identity as an explanation for politics are undisciplined and undiscriminating. Our effort to impose greater discipline and discrimination on the identity-to-politics link focuses on the following steps: categorization, identification, consciousness, politicization, and coordination (see also Lee 2008).

First is the act of categorization. As numerous scholars have observed, the categories that have been used to define a given group have been quite variable across the history of ethnoracial classification in the decennial census (see, e.g., M. Anderson 1988; Anderson and Feinberg 1999; Nobles 2000; Rodriguez 2000; Snipp 2003). Across past census enumerations, individuals of African descent have been counted in fractions (as "three-fifths" of a person) and by gradations of bloodline ("mulatto," "quadroon," and "octaroon"); individuals of South Asian descent have been, at different times, classified as Caucasian, Native American, "Hindoo," and Asian; Mexicans in the United States have been, at different times, classified as white, Mexican, "Spanish-surname," other race, and Hispanic. There are countless other examples. While the insight that we often take our racial and ethnic categories as given may be trivially true in the context of contemporary African American party identification, it is a potentially more consequential consideration in the broader historical sweep of racial and ethnic politics.

A second important step is that of identification. That is, does a given menu of ethnoracial categories in fact correspond with how individuals see themselves? This, too, may seem like a trifling point, but numerous studies have shown that the set of individuals who might conceivably identify with a given category does not correspond perfectly or sometimes even reliably with the subset of individuals who actually identify with that category (Waters 1990; Lieberson and Waters 1993; Goldstein and Morning 2000; Lee 2005). The potential divergence between categorization and identification is especially meaningful with the inclusion of a multiracial identifier in the 2000 census (Perlmann and Waters 2003; Lee 2005). For the purposes of our current study, which analyzes data in which racial boundaries are self-defined in social surveys, we simply take the prior steps of identification and categorization as given. But it is important to note that they are not always automatic.

A third important step is consciousness. Self-identification with a group and sharing a sense of solidarity and common interests with that group are potentially distinct steps. As Dennis Chong and Reuel Rogers argue, "There is no theoretical reason to expect that group identification by itself—without the mobilizing ideology of group consciousness—would increase an individual's propensity to participate in politics" (2003, 12). In explaining racial differences in political participation, for instance, a simple comparison of voting behavior showed whites on average to be

more active than African Americans. Since white Americans had disproportionately greater socioeconomic resources than their black counterparts, this result raised few eyebrows. Once the levels of group consciousness among African Americans was controlled for, however, blacks
actually appeared to be *more* active than their white counterparts, suggesting that a strong sense of racial solidarity could effectively counter-
balance a person's socioeconomic status (Olsen 1970; Verba and Nie
1972; Shingles 1981).[12]

The notion of a linked-fate heuristic is an especially powerful elaboration of how persons who share a group identity also share a collective
worldview. This theoretical articulation of racial group consciousness as
a cognitive heuristic is especially likely to be a significant determinant in
African Americans' political choices, such as which party to identify with.
That is, if African Americans increasingly view their individual well-being
as decoupled from the welfare of the entire black community, we should
expect to see divergent interests and a general attenuation of the collective rationale for unity in the political arena. Irrespective of whether race
has in fact diminished as a defining factor in the life chances of African
Americans, the *perception* that the collective fates of persons of African
descent are no longer hinged as tightly would probably attenuate the collective, coordinated attachment of party loyalties to the Democratic
Party. Thus, a third hypothesis about partisanship is as follows:

*Hypothesis 3: The weaker a person's sense of racially linked fate, the
greater the likelihood of not identifying with the Democratic Party.*

A sense of group consciousness or even the more precisely defined notion of a linked-fate heuristic, however, does not automatically translate
into political identification as a Democrat, especially not in the overwhelming proportions that African Americans sometimes demonstrate.
Specifically, we contend that the link between group interests and party
identification is contingent on two additional logical steps. The fourth
important step in the chain of reasoning from demographic categorization to Democratic identification is politicization. By "politicization" we
mean the recognition of the legitimacy of mainstream electoral politics as
a venue for the pursuit of group-based interests. That is, an often un-
stated and unexamined step in linking group status to collective mobilization is an assumption of the legitimacy of a political regime, the viabil-

---

[12] More recent studies—e.g., Verba, Schlozman, and Brady (1993); Leighley and Vedlitz
(1999)—suggest that group consciousness may not be as forceful a counterweight to socioeconomic status. As Chong and Rogers (2003) point out, however, this is attributable in
part to differences in how consciousness is operationalized across studies as well as shifts in
the venue for group mobilization—from the electoral arena of voting behavior in the civil
rights era to the other modes of political participation.

ity of pluralist politics, and the efficacy of political participation. This liberal democratic conception of citizenship may seem so obvious to a political scientist as to be unworthy of elaboration, but consider the long-standing debate between W.E.B. DuBois and Booker T. Washington about how best to advance the cause of African Americans in the late nineteenth and early twentieth centuries, or the prominence of separatist groups such as Marcus Garvey's United Negro Improvement Association or the Nation of Islam.

This is a critical step because, as we will see, there is a strong sense of mistrust of mainstream white institutions within the African American community and strong sentiment in favor of autonomous black organizations. If a large segment of the black community is suspicious of alliances with those outside the black community, there is every reason to believe that support for black autonomy could promote Independence and severely undercut the link between black group interests and the majority-white Democratic Party. This leads to the following hypothesis:

Hypothesis 4: The stronger a person's support for black separatism, the greater the likelihood of not identifying with the Democratic Party.

The final step is coordination. That is, after African Americans identify with a given racial category, share a worldview through that identification, and believe in the legitimacy of electoral politics as a site for pursuing commonly defined interests, they must still choose sides, and do so *collectively*. With this last step, we mean to distinguish between acting as individuals in the best interests of one's in-group and acting collectively in the best interests of one's in-group. The key to this coordination is comparing the relative work of each party toward achieving the political interests of African Americans. Although it may be readily apparent to many that the Democratic Party, as the "minority" party, works harder for African American interests, it may be less obvious to others. Indeed, given the publicized (if symbolic) efforts by the Republican Party to target minority voters, and the growing chorus of critics who view the Democratic Party as reluctant to actively cater to its African American base, there may be some real ambivalence about which partisan option best serves the black community. Our final pair of hypotheses thus concerns the evaluation of party differences.

Hypothesis 4.1: The less a person views the Democrats as working for the interests of black Americans, the greater the likelihood of not identifying with the Democratic Party.

Hypothesis 4.2: The more a person views the Republicans as working for the interests of black Americans, the greater the likelihood of not identifying with the Democratic Party.

To sum up this rather lengthy discussion, we focus on three key factors that we think—beyond socioeconomic status and ideological self-placement—are likely to influence the non-Democratic identification of African Americans: the attenuation of group consciousness, the intensification of black separatism, and the evaluations of how the Democratic and Republican parties are serving the interests of African Americans.[13]

TRENDS OVER TIME: CLASS, CONSERVATISM, SOLIDARITY, SEPARATISM, AND PARTY EVALUATIONS

Can any of these accounts plausibly explain the movement of large numbers of African Americans from the Democratic Party to Independence? In the current section, we review the secondary evidence on the roles that class, conservatism, linked fate, black solidarity, and party evaluations play in defining the politics of the black community. In each case, we assess whether or not substantial segments of the black community fit each account and, where possible, whether the number of blacks who fit has increased markedly in recent decades. Where survey data are used, we rely principally on three in-depth national surveys of African American political attitudes and behaviors: the 1984 National Black Election Study, the 1993–94 National Black Politics Study, and the 1996 National Black Election Study.[14] These data are also used in our multivariate statistical analyses in the ensuing sections. Details of each survey and the questionnaire items examined are contained in the online appendix (http://press .princeton.edu/titles/9468.html).

Class Divisions

Might class divisions provide a plausible explanation for the growing black partisan diversity? Historically, class divisions in the black community have been evident and have often played at least somewhat of a

[13] In focusing on a linear chain linking ethnoracial classification to racially based collective action, our primary aim is to be deliberate about logical steps that are often assumed. In reality, of course, these steps are highly unlikely to constitute a universal, uniform, necessary-and-sufficient developmental sequence. As numerous studies of social movements show, the causal web of relationships is likely to be inextricably endogenous: it is quite often the act of doing politics, collectively, that motivates the fact of perceiving a group identity, individually (Melucci 1987; Snow and Benford 1992; McAdam et al. 2002).

[14] Since the ANES does not include an adequate set of questions on racial identity, has no questions relating to black autonomy, and each year includes an inadequate number of African American respondents to allow for a more in-depth analysis, we are unable to repeat most of the analysis on the ANES.

role in black politics. As Welch and Foster note, "Every study that has looked closely at the black community has found a gulf between the black middle classes and the mass of impoverished black citizens" (1987, 447). This divide was evident in the antebellum period when slaves and free blacks pursued different agendas. It was evident in the early twentieth century in southern cities such as Birmingham, where poor blacks shunned mainstream black organizations in favor of more radical organizations like the Communist Party (Kelley 1994). It was evident in northern cities later in the twentieth century, when middle-class blacks were often accused of serving their own interests rather than those of residents of poor, urban ghettos (Drake and Cayton 1945; Frazier 1957).

But scholars hold divergent views over the extent to which class divisions translate into distinct political views among African Americans today. Some suggest that class does matter in important ways for the black community (Tate 1994, Dawson 2001). Dawson (2001) finds fairly sharp class divisions across core black ideologies, and Cohen and Dawson (1994) find distinct political views among blacks living in neighborhoods of concentrated poverty.[15] Some claim that even larger differences are evident: "There are no longer two Americas in conflict, one black and one white. There's also the conflict between a prospering and expanding black middle class and an increasingly desperate and destitute black poor. . . . [The] political rift between them is as deep and wide as the Grand Canyon" (Hutchinson 1999).

Others disagree. A range of other studies has found few real class divisions in black public opinion (Gilliam 1986; Gurin et al. 1989; Welch and Foster 1987; Parent and Steckler 1985; Hwang et al. 1998). Many studies of the black vote have also uncovered little divergence between the preferences of middle- and lower-class blacks (e.g., Gurin et al. 1989). As Susan Welch and Michael Combs conclude, "The much debated political schism along class lines in the black community has not materialized in any general way" (1985, 96). If anything, this latter group of scholars is likely to argue that higher-status blacks are more, rather than less, racially conscious (Hajnal 2007). The claim is that for many middle-class blacks, economic gains mean living in a primarily white world where racial discrimination and racial differences are more pronounced and more incessant (Hochschild 1995, Feagin 1991, Cose 1995). Thus, while economic divisions are clearly growing, it is not at all clear how much impact this growing class divide is having on black partisanship.

---

[15] See also Wilson (1987) and Anderson (1991) on the divide in today's inner-city black neighborhoods between "street" and "decent" subcultures.

Conservatism

A variant of the upward class mobility thesis, as we noted, is the possibility that growing conservatism within the black population is the engine behind the growing partisan diversity among African Americans. African Americans have traditionally been viewed as one of the most politically cohesive and liberal groups in the nation (Gilliam 1986; Welch and Foster 1987; Dawson 1994; Kinder and Sanders 1996; Schuman et al. 1997; Tate 2003). Certainly, when compared with whites, African Americans appear to be firmly entrenched to the left of the mass of white Americans (Dawson 1994; Kinder and Sanders 1996; Schuman et al. 1997; Hochschild and Rogers 1999; Kinder and Winter 2001). In the ANES, for instance, African Americans as a group stake out positions that are substantially more liberal than those of whites on government assistance to blacks, urban unrest, spending on social services, providing guaranteed jobs, health services, and overall government spending. On each of these questions, the proportion of blacks who express liberal policy views was over twenty points higher than the proportion of whites who expressed similar views (Kinder and Winter 2001). Thus, it would still be fair to characterize blacks as a largely liberal community.

But this liberal orientation is in many ways limited. First, outside of implicit and explicit racial issues and questions related to redistribution, there is much less unity. On moral issues, in particular, black respondents hold views that are as conservative or even more conservative than those of whites (Hamilton 1982, Bositis 2000, Tate 1994). This appears to be true in the ANES for abortion rights and women's equality. Other data find that a majority of blacks favor school prayer (Bositis 2000), oppose certain aspects of gay rights (C. J. Cohen 1999), favor restrictions on immigration (Hajnal and Baldassare 2001), and support tougher sentencing laws (Bositis 2000). Moreover, even on core social welfare questions, cracks in black liberalism can be found (Hajnal and Baldassare 2001). For example, in our surveys, one-third of blacks feel that "black people depend too much on government programs."[16]

Furthermore, there are signs that black liberalism is waning. In the 1972 ANES, 31 percent of African Americans self-identified as "liberal," 18 percent as "moderate," 8 percent as "conservative," and 43 percent reported not having "thought much about it." By the 1982 ANES, only about 16 percent of African American respondents identified as "liberal"

---

[16] Some even claim that outside a core set of racial policy questions, blacks are not at all ideologically distinct from whites (Canon 1999). Hajnal (2007), however, has shown that across the range of issues addressed in direct democracy, blacks are significantly more likely to end up on the liberal side of the vote than whites are.

and 18 percent again as "moderate"; there was a doubling of conservatives at 16 percent; and 50 percent chose none of these ideological self-placement options. This shift has remained relatively steady since, with the primary change being an increase in the number of self-identified moderates: in the 2004 ANES, 13 percent of African Americans declared themselves "liberal," 30 percent "moderate," 15 percent "conservative," and 42 percent reported not having "thought much about it." This shift is also evident when we examine views about the larger role of government. On the question of whether the "government in Washington should see to it that every person has a job and a good standard of living," 65 percent of African Americans agreed that government should have such a role, whereas only 6 percent believed that African Americans should be self-reliant. In the 2000 ANES, by contrast, only 30 percent supported an activist government role, and 32 percent agreed that "government should let each person get ahead on his own." The percentage of African Americans who staked a middle ground between these two positions increased from 12 percent in 1972 to 21 percent by 2000. To put it provocatively, African Americans today are almost as disproportionately moderate, ideologically, as they are disproportionately Democratic, institutionally.

Some have questioned what these labels mean for blacks and whether these changes represent a real shift in policy views (Hamilton 1982, Tate 1994, Dawson 2001).[17] However, an analysis of individual policy positions reveals a similar shift to the right. Both the ANES and the three political surveys of African Americans we examine in this chapter indicate that blacks are also becoming more conservative on a range of specific policy issues including overall government spending, aid to blacks, ensuring full employment, and health services.[18] The proportion of blacks, for example, who think "the government should provide fewer services, even in areas such as health and education, in order to reduce spending" has tripled from only 7 percent in 1972 to 21 percent in 1998. Similarly, the number who oppose special government assistance to the black community has grown dramatically from 12 percent in the 1970s to 29 percent in the 1990s. There is little denying that blacks are still more cohesive and more liberal than other groups on most issues, but there is also little denying that elements of a conservative agenda have crept into sub-

---

[17] Dawson (2001), for example, argues that even today only 1 percent of blacks can be considered true believers in black conservatism. However, this figure ignores the fact that large segments of the black community support at least some elements of a conservative agenda.

[18] On only one issue in the NES, women's rights, were blacks markedly more liberal over time.

stantial segments of the black community.[19] In this regard, African Americans are perhaps no different from the rest of the nation, which has taken a similarly rightward turn in recent decades. Thus, there is reason to believe that growing black conservatism could be a central force in driving blacks away from the Democratic Party.

Racial Solidarity

What of our own account of exit from the Democratic Party? Can group interests actually push blacks away from the Democratic Party? Is black autonomy sufficiently popular to sway significant elements within the black community toward Independence? And are many blacks ambivalent enough about how well the Democratic Party serves black interests to choose another option? We suggest that racial solidarity and group-defined interests remain powerful in the African American community today, but that there are growing signs of racial separatism and diminishing marginal perceived differences between the parties, which may play a role in the increase in the number of black Independents in America today.

First, there is little doubt that racial identity plays a central role in black politics today. Not only do blacks believe that racial inequality is a near permanent feature of American society, they also tend to see whites and racial discrimination as key factors behind the plight of blacks. The numbers across the three surveys are in many cases almost overwhelming. Almost all blacks (95 percent) recognized that the black community has not achieved racial equality. There is also near consensus about the root of the problem. Almost 80 percent agreed that "American society is unfair to black people," and another 86 percent believed that "discrimination against blacks is still a problem." About a third even questioned whether there had been any racial progress at all in the last twenty years. Furthermore, there was not much optimism about the future. Some 38 percent of blacks believed that "blacks will never achieve equality." Underlying this pessimism were strong suspicions about the interests and intentions of the white community. Only 23 percent of blacks felt that most whites want to "see blacks get a better break," and 35 percent thought that "most white people want to keep blacks down."

There is also little doubt that blacks tend to express group consciousness and feel closely tied to the well-being of the larger black community. Almost all blacks (94 percent) indicated they felt very close or somewhat

---

[19] An snalysis of the General Social Survey data reveals an almost identical trend in black public opinion over time.

TABLE 4.1
Distribution of Linked Fate among African Americans

	1984 NBES	1993 NBPS	1996 NBES	Total
A lot	31.3%	36.3%	36.1%	34.6%
Some	31.0	31.6	36.5	33.0
Not very much	11.1	9.9	10.0	10.3
Not at all	26.7	22.3	17.4	22.1

Data: 1984 National Black Election Studies, 1993 National Black Politics Study, 1996 National Black Election Studies.

close "in ideas and feelings about things to Blacks."[20] As table 4.1 shows, across the three surveys that we focus on in this chapter, two-thirds of blacks (68 percent) agreed that "what happens to black people in this country has [something] to do with what happens to me." Two more recent points of reference, the 2004 "Racial Attitudes Study" (Dawson and Popoff 2004) and 2005 "Katrina, Race, and Poverty" survey (Dawson 2006), found that roughly 74 and 70 percent of its respondents, respectively, perceived a linked fate "somewhat" or "a lot." This sense of racial identity is also consequential for black politics. Racial identity has been linked to liberal-conservative ideology, views on racial policy, and preferences across a host of nonracial policy dimensions (Tate 1994, Dawson 2001). Identity has also been tied to presidential vote choice and support for a range of core black ideologies from black separatism to economic conservatism (Dawson 1994, 2001; Gurin et al. 1989).

The fact that group consciousness and a sense of linked fate remain high among the black community today suggests that neither factor can account for the recent exit of large numbers of African Americans from the Democratic Party. This conclusion is reaffirmed by an analysis of trends over time. There is no sign of a decline in a perception of linked fate. As table 4.1 shows, the distribution of blacks' linked-fate orientation in the separate political surveys of African Americans is quite consistent across time and surveys: a little above a third of African Americans strongly believe that "what happens generally to black people in this country will have something to do with what happens in my life," with another third believing the statement somewhat, and more than one fifth rejecting any coupling between individual and collective destinies. More recent surveys—although not strictly comparable—suggest that little has

[20] A comparative analysis indicates that black racial identity is stronger and more pronounced than the identities of other groups (Gurin 1995).

changed in the ensuing decade. In the 2004 National Politics Survey, about two-thirds of blacks expressed a sense of linked fate.

Indeed, if the focus is on African Americans who think that blacks' interests are linked "some" or "a lot," there is actually an increase over the two-decade period of our three polls toward a trend of more blacks seeing race as a defining influence in their lives—exactly the opposite of what we would expect given changes in party identification. The proportion of blacks who believe that "what happens generally to black people" has at least "some" effect on their own life chances increases from 62 percent in 1984 to 68 percent in 1993 and 73 percent in 1996. Similarly, the number of African Americans who are hopeful that blacks will eventually achieve racial equality fell from 53 percent in 1984 to 39 percent in 1996. Over time, more blacks also believed that "most whites want to keep blacks down" (40 percent in 1984 and 47 percent in 1996). Thus, while we expect black identity to figure prominently in black partisanship, at first glance it seems unlikely that group interests could provide a clear explanation of blacks' Democratic defection.

Racial Separatism

As we noted earlier, a separatist ideology has been and continues to be an important driving force in black politics. The long history of black nationalism as a popular and powerful ideology spans early evocations such as Martin Delaney's efforts to reestablish a colony of freed slaves in Africa; Booker T. Washington's late-nineteenth-century ideology of black self-help; Marcus Garvey's efforts to build an African nation-state in the 1920s and 1930s; later instantiations such as Malcolm X, Elijah Muhammad, and the rise of the Nation of Islam and Huey Newton, Bobby Seale, and the Black Panther Party's campaign to empower inner-city black communities; and, most recently, echoes of black nationalism in the rap and hip-hop music of KRS-One, Sister Souljah, Ice Cube, and others (Kelley 1994, Rose 1994, Henderson 1996, Dawson 1999). The belief that black politics must be understood from the standpoint of an existing system of racial domination and that racial progress must be achieved in the form of economic, political, and cultural autonomy is, according to Michael Dawson, "the second oldest ideological tendency found within black political thought" (2001, 85).

Black nationalism, in short, is much closer to the political philosophy of Charles Mills (1997) than it is to the political philosophy of John Stuart Mill (Thompson 1976). And it has widespread support among African Americans today. In the three surveys of black politics we examine, a large minority of African Americans supported key elements of a black nationalist ideology. Well over half of all blacks felt that blacks "should shop in black owned stores" and that "black children should study an African language." Almost half of all African Americans agreed that "black people form a nation within a nation," 40 percent called for blacks to "participate in black-only organizations whenever possible," and 38 percent expressed support for a black political party. As Dawson provocatively claims, "Black nationalism, not the various black liberal ideologies, is the most important ideological determinant of black public opinion" (2001, 349).

There are, however, limits to how far some black Americans will go in support of nationalist beliefs. Few African Americans (3 percent) agreed that blacks "should not have anything to do with whites"; only 14 percent agreed or strongly agreed that "blacks should have their own separate nation"; and only 27 percent agreed or strongly agreed that "blacks should *always* vote for black candidates."

More important, as recent work by Robert Brown and Todd Shaw (2002) suggests, black nationalism may not be a single overarching ideology. Specifically, Brown and Shaw demonstrate a multidimensional structure to black nationalism that distinguishes "community nationalism" (local economic, social, and political self-determination in predominantly African American communities) from "separatist nationalism" (race-based sovereignty and a literal or figurative separation from the economy, politics, and culture of white-dominated America).[21] These two dimensions of black nationalism are especially germane to our study because the effects of community nationalism and separatist nationalism on one's party identification are likely to run in opposite directions. Specifically, as Brown and Shaw put it, "Community nationalism rests on a premise that is almost a truism," given a basic level of racial group consciousness. As such, it is more of a "mainstream" ideology within the black community and finds greater support among African Americans who are better off and more liberal—that is, there is no obvious inconsistency between adhering to community nationalism, perceiving a strongly linked fate, and identifying with the Democratic Party. By contrast, it is almost a truism that a separatist nationalism will reject the relevance of mainstream electoral politics and white-dominated political parties as a venue for the advocacy of racial group interests. Concomitant with this logic, Brown and Shaw find greater support for separatist nationalism among African Americans who are younger, poorer, and male. Thus, to be more precise about our expectations from hypothesis 4, separatist nationalists should be more likely to move away from identifying with the Democratic Party,

---

[21] Brown and Shaw also posit the possibility of a third dimension of what might be called cultural nationalism, formed around attitudes toward Africa as a "homeland" and the value of learning African languages and cultures.

but community nationalists may actually be more likely to identify with the Democratic Party.

What about changes in the salience of, and adherence to, black nationalism in the last few decades? Here, it is difficult to say much with the available survey data. Prior to 1980, there was no systematic public opinion data on black nationalist sentiments. Since 1980, the available polls present a mixed picture. In the 1984 National Black Elections Study, for instance, 29 percent of African Americans supported the idea of a black political party. This proportion increased to 50 percent in the 1993 National Black Politics Study, but then nosedived to 34 percent by the time of the 1996 National Black Elections Study. Outside the realm of what public opinion data have to say, there certainly seems to be a rise in the publicity given to nationalist sentiments in the African American community. As scholars such as Errol Henderson (2000) have suggested, African American political movements have cycled between periods of liberal integrationism and black separatism. There is little debate, from this broad historical view, that at least since the civil rights movement evolved into the black power movement, we have witnessed a strong tide of black nationalist sentiments (Carmichael and Hamilton 1967). One could go so far as to claim that black nationalism was the primary public face of African American politics throughout the 1990s, as seen in the lingering, sometimes obsessive, focus of mass media coverage of events and phenomena such as the African American–led boycotts of Korean "mom-and-pop" grocers in New York City and then Los Angeles (Freer 1994, Kim 2000, Joyce 2003), Minister Louis Farrakhan's rise to the national stage with the Million Man March (Taylor and Lincoln 1997; McCormick and Franklin 2000), the legal status of black male academies (Grant-Thomas 2000), the allegedly illiberal and intolerant strains of Afro-centrism as articulated by Leonard Jeffries and Molefi Asante, and the commodification and cultural rebirth of Malcolm X (Dyson 1995). While this discussion is admittedly nonscientific, it strengthens our suspicion that the central place of black separatist ideologies in the African American community might condition the willingness of African Americans to exit from party identification.

Coordination

The final dimension of black party identification that we consider is the pairwise choice between the Republican and Democratic parties. As we noted earlier, the final step in the logic of a group basis to party identification is that once African Americans have decided to act on the basis of their group identification and decided to so act in the venue of main-

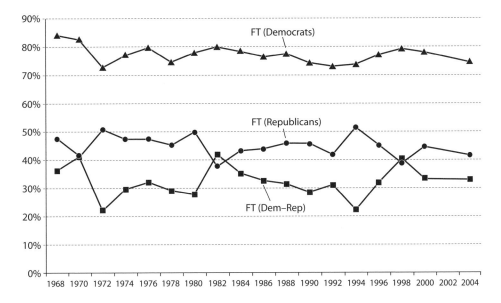

Figure 4.4. Party affect for African Americans, 1964–1998

stream, electoral politics, they must still coordinate and choose sides. This act of evaluating both the Democratic and the Republican parties is, we posit, a vital intermediary between a linked-fate orientation and the partisan identification of most African Americans with the Democratic Party. In the American National Election Studies, two common metrics are used to measure how individuals gauge the two parties—an affective measure based on how "warm" or "cold" respondents feel toward the Democratic and Republican parties (the "feeling thermometer") and a more cognitive measure of how many positive or negative characteristics of each party a respondent can volunteer (up to five mentions). Based on these two measures, there are no obvious trends over time to guide our understanding of the growing tendency of African Americans to identify as Independents.

Figure 4.4 shows the over-time trends in party affect among African Americans, using the feeling thermometer items in the ANES.[22] As the figure quite plainly demonstrates, there is very little variation in the affect of either party. Regarding the affect toward the Democratic Party, there is, however, a discernible downward trend, from an average warmth toward the Democrats in the 80s (during the late 1960s) to an average

[22] Figure 4.4 shows a moving average (three years) of feeling-thermometer (FT) ratings in each biennial ANES survey.

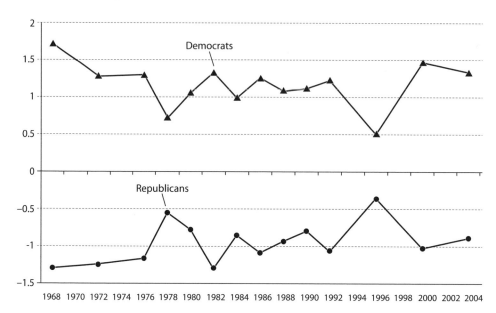

Figure 4.5. Party cognition for African Americans, net likes/dislikes, 1952–2004

warmth in the 70s. Most of this decline, however, occurs in the early 1970s (and thus does not correspond very tightly with the period of growing identification as Independents). On the Republican side of the partisan aisle, and in the overall difference in party affect between the Republican and Democratic parties, there is only the slightest hint of a downward "cooling" of party affect over time.

When we turn to party cognition, as measured by the number of likes and dislikes for each party, there is somewhat more evidence of changes over time that are consistent with the trends in party identification among African Americans. Recall that in figure 4.2, the level of party identification with the Democratic Party is at its highest in 1968, then gradually falls, with a particularly low trough in 1992. This is roughly (with far greater changes from one biennial ANES to another) the trend we find in figure 4.5, which charts the net of likes and dislikes mentioned for both the Democratic and the Republican parties from 1968 to 2004. The weighted average of likes and dislikes for the Democratic Party peaks in 1968, and this net statistic drops (with some fluctuation) until it hits its nadir in 1996. This trend is paralleled in the opposite fashion for the weighted average of likes and dislikes for the Republican Party. Thus, by at least one measure of the rational, pairwise evaluation of the Democratic and Republican parties, we might expect to see the general patterns in party identification we see in figure 4.2.

There is, however, a real problem with both of these measures of partisan affect. Neither the feeling thermometer nor the mention of likes and dislikes is conditioned on a racial group calculus; thus it provides a limited test of our theoretical expectations. We now turn to a measure of party evaluation that is directly related to black group interests. Using this latter measure—available only in the black politics surveys we use in this chapter—we find some real ambiguity about which party serves blacks' group interests. When asked how hard they think the Republican and Democratic parties "really work on issues black people care about," most blacks expressed a slight preference for the Democratic Party, but the gap was not nearly as wide as one might expect. Almost 30 percent of blacks felt that the Democratic Party did not work hard for black interests. Another 20 percent believed that the Republican Party does work hard for blacks' interests. When responses to the two questions were combined, fully 31 percent of the black community believed that the Republican Party works as hard as or harder than the Democratic Party for blacks' interests. In particular, only a small proportion of African Americans saw the Democratic Party as a clear-cut partisan choice for the African American community. Only 7 percent felt that the Democratic Party worked "a lot harder" than the Republican Party on issues that are important to blacks.[23] Finally, a substantial number felt that neither party was working especially hard on issues that blacks care about. Over a quarter felt that both parties work "not too hard" on black issues, and 6 percent felt that both parties ignore issues that are important to the black community. In short, there is ample room for a race-based evaluation of the two major parties to account for the exit of more and more blacks from the Democratic Party.

In this section, we have considered an array of evidence—most of it in the form of a review of secondary analyses—on background factors that may help us to understand the growing flight of blacks from the Democratic Party. None of our discussions here gives a conclusive account of changes in African American party identification over time. That sort of discriminating analysis would require careful time-series analyses, an especially high hurdle to overcome given the relative lack of time-series data on African American politics. Specifically, data on three key factors—racial solidarity, racial separatism, and the pairwise evaluation of each party's advocacy for African American political interests—are avail-

[23] There is no clear trend over time across our three surveys in how well each party is viewed as an advocate of black issues.

able at only three points in time: 1984, 1993, and 1996. These data, however, do allow us to assess the relative contribution of each of the five factors we have considered to the microfoundations of blacks' party identification. It is to this task that we now turn.

Explaining Blacks' Partisan Choice

We begin this analysis by looking at a simple model of partisan choice that tests only conventional accounts of black politics and ignores our more complex, multidimensional account of black partisanship. Thus, in the first half of table 4.2, we present the results of an ordered logit regression that uses the standard seven-point linear scale of partisanship as the dependent variable, with Democrats on the left, Independents in the middle, and Republicans on the right. A higher value thus indicates movement away from the Democrats and toward identifying as Independent or Republican. Later in the chapter, we will examine whether this assumption about the linearity of the choice is warranted.

Based on our earlier discussion, we explain African American partisan choice as a function of five sets of factors.[24] First, to determine the extent to which party identification is based on a traditional liberal-conservative ideological dimension, we include responses to a question asking respondents how they self-identify in ideological terms. Since one of our central contentions is that the relationship between ideology and party identification is not linear, we examine the effects of ideology through a series of "dummy" variables that allow us to estimate, separately, the effects of self-identifying as a strong liberal, a weak liberal, a weak conservative, or a strong conservative (compared with the effect of being an ideological

[24] In tables 4.2 and 4.3, we cannot consider two other factors that make up much of the Michigan School account of partisanship: childhood socialization and the effects of being apolitical. Unfortunately, none of the three surveys of black Americans includes data on parental partisanship or other measures of childhood socialization, and the three surveys do not contain consistent measures of political involvement. We can, however, make some remarks about the relevance of both factors to black partisan choices. Based on the earlier results from the NES that we presented in chapter 2, we believe that parental cues are an important influence on black partisanship. There also appears to be a link between political engagement and black partisanship. In alternate tests, using individual surveys, we found a weak relationship between political participation and political interest and black partisanship. Namely, nonvoters, those who do not trust government, and those not interested in national campaigns are more apt to be Independents. It is, however, unclear how to interpret this last set of results. We contend that for many African Americans limited engagement in national politics and nonpartisanship are the result of rational skepticism about what the two parties are doing for their interests or for the broader interests of the black community. In this case it is not being apolitical that leads to nonpartisanship. Rather, having no clear partisan option to choose leads to political disengagement and nonpartisanship.

moderate). Second, to examine the effect of socioeconomic background on partisan choice, we test for the independent effects of four dimensions of class status: family income, educational attainment, home ownership, and employment status.

In addition to class and conservatism, we test for the three factors that we believe are key mediators between a demographic group definition and one's political organizational identification: racial group consciousness, black autonomy, and the racially based evaluation of the Republican and Democratic parties. Racial group consciousness is measured by the standard linked-fate question that asks respondents how much their personal well-being is defined by the well-being of the larger black community. Following Brown and Shaw (2002), we test two separate dimensions of black nationalism.[25] First, we constructed an index of nationalism as support for community control, measured by four items—"blacks should shop in black-owned stores whenever possible," "blacks should have control over the government in mostly black communities," "blacks should have control over the economy in mostly black communities," and "blacks should rely on themselves and not on others." Second, we constructed an index of nationalism as a more explicitly political, separatist movement, measured by four items—"black people should always vote for black candidates when they run," "blacks should form their own political party," "black people should have a separate nation," "black people form a nation within a nation."[26] Finally, to see if perceptions about either party's efforts on behalf of the black community affected partisan choice, respondents were asked, "How hard do you think the Republican/Democratic Party works on issues black people really care about?" Given our strong theoretical belief that party identification (and party evaluation) is not linear, we specify separate variables for African Americans' evaluation of the Democratic and Republican parties (rather than taking a measure of the difference in party evaluations).[27]

[25] The use of Brown and Shaw's scales are admittedly somewhat controversial, given the counterevidence by Davis and Brown (2002) that black nationalism is a unidimensional, not multidimensional, scale. Although we do not contest the findings of Davis and Brown or attempt to adjudicate the differences between the two interpretations of black nationalism, there are valid conceptual grounds for distinguishing the two dimensions of nationalism that Brown and Shaw identify vis-à-vis one's party identification, and as table 3.3 shows, the two dimensions can lead to quite opposite effects on one's partisan attachments.

[26] The alpha reliability coefficient for the community nationalism scale is 0.65, and for the separatist nationalism scale it is 0.54.

[27] In addition to these five factors, we included several control variables—the age and gender of respondents, the race of the interviewer (see, e.g., Davis 1997 for the importance of controlling for the potential social interactive effects of an interviewer's race), and the fixed effects of each survey (measured by dummy variables for the 1993 National Black

Table 4.2 presents three different models of African American party identification: a baseline model (with measures of ideology, class, linked fate, and our control variables), a variant that includes our two black nationalism scales (Model Two), and our full account, which also includes the evaluation of how well the two parties represent the interests of African Americans (Model Three). The results from the first column of table 4.2 do confirm some of the conventional views of partisanship and blacks' partisan choices. First, there is a clear link between liberal-conservative ideology and partisan choice.[28] The effect is discernible on only one end of the ideological continuum, however. That is, extreme liberals are about 16 percent more likely to identify as strong Democrats than they are as moderates, and moderate liberals are somewhat more likely to do so as well.[29] But there are no differences between moderates and conservatives, ideologically, in their partisan attachments. This one-sided relationship is especially meaningful given the over-time trend in African American ideological self-placement as seen in figure 4.4, where there is a conspicuous rise of ideological moderates and a decline of ideological liberals. The fact that there are both fewer ideological liberals and fewer partisan Democrats in the African American population today no longer seems coincidental. As one might have predicted, alternate tests indicate that fiscal and social liberalism—as opposed to moral or religious liberalism—is the main reason for the link between liberal-conservative ideology and party identification among African Americans. Specifically, views on the government's role in creating jobs, assisting blacks, and spending on crime all affected partisanship, whereas views on gay rights and handguns had no significant effect (the analysis is not shown).

Class effects are more complex. Specifically, in Model One we find no support for the upward-mobility thesis, except in its obverse. That is, the

Politics Study [NBPS] and the 1996 National Black Election Study [NBES]). In alternate tests, we also tested for a range of contextual effects including region (South versus non-South), racial context (the percentage who are black in the respondents' neighborhood), and poverty context (the percentage who are poor in the neighborhood). Blacks in the South were marginally more Democratic than blacks elsewhere. Other contextual effects are noted in the text.

[28] There is some concern that the relationship between liberal-conservative ideology and party identification is reciprocal and thus that liberal-conservative ideology is in part the result rather than the cause of party identification. However, existing research that tests for this reciprocity has generally found that party identification has only a very small effect on most individual policy positions and has never found an effect of partisanship on overall liberal-conservative ideology (Franklin 1984; Page and Jones 1979; but see Goren 2005).

[29] For this and all other predicted probabilities detailed in the book, we utilize a simulation procedure developed by King, Tomz, and Wittenberg (2000). In each case, we vary values on the dimension of interest (i.e., moving from strongly liberal to strongly conservative views) while holding constant all other factors at their mean (or modal value for categorical variables).

TABLE 4.2
Determinants of Black Partisan Choice (Ordered Probit)

	Model One		Model Two		Model Three	
Ideology						
Extreme liberal	−.425	(.065)**	−.410	(.069)**	−.354	(.071)**
Moderate liberal	−.144	(.073)*	−.147	(.078)^	−.121	(.079)
Moderate conservative	−.069	(.079)	−.085	(.084)	−.072	(.086)
Extreme conservative	0.006	(.070)	0.028	(.075)	0.022	(.077)
Class						
Income	0.004	(.011)	0.015	(.011)	0.026	(.012)*
Education	−.012	(.016)	−.010	(.017)	−.012	(.017)
Home ownership	−.056	(.050)	−.092	(.053)^	−.104	(.055)^
Unemployed	0.414	(.090)**	0.457	(.096)**	0.462	(.098)**
Black group interests						
Black linked fate	−.059	(.021)**	−.046	(.022)*	−.038	(.023)^
Community control	—		−.079	(.031)**	−.066	(.032)*
Racial separatism	—		0.050	(.051)	0.036	(.052)
Democrats work for blacks	—		—		−.294	(.032)**
Republicans work for blacks	—		—		0.246	(.031)**
Background controls						
Age	−.016	(.002)**	−.016	(.002)**	−.015	(.002)**
Male	0.221	(.048)**	0.208	(.051)**	0.164	(.053)**
Black interviewer	0.002	(.050)	0.026	(.054)	0.061	(.056)
Year 1993	0.115	(.063)^	0.112	(.070)^	0.073	(.072)^
Year 1996	0.059	(.061)	0.064	(.066)	0.057	(.068)
Cut 1	−.783	(.117)	−.821	(.147)	−1.09	(.187)
Cut 2	−.183	(.117)	−.222	(.147)	−.461	(.186)
Cut 3	0.398	(.118)	0.343	(.147)	0.146	(.186)
Cut 4	0.725	(.119)	0.676	(.148)	0.472	(.187)
Cut 5	1.088	(.122)	1.051	(.151)	0.839	(.190)
Cut 6	1.410	(.128)	1.357	(.156)	1.116	(.195)
Pseudo R-squared	0.032		0.034		0.055	
Chi-squared	217.19**		204.44**		314.70**	
LR-test chi-squared	—		738.03**		364.36**	
N	2427		2159		2086	

Significance levels: **$p < .01$ *$p < .05$ ^ $p < .10$. Data are from the 1984–88 National Black Election Study, 1993 National Black Politics Study, and the 1996 National Black Election Study. Party identification is measured as seven categories from a minimum value for strong Democrats to a maximum value for strong Republicans. The statistical model is estimated using Intercooled Stata v8.1.

first column of table 4.2 shows that unemployed African Americans are significantly more likely to identify with the Republican Party than they are with the Democratic Party. This effect, moreover, is rather substantial: unemployed blacks are about 16 percent less likely to identify as strong Democrats than are working African Americans. Once we control for our three racial factors in Model Three, however, family income and home ownership become significant determinants of party choice. Consistent with the expectation of the upward-mobility thesis, we find that African Americans who garner higher wages are more likely to seek alternatives to Democratic Party identification. The effect here, however, is modest: African Americans in the highest income bracket in our surveys are 8 percent less likely to identify as strong Democrats than are their counterparts in the lowest income bracket. The effect of home ownership, like unemployment, again runs counter to the logic of the upward-class-mobility thesis: black home owners are actually about 4 percent *more* likely to identify as Democrats than are African Americans who do not own the homes they live in. The contrarian results on employment and home ownership suggest a potential counternarrative to the usual story that is told about class and politics. It may be the case that with the attainment of economic security, such as owning a home and being gainfully employed, black Americans may be more inclined to reward their party of choice (much like retrospective voters) than to set up new partisan roots.

Table 4.2 also confirms the importance of a group-based political calculus. Consistent with prior work by Dawson (1994) and Tate (1994), a sense of racial linked fate influences party identification.[30] The effect, however, is relatively small: African Americans who believe that their own well-being is strongly linked to that of other African Americans are between 7 percent (Model One) and 4.5 percent (Model Three) more likely to identify as strong Democrats than are African Americans who believe that their fates are unlinked. With black nationalism, only our community nationalism scale appears to be a significant factor. Specifically, African Americans who strongly advocate local control and autonomy in predominantly black communities are between 10 percent (Model Two) and 8 percent (Model Three) more likely to identify as strong Democrats than are blacks who reject all aspects of community nationalism.[31]

---

[30] As one might expect, we found that the dominant factor explaining linked fate is assessments of the racial fairness of American society. The more that blacks believe that discrimination is prevalent and that the American system will never be fair, the stronger their sense of linked fate. African Americans who are more actively involved in social institutions and who presumably interact more regularly with other members of the black community also tend to have a stronger sense of linked fate (the analysis is not shown).

[31] Black separatism is itself a function of at least two kinds of factors. Both concerns about widespread racial discrimination and a strong sense of black linked fate, as expected,

By far the strongest influence on black partisanship, however, is the evaluation of how hard the Democratic and Republican parties work for African Americans. Table 4.2 shows that African Americans who strongly think that the Democratic Party works harder for blacks' interests are 34 percent more likely to identify as strong Democrats than are those who disagree; African Americans who strongly think that the Republican Party works harder for blacks' interests are 28 percent less likely to identify as strong Democrats than are those who disagree.[32]

These results, taken together, give moderate support to our main story line. Class and ideology do influence the partisan choices of African Americans, but not as forcefully, consistently, or coherently as we might think. The evidence for a racially based political calculus is somewhat stronger. The rational and racially conditioned evaluation of both parties—that is, a pairwise comparison of the Democratic and Republican parties conditioned on each party's advocacy of African American *group* interests, not the interests of an individual per se—is easily the most potent influence on one's party identification. However, racial solidarity itself, as measured by the belief in a linked fate, is only modestly predictive. Moreover, black nationalism is an influence on party identification, but only in its community-control dimension. Racial separatism, at least in this linear, ordered probit specification, appears to have no influence on one's party identification.[33] Perhaps the most conspicuous evidence of the mixed success of the results in table 4.2 is that very little of the variation in black party choice is explained; even our full model explains only 5.5 percent of the variation in our dependent variable.

THE STRUCTURE OF BLACKS' PARTY CHOICE

In this section, we show that this limited explanatory power and the sometimes varied success of our theoretical expectations are the result of

---

led to increased support for black separatism. Younger and lower-class blacks were also more apt to express separatist views (the analysis is not shown).

[32] Race is also the dominant factor in trying to explain why some African Americans are skeptical about how well the Democratic Party serves black interests. Those who did not see discrimination as a real problem were less likely to see Democrats as working harder for blacks. By contrast, younger African Americans and those more involved in politics were much more apt to see the Democrats as strong advocates of black interests.

[33] Among our control variables, age and gender are both significantly related to party identification. Younger African Americans and black men are more inclined to move away from the Democratic Party. The age effect in particular suggests that black political unity may be fading over time and that African American political choices may be responsive to changes in the nature of American race relations. For a more detailed explanation of how and why age affects black partisanship, see Luks and Elms (2003).

estimating our parameters on a linear, ordered dependent variable. The multiple pathways to partisanship that we put forward in this book have implications not only for *which* partisan option African Americans ultimately choose to align with but also for *how* African Americans go about choosing between the three options of Democrat, Independent, and Republican. African American choices should not only differ from conventional accounts of white party identification in terms of the dimensions that predict partisanship, but more fundamentally, they should differ in terms of how African Americans structure the choice. The relevance of multiple, orthogonal dimensions means that most blacks do not perceive the parties the way many whites might. For many whites, the choice may be one of simply deciding where to place themselves along a linear continuum ranging from strongly Democratic on the left to Independent in the middle and to strongly Republican on the right. For blacks, the three options are not likely to be neatly ordered along this linear continuum. Indeed, the three choices may not be ordered at all, but different dimensions may come into play at different points in the decision-making process. For many blacks, Independent will not fall in the middle.

To more closely examine the structure of black partisan choices and to better test the role of black autonomy, we drop the assumption that party identification is linear and instead test a multidimensional model of partisanship. The estimator we use to test the nonlinearity of party identification is multinomial logit, which allows us to capture the effect of each independent variable on each pairwise combination among possible party identification categories (see Aldrich and Nelson 1984; S. Greene 2000). That is, rather than modeling party identification as a continuum from Democrat to Independent to Republican, a multinomial logit allows us to estimate the relative probability of identifying between each pair of choices. The categories of party identification that are examined here are "Democrat," "Republican," and "Independent," so the pairwise choices that we model are Independent or Democrat, Republican or Independent, Democrat or Republican.[34] Unlike many other studies of party identification, we have chosen not to separate out partisan leaners from other Independents because we view the choice to identify first as an Independent as meaningful in its own right and also because the results do not differ markedly by reserving the category for only "pure Independents."[35]

---

[34] The results in table 4.3 also exclude the interviewer's race and survey year fixed effects. In specifications that include these variables, they are not significant factors, so we allow the greater parsimony of the model specified in table 4.3 to prevail.

[35] When we repeated the analysis in table 4.3 with Independent leaners included as partisans, we reached essentially the same set of conclusions regarding black partisan choices. The results of this alternate specification are included in table 4.A.1 in the online appendix (http://press.princeton.edu/titles/9468.html).

A few other points on the interpretation of table 4.3 bear note. First, because multinomial logit is an explicit nonlinear statistical estimator, the parameter estimates can be somewhat of a challenge to interpret. To make the result clearer, we transform these parameter estimates into odds ratios ("relative risk ratios") that allow for assessments of relative magnitude—the relative odds of, say, identifying as a Republican or an Independent, given a one-unit change to an independent variable of interest, say, of being employed or unemployed.[36] Also, table 4.3, unlike most presentations of multinomial logit regressions, presents estimates for every pairwise combination of the three categories.[37]

There are two claims we make based on the results in table 4.3. The first is that black nationalism represents a new and important dimension in blacks' partisan choice and works orthogonally to conventional linear models of party identification. That is, support for black nationalism in its various forms can lead both to support for and opposition to the Democratic Party. The second claim is that an unordered model of partisan choice better fits blacks' party identification. In other words, blacks' partisan choices are not neatly ordered along a single dimension.[38]

As table 4.3 demonstrates, once the assumption of an ordered dependent variable is discarded, the importance and orthogonality of black nationalism become evident.[39] Specifically, we find significant and con-

[36] For each pairwise comparison, say between identifying as a Democrat or as an Independent, table 4.3 shows three statistics—the parameter estimate and its corresponding standard error and relative risk ratio.

[37] Technically, a "baseline" category against which other alternatives are compared must be chosen for the model to be statistically "identified," and in many cases, there are strong theoretical grounds for choosing that optimal base category. In our case, the theory argues that each pairwise choice is significant. Hence columns one, two, and three show the results from two separate estimates—first, with "Independent" and then with "Democrat" as the base category.

[38] The structure of black partisan choices may be even more complicated than table 4.3 suggests. Different segments of the black population differ not only in terms of which partisan option they prefer but also in how difficult it is to choose a party in the first place. For black nationalist separatists, in particular, we might expect an especially high level of ambivalence and uncertainty, given that there is no viable black party at the national level and thus no obvious partisan choice. A heteroskedastic probit analysis of party identification supports this view and reveals that of all the subgroups in the black community, it is most difficult to predict the partisan choices of those who believe strongly in black autonomy (the analysis is not shown).

[39] Further evidence of the orthogonality of black nationalism emerges from an analysis of those who respond "don't know" or "no preference" to the party-identification question. One of the strongest predictors of not providing a clear answer to the question is holding black nationalist views (the analysis is not shown). The fact that nationalists are particularly likely to answer "don't know" suggests that their views do not fit neatly along the liberal-conservative dimension separating the two parties. Overall, about 5 percent of all blacks answer "don't know" or provide no answer to the party-identification question.

Table 4.3
Determinants of Black Partisan Choice (Multinomial Logit)

	Pr(Ind) vs. Pr(Dem)		Pr(Rep) vs. Pr(Dem)		Pr(Rep) vs. Pr(Ind)	
	MNL	RRR	MNL	RRR	MNL	RRR
Extreme liberal	−.519	0.60**	0.116	1.12	0.634	1.89^
	(.153)		(.357)		(.370)	
Moderate liberal	−.519	0.60**	−.032	0.97	0.487	1.63
	(.176)		(.450)		(.465)	
Moderate conservative	−.405	0.67*	0.257	1.29	0.661	1.94
	(.186)		(.409)		(.426)	
Extreme conservative	0.025	1.02	0.982	2.67**	0.958	2.61**
	(.161)		(.320)		(.331)	
Income	0.017	1.02	0.092	1.10	0.076	1.08
	(.025)		(.058)		(.060)	
Education	0.039	1.04	−.131	0.88	−.170	0.84^
	(.036)		(.094)		(.097)	
Home ownership	−.162	0.85	0.285	1.33	0.447	1.56^
	(.116)		(.263)		(.272)	
Unemployed	0.417	1.52*	1.622	5.06**	1.205	3.34**
	(.211)		(.332)		(.347)	
Black linked fate	−.001	1.00	−.207	0.81*	−.208	0.81^
	(.049)		(.103)		(.107)	
Community control	−.010	0.99	−.454	0.65**	−.443	0.64**
	(.068)		(.154)		(.159)	
Racial separatism	−.002	1.00	0.550	1.73*	0.552	1.74*
	(.098)		(.225)		(.233)	
Democrats work for blacks	−.502	0.61**	−.558	0.57**	−.055	0.95
	(.069)		(.150)		(.153)	
Republicans work for blacks	0.349	1.42**	0.925	2.52**	0.576	1.78**
	(.066)		(.133)		(.137)	
Age	−.026	0.97**	−.017	0.98*	0.009	1.01
	(.004)		(.009)		(.009)	
Male	0.490	1.63**	0.174	1.19	−.316	0.73
	(.110)		(.257)		(.263)	
Constant	0.516		−2.26		−2.78	
	(.389)		(.866)		(.893)	

Pseudo R-squared	.099
Chi-squared (df = 24)	297.98**
N	2,147

Significance levels: ** $p < .01$ * $p < .05$ ^ $p < .10$. Data are from the 1984–88 National Black Election Study, 1993 National Black Politics Study, and the 1996 National Black Election Study. Party identification is measured as three categories: Democrats, Independents (including partisan leaners), and Republicans. The statistical model is estimated using Intercooled Stata v8.1.

trasting effects for the two aspects of black nationalism. Once again, as in table 4.2, belief in nationalism qua community control significantly increases one's likelihood of identifying as a Democrat. But here we also find that belief in nationalism qua racial separatism works in essentially the opposite direction by increasing one's likelihood of identifying as a Republican. Race, at least in the sense of support for black autonomy, can work for or against the Democratic Party.

Table 4.3 also sheds significant light on the unordered nature of blacks' partisan choices. The chief criterion for assessing the utility of estimating a given model of choice assuming an ordered or unordered dependent variable is what one might call the "transitivity" of the coefficients across pairwise choices in the unordered condition. That is, if party identification is in fact an ordered sequence of choices from identifying as a strong Republican to identifying as a strong Democrat, then the estimated parameters for the intermediate choices—Democrat or Independent, Independent or Republican—should reflect lighter shades of the more boldly colored estimates we derive for the full spectrum of choices. There are strong and weak criteria for gauging the utility of our multinomial logit estimates. The strong criterion is that we should not see relationships that appear to switch from night to day—to reverse signs while retaining significance. The weaker criterion is that relationships that did not exist in the ordered probit estimates should not come to light in the multinomial logit estimates.[40] In both cases, table 4.3 shows compelling evidence that partisan choices are not neatly ordered for African Americans.

The strongest evidence for this is found in the relationship between ideological self-identification and party identification. For the pairwise choice between identifying as an Independent or a Democrat, extreme liberals and moderate liberals are more likely to identify as Democrats than are ideological moderates, as we might expect. But table 4.3 shows that moderate *conservatives* are also more likely to identify as Democrats than are staunch moderates, and by almost the same magnitude of effect as we find among the liberal categories. In the choice between Republicans and Independents, extreme conservatives, as we might expect, are significantly more likely to choose to identify as Republicans. Quite surprisingly, however, extreme *liberals* also appear more likely to choose to identify as Republicans rather than as Independents (although the statistical significance of this result is much weaker).[41] The relationship be-

---

[40] The latter is a weaker condition because the premise that a dependent variable is ordered could be consistent with the uncovering of new statistically significant relationships under the multinomial logit if there are strong nonlinearities in the relationship of the dependent variable to a given explanatory variable.

[41] For the pairwise choice between Republicans and Democrats, the results are straightforward: only extreme conservatives are distinct from moderates, and they are significantly more likely to choose to identify as Republicans. This effect is strong.

tween ideology and partisanship is anything but linear. This nonlinear relationship, coupled with the earlier nonlinearities we found between partisanship and black nationalism, make a convincing case for the added value of estimating African American party identification as an unordered phenomenon.

The analysis presented in table 4.3 also suggests an answer to our question about the declining rates of identification with the Democratic Party over time. As we saw in figures 4.2 and 4.3, much of the change in black partisanship since the 1960s is the exit of black Democrats who identify as Independents and, among Independents, the increasing proportion of Democratic leaners. Thus, to explain the out-migration of African Americans from Democratic Party identification, the critical comparison is not between Democrats and Republicans but between Democrats and Independents.

Here table 4.3 points to two principal factors: ideology and the evaluation of each party's efforts vis-à-vis African Americans. These findings must be interpreted with care, however. The quick-and-dirty conclusion to draw would be that African Americans are increasingly becoming conservative and that race is declining in significance for African Americans. Let us take each of these in turn. The danger in reading too much into a conservative turn in black political ideology is that, as we see from figure 4.4, most of the variation over time and across individuals comes from liberals who now self-identify as moderates. Similarly, in table 4.3 we see that most of the variation in the choice between identifying as a Democrat and Independent comes from the distinctiveness of ideological moderation, not conservatism. Thus, the explanation for blacks' exit from the Democratic Party, to the extent that it is driven by ideology, is not a more conservative black polity but a growing consensus on ideological moderation within the African American community.

The story of the relevance of a racial-group calculus is similarly nuanced. Our findings in table 4.3 underscore several parts to the story. First, African American partisan choice is in substantial measure a reflection of considerations beyond a person's class status and orthogonal to his or her liberal-conservative orientation. Second, it shows once again that racial considerations can and do push African Americans away from the Democratic Party. But it is a more consistent factor in pushing African Americans who identify as Republicans. This finding, coupled with the selective effect of our measures of a racial group calculus on the pairwise choice between Democrat and Independent—recall that neither linked fate nor racial separatism is a factor in this choice—points, rather persuasively, to the conclusion that the lion's share of the decline in black Democratic identification, vis-à-vis racial considerations, is not the result of the diminishing significance of race per se but of a shift in the pairwise evalu-

ation of how hard the Democratic and Republican parties work on behalf of African Americans. This evaluation, importantly, is a perfectly
reasonable response to the rise of "Third Way" new Democrats, who
have relegated issues of race to the periphery of the Democratic policy
agenda, if not offstage altogether (Walters 1988, Frymer 1999).

The Impact of a Black Democrat as President

Barack Obama's electoral victory on November 4, 2008, was arguably
one of the most important events in the history of black politics in this
nation. In a country that has engaged in repeated, often passionate,
and sometimes violent battle over the rights of African Americans to participate equally in the democratic process, the ascension of a black man
to the nation's highest office was both startling and potentially earth-
shattering.[42] Given the promise of a black presidency, it is important to
ask how much the outcome of the 2008 contest will change the patterns
that we have reported in this chapter. Does a black Democratic president
mean the end of the decline in African American attachment to the Democratic Party? Does it reshape the racial, ideological, and partisan views
of individual black Americans? In short, does it change everything? With
Barack Obama having spent less than a year in office as of this writing, it
is far too early to offer a definitive assessment of the impact of a black
presidency on the politics of the black community. Nevertheless, there are
already signs of both change and retrenchment that may provide some
insight into the long-term consequences of the 2008 elelction.

In the immediate aftermath of the 2008 presidential contest, the indica-
tions were of widespread euphoria and dramatic change in the black
community. According to one poll, fully 71 percent of African Americans
said that Obama's election was either "the most important advance that
has taken place for blacks in the last 100 years" or "one of the two
or three most important advances" (Saad 2010). Among blacks, the
Gallup poll's index-of-life satisfaction demonstrated a remarkable rise
from a mean value of -1 before the election (October 2008) to 62 shortly
after the election (April 2009). In a dramatic reversal, blacks went from
being substantially less optimistic about the direction of the nation's
economy (11 percent positive versus 31 percent positive for whites)
to being more than twice as likely as whites to expect their economic
fortunes to improve (47 percent versus 22 percent for whites). Although
the data are sparse and the evidence of change is not dramatic, all of

---

[42] Despite Obama's mixed racial heritage, it seems clear that most Americans see him as
an African American.

this may have had some influence on black partisanship. The Gallup party-identification series reveals a small increase in Democratic Party identification. According to the Gallup poll, black attachment to the Democratic Party grew from 75 percent before Obama's election to 82 percent in November 2009.

But only a short time into Barack Obama's presidency, there are already signs of growing impatience and even some discontent within the black community. Polling data suggest that with Obama's apparently conscious strategy to avoid the potentially divisive issue of racial inequality and with no significant racially focused legislation on the horizon, many blacks are getting restless with the pace of change under Obama and the Democratic Party. The perception that Obama could help racial relations has fallen steeply from its high in November 2008, when three-quarters of all blacks believed that Obama would improve race relations, to November 2009, when a slim majority (51 percent) agreed with the same statement (ABC News 2010).[43] And on questions about the future of race relations, blacks' attitudes are essentially right where they were before the election. After declining significantly during the 2008 campaign, the number of African Americans who think that we will never find a solution to the nation's racial problem has returned to its pre-Obama levels. According to ABC News / *Washington Post* polls, the proportion of blacks who believe we will always have a racial problem fell from 56 percent in 2007 to 49 percent during the campaign but then rose to 55 percent in October 2009 (ABC News 2010). In an even more ominous sign for Obama and the Democratic Party, the percentage of blacks who think "the policies of Barack Obama will not go far enough in promoting efforts to aid the black community" has risen sharply from 20 in June 2008 to 32 in October 2009 (Saad 2010). The same two polls also showed a small increase in the number of blacks who think race relations have gotten worse.

The vast majority of blacks still approve of President Obama, and there is as yet no indication of any increase in black defection from the Democratic Party under his stewardship, but the euphoria and high expectations that marked the beginning of his term are clearly gone. There is obviously a long way to go, but based on these patterns it is not at all clear that Obama's time in office will greatly reshape the partisan politics of black America. Indeed, it seems likely that even though the Democrats were the first party to advance an African American presidential nominee, the partisan battle for black allegiances will continue. For Obama and the Democratic Party more generally, the key will still be to try to

---

[43] Similarly, Gallup reports that the proportion of African Americans who think race relations have gotten better shrank from 23 percent in late 2008 to 11 percent in October 2009.

convince black Americans that black interests can best be served under the auspices of the Democratic Party.

SUMMARY AND DISCUSSION

What do our findings imply for our understanding of black politics and partisan identification? First, let us restate our basic conclusion: Black partisan choices often do not fit neatly into the ideologically driven Downsian model or the socialization story of the Michigan School. There is some evidence that conventional nonracialfactors such as class and conservatism do work to divide the black community. But the effects for these conventional factors are inconsistent and often weak. In particular, our results indicate that the relationship between liberal-conservative ideology and blacks' party identification is anything but linear. In short, conventional, nonracial politics matters, but it is not the driving force of black politics.

Our analysis indicates instead that race remains the central factor in black partisan decision making. How African Americans view American society and the degree to which they think their own well-being is tied to the fate of the larger black community underlie much of black partisan politics. But as we have shown, the connection between group interests and the Democratic Party is not at all automatic. In fact, racial identity can and does cut both ways. Racial identity can lead to linked fate and support for the Democratic Party, but it also seems to lead to a support for black separatism and distance from both the Democratic and the Republican Party. This latter dimension—autonomy versus integration—is one that previous accounts of black partisanship have largely ignored.

All this leads to a second conclusion. African Americans may differ from other groups not only in terms of which factors determine their partisan identification but also in the structure of their choices. For many whites, a unitary decision about where to place themselves on a linear scale ranging from liberal on the left to conservative on the right may still be appropriate. But for African Americans, a multidimensional, unordered model more accurately depicts partisan choices. Unless we model black partisan choices in this more complex manner, we reach a series of inaccurate conclusions, and we may miss important insights.

The implications of all this for the future of black politics are not at all clear. On one hand, there is little evidence that black group consciousness is waning. In fact, in our 1996 survey, some 73 percent of African Americans indicated that they felt a sense of linked fate, a substantial increase from the 62 percent who felt similarly in 1984. Black unity in the political arena is waning by some measures, but this is certainly not because large numbers of African Americans believe that race is no longer relevant. Moreover, economic heterogeneity does not appear to be driving blacks apart in any major or consistent way. At the same time, there are other signs that blacks are divided and that they could become more divided politically in the future. The decline of liberalism among the black population may begin to push African Americans apart politically. And younger blacks are less happy with the Democratic Party and more supportive of black separatism. In short, there are reasons to expect that we will see ongoing unity and other reasons to expect greater division in the future.

Ultimately, how these factors combine and play out is likely to depend on the actions of the Democratic and Republican parties. How each party is perceived to serve group interests is a critical intervening variable in black partisan decision making. If individual blacks believe the Republican Party works hard for black interests, they will support the Republican Party. The critical question is thus not whether black class structure will continue to change or whether blacks will continue to become more conservative in their views. The critical question is how well either party can make the claim that its agenda serves black interests. So far, the Republican Party has not been particularly successful at making this claim, but there is at least the potential that it will win more hearts and minds in the future. The Democratic Party has been very successful at making this claim in the past, and the election of Barack Obama has the potential to further solidify it. But the reluctance of the president and the Democratic Party to push forward major reforms that address racial injustice has clearly been noticed by many members of the African American community. It is not clear how long the Democratic Party can continue to put racial issues near the periphery of its agenda before it begins to lose substantial black support. This is something that both parties need to seriously consider if they want to attract more black support.

CHAPTER 5

What Does It Mean to Be a Partisan?

> What does it mean to be an American?
> —J. Hector de St. John de Crèvecoeur

> I'm Indian first. Sikh second. Politician third. No, I'm American
> first. I must be grateful to this flag. Actually, I'm a human being
> first. American second. Indian third. I mean, Sikh third. Indian
> fourth. Irish, maybe fifth or sixth. I may not look it, but Duggal
> is an Irish name.
> —Harjinder Singh Duggal

MORSHED ALAM—AN IMMIGRANT, Laundromat owner, former electrical engineer, one-time student leader in Bangladesh's struggle for independence, and now a New Yorker and an aspiring politician—describes his rocky initiation to party politics in the United States: "In 1996, the Republican State Senator from my district wrote a book saying there are too many immigrants in America. It's time to put a padlock at the gates to this country. . . . I thought, I will challenge this guy for his Senate seat" (quoted in Lehrer and Sloan 2003, 373). Rather than being greeted with open arms as a Democratic challenger or even grudging recognition as a legal entrant into the electoral playing field, however, Alam faced a relentless stream of pressure from the Queens County Democratic Party and others to quit the race. The pressure ranged from a legal challenge to the Board of Elections to physical threats and bodily harm. As Alam puts it, "Even when I won the Democratic primary, and was legally the party's candidate, the party machine didn't help me. I'm thinking, is this a real democracy? I went through every kind of hell in that race. . . . I was sent to the hospital with two broken bones around my eyes" (Lehrer and Sloan 2003, 373–74).

Alam survived the physical attacks but was outspent by the Republican incumbent by $500,000 to $35,000, never received the backing of the county Democratic Party, and ultimately failed to prevail in the election. Nonetheless, he won 42 percent of the vote in the general election and put the predominantly white Democratic establishment in Queens County on notice that naturalized immigrants like himself and Harjinder Singh Duggal (quoted in the epigraph to this chapter) could no longer be ignored. Alam attributes his success to patchwork coalition building: "No one ethnic group will ever have a majority again in this borough. Now you have to have a coalition. My campaign committee was made up of a Colombian-American, a Jewish-American, a Black-American, a union worker, and a conservative Republican. It's not like years ago when you were Irish in an Irish neighborhood, or Italian in an Italian neighborhood" (Lehrer and Sloan 2003, 373–74).

How emblematic is Alam's story of the state of affairs between immigrants and political parties in America today? Are local party organizations like the Queens County Democratic Party aloof, if not outright hostile, toward political newcomers, in stark contrast to our ballyhooed views of their central role in incorporating previous waves of immigrants from the late nineteenth and early twentieth centuries? Alam's travails are of course but a single anecdote, and the demographic changes in the United States described in chapter 1 make it seem near impossible for either major party to ignore. If the Democratic and Republican parties are in fact ignoring new immigrants to America, they do so at their peril, given the razor-thin electoral margins that have decided recent presidential contests and the organizational imperative of both parties to sustain their membership rolls and maintain a base of party activists. These questions and considerations have generated a welter of new scholarship on "immigrant political incoporation," most of which has focused on the role of political parties and—in the absence of evidence of an incorporating role of parties—organizations that constitute civil society in local and transnational arenas.

In the next two chapters, we adopt a different tack. We invert the lens on immigrant political incorporation. Rather than peer from the top down to see if key political institutions are bringing new Americans into active political life, we rake through individual-level survey data to see what relationship these new Americans have to political parties, if any. Do Latino and Asian American immigrants and subsequent generations of Latinos and Asian Americans think in terms of political parties? If so, will Asians and Latinos ally with the Democratic Party on the basis of collective racial interests as African Americans have since the civil rights era? Or will their ties to a political party be determined instead by policy differences and liberal and conservative beliefs, as they are for many white Americans? Or something else? Such questions are of vital interest to scholars and practitioners of politics alike. The ties that Latinos and Asian Americans have (or do not have) will affect their potential to reconfigure existing party alignments, to act as swing voters, and the like.

Our two epigraphs for this chapter capture the kernel of our answer to these questions. It is both implicit and explicit in the existing literature that party identification is a key (if not *the* key) answer to de Crèvecoeur's query, politically speaking. Yet in the excerpt from Lehrer and Sloan's collection of immigrant oral and visual histories, *Crossing the Boulevard,* Duggal voices plainly and powerfully how complex, ambiguous, and numerous are the political identities of immigrants in our present-day, post–civil rights ethnoracial landscape. Yet for Duggal—who, as a member of the Queens Democratic County Committee (and, in that position, one of the first Sikhs to be elected to political office in New York City), is clearly a political being—party identification is nowhere reflected among the identities he defines himself by.

This chapter begins with a review of the historical and present-day debate on whether party organizations are bringing immigrants into their fold and by surveying existing data and research on Latino and Asian American partisanship. Our focus here is on a relatively unconsidered aspect of party identification—namely, why a plurality of these new Americans, in most polls, choose not to identify with a political party. The modal Latino and Asian American is what we call "uncommitted" or "nonidentifier." We consider several explanations for why party politics has not become the "unmoved mover" that it is for most other Americans. We argue that, rather than presenting a portrait of Latinos and Asian Americans as threats, political unknowns, or apolitical bystanders, their nonpartisanship reflects an ongoing process of learning in a still unfamiliar and uncertain political milieu. That is, the relationship that Latinos and Asian Americans have or fail to have with political parties reflects the multiple processes by which immigrant-based groups become incorporated into life in the United States. In our account, in addition to considering basic elements of the straight-line assimilation model such as time and class, which others have investigated, we integrate a series of explicitly political factors related to a more contingent or segmented model of assimilation. Within this political account of immigrant incorporation, we assess the roles played both by emerging institutional ties and by attitudinal incorporation. Specifically, in terms of attitudinal incorporation, we consider the importance of information acquisition, ideological leanings, and racial identities in fostering Latino and Asian American partisanship. Near the end of this chapter we begin to empirically examine the relationship between different aspects of incorporation and partisanship, and in the next chapter we test a full model of Latino and Asian American party identification.

WHY LATINOS AND ASIAN AMERICANS?

One prefatory matter is on the two groups that are of primary interest in this chapter. We focus here on the party identification of Latinos and

Asian Americans. Much of our theoretical framing of *why* these two groups ought to be examined together is a story about party identification in the context of immigrant political incorporation. Clearly, not all Latinos and Asian Americans are foreign-born. Both Latinos and Asian Americans, however, are *immigration-based* communities. That is, most individuals described by these panethnic categories were either born outside the United States or born to a foreign-born parent, and the experience of being "strangers from different shores" is widespread. Thus, according to the most recent American Community Surveys, roughly two-thirds of Asians in the United States are first-generation immigrants, and roughly 40 percent of Latinos are foreign-born. More than two-thirds of Latinos and 87 percent of Asian Americans are either first- or second-generation Americans. In this regard, while not everyone who self-identifies as Latino or as Asian American is an immigrant, both Latinos and Asian Americans, as groups, are newcomers to the American political scene.

There is, to be sure, a great deal of variation in immigration patterns and political histories among ethnic/national origin groups that comprise the Latino and Asian American communities. We need not dig farther down than the three most prominent Latino ethnic/national origin groups—Cubanos, Puertoriqueños, and Chicanos—to make this case. Thus, by our use of "Asian American" and "Latino" we do not mean to imply that the national origin/ethnic subgroups that make up these panethnic demographic populations are either homogeneous vis-à-vis one another or alike in their attachments to political parties. Furthermore, almost by definition (in designating Latinos and Asian Americans as two separate populations with separate demographic labels), there is more that differentiates Latinos from Asian Americans than is common to both groups. We do not mean to imply, therefore, that in combining our analyses of Latinos and Asian Americans in this chapter that the two groups are similar in some fundamental respect vis-à-vis their partisanship patterns. That matter is an empirical one.

We do combine both groups in our analysis, however, because our theoretical account of whether and why predominantly immigrant-based groups such as Latinos and Asian Americans identify with a political party is a shared one. It is also a theoretical account that is discernibly distinct from the patterns of partisanship we propose and find evidence for among African Americans and whites. Finally, although our empirical results do show important points of departure between Latinos and Asian Americans vis-à-vis party identification, both groups have a great deal in common, including the starting point—an aversion to party labels rooted in the institutional- and individual-level processes of immigrant political incorporation.

BACKGROUND: IMMIGRANT POLITICAL INCORPORATION IN AMERICA

How politically incorporated are Latinos and Asian Americans? A common approach is to determine the present by looking to the past. As many accounts have it, the late nineteenth and early twentieth centuries in America represented a golden age of immigration. Immigrants came from distant lands (predominantly European) and were absorbed in America's economic markets, assimilated into its social customs, and incorporated by its political institutions. This period is, at least in our collective memory, one that represents a model for the inclusion of newcomers into a pluralist political system, with local political parties playing the critical intermediary role in this process of incorporation. Scholars have documented how urban political machines actively mobilized immigrants into new citizens, wheedled favors and employ for them, enrolled them as newly registered voters, maneuvered their electoral choices, and, in due course, moved them up the rank and file of the party machine (Dahl 1961a, Allswang 1977, Andersen 1979, Cornwell 1960, Archdeacon 1983, Sterne 2001). In this era of immigration, roughly a half million to a million newcomers disembarked at Ellis Island and other points of entry each year, a reserve army of potential partisans whose mobilization was, by some accounts, sufficient to tip the balance in the New Deal party realignment to the Democrats (Andersen 1979).

This rose-tinted view of our democratic history has come under considerable scrutiny in recent years. America, so the revisionist accounts now tell us, was never as welcoming of immigrants into the political system as our myths of a "nation of immigrants" would have it. At the very highest political offices, there was widespread disdain for the inclusion of new immigrants in the American political process. Woodrow Wilson and Theodore Roosevelt, bitter rivals in politics, agreed on the question of immigration. In his 1902 text, *A History of the American People,* Wilson remarked grimly on the influx of "men of the lowest class from the south of Italy and mean of the meaner sort out of Hungary and Poland" and offered the view that these southern and eastern European migrants had "neither the skill nor energy nor any initiative of quick intelligence."[1] A somewhat less welcoming party structure is also reflected in more scholarly revisions of the epoch of machine politics (Erie 1990, Sterne 2001, Trounstine 2006). Scholars of urban politics have noted that not all immigrant groups from Europe were equally incorporated (see, e.g., Igna-

---

[1] Wilson was not excoriated for these views until 1912, when William Randolph Hearst, who opposed his presidential candidacy, brought them to light. Wilson eventually recanted his views on southern and eastern European immigrants.

tiev 1995, Jacobson 1998), that the willingness of party machines to incorporate new immigrants varied across historical contexts (Mayhew 1986) and with the degree of party competition in a city (Wolfinger 1965, Erie 1990), and that nonparty organizations such as neighborhood associations, unions, churches, and ethnic voluntary associations were vital in incorporating new immigrant groups (Oestreicher 1988, Sterne 2001). Moreover, even much celebrated groups like the Irish (with Tammany Hall in New York and Boss Curley in Boston) succeeded by claiming whiteness and explicitly positioning themselves against blacks, Mexicans, and Asians.

Among political scientists today, much of the burgeoning literature on contemporary immigrant political incorporation is anchored by careful theorizing and analysis on how today's political parties compare with those of yesteryear (e.g., Jones-Correa 1998, Gerstle and Mollenkopf 2001, Kim 2006, Rogers 2006, Wong 2006). For the most part, the scholars behind these works conclude that today's parties lack the organizational capacity, the cultural understanding, and perhaps even the political motivation to shepherd new immigrants into the political process and nurture secure attachments with a particular political party. As one study recounts the words of a community leader of Mexican American descent in East Los Angeles, "Stop anybody walking down the block, ask them, 'Can you please tell me where is the local chapter or the local office of the Democratic Party in your neighborhood?' Everybody will look at you with bewilderment: 'What is this crazy guy talking about?'" (Wong 2006, 510).

The result of this underwhelming presence of political parties in the everyday lives of Latinos and Asian Americans is putatively reflected in the underwhelming rates of political participation among Latinos and Asian Americans and in the corresponding underrepresentation of Latinos and Asian Americans in elected and appointed political offices (see, e.g., Uhlaner et al. 1989; Verba et al. 1993; DeSipio 1995; Leighley and Vedlitz 1999; Ramakrishnan 2005; Lien et al. 2007). Table 5.1 shows the basic patterns of underparticipation in terms of the three widely studied stages of formal political incorporation. The three key steps here are whether a newcomer to the United States has established citizenship, whether that citizen (if eligible) registers to vote, and whether that registered voter actually casts a vote come Election Day. The table compares the levels of incorporation of whites, African Americans, Latinos, and Asian Americans.

The main point of this table is quite clear. Latinos and Asian Americans lag well behind both whites and African Americans at each step in this process of political incorporation. The citizenship numbers are not unex-

TABLE 5.1
From Citizenship to Voting, 2008

	Whites	African Americans	Latinos	Asian Americans	Total
% citizen	98	94	63	68	91
% registered	72	66	38	37	65
% voted	65	61	32	32	58
% registered I citizen	74	70	59	55	71
% voted I registered	90	93	84	86	90

Source: 2008 Current Population Survey. The "% registered" and "% voted" rows show the proportion of all adults in that group; the rows with "% registered I citizen" and "% voted I registered" show the proportion of citizens who registered and the proportion of registered voters who turned out to vote, respectively.

pected, as there is a substantially higher proportion of Latinos and Asian Americans who are foreign-born than there are immigrant whites and blacks. (According to 2008 American Community Survey data, 67 percent of Asian Americans and 38 percent of Latinos were foreign-born, and only 4 percent of non-Hispanic whites and 8 percent of blacks were foreign-born.) Nativity alone, of course, does not explain the patterns we see, since the citizenship rates of Asian Americans exceed those of Latinos, despite the significantly greater proportion of foreign-born Asian Americans.

This underparticipation in politics is also mirrored by data on the levels of political representation across racial and ethnic groups. If representation is measured by matching the proportion of legislators in a group to the population proportion of that group, African Americans come the closest to parity in representation, with Latinos and Asian Americans lagging substantially behind. This underrepresentation is shown quite clearly in table 5.2: according to the 2008 American Community Survey, Hispanics constituted more than 15 percent of the U.S. population, but only 5.7 percent of members of Congress in the House of Representatives and 3.1 percent of state legislators in 2006; Asian Americans (even allowing for the more inclusive "alone or in combination" categorization) were just under 5 percent of the U.S. population but roughly 1 percent of members of the House and of state legislatures.[2]

[2] African Americans made up roughly 13 percent of the U.S. population by the "alone or in combination" grouping (and 12.4 percent if counted as "Black or African American alone"). Native Americans constituted 1.4 percent of the population when counted "alone or in combination," and 0.8 percent when counted "alone."

TABLE 5.2
Minority Representation in Elected Office, 2006

	African Americans	Latinos	Asian Americans	Native Americans
House	41	25	4	1
	(9.4%)	(5.7%)	(0.9%)	(0.2%)
State legislature	530	229	85	47
	(7.2%)	(3.1%)	(1.1%)	(0.6%)

PATTERN AND DISORDER IN LATINO AND ASIAN PARTY IDENTIFICATION

Thus, although much has been made of the growing numbers of Latinos and Asians in the United States, these numbers have yet to readily translate into political power. Nor do they reflect the levels of democratic inclusion and political incorporation that native-born whites and African Americans experience. Beyond these institutionally rooted markers of incorporation, we examine what implications the less-than-complete commitments of political parties to the incorporation of immigrants have for how immigrants and their subsequent generations come to view political parties and the party system. If party identification is the bedrock of American democracy, what do we know about the party attachments of Asian Americans and Latinos?

The answer, it turns out, is a contingent one. One contingency is the availability of data. In general, there is substantially greater data on Latino partisanship than there is on Asian American partisanship. Simply on the basis of their relative proportions of the general population, the number of Latino respondents to a typical national survey such as the General Social Survey (GSS) and the American National Election Studies (ANES) allow for reasonably valid estimates of Latino party identification; the number of Asian American respondents do not. This relative effect also holds with most media polls, where it is commonplace, if not *de rigueur*, to disaggregate survey results between white, African American, and Latino respondents. Moreover, a number of surveys focus exclusively on the opinions of Latino and Latina Americans in the realm of political science research, starting with the 1989–90 Latino National Political Survey and followed by the *Washington Post*/Kaiser Family Foundation/Harvard University 1999 Latino Survey, the Pew Hispanic Center/Kaiser Family Foundation 2002 National Survey of Latinos and 2004 National Survey of Latinos, three surveys by the Latino Policy Coalition in April, June, and October 2006, and the 2005–6 Latino National

Survey. By contrast, although there are now a few surveys with reasonably large samples of Asian American respondents, the number is substantially fewer than for Latinos, and the quality of data is substantially poorer. To date, there have been only two serious attempts to systematically survey the opinions of Asian Americans: the 2001 Pilot National Asian American Political Survey and the 2008 National Asian American Survey.[3]

A second important contingency is the representativeness of the sample. Some surveys poll likely voters, others poll only adults living in metropolitan areas with a high proportion of Asians or Latinos, still others poll only Asians and Latinos with certain surnames, and finally some poll only certain ethnic subgroups within these panethnic groups, and so on. For example, many of the existing surveys of Asian Americans are geographically specific samples that do not allow us to draw valid inferences for the national Asian population (e.g., academic surveys such as the Los Angeles Study of Urban Inequality, the Immigrant Second Generation in Metropolitan New York project, the polls of the Institute for Asian American Studies at the University of Massachusetts in Boston, and media polls like the Los Angeles Times surveys of the 1990s and the 2004 San Jose Mercury News survey). These surveys also do not reflect the significant suburbanization of the Asian and Latino populations or their dispersion from traditional gateway cities such as New York, San Francisco, Chicago, and Los Angeles to new destinations in North Carolina, Georgia, Minnesota, and other less traditional targets of migration.

Finally, a third contingency is the quality of the data. Some surveys tolerate response rates as low as 25 percent for a telephone interview, and others endeavor to reach much higher response rates and conduct face-to-face interviews. That is, in some surveys, three out of the four target respondents in a randomly drawn sampling frame refused to be interviewed. These nonresponders are, importantly, not randomly distributed in the general population (Brehm 1993; Groves 2007; Groves et al. 2007; Keeter et al. 2007). Moreover, some surveys conduct interviews only in English, and others allow non-English interviews. The language in which an interview is conducted can have significant and sizable effects on what we infer about a given outcome of interest. For instance, in a simple cross-tabulation of party identification by language of interview, Latinos interviewed in Spanish are almost 19 percent more likely to self-identify as Republican than their counterparts interviewed in English (Lee 2001).

---

[3] Worse still, the validity and utility of inferences from these surveys are limited by the small sample size for particular national groups, the disproportionate representation of foreign-born Asians and of respondents who selected a non-English language for interview, and the heavy reliance on Asian Americans living in large central cities.

These contingencies aside, we can say with significant confidence that Latinos lean more heavily toward the Democratic Party in their partisan attachments than they do toward the Republican Party (Alvarez and García Bedolla 2003; Uhlaner and García 2005; de la Garza 2004). Over a twenty-six-year period of the ANES from 1978 to 2004, 46 percent of Latinos in the ANES self-identified as Democrats, 17 percent as Republicans, and 37 percent as Independents (without any follow-up on the partisan leanings of self-reported Independents). This preference for the Democratic Party is even more pronounced at the ballot box, with exit polls finding a consistently strong margin of preference among Latino voters for Democratic candidates over their Republican counterparts.

There is, we should note, some disagreement on whether or not there is a trend away from Democratic partisanship among Latinos. Gimpel and Kaufmann (2001) pooled network exit polls of presidential elections from 1976 to 2000 and found that in the 1976 election between Jimmy Carter and Gerald Ford, Latinos voted overwhelmingly Democratic over Republican, 82 percent to 18 percent. By the 2000 election between Al Gore and George W. Bush, this gap had slimmed to a margin of a 62 percent Democratic vote and a 35 percent Republican vote among Latinos. The real firestorm here was fueled by the striking contrast in exit poll data between the 2000 and the 2004 presidential elections. In 2004 the exit polls of the National Election Pool (NEP, the successor to the Voter News Service) initially reported that this 27-percentage-point gap had been narrowed to 9, with a 53-to-44 split in the Latino vote share between the Democratic loser John Kerry and the Republican incumbent George W. Bush.[4]

---

[4] Even the National Association of Latino Elected and Appointed Officials' (NALEAO) most recent *2004 Latino Election Handbook* similarly observes an increasing trend toward registration with the Republican Party among California Latinos since 2000. Importantly, the 2004 NEP exit poll also found a closing of the gap in party identification among Latino respondents: in the 2000 Voter News Service (VNS) exit poll, Latinos favored the Democratic Party over the Republican one by a 55-to-24-percent split; in the 2004 NEP exit poll, this split had seemingly shifted to 49 to 27- percent. This seemingly sizable shift in Latino voters' preferences led to controversy and objections from the National Council of La Raza, the William C. Velasquez Institute, the Southwest Voter Registration Education Project, and a number of scholars (Gimpel 2004; Leal et al. 2005; Suro et al. 2005). In response to several pertinent objections to the 2004 NEP exit poll methodology, the 2004 vote-share results were "re-weighted" and revised to show a 39 percent Latino vote share for President Bush. There were two primary issues here. First, the NEP Election Day exit polls differed quite a bit from the expectations of preelection polls, which suggested something closer to a 60-30 split in vote share (Leal et al. 2005). Second, the sampling of precincts appeared to produce a nonrepresentative sample of Latino voters, including a disproportionate number of Cuban voters in the Miami area, fewer young voters, fewer urban voters, fewer self-identified Democrats, fewer women, and fewer opponents of the war in Iraq—all correlates of a vote preference for Kerry over Bush (Suro et al. 2005).

Before bowing to the temptation to infer that Latinos are becoming more "white" as an electorate, more attentive to their social conservatism as a guide to their partisanship, or more responsive to the strategic and aggressive efforts of the Republican Party to woo Latino voters, it is important to note that still other studies argue that Latino Americans are actually growing more Democratic. Matt Barreto and Nathan Woods (2005), for example, find that the proportion of registered Latino Democrats to registered Latino Republicans in Southern California increased substantially between 1992 and 1998. Moreover, there is good evidence that California's divisive ballot initiatives (especially Propositions 187 and 209) have had a galvanizing and mobilizing effect in the Latino community, inducing noncitizens to naturalize, nonvoters to mark their ballots, and nonpartisans to identify with the Democratic Party (Bowler et al. 2006; Segura et al. 1997; Pantoja et al. 2001; Ramírez 2002). And still other studies suggest that Latino partisanship is sensitive to the party-specific issue positions and agendas (Alvarez and García Bedolla 2003; Nicholson and Segura 2005).

The point of this discussion is not to settle any scores on the question of whether there is a shift among Latino voters away from the Democratic Party. As a Pew Hispanic Center report on the 2004 Latino vote concludes, "Whether the decline in the fortunes of the Democrats among Hispanic voters from 2000 to 2004 simply reflects the relative popularity of George Bush among Hispanic voters or a more permanent shift in Hispanic party loyalties remains an open question" (Suro et al. 2005, 14). It is, indeed, an open question, and one whose premises keep shifting. In the 2006 election cycle, the NEP exit poll data indicated another swing of the pendulum with a 69–30 split in the Latino vote share in favor of Democratic congressional candidates. And in the 2008 presidential elections, the pendulum remained arced toward the Democratic Party, with the NEP exit polls finding a split of 67 to 31 percent in favor of Barack Obama over John McCain.

Rather than settle this score, we aim here to make a few initial points. First, Latinos are, on the whole, more Democratic in their partisanship than they are Republican. Second, while the direction of Latinos' partisanship is unambiguous, the strength of that tendency is possibly in flux. Importantly, a key point of this chapter is that this potential ambiguity in how stalwartly Democratic Latinos are stems in part from the very large proportion of Latinos who do not identify with either party. The net result is a segment of the electorate whose partisan vote share may vary from presidential election to partisan election, subject to the contingencies of specific elections and candidates and to the dynamic political evolution and maturation of Latinos. These points aim toward yet another feature of party identification among Latino Americans and Asians—

namely, the conspicuous absence of such institutional attachments for so many—that is at the heart of our analysis. Before we fully explore the conspicuously uncrystallized partisan attachments of so many Latino Americans, let us look at the case of Asian Americans.

This theme of discernible partisan patterns, together with conspicuous ambiguities, is also characteristic of the relationship that Asian Americans have to political parties. As we suggested earlier in this chapter, speaking with any precision or predictive punch about how Asian Americans are likely to vote come November can be pretty dodgy. There are myriad reasons why this is so. Chief among these is the dearth (until only very recently) of systematic, reliable data on which to base our expectations. A large random sample of U.S. adults—say in a preelection survey or an exit poll—will contain only a handful of persons of Asian descent and most likely have a bias for those Asians who are more educated, well off, assimilated into life in the United States, and proficient in English. The costs of obtaining a larger, unbiased sample, moreover, can be prohibitive. Thus, it is difficult to find a sample design for a population that is linguistically heterogeneous and geographically dispersed across ethnic subgroups yet locally concentrated within ethnic subgroups and remarkably diverse linguistically (e.g., see Lien et al. 2001). Simple random sampling methods such as random digit dialing is hugely inefficient; more selective and stratified sampling methods like cluster sampling on high-density Asian population areas will yield an unrepresentative sample of Asian Americans nationally; interviews conducted only in English (the norm in survey practice today) will yield even more biased estimates of Asian American opinion and behavior.

As a result, the quality of data on Asian Americans is typically suspect. A powerful example of how varied and suspect the quality of data is on Asian Americans is the striking "house" effects between two exit polls fielded in California following the 1996 general elections. The Voter New Services found Asian Americans to be more Republican than Democratic (48 percent to 32 percent), whereas the Los Angeles Times found the opposite—Asian American Democrats appeared, by this exit poll, to outweigh Asian Republicans (44 percent to 33 percent). Even the recent 2001 Pilot National Asian American Politics Survey and 2008 National Asian American Survey—the two most rigorous and systematic academic surveys of Asian Americans to date—are perhaps closer to alchemic coups de moment than gold standards for the field.

Notwithstanding these seemingly intractable challenges of finding reliable, valid data on Asian American public opinion, a clear and emerging pattern is apparent. As with Latinos, Asian Americans appear to favor the Democratic Party, and this partisan pattern has developed over the last

TABLE 5.3
Exit Poll Data on Asian American Vote Choice, 2000–2008

	2000	2004	2006	2008
Democrat	55	56	62	63
Republican	41	44	37	34

few decades. In the first study of Asian American partisanship acquisition, Cain and his colleagues (1991) found—using data from a 1984 survey of Asian Americans in California—a roughly even split in partisanship and that Asian Americans were far more Republican in their partisanship than Latinos. The authors argue that this effect resulted from the salience of foreign policy concerns among Chinese, Koreans, and Southeast Asians and that there was no discernible effect of being a racial/ethnic minority that pulled Asians toward the Democratic Party among their second- and third-generation respondents.

Yet according to one review of twelve national, state-level, and metropolitan-level surveys in the 1990s, the roughly even split in Asian American partisanship began to take a discernibly Democratic turn by the 1998 off-year elections (Lien 2001). This leaning has become solid in recent years. In the postelection 2000–2001 Pilot National Asian American Politics Study (PNAAPS)—the first multicity, multiethnic, and multilingual academic survey of Asian Americans—Democratic identifiers outnumbered Republican identifiers by more than two to one, and across all ethnic subgroups except for Vietnamese Americans (who lean modestly toward the Republican Party).

This partiality is mirrored too in how Asians vote, shown by exit poll data given in table 5.3.[5] According to Voter New Service (VNS), a solid majority of Asian Americans voted for Al Gore over George W. Bush in 2000 (55 percent to 41). The partiality toward Democratic presidential candidates then rose steadily with successive elections, with the NEP finding a decisive split of 63 to 34 percentage points in favor of Barack Obama over John McCain in the most recent (2008) presidential election. This emerging pattern is also mirrored by voter registration studies in 2004 and 2006 by the Asian American Legal Defense and Education Fund in New York and the Asian Pacific American Legal Center in South-

[5] As with Latinos, there are strong reasons to use exit poll data on Asian Americans with caution. The data are biased by a reliance on sampling selective precincts, sampling based on past voting behavior, and interviewing only in English with a predominance of particular ethnic/national-origin groups. In more local, multilingual, multiethnic polls in Los Angeles, San Francisco, and New York City, the margins are even more decisive for Democratic candidates.

ern California, which found marked increases in the number of Asian Americans who are registered Democrats.

With both Asian Americans and Latinos, there are several critical caveats to these general facts about the direction of partisanship. Perhaps the most commonly raised qualification is that patterns of party identification vary substantially by ethnic/national origin groups. Among the primary Latino subgroups, it is Cubans, and among the primary Asian subgroups, it is Vietnamese (and, by some accounts, Koreans) who are the most likely to identify as Republicans (Cain et al. 1991; de la Garza et al. 1992; Uhlaner and García 2005; Lien et al. 2004). Moreover, party identification varies by immigrant status (foreign-born and generation in the United States), the number of years lived in the United States, and naturalization. Last, we also know that issues and interests matter—most obviously in the arena of foreign policy—as an explanation for why Cubans, Vietnamese, and Koreans tend to identify as Republicans more often than do other Latino and Asian subgroups.

Thus far we have highlighted two defining features of Latino and Asian American partisanship: its contingency across time and data sources and its partiality for the Democratic Party in the dyadic choice between identifying with the Republican or Democratic Party. But these features, important as they are, mask what we think is an even more central one—the tendency of members of both populations to remain outside the partisan scale.

NONIDENTIFIERS

While professors and pundits alike chomp at the bit to proclaim partisan colors, for many Americans there is a critical prior question. Many Americans must first ponder what it means to be a partisan. The willingness to think in partisan terms—by which we mean the willingness to place oneself on a party-identification spectrum at all—is a separate and important prior factor to the specific self-placement on the spectrum from strong Democratic to Independent to strong Republican identification.

This decision is relatively inconsequential when we consider the white or African American populations. In the American National Election Studies cumulative file from 1948 to 2004, less than 7 percent of the black and white sample chose one of the following nonpartisan responses—"no preference," "none," "neither," "other," and "don't know"—or otherwise refused to answer the question. Thus, it is not surprising to find that most studies of partisanship simply dismiss this group as an anomaly, code them as missing, and drop them from analysis altogether.

For expository purposes, we refer interchangeably to Latinos and

TABLE 5.4
(Non)Partisanship among Latinos and Asian Americans

	Latinos	Asian Americans
Democrats	34%	30%
Republicans	10	14
Independents	17	20
Nonidentifiers	38	36

Source: 2006 Latino National Survey and 2008 National Asian American Survey.

Asian Americans who opt for these "noncompliant" response categories—"no preference," "none," "neither," "other," "don't know," or some other mode of refusal to self-identify as Democrat, Republican, or Independent—as "nonidentifiers." While the phenomenon of nonidentifiers may be rare enough among whites and African Americans to treat as a residual response category, for immigrant-laden groups such as Latinos and Asian Americans placing oneself somewhere on the conventional partisan scale is an often difficult, if not impossible, task.[6] In fact, in looking at the 2006 Latino National Survey and the 2008 National Asian American Survey—the two most recent national scholarly surveys of Asian American and Latino politics—it becomes readily apparent that indecision is the modal response in these populations. As table 5.4 shows, fully 38 percent of Latinos and 36 percent of Asian Americans are uncommitted to a partisan response category.

If we add Independents—that is, those who are able to answer the root-party identification question but then claim no attachment to either party—we arrive at the conclusion that a solid majority of Latinos and Asian Americans are nonpartisans. In both the 2006 LNS and the 2008 National Asian American Survey (NAAS), only 44 percent of all respondents identified with one of the two major parties. For Latinos and Asian

[6] To be more precise, the phenomenon of refusing to answer the party-identification question or indicating a "don't know" response is quite rare (an incidence of 0.46 percent in the ANES from 1968 to 2004), as is indicating some preference other than Democrat, Republican, or Independent (an incidence of 0.58 percent over the same years). Indicating no preference, however, is decidedly more common (7.8 percent). In total, even in the representative U.S. population sample of the ANES, almost 9 percent of Americans would be classified as "nonidentifiers" by our account. In the ANES, those indicating no preference or registering a "don't know" response are asked the follow-up question given to Independents, about whether they in fact lean toward one party or the other. Thus, in the conventional construction of a seven-point party identification scale in the ANES, only those respondents who simply refuse to answer the party-identification question or the follow-up on partisan leaners are treated as truly missing data and deleted from subsequent analyses (an incidence rate of less than 1 percent between 1968 to 2004).

Americans, the two categories that studies of partisanship largely concentrate on are only a minority of the population. The response categories that are usually treated as a residual and dropped from a detailed analysis—which we pool together under the label "nonidentifiers"—are in fact the modal kind of response for these groups. This finding, importantly, is not limited to just these two surveys. Most previous surveys of Latinos and Asian Americans—for example, the 2001 Pilot National Asian American Survey, the 1989 Latino National Political Survey, and the Pew Hispanic Center's 2002 *National Survey of Latinos* and 2004 *National Survey of Latinos*—all find that a majority or near-majority of respondents are either nonidentifiers or Independents.

EXPLAINING THE PARTISAN CHOICES OF LATINOS AND ASIAN AMERICANS

How can we explain the distribution of Asian American and Latino partisanship that we find? To answer this question, we briefly revisit explanations that emerge from the traditional party-identification literature. We then move on to consider the relevance of explanations that arise out of what we think is a core process delimiting Latino and Asian American partisan choices—immigrant incorporation. Finally, we adopt key features of existing models of partisanship and our understanding of the process of immigrant incorporation to specify our own model of partisanship for these two groups. The key to our account is a more nuanced and multidimensional story of how incorporation does (or does not) occur across different segments of the population. In particular, we apply our larger theoretical account of (non)partisanship in America and our three elements of information, identity, and ideology to the specific case of the immigrant-based Latino and Asian American populations.

Since traditional accounts of partisanship either overlook nonidentifiers altogether or dismiss them as irrelevant to the political arena, it is not surprising to find that traditional theories offer little in the way of a direct explanation of this phenomenon. Nevertheless, one can extrapolate a story from these theories. A Downsian might infer that Americans with decidedly moderate views would be the most likely to remain nonpartisans or end up as nonidentifiers. For these middle-of-the-road Americans with few strong policy positions, there may not be sufficient motivation to make a partisan choice in the first place. An alternative extrapolation from the Downsian theory might be to adopt Albert O. Hirschman's critique of Hotelling (1929) and subsequent median voter accounts of duopolies. Specifically, Hirschman articulates "exit" and "voice" as alternatives to "loyalty" and thus alternatives to the view that "*the 'captive'*

*consumer (or voter) who has 'nowhere else to go' is the epitome of pow-
erlessness"* (1970, 70 [emphasis in original]).

These possibilities do not take us very far. The view that nonidentifiers
are ideological moderates is easily rebutted. In both the 2006 LNS and
the 2008 NAAS, there is a striking parallel between the high proportion
of Latinos and Asian Americans who do not identify as Democrats, Independents, or Republicans and the proportion who do not identify as liberals, moderates, or conservatives. In the 2006 LNS, 21 percent of respondents identify as conservatives, 13 percent as liberals, 17 percent as
moderates, and fully 49 percent indicate that they either do not know
how to place themselves in the traditional ideological spectrum or do not
think in ideological terms. Fully 69 percent of Latinos who refuse to identify as Democrats, Independents, or Republicans also refuse to identify as
liberals, moderates, or conservatives. Self-identified moderates make up
only 9 percent of Latino nonidentifiers. The companion figures in the
2008 NAAS are not quite as remarkable but make a clear case nonetheless. The basic distribution of ideological views is 13 percent conservative, 21 percent liberal, 32 percent moderate, and 34 percent nonideologi-
cal identifiers. Fully 55 percent of Asian Americans uncommitted to a
partisan identity are also uncommitted to an ideological identity; only 24
percent self-identify as moderates, with 12 and 9 percent identifying as
liberal and conservative, respectively.

Hirschman's account of exit from noncompetitive duopolies is more
promising because it specifies a mechanism through which individuals
can opt not to identify with either firm in the market—that is, it allows a
dissatisfied consumer to exit from a market altogether. This view of nonidentification as the exercise of an exit option, however, presumes preex-
isting preferences of the commodities produced by political parties in a
duopolistic marketplace. Most Asian Americans and Latinos—as foreign-
born and second-generation Americans—are relative newcomers to this
marketplace, and the stability of consumer preferences cannot easily be
presumed.

Thus, a missing element in the information- and market-based approach to explaining party identification is a prior account of how newcomers form preferences for partisan goods. Here, the reliance on political socialization in the Michigan School of party identification would
seem felicitous. From the standpoint of *The American Voter,* one might
think of nonidentifiers as those who fail to identify with a party by virtue
of their having been raised by parents who were also uncommitted and
apolitical, or in social and institutional settings that fostered inattention
to or disdain for party politics. This raises an interesting question about
whether nonidentification is a habit that is passed on from generation to
generation—a question that is not explicitly raised by advocates of the

Michigan School. But it still fails to account for nonidentification among foreign-born Latinos and Asian Americans. If the population in question is not politically socialized (especially in one's preadult years, according to *The American Voter*) in the United States, then socialization per se cannot explain the remarkably high proportion of nonidentifiers among Latinos and Asian Americans.

What is obviously absent from these traditional models is a consideration of the immigrant experience and its aftermath. As we noted in chapters 1 and 2, this is not prima facie the result of an explicit omission on the part of the Michigan and Downsian schools of thought, as these theories originated during a period of far lower rates of immigrant stocks and flows. If one's immigrant experience does have a bearing on one's status as uncommitted and unattached to either of the two parties, then we need to integrate key elements of this immigrant experience into any discussion of the party identification of Latinos and Asian Americans. More to the point, the argument we develop in this chapter is that the process of *immigrant political incorporation* is critical in understanding the partisan choices of immigrants and their offspring. In the next section, we begin the process of trying to understand what political incorporation is and in turn what it means for questions of party identification.

Immigrant Incorporation and Partisan Politics

We argue that the questions "what does it mean to be a partisan" and de Crèvecoeur's "what does it mean to be American" are deeply interconnected. What it means to be an American, politically, is identifying as a Democrat, Republican, or Independent. For the modal Latino and Asian American, this institutional attachment with and incorporation into American political life remains unformed. The attachments that immigrant-based ethnic communities such as Latinos and Asian Americans form, *or fail to form,* to a political party are an important and underexamined dimension of immigrant political incorporation.

We use the term "political incorporation" broadly to denote the process of successive stages of inclusion into arenas of democratic voice and choice—from the political freedoms conjured in the imaginary of a newcomer to America's shores to a literal seat at the table of a governing political coalition. This definition covers traditional measures of legal membership (citizenship), formal political participation (registration, voting, campaigning), and informal participation (volunteering, community problem solving). We also see it as covering direct inputs into decision-making and authorizing institutions (descriptive and substantive representation, legal recognition, bureaucratic capture).

Beyond the formal institutional dimensions of political incorporation, we are also keen to examine the extent to which political incorporation is reflected in an immigrant or second-generation American's subjective sense of membership. This sense of belonging, agency, and voice is, we posit, fostered access to basic knowledge concerning the political process, recognition of and attachment to the key issues and core ideological dimensions that delineate partisan politics in this nation, and the development of social and racial identities that can be linked to the available partisan options.

In explicitly defining a role for processes of institutional and attitudinal incorporation, we hope to expand upon the rich body of work—in large measure by sociologists—on the pathways that immigrants follow during their journey through successive lived experiences in their adopted nation. In general, in this corpus the main line dividing competing accounts is whether immigrants become fully absorbed into and included in their receiving contexts, whether they retain cherished aspects of their ethnic identities and cultural beliefs from their country of origin, or whether some hybrid of acculturation and ethnic resilience occurs. We briefly discuss each of these three primary theoretical variants on immigrant incorporation below.

STRAIGHT-LINE ASSIMILATION

The first of these variants is the "straight-line" assimilation model. This perspective is a process by which immigrants gradually and inexorably absorb the norms, values, and practices of the adopted society (Park 1926, Gordon 1964). In Robert Dahl's oft-cited account of political incorporation, the process of incorporation begins with the incentives presented to elites by the salience of ethnic identity for most immigrants. Thus Dahl observes in *Who Governs,* his study of Irish and Italian Americans in New Haven, that "the 'ethnic' . . . found that his ethnic identification colored his life, his relations with others, his attitudes toward himself and the world. . . . Any political leader who could help members of an ethnic group to overcome the handicaps and humiliations associated with their identity, who could increase the power, prestige, and income of an ethnic or religious out-group, automatically had an effective strategy for earning support and loyalty" (1961a, 33).

Dahl further notes that the short-term benefits of recruiting or pandering to these identitarian concerns have long-term costs, as subsequent generations who enjoy the fruits of full social, civic, economic, and political inclusion may be unresponsive. Thus Dahl concludes: "Ethnic politics . . . is clearly a transitional phenomenon. The very success of politicians who use the ethnic approach leads to the obsolescence of their strategy" (34). Under this view, the passage of time serves not only to lift the socioeconomic circumstances of new ethnic Americans but also to "normalize" their political priors to those of native-born (white) citizens. One implication of this normalization, in the political arena, is that partisanship should become more salient with the passage of time. Another implication is that Latinos and Asian Americans will, in the long run, begin to look a lot like white Americans in their partisan proclivities. Although most contemporary scholars find this linear model problematic, its vestiges remain in many empirical studies of the Latino and Asian American populations that tie partisanship acquisition and choice to time lived and generation in the United States (Cain et al. 1991; Cho 1999; Wong 2000; Welch and Sigelman 1993; Uhlaner and García 2005; de la Garza et al. 1992).

A slightly more nuanced version of this assimilationist model identifies a specific mechanism through which ethnic interests become less effective as a means for party elites to recruit and mobilize electoral support. A close reading of *Who Governs* thus finds that, in Dahl's view, it is the presumed homogeneity of class interests in the immigrant first generation that enables ethnicity to become a focal point for organizing and activating politics. Once class interests within an ethnic community become heterogeneous with the upward mobility of second- and third-generation immigrants, the salience of ethnicity recedes. This heterogeneity and upward mobility is the mechanism that is hypothesized in the sociological literature on how the ethnic identities of previous generations of immigrants have receded into the twilight (Alba and Nee 2003, Waters 1990). It is also the basis for more controversial debates over whether the rise of a black middle class in the twentieth century has led to a decline in the significance of race as a foundation for the politics of African Americans in the post–civil rights era (Wilson 1978; Thernstrom and Thernstrom 1997; Dawson 1994; Shelby 2005). Class, too, has found its way into recent empirical studies of the Latino and Asian American populations, but here findings about its relationship to partisanship are more mixed (Welch and Sigelman 1993; Kosmin and Keysar 1995; Cain et al. 1991; York 1999; Alvarez and García Bedolla 2003).

Ethnic Resilience

A second, separate view on immigrant incorporation is that ethnicity does not fade in a linear way across generations. Rather, it is a resilient and persistent factor in the lives and politics of newer immigrant-based groups such as Latinos and Asian Americans. In this "ethnic resilience" model (see, e.g., Portes and Bach 1985; de la Garza and DeSipio 1999), we can expect an awareness of discrimination and barriers to full inclusion to grow with the third and subsequent generations, rather than melt away into the color-blind experience of unhyphenated Americans. Under this racialized or ethnic view of incorporation, the passage of time and the accretion of information and experiences serve to further "marginalize" new ethnic immigrant groups such as Latinos and Asian Americans and remind them of their station in American life.[7] The effect of this continued "minority group status" will presumably be the alignment of the political interests of Latinos and Asian Americans with those of Democrats to the extent that the Democratic Party is perceived to advocate more vigorously on behalf of racial and ethnic minorities.

SEGMENTED ASSIMILATION

A third variant of assimilation sees the incorporation of immigrants as a contingent outcome. This "segmented assimilation" model maintains that the process of incorporation is a "bumpy" one, with multiple pathways that depend on the specific opportunities and contexts that individual immigrants face (Zhou 1997; Gans 1992; Portes and Rumbaut 1996). Some immigrants will find avenues to economic advancement and will be given opportunities to obtain key markers of mainstream status. Other immigrants will find these pathways blocked and will come to view themselves as racialized minorities. The pathways that immigrants and their offspring travel are contingent on any number of factors from spatial contexts (Massey 1995; Portes and Zhou 1993) to family socioeconomic origins (Portes 1995) to social interaction and the degree of ethnic isolation that defines an immigrant's surroundings (Zhou and Logan 1991).

POLITICAL INCORPORATION AND THE DIMENSIONS OF INFORMATION, IDEOLOGY, AND IDENTITY

In our analysis, we view information, ideology, and identity as capturing relevant dimensions of the process of immigrant incorporation into American society and potentially in politics. We hope to add a deeper understanding of the factors that are particularly important in guiding *partisan* incorporation. The literature offers reasonably complete ac-

---

[7] In the case of Mexican Americans, competing accounts have emerged on whether the basis for the maintenance of ethnic identity is persistent anti-Latino discrimination and minority-group status well into the third generation and beyond or whether it is the result of the replenishment of new immigrants and, consequently, the maintenance of social ties and networks across generations of Mexican Americans (Jiménez 2008; Telles and Ortiz 2008).

counts of how and why immigrants and their offspring take different pathways in the economic and social spheres. We continue, however, to have an inadequate sense of how and why members of the Latino and Asian American populations travel at different paces to different destinations along the route from their status as nonidentifiers to full-fledged partisan loyalists; similarly, we have sparse knowledge of why they choose one party over the other, if and when they establish a partisan attachment.

To understand the political arena, we first borrow from sociology. As we have noted, the sociological literature is replete with studies that highlight different factors integral to the incorporation of immigrants. First among these are the "straight-line" assimilation factors of time spent in the United States and socioeconomic advancement. In addition, sociologists have focused on the friendship networks, organizational ties, and various other modes of civic engagement. These modes of social interaction are likely to have an effect on immigrants' information environment, ideological assimilation, and identity formation.

Beyond these sociological factors, we also stress the centrality of more explicitly political factors that shape political incorporation. Here we see two key dimensions of incorporation and two key sets of measures of incorporation. The first is the degree to which newcomers are formally included or excluded by a receiving society's social, economic, and political *institutions*. In the realm of political incorporation, the primary focus here will be on institutions, laws, and policies—among other things, naturalization laws, electoral rules, multicultural policies, and political markets (especially the degree of local and national party competition).

The second dimension aims to capture the varying degrees of agency held by individuals in a political system. Even if institutions, laws, and policies opened their arms far and wide, Latinos and Asian Americans might not to be well incorporated if they did not feel a sense of belonging in the political sphere. There are unequal degrees in the "socially authorized and encouraged sense of being entitled to be concerned with politics, authorized to talk politics" (Bourdieu 1984, 409). The spectrum here might be described as ranging from a sense of alterity (or "otherness") to feeling fully authorized to be political. For Latinos and Asian Americans, the degrees of social authorization are likely to vary depending on their immigrant socialization and racial and ethnic minority status.[8] The point

---

[8] The two groups we examine in this chapter may be particularly given to a sense of political "otherness," which may explain their reluctance to self-identify with a party or with the two-party system. For Latinos, there is the history of conquest and colonization (for Latinos of Mexican and Puerto Rican descent) and the present reality of the public's exaggerated perceptions about the prevalence of illegal immigration and the degree to which undocumented entrants to the United States are an exclusively Latino phenomenon. For

here is that even if the Democratic and Republican parties were clamoring for the attention of Latinos and Asian Americans (and there is plenty of evidence that they are not), we are not likely to see a great deal of partisan activity without their having some sense of agency and authorship over their political fates.

This is a realm of attitudinal acculturation in which we continue to believe that our two key indicators of political predispositions (ideology and identity) and the one additional key indicator of political awareness (information) will be crucial. To have a sense of voice and agency as a political actor in the American partisan system requires the tools to decipher how politics is discussed and defined in the United States. To this end, immigrants' ability to place themselves along the traditional American *ideological* spectrum from fervent liberals to ardent conservatives is likely to influence not only how these political newcomers place themselves on issues, but also whether they deem politics to be a civic activity worth pursuing. As we have already intimated, a large proportion of Latinos and Asian Americans simply do not place themselves on this spectrum. Yet as we shall see, for those who do, this ideological predisposition will strongly shape their decision to identify with a partisan category or remain uncommitted and define the category to which they attach themselves.

There are two aspects to the effect of ideology. The direct effect acts on those Latinos and Asian Americans who are able to place themselves along the liberal-to-conservative spectrum. The indirect effect acts on those who fall outside this ideological spectrum. Immigrants and their offspring will often have distinct issue concerns that are apt to garner limited attention from the major parties and mainstream media outlets. Issues such as Puerto Rican statehood, regionalism in Mexico, Korean reunification, and the ongoing dialectics of China's continuing conflicts with Taiwan might matter intensely to Latino and Asian American subgroups but rarely attract commensurate attention in partisan political discourse. To the extent that immigrants and their offspring remain attached to these orthogonal issues, their incentives to identity with and invest in a partisan attachment will be limited.

As we noted earlier, we further believe that for racially and ethnically defined minorities, *identity* is another key predisposition that may help to shape partisan choices. Group consciousness, as we see it, is neither inevitable nor inevitably important. For some, race will have little significance, but for others, experiences in America will establish a link between their own life chances and the status of the larger group and will awaken a

---

Asian Americans, there is a similarly long history of treatment as "perpetual foreigners" and a "yellow peril" that extends into the present day with incidents such as the 1996 campaign finance controversy, in which legal contributions from citizens and permanent residents of Asian background were framed in media coverage as influence buying by foreign interests.

strong racial identity. The presence of in-group solidarity, out-group differentiation, and intergroup conflicts should help raise the salience of politics as a forum in which collective interests are pursued and intergroup conflicts might be mediated. Thus, strong racial identification will potentially help define partisanship for Latinos and Asian Americans. Given that racial policy questions often delineate the two parties and given the Democratic Party's clear association with what is widely perceived to be a "prominority" policy agenda, we further expect that experiences with racial discrimination, a strong sense of racially linked fates, and political commonality will lead to greater Democratic allegiance and diminished nonpartisanship (Carmines and Stimson 1989; Lee 2002; Edsall and Edsall 1992).

Finally, predispositions—whether ideological or identitarian—are either crystallized or fade into insignificance, depending on relevant *information* about the political arena and the partisan choices that are available to the American public. Immigrants are apt to arrive with the barest of knowledge of the American political system. Until they are able to update their priors on what U.S politics is, why it matters, and how parties represent (or fail to represent) their interests, they have little incentive to travel along the partisan pathway and many reasons to remain uncommitted to either party. Information is critical here because it clarifies choices, encourages efficacy (it is difficult to believe our choices matter until we have witnessed some measure of responsiveness from the system), enables trust (it is difficult to trust that which we do not know), and facilitates participation in a complex, multilevel political system. Thus, we expect information to be a key factor in the partisanship patterns for Latinos and Asian Americans. Latinos and Asian Americans who remain less familiar with U.S. parties and the political system or who have not seen enough to trust the system will be more likely to remain nonidentifiers.

RESEARCH PLAN AND DATA DESCRIPTION

In the coming pages, we present evidence in support of our account of Latino and Asian American partisanship in several stages. In the remainder of this chapter, we offer some basic tables that illustrate the first-order relationships between Latino and Asian American partisanship on one hand and a range of different factors highlighted by the literature and our own account on the other. These simple, bivariate tests indicate that traditional explanations of partisanship only weakly predict Latino and Asian American partisanship, whereas factors related to political incorporation and, in particular, measures of information, identity, and ideology tend to be strongly linked to the partisan status of both populations.

In the next chapter, we test these conclusions more systematically, using a multivariate model that incorporates each perspective simultaneously.

This account of party identification is examined using data from the primary political surveys of the groups in question—the 2006 Latino National Survey (Fraga et al. 2006) and the 2008 National Asian American Survey (Wong et al. 2009). The 2006 Latino National Survey (LNS) completed 8,634 telephone interviews of self-identified Latinos/Hispanics between November 17, 2005, and August 4, 2006. Of this sample, 5,704 respondents were Mexican, 822 were Puerto Rican, 420 were Cuban, 407 were Salvadoran, 335 were Dominican, 333 were Central American, and the remaining 613 belonged to some other Latino ancestry.[9] The 2008 National Asian American Survey (NAAS) included 5,159 telephone interviews of self-identified Asian Americans between August 18 and October 29, 2009. Of this sample, 1,350 respondents were self-identified Chinese, 1,150 were Asian Indian, 719 were Vietnamese, 614 were Korean, 603 were Filipino, 541 were Japanese, and 182 identified with some other ethnic ancestry or national origin group.[10]

DESCRIPTIVE PATTERNS OF PARTY IDENTIFICATION

We first describe the general distribution of party identification across different subsets of the Latino and Asian American populations. Our aim here is to see how well our expectations stand up to a rough cut of the data. Unadorned cross-tabulations, when carefully matched to sound reasoning and coherent theorizing, are often remarkably robust compared with fancier statistical modeling. So we check here to see if our data push us past this important first post. Specifically, we compare indicators of straight-line assimilation with alternative dimensions of political incorporation.

Our four categories of party identification are self-identification as a Democrat, as a Republican, and as an Independent or identification with none of these conventional forms of identification. In the analysis, the nonidentifiers' category is a combination of residual nonpartisan catego-

---

[9] The stratified sample was drawn from fifteen states and the District of Columbia metropolitan area and was designed to be fully representative of each state/metro area's Latino population. The target population for the LNS covers 87.5 percent of the total U.S. Latino population. Fully 62 percent of respondents chose to be interviewed in Spanish.

[10] The NAAS sample was drawn from an extensive ethnic name list (matched to first name and surname). There is an oversample of respondents from California, the New York/New Jersey metropolitan area, and metropolitan areas that represent "new destinations" for Asian American immigrants. Interviews were conducted in English and seven non-English languages (Cantonese, Mandarin, Hindi, Japanese, Korean, Tagalog, and Vietnamese); 40 percent of our sample opted for a non-English-language interview.

TABLE 5.5
Partisanship by Longevity and Generation in the United States

	1–8 yrs	9–16 yrs	17–26 yrs	27 + yrs	Foreign-born	2nd gen
2006 LNS						
Republican	5.1%	6.5%	11.1%	15.4%	8.1%	13.7%
Democrat	17.3	25.4	32.3	45.8	26.1	45.0
Independent	21.5	19.2	18.5	13.9	19.1	15.4
Nonidentifier	56.1	49.0	38.2	25.0	37.9	26.0

	1–12 yrs	13–20 yrs	21–29 yrs	30 + yrs	Foreign born	2nd gen
2008 NAAS						
Republican	4.6	13.2	16.1	18.5	11.7	14.7
Democrat	23.8	30.7	26.9	36.8	28.7	39.6
Independent	21.2	19.6	23.2	17.0	20.3	22.4
Nonidentifier	50.4	36.5	33.8	27.8	39.4	23.3

Cell entries are column percentages.

ries that included "don't care," "don't know," and "other party" in the 2006 LNS and those who chose "do not think in these terms" or "not sure" or refused to answer the question in the 2008 NAAS. We start with key measures of social incorporation. Existing studies of Latinos and Asian Americans highlight the role that lived experience in the United States plays in structuring partisan attachments (Bowler et al. 2006; De-Sipio 1995; Cho 1999; Pantoja et al. 2001; Wong 2000).

Table 5.5 shows the distribution of the four partisanship categories by the number of years lived in the United States among immigrants and also between immigrants and second-generation Latinos and Asian Americans. The number of years in the United States among immigrants is grouped into rough quartiles.[11] This preliminary table broadly supports the straight-line assimilation model. For both Latinos and Asian Americans, time lived in the United States translates into a greater likelihood of having partisan attachments. Latino immigrants who have lived here for 27 years or longer, for example, are more than half as likely to be uncommitted about their partisanship than are their counterparts who have lived here for 8 years or less (25 percent versus 56 percent). The effect of length of time lived in the United States for Asian Americans is almost as pro-

[11] For the LNS, the quartiles are divided roughly into Latino immigrants who have lived in the United States for 8 years or less, between 9 and 16 years, 17 and 26 years, and 27 years and longer; for the NAAS, the quartiles split the sample between Asian immigrants who have lived in the United States for 12 years or less, between 13 and 20 years, 21 and 29 years, and 30 years and longer.

nounced: more than 50 percent of Asian Americans who have lived in the United States for 12 years or less do not identify as Republicans, Democrats, or Independents; only about 28 percent of those who have lived in the United States for 30 years or longer are similarly uncommitted.[12]

Our initial analysis of partisanship by longevity and generation confirms the general expectation of a straight-line assimilationist account. Earlier we also described a more nuanced version whereby immigrant incorporation would follow from class mobility. In table 5.6, we begin to test this alternative version by focusing on the partisanship of high- and low-income and high- and low-education respondents.[13]

The results suggest that class gains are related to partisan incorporation. For both Latinos and Asian Americans, high-class status (in the form of either greater education or higher income) is associated with declines in the nonidentifier category. Latinos at the highest levels of family income and education attainment are roughly three times less likely to remain uncommitted in partisan terms. For Asian Americans, the ratio is closer to twofold. As table 5.6 shows, most of this decline is parlayed into a greater likelihood of identifying either as a Democrat or as a Republican (and not identifying as an Independent, with the lone exception of an increase in self-identified Independents among the most highly educated Asian Americans).[14]

Tables 5.5 and 5.6 show that the traditional markers of immigrant assimilation—length of time in one's new country and socioeconomic advancement—help to define whether Latinos and Asian Americans commit to a partisan category or remain as nonidentifiers. What about the role of political factors? For many scholars of American politics, partisan choices are, at their heart, about issue positions and ideology. We choose the party closest to our views on the main liberal-conservative divide that separates the two parties. Thus, liberals should identify as Democrats, Republicans should end up with ties to the Republican Party, and moder-

---

[12] Table 5.5 also shows that for Latinos time lived in the United States benefits the Democratic Party more than it does the Republican Party, whereas for Asian Americans the gains are roughly equal.

[13] For the 2006 LNS, the cutoff points for low and high income are respondents making a household income below $15,000 a year and above $65,000 a year; for low and high educational attainment, these cutoffs are respondents with an eighth-grade education or below and a graduate or professional degree. For the 2008 NAAS, the equivalent cutoffs are between respondents making a household income below $20,000 and those making above $150,000; for low and high educational attainment, they are between respondents with only some high school education and those with an advanced graduate or professional degree.

[14] Importantly, as table 5.6 indicates, class gains do not appear to be associated with a clear shift to the Republican Party for either Latinos or Asian Americans. The two parties benefit roughly equally from class gains.

TABLE 5.6
Partisanship by Socioeconomic Status

	Low income	High income	Low education	High education
2006 LNS				
Republican	6.1%	20.3%	5.7%	14.5%
Democrat	28.1	46.5	21.7	48.3
Independent	20.4	18.5	18.3	18.7
Nonidentifier	45.5	14.8	54.2	18.5
2008 NAAS				
Republican	11.9	20.2	10.8	9.4
Democrat	30.3	38.7	25.8	35.1
Independent	18.4	21.7	11.4	26.1
Nonidentifier	39.5	19.4	52.0	29.3

Cell entries are column percentages.

ates should choose Independence or perhaps remain uncommitted. Is this account of American politics true for the two groups we examine in this chapter?

Table 5.7 examines this question by dividing Latinos and Asian Americans into four groups: those who self-identify as liberal, moderates, or conservatives and those who reject any of these conventional categories of ideological self-identification. The table shows very mixed support for the claim that partisanship is anchored by ideology. For both Latinos and Asian Americans, roughly a majority of liberals self-identify as Democrats (51 percent in the LNS and 50 percent in the NAAS). Also, for both groups, a majority of those uncommitted to a partisan category refuse to identify with an ideological category: 54 percent of the uncommitted are "ideological nonidentifiers" in the LNS, and this figure is 58 percent in the NAAS.

At the same time, identifying as a moderate or conservative has no clear bearing on one's partisanship. The modal Latino and Asian American moderate self-identifies as a *Democrat* (43 percent in the LNS, 33 percent in the NAAS), not as an Independent or uncommitted. Similarly, self-identifying conservatives are not especially likely to ally with the Republican Party. Among Latino respondents in the LNS, only 22 percent of conservatives self-identify as Republicans, with 34 percent identifying as *Democrats* and the remaining 44 percent either identifying as Independents or remaining uncommitted in partisan terms. Similarly, among Asian Americans in the NAAS, 31 percent self-identify as Republican, 25

TABLE 5.7
Partisanship by Ideology

	Liberal	Moderate	Conservative	Nonidentifier
2006 LNS				
Republican	7.9%	11.5%	21.5%	6.1%
Democrat	51.2	42.5	34.4	26.4
Independent	23.1	25.6	17.1	13.6
Nonidentifier	17.9	20.4	27.1	54.0%
2008 NAAS				
Republican	9.7	11.7	31.2	6.3
Democrat	49.7	32.8	25.1	20.2
Independent	20.2	28.0	18.4	15.4
Nonidentifier	20.3	27.5	25.4	58.1

Cell entries are column percentages.

percent identify as Democrats, and an identical 44 percent identify as Independents or are uncommitted.[15]

So far, we can understand some of what is going on with Latino and Asian American partisanship using conventional markers of socioeconomic status, linear time in the United States, and ideology. Beyond these factors, we are also interested in the extent to which other factors help to explain patterns of partisanship. Previously, we noted that scholars generally focus on the three key stages of formal political incorporation at the individual level: whether immigrants have naturalized as citizens of the United States, whether they have registered to vote, and whether they vote. We also already described the basic patterns of Latinos and Asian Americans on these measures based on the 2004 American Community Survey: compared with both whites and African Americans, Latinos and Asian Americans are both woefully "underincorporated" at each stage of the process. Do patterns of partisanship then also change across these stages of political incorporation? The next table offers some revealing clues to this question.

First, citizenship does not appear to significantly change patterns of partisanship. We see this by comparing the distribution of partisanship for noncitizens with that for citizens who are not registered to vote. For

---

[15] One final way to make this point is to treat partisanship and ideology in the conventional way—uncommitteds and nonidentifiers as nonvalid responses—and create sevenpoint scales that can be correlated with one another. Even in this case, the pairwise correlation is positive but relatively smaller (0.24 for the LNS and 0.23 for the NAAS). By comparison, in figure 2.5 we saw that the correlation of partisanship and ideology in the ANES is typically around 0.50.

TABLE 5.8
Partisanship by Citizenship and Registration Status

	Noncitizen	Citizen, not registered	Registered to vote	Voted in last election*
2006 LNS				
Democratic	21.1%	27.8%	50.5%	53.1%
Republican	4.9	9.7	16.8	18.0
Independent	19.8	17.2	15.3	14.0
Nonidentifier	54.2	45.3	23.5	14.9
2008 LNS				
Democratic	26.3	24.9	36.0	38.6
Republican	5.6	10.1	17.1	16.6
Independent	19.5	24.4	20.9	21.3
Nonidentifier	48.6	40.6	26.1	23.7

*Figures represent self-reported voting behavior in the 2004 elections.

both Latino and Asian American respondents, the rank order is exactly the same between noncitizens and unregistered citizens: the greatest number are nonidentifiers, followed by Democrats, Independents, and, last, Republicans. The one shift that is consistent between the two groups here is that the proportion of nonidentifiers falls modestly between noncitizens and unregistered citizens (from 54 percent to 45 percent in the LNS; from 49 percent to 41 percent in the NAAS).

The far more dramatic effect occurs with the act of registering to vote and voting itself. In the LNS, the proportion of nonidentifiers drops from 45 percent among unregistered citizens to 24 percent among registered citizens; in the NAAS, this drop is from 41 percent to 26 percent. With both Latinos and Asians, there is a moderate increase in the proportion of self-identified Republicans (from 10 percent to 17 percent in both the LNS and the NAAS), and a relatively bigger increase in the proportion of self-identified Democrats (from 28 percent to 51 percent in the LNS and from 25 percent to 36 percent in the NAAS). This distribution in partisanship among those Latinos and Asian Americans registered to vote, moreover, looks very similar to that for voters themselves, as table 5.8 shows.

One fair objection to inferring too much from these figures is that many states allow individuals to identify a party affiliation when they register to vote. Thus, the close correspondence between partisanship and voter registration may reveal little more than a tautology. Indeed, almost 80 percent of Latinos and Asian Americans in both surveys who are registered to vote indicated that they are registered as Democrats, Republicans, or Independents/nonpartisans. Moreover, in the LNS, 86 percent of self-identified Democrats are registered as Democrats, and 80 percent of self-identified Republicans are registered as Republicans. Similarly, in the NAAS, the percentage of respondents whose party identification matches their voter registration is 84 for Democrats and 81 for Republicans.

Whether or not partisanship is determined before one registers to vote and turns out on Election Day, these acts represent clear institutional moors that help tie down Latinos and Asian Americans to political parties in the United States. Beyond these formal electoral institutions, we also consider the role of other institutional influences (in particular, institutions within civil society such as churches and community organizations) and the racial group identities that Latinos and Asian Americans form as additional influences on their partisanship. These factors appear to move only modestly with the distribution of party identification at the bivariate level and, as we shall see in chapter 6, yield mixed results in multivariate analyses.

One other factor that appears unambiguously to sharpen the partisan focus of Latinos and Asian Americans is information. As we argued earlier, because Latinos and Asian Americans are predominantly immigrants or their offspring, a common base of knowledge about and attentiveness to politics cannot be assumed. In the absence of familiarity with what parties have to offer, it is entirely reasonable for these groups to maintain a skeptical stance toward partisanship and withhold judgment. Table 5.9 shows this effect on two measures: (1) perception of differences between the two parties and (2) the groups' general level of political interest.[16]

The results here are unambiguous: with both attentiveness and perceived differences between the parties, respondents' likelihood of identifying as a Democrat or Republican increases sharply, and their likelihood of remaining uncommitted falls equally dramatically. Roughly one in two Latinos and Asian Americans who fail to see differences between the parties, do not possess basic knowledge about the parties, or are generally inattentive to politics are nonidentifiers in partisan terms. Among those with high levels of information and attentiveness, this proportion diminishes to roughly one in five. Among the highly informed and attentive, the proportion who identify as Democrats or Republicans roughly doubles, with the highest preponderance among self-

---

[16] The measures of political interest in the LNS and NAAS are identical, but we use different measures to look into perceptions of party differences. In the LNS, this perception is measured indirectly by asking respondents about their basic knowledge of party politics—specifically, which party was in control at the time in the House of Representatives and which presidential candidate in 2004 garnered the highest number of votes in the respondent's state.

TABLE 5.9
Distribution of Partisanship by Political Information

	Perceived party differences		General political attentiveness	
	Low	High	No	Yes
2006 LNS				
Democratic	22.0%	46.1%	22.2%	46.6%
Republican	4.6	22.1	7.1	17.6
Independent	16.9	18.5	13.6	15.9
Nonidentifier	56.5	13.2	57.2	20.0
2008 NAAS				
Democratic	23.9	38.8	19.1	38.2
Republican	8.7	15.2	8.5	15.7
Independent	18.7	23.5	17.0	26.5
Nonidentifier	48.7	22.5	55.4	19.6

identified Democrats (between 38 percent and 47 percent, depending on the measure and the group in question).

Finally, our account also details the role of identity. Although we do not expect all members of these two groups to become racialized, we argue that recognizing the importance of race and developing a strong racial or panethnic identity should create the motivation for party ties (primarily Democratic ones) among subsets of the Latino and Asian American populations. The role that racial identity plays in altering the contours of both groups' partisan positions is displayed in table 5.10.

The main conclusion to draw from the table is that identity does help to shape Latino and Asian American partisan choices. Perceiving discrimination and feeling a sense of linked fate with other members of their panethnic group affect their partisan status to one degree or another. The strength of the pattern varies from question to question and from group to group, but generally speaking a stronger sense of racial identity is linked to diminished nonidentification and greater attachment to the Democratic Party. For example, Latinos who perceive a lot of discrimination are more than twice as likely to identify as Democrats than those who perceive little discrimination (47 percent versus 22 percent). Among Asian Americans, the strongest relationship is with the linked-fate question. Among Asians who have little sense of a linked fate, nonidentifiers (44 percent) greatly outnumber those who have ties to the Democratic Party (31 percent). By contrast, among Asian Americans who believe that their own well-being is connected to the fate of the larger Asian American

TABLE 5.10
Distribution of Partisanship by Racial Identity

	Experienced discrimination		Panethnic linked fate	
	Low	High	Low	High
2006 LNS				
Democratic	21.6%	47.3%	39.9%	47.3%
Republican	51.6	23.1	27.1	23.1
Independent	10.1	11.3	14.4	11.3
Nonidentifier	16.7	18.3	18.6	18.3
2008 LNS				
Democratic	31.0	47.0	30.5	47.0
Republican	14.5	18.2	13.6	18.2
Independent	13.3	10.6	12.4	10.6
Nonidentifier	41.2	24.2	43.5	24.2

population, the reverse is true—Democrats greatly outnumber nonidenti-fiers (47 percent versus 24 percent). For these two groups, partisanship is not simply about class or ideology or even institutions and information. It is also very much about race and identity.

CONCLUSION

In this chapter, we have begun to dissect in earnest the theoretical and empirical implications of the growing diversity of the American body politic. This investigation has entailed extended discussions of the exist-ing data (or the insufficiencies thereof) on Latinos and Asian Americans and the existing literatures on immigrant political incorporation and on the partisanship of Latinos and Asian Americans. We have advanced the position that the question of Latino and Asian American partisanship should be viewed together with the question of Latino and Asian Ameri-can political incorporation, and vice versa. In short, we view the question "What does it mean to be partisan?" and de Crèvecoeur's "What does it mean to be an American?" as close cousins. To understand whether and why Latinos and Asian Americans come to hold a view of political parties in the United States is to understand whether and why Latinos and Asian Americans come to feel included, at the institutional level, and autho-rized, at the individual level, to do the work of politics. We spent some time in this chapter detailing the implications of this view vis-à-vis our general argument about the role of identity, ideology, and information in shaping (non)partisanship.

We then concluded the chapter by examining, descriptively, the rough fit between our general discussion of Latino and Asian American partisanship and the best available data. We found, for example, that longevity in the United States, generation, socioeconomic status covary quite noticeably with the patterns of partisanship among Latinos and Asian Americans. These results, taken together, present a portrait of Latino and Asian American partisanship that is broadly consistent with past research on "straight-line" and "segmented" immigrant assimilation. This should come as no surprise, given the dominance and durability of these accounts.

A few additions and qualifications are less common but crucial nonetheless. First, to the immigrant assimilation literature, we add the important role that political institutions and political information play in forming partisan attachments. Partisanship is not just a new social norm or civic practice that immigrants acquire independent of politics. Second, to the party identification literature, we add the critical importance of understanding the absence of any partisan commitments in its own right, rather than treating nonidentifiers as a residual outcome. We also add the potentially mixed influence of ideology on partisanship. Finally, to the often disconnected literatures on Asian American and Latino politics, we add the timely reminder that the process by which these groups come to acquire partisan habits may share more than they hold distinct. In a surprising number of instances, the distribution of partisanship across key factors for Latinos and Asian Americans is strikingly similar in both groups.

These claims are, of course, only propositional, given the preliminary nature of our analysis thus far. To further refine and more rigorously test our views on Latino and Asian American party identification, we turn to a multivariate analysis of our sequential account of party identification in chapter 6.

The Sequential Logic of Latino and Asian American Partisanship

> The Chinese do not desire to become citizens of this country, and have no knowledge or appreciation of our institutions. . . . To admit these vast numbers of aliens to citizenship and the ballot would practically destroy republican institutions on the Pacific coast, for the Chinese have no comprehension of any form of government but despotism, and have not the words in their own language to describe intelligibly the principles of our representative system.
>
> —1877 Report of the Joint Special Committee to Investigate Chinese Immigration

> Yes, it's true. Because most of our compatriots have the same experience . . . that the state has been inefficient and irresponsible, and it hasn't responded to the demands of its people. . . . So they come here and they say "I'm not going to get involved in politics [*no voy a vivir lo politico*—literally, "I'm not going to live the political"].
>
> —Anonymous

AS WE LEARNED in the last chapter, the partisan choices of Latinos and Asian Americans are, in important ways, different from those of whites and blacks in America. Not only are Latinos and Asian Americans particularly unlikely to identify with the Democratic or Republican Party, they are also especially prone to expressing uncertainty and ambivalence about all of the available partisan options. The prevalence of uncommitted nonidentifiers in both groups sets them apart. Conventional explanations of party identification do help to account for at least some of these patterns. But the accounting is far from complete. Our initial foray into Latino and Asian American partisan choices also pointed to the important role incorporation played. The partisan patterns that we saw in chapter 5 appear to reflect the role of information acquisition, racial identity formation, and other factors related to the contingent process of immigrant adaptation. In this chapter we investigate, in a more systematic way, how each of these elements affects the party identification of

Latinos and Asian Americans. Our goal is to develop and test a more complete model of partisanship that simultaneously considers each of these possible explanations.

FROM NONPARTISAN THINKING TO PARTISAN CHOICE: MODELING PARTY IDENTIFICATION

How, then, do Latinos and Asian Americans choose different partisan and nonpartisan options? In chapter 5 we noted that the modal response among these Americans to the standard party-identification question is nonidentification. We believe that the widespread preference for this residual category implies a sequential process to partisan choice. We suggest that the process of partisanship acquisition follows two steps: one in which a political newcomer comes to see the triad of Democrat-Independent-Republican as a meaningful choice, and a second in which one of these categories is actively chosen.

This sequential logic is ignored in most statistical approaches to modeling party identification. The most common approach, as we mentioned in chapter 1, is to simply place the different categories of party identification side by side in a spectrum that ranges from strong identification with the Democratic Party on one end, with Independents in the middle, and strong identification with the Republican Party on the other end. Under this common practice, the "residual" categories of nonpartisanship that we have been considering in the context of Latino and Asian American partisanship—"don't know," "not sure," "refused," and so on—are treated as missing values and excluded from the statistical analyses. Multivariate tests then usually deploy least squares regression or an ordered, polychotomous choice (probit or logit) regression.

These types of estimators, however, all assume that partisan choices are neatly ordered along a singular continuum—an assumption that we have repeatedly questioned. For example, are all those who claim to be Independent really "in the middle" between Democrats and Republicans? A more recent and more careful line of scholarship has begun to model partisanship in an unordered fashion (Alvarez and García Bedolla 2003, Uhlaner and García 2005, Lien et al. 2004). The estimator that most of these scholars use and that we employ in other analyses in this book is multinomial logit. This type of estimator allows analysts to capture the effect of each independent variable on each pairwise combination among possible party-identification categories without assuming any ordering to the choices (see Aldrich and Nelson 1984, S. Greene 2000).

But the problem with even this latter option is that respondents who opt not to identify with a partisan category—by indicating that they "don't know," are "not sure," or "do not think" in partisan terms or who simply refuse to answer the question—are treated as missing values. There is a long and contested methodological debate over how to deal with "missing data." A typical approach is to simply exclude these respondents from the statistical analyses, but the wisdom of this depends on whether the cases are "missing completely at random," "missing at random," or "missing not at random." The fact that these omitted cases represent the plurality of the Asian American and Latino populations in itself indicates nonrandomness in these missing observations. Moreover, simply imputing answers where they were not given—whether by mean, deterministic regression, hot deck, or multiple imputation—is unlikely to lend empirical verisimilitude to such a high-incidence phenomenon.

As we noted earlier, in the case of party identification for immigration-based groups such as Latinos and Asian Americans, we believe that the choice not to self-identify as Democrat, Republican, or Independent is meaningful and not random. Specifically, we posit that these "noncompliant" responses represent a choice in the first of a two-stage process of coming to terms with two-party competition in the United States. Before they can place themselves at a point somewhere along the traditional partisan spectrum, political actors must begin to see meaning, content, or value in the partisan options that are typically offered. Only after passing through this stage can individuals engage in the second stage, where they choose between the three unordered options of Independent, Democrat, and Republican. This sequential logic is ignored in most statistical approaches to modeling party identification.

To help understand these distinctions, we present the four partisan choices graphically in figure 6.1. Schematically, there are three possible ways in which the choice of partisanship can be represented. The first decision tree, 6.1a, presents all four categories of partisanship as a simultaneous choice. This model mirrors most of the existing studies of the party identification of Latinos and Asian Americans (and of party identification writ large) and implicitly adopts a limited case in which two conditions are met: (1) the branch leading to residual categories of nonpartisanship are truncated as "missing values" for the purposes of analysis; (2) the remaining three categories are ordered in a linear fashion from "Democrat" on one end of the spectrum to "Republican" on the other, and "Independent" in the middle. An alternative rendering of the simultaneous model would be one in which all four categories are taken together, but the idea of simultaneously choosing between six pairwise trade-offs, including odd couplings such as refusing to answer the question or identifying as a Republican, independent of all other alternatives,

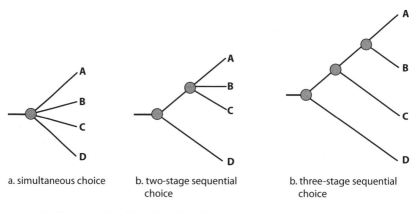

a. simultaneous choice   b. two-stage sequential   b. three-stage sequential
                              choice   choice

A = "Democrat," **B** = "Republican," **C** = "Independent," and **D** = "apartisanship"

Figure 6.1. Simultaneous and sequential models of partisan choice

makes this an unattractive approach to modeling Latinos' and Asian Americans' partisan choices.[1] This representation, we suggest, misses the sequenced nature of partisan choice, where the partisan thinking and, more broadly, the sense of authorization and authorship over the political realm is prior to the actual choice of identifying with a major party or identifying as an Independent.

That is, we think the actual process by which Latinos and Asian Americans come to terms with their partisanship in the U.S. context is better represented by figures 6.1b and 6.1c. The second decision tree, 6.1b, depicts a first stage where individuals either think in partisan terms or do not. Those who do not think in partisan terms opt to remain uncommitted. Among those who are able to make a meaningful choice between the three primary response categories, the second stage is represented as an unordered choice (with pairwise trade-offs between "Democrat," "Independent," and "Republican"). Finally, a third decision tree is to represent partisan choice in the three stages shown in figure 6.1c. The first step, as in figure 6.1b, is deciding whether the triad of choice categories is meaningful or not. Next, respondents decide whether to identify with a major

---

[1] Another reason it is unwise to simply add residual categories of nonpartisanship together with the choice between "Democrat," "Independent," and "Republican," in a conventional multinomial logit model with a combination of eight pairwise choices, is that the model presumes what is called the "independent of irrelevant alternatives" (IIA). It is, however, quite possible that the distribution of Independents, Democrats, and Republicans within the Latino and Asian American populations will differ depending on whether the category of nonidentification is an available option.

party or not. Finally, in figure 6.1c, respondents choose to identify either as Democrats or as Republicans.

Figure 6.1, if you will, presents us with three different ways to think about our dependent variable—each of which comes with a very specific implication about what kind of statistical estimation is appropriate. We are firm in our view that partisan choice for Latinos and Asian Americans is not simultaneous, as shown in figure 6.1a, but more agnostic between the two sequential models shown in figures 6.1b and 6.1c, since on conceptual grounds, a simultaneous choice between "Democrat," "Republican," and "Independent" strikes us as similarly plausible for a further sequential choice between "Independent/partisan" and "Democrat/Republican." In the models that follow, we employ the decision tree depicted in figure 6.1b, but it is worth noting that our results are strikingly similar whether we model a two-stage or a three-stage sequence. Critically, the results for the first stage—a key to our argument, given that nonidentification at this stage is commonly dropped out of the analysis as "missing observations"—are quite distinct from the results for any other stages, regardless of how many stages we model.

Having discussed in some depth how we should think about the "dependent variable" of party identification, our next task is to specify the factors that will explain how individuals make decisions about partisan choice. Each of the factors that we outline in some way reflects a process of incorporation into the American political arena and the partisan choices that the arena offers. We start with factors central to classical assimilation theory: time, generation, and socioeconomic attainment. In line with this straight-line assimilation model, we consider whether party identification varies by nativity (whether foreign-born or born in the United States), the number of years one has lived in the United States as an immigrant, third-generation (or higher) status, educational level, and family income. Our expectations here are straightforward: Latinos and Asian Americans who are more deeply rooted in American soil by virtue of having lived in the United States longer, being wealthier, or being better educated are all more likely to have stronger partisan commitments and, at least in the case of class gains, to be more prone to identifying with the Republican Party.

Beyond this traditional account, we test for four clusters of variables that we view as associated with a more contingent view of incorporation: ideology, information, identity, and institutions. In terms of ideology, we focus on the role played by assimilation into the basic liberal-conservative divide that separates the two parties. To assess the relevance of both the strength and the direction of views on this central ideological dimension, we measure liberal-conservative ideological leaning with a series of dummy variables for strong liberalism, weak liberalism, strong conservatism, and weak conservatism—with ideological moderates as the baseline for comparison. As we saw in chapter 5, with both Latinos and Asian Americans, nonidentification with ideological terms that are familiar in the U.S. context—"liberal," "conservative," and "moderate"—is very commonplace. In the NAAS, 28 percent of respondents did not identify with any of these categories; in the LNS, the figure was a whopping 48 percent. Accordingly, we also add a dummy variable for ideological nonidentifiers.

The second cluster of variables relates to information and other attributes that individuals acquire through political incorporation. As we have noted, we believe that direct experience with and knowledge of a political system that is unfamiliar to immigrants and their offspring is a vital precursor of partisan attachments. With political information, we test for party-specific effects as well as a general interest in politics. In the 2008 NAAS, our measure of party-specific information is whether or not respondents perceive important differences between the two major political parties on an issue of special importance to them. In the 2006 LNS, the measure is an index of two political knowledge items: which party (Democratic or Republican) is more conservative at the national level and which party holds the majority of the seats in the House of Representatives.

Third, we consider the extent to which the identity formation of Latinos and Asian Americans shapes their partisanship. Here our main focus is on racial identity. As with most of the extant political science research on racial identity, our model specification is heavily informed by the concepts of social group identity (Tajfel 1981; Turner et al. 1987) and racially linked fate (Dawson 1994). Social group identity theory posits three key, interrelated factors: in-group favoritism, out-group differentiation, and intergroup competition. Linked-fate theory posits the key role of a racial-group heuristic in the cognitive calculus of well-differentiated social groups such as African Americans.

To test for these possible effects of identity formation in this chapter, we specify four variables: (1) panethnic linked fate, (2) perceptions of in-group political commonality, (3) perceptions of out-group political commonality, and (4) the personal experience of being discriminated against. Panethnic linked fate and the belief that Asian Americans have common political interests are two group-specific and context-specific indicia of in-group solidarity. The belief that Asian Americans have common political interests with non-Asians is our context-specific measure of out-group differentiation.[2] The experience of discrimination is used to tap into the

---

[2] This variable is measured as an additive index of three items: perceived political commonality with whites, African Americans, and Latinos.

experiential bases of intergroup competition. "Groupness" here is presumed to be panethnic (i.e., vis-à-vis the umbrella categories of Asian American and Latino), but obviously the same factors could be salient at the level of groupness defined by ethnic/national origin.

Finally, we also recognize that ideology, information, and identity are not prefigured factors for immigrant-based populations such as Latinos and Asian Americans. As we described these factors in chapter 5, ideology and identity reflect underlying political predispositions, and information reflects the role of political information—cognitive psychological determinants of party identification. As elements in our full account of party identification as political incorporation, these individual-level factors act together with institutionally located factors. Specifically, we also test for the influence of five institutional measures. Two are within the realm of formal institutional politics: one's voter-registration status and one's degree of trust in government.[3] Voter registration is a critical point of entry into formal political participation for Latinos and Asian Americans (DeSipio 1996, Alvarez and Ansolabehere 2002, Nakanishi and Ong 1996). Trust is a foundation of the principal-agent relationship that forms the core dyad of representative government and also the basis for deciding which sources of political information to rely on and which to discount (Lupia and McCubbins 1998).

The remaining institutionally based measures we test for are within the realm of civil society: membership in civic organizations, ethnic media use, and religiosity. As we noted in chapter 5, in the absence of responsive and responsible parties, one place that many scholars have recently turned to is the institutional influence of organizations within civil society—community organizations, religious institutions, independent media, labor unions, voluntary associations, and the like. From political philosophers like Carole Pateman (1970) to empirical political scientists such as Sidney Verba, Kay Scholzman, and Henry Brady (1995), civic engagement is seen to develop key civic skills like political communication and organizing and in nurturing a sense of psychological engagement and efficacy in the realm of public affairs. These are skills that probably heighten, vis-à-vis our earlier discussion, an immigrant's sense of authori-

[3] Citizenship is another key institutional marker of political incorporation. Both citizenship and voter registration are potentially important factors in forming partisan attachments. We focus on voter registration for several reasons. First, statistically, the two factors are too closely correlated to allow for both to be profitably specified in the same model. Second, people choose to become citizens of the United States for manifold reasons—economic, social, cultural, and political—but voter registration is almost singularly political. So much so that the worry about including voter registration in our analysis is that it may be conceptually unclear whether identifying with a party (or thinking in partisan terms) may induce someone to register to vote or whether being registered to vote propels someone to be a partisan.

zation to become informed and involved in politics and consequently, we posit, to develop a sense of partisanship. These institutional markers, important in their own right, are also potentially key mediators of identity and ideological belief formation and fonts of information.

Taken together, these dimensions of immigrant incorporation—ideology, information, identity, and institutions—allow for a fuller consideration of the contingent and segmented process of immigrant acculturation. Our expectations here vary across the two stages of party identification we examine. In the first stage of thinking in partisan terms, the expectations are straightforward. Latinos and Asian Americans who are more incorporated—whether in terms of ideology, information, identity, or institutions—are more likely to have developed some partisan attachments. In the second stage, we expect incorporation to recede somewhat in importance, while other, more conventional partisan factors emerge as significant. We also expect our results to diverge slightly between respondents who are considering Independence and those who engaged in a comparison of the Democratic and Republican parties. In the former case, we believe that different aspects of incorporation will be more central.[4] In contrast, in the final pairwise decision between Democratic and Republican Party affiliation, we expect our results to roughly mirror the basis of partisan choice for the general population and say less about immigrant incorporation per se. For instance, to the extent that racialized minorities in America are generally more likely to self-identify with the Democratic Party, we might expect the same for Latinos and Asian Americans. Similarly, to the extent that the Republican Party has "captured" the interests of highly religious Americans, we might expect the same for Latinos and Asian Americans. Finally, to the extent that liberals are more likely to identify as Democrats and conservatives are tied to the Republican Party, we should expect similar links within the Latino and Asian American population.

Finally, we also include background demographic factors that are important statistical control factors—gender, age, and ethnic/national origin—given their salience in racial politics and political behavior research. For Latinos, we test for the independent effects of being Mexican, Cuban, or Puerto Rican, with a mix of Salvadorans, Dominicans, Central Americans, and Hispanics from elsewhere in Latin America as the baseline ethnic/national-origin group. For Asian Americans, we include dummy vari-

---

[4] To further complicate matters, we also expect that Latinos and Asian Americans may also identify as Independents for some of the same reasons as the extant literature suggests to us that whites do—out of apathy, a sense of alienation, an inability to differentiate between the two major parties—or identify as Independents for the same reasons that our chapter on African Americans suggests—because their view of politics is not as deeply racialized as that of partisans themselves.

ables for Asian Indians, Chinese, Filipinos, Koreans, and Vietnamese, with Japanese Americans as the baseline ethnic / national-origin group.

RESULTS AND DISCUSSION

Our results are displayed in two tables that sketch the relationships between all of these different factors and partisan choices in the two partisan stages that we have outlined. Each table is derived from a logistic regression and a multinomial logit regression.[5] The first-stage logistic regression distinguishes between respondents who do not think in partisan terms (i.e., our "residual" uncommitted category) and everyone else (i.e., all those who are willing to offer a response that indicates at least a minimal sense of partisan thinking). The second-stage multinomial logit models the three unordered pairwise choices of Independent, Republican, and Democrat. Unlike most presentations of multinomial logit regressions, we offer estimates for every pairwise combination of the three categories.[6] For each variable in a regression, we present the parameter estimate and standard error. To help the reader more easily understand the relative impact of each variable, figures 6.2 and 6.3 show the strength of statistically significant relationships graphically. These figures show "min-max" predicted probabilities: the difference in the relationship to the dependent variable between respondents at the maximum value and minimum value of the explanatory variable.

Incorporation and Partisanship

Rather than summarizing the effect of each independent variable in each stage, for each panethnic group, we begin by highlighting the main conclusions that emerge from this analysis. Perhaps the clearest and most

[5] One concern with these regressions is the possibility of reciprocal causation. Particularly in the case of our identity and institutional variables, it is possible that party identification may affect rather than be affected by the independent variables. Unfortunately, as other scholars have noted, "It is virtually impossible to sort out the precise causal mechanisms that govern relationships" between party identification and other factors (Niemi and Jennings 1991, 973; see also Miller and Shanks [1996] on this point). What we have done is rerun the analysis dropping different sets of potentially endogenous variables to show that other relationships in the model are largely unaffected.

[6] Technically, a baseline category against which other alternatives are compared must be chosen for the model to be statistically "identified," and in many cases, there are strong theoretical grounds for choosing that optimal base category. In our case, the theory argues that each pairwise choice is significant. Hence, tables 6.1 and 6.2 show the results from two separate estimates—first with "Independent" and then with "Democrat" as the base category.

TABLE 6.1
Determinants of Latino Party Identification: Two-Stage Model

	Stage one	Stage two		
	Identifier or nonidentifier	Democrat or Independent	Republican or Independent	Republican or Democrat
Straight-line assimilation				
Foreign-born	-.44 (.13)**	-.73 (.14)**	-.46 (.19)*	n.s.
Years in U.S. if immigrant	.008 (.004)*	.009 (.004)*	n.s.	n.s.
Educational level	n.s.	.07 (.04)^	n.s.	-.10 (.04)*
Family income	n.s.	n.s.	n.s.	.08 (.03)**
Contingent incorporation				
Ideology				
Strong conservative	n.s.	.26 (.14)^	1.63 (.17)**	1.37 (.14)**
Weak conservative	-.52 (.13)**	n.s.	.77 (.18)**	.66 (.16)**
Weak liberal	n.s.	n.s.	n.s.	n.s.
Strong liberal	n.s.	.30 (.15)*	n.s.	-.54 (.22)**
Ideological nonidentifier	-1.03 (.10)**	.26 (.10)**	.49 (.15)**	.24 (.14)^
Information				
Perceived party differences	.63 (.05)**	.11 (.05)^	.51 (.07)**	.43 (.07)**
General political attentiveness	n.s.	n.s.	.07 (.03)*	.08 (.03)**
Identity				
Panethnic linked fate	.07 (.03)*	.08 (.04)*	n.s.	-.13 (.04)**
Political commonality, in-group	n.s.	.16 (.04)**	.10 (.06)^	n.s.
Political commonality, out-group	.08 (.02)**	n.s.	n.s.	n.s.
Experienced discrimination	n.s.	n.s.	-.26 (.12)*	-.26 (.11)*

	Model 1		Model 2	
Institutions				
Trust in government	.10 (.04)**	n.s.	.54 (.07)**	.34 (.05)**
Registered to vote	.87 (.09)**	.33 (.10)**	.59 (.15)**	.26 (.13)*
Ethnic-media consumption	-.09 (.05)^	n.s.	-.17 (.08)*	-.13 (.07)^
Civic participation	n.s.	n.s.	.09 (.05)^	n.s.
Religiosity	n.s.	n.s.	.18 (.04)**	.15 (.04)**
Background controls				
Age in years	.013 (.003)**	.021 (.003)**	.010 (.004)*	-.010 (.004)**
Female	-.26 (.07)**	n.s.	n.s.	-.22 (.09)*
Cuban	n.s.	-1.03 (.21)**	.40 (.23)^	1.43 (.20)**
Puerto Rican	n.s.	-.50 (.18)**	n.s.	n.s.
Mexican	n.s.	-.40 (.10)**	-.42 (.14)**	n.s.
Constant	-.51 (.34)	-.54 (.39)	-3.19 (.53)	-3.05 (.48)
Number of observations	5894		4156	
Log likelihood	-2860.32		-3636.62	
Pseudo R-squared	0.20		0.11	

Note: Cell entries are parameter estimates and their corresponding standard errors. Significance levels: ^ = $p < .10$ / * = $p < .05$ / ** = $p < .01$.

TABLE 6.2
Determinants of Asian American Party Identification: Two-Stage Model

	Stage one	Stage two		
	Identifier or nonidentifier	Democrat or Independent	Republican or Independent	Republican or Democrat
Straight-line assimilation				
Foreign-born	−.44 (.21)**	n.s.	n.s.	n.s.
Years in U.S. if immigrant	.012 (.005)*	n.s.	n.s.	n.s.
Educational level	n.s.	−.11 (.05)*	−.17 (.06)**	n.s.
Family income	n.s.	−.07 (.03)*	n.s.	.08 (.04)*
Contingent incorporation				
Ideology				
Strong conservative	.65 (.25)**	n.s.	1.22 (.23)**	1.54 (.23)**
Weak conservative	n.s.	−.38 (.20)*	.72 (.20)**	1.10 (.20)**
Weak liberal	n.s.	.65 (.16)**	n.s.	−.81 (.23)**
Strong liberal	.56 (.19)**	.77 (.18)**	n.s.	−.42 (.20)*
Ideological nonidentifier	−.93 (.12)**	.33 (.16)*	n.s.	
Information				
Perceived party differences	.58 (.10)**	.34 (.12)**	n.s.	−.30 (.14)*
General political attentiveness	.13 (.07)^	n.s.	n.s.	n.s.
Identity				
Panethnic linked fate	n.s.	n.s.	n.s.	n.s.
Political commonality, in-group	.10 (.06)*	.19 (.06)**	.14 (.07)*	n.s.
Political commonality, out-group	.04 (.01)**	n.s.	−.06 (.02)**	−.03 (.02)^
Experienced discrimination	n.s.	n.s.	−.16 (.07)*	n.s.

Institutions	Model 1	Model 2	Model 3	Model 4
Trust in government	n.s.	n.s.	.23 (.05)**	.24 (.05)**
Registered to vote	.74 (.10)**	.25 (.13)*	.55 (.17)**	.30 (.16)^
Ethnic-media consumption	n.s.	n.s.	n.s.	n.s.
Civic participation	n.s.	n.s.	n.s.	n.s.
Religiosity	n.s.	.05 (.03)^	.11 (.03)**	.08 (.03)*
Background controls				
Age in years	n.s.	n.s.	n.s.	n.s.
Female	−.17 (.10)^	n.s.	n.s.	n.s.
South Asian	.44 (.21)*	n.s.	−1.33 (.31)**	−1.03 (.29)**
Chinese	n.s.	−1.11 (.24)**	−1.38 (.32)**	n.s.
Filipino	n.s.	−.53 (.26)*	.54 (.32)^	n.s.
Korean	n.s.	.48 (.29)^	n.s.	n.s.
Vietnamese	.68 (.24)**	−1.57 (.28)**	n.s.	1.47 (.30)**
Constant	.04 (.39)	.87 (.45)	1.48 (.58)	−2.35 (.55)
Number of observations	2890		2139	
Log likelihood	−1422.98		−1951.06	
Pseudo R-squared	0.14		0.14	

Note: Cell entries are parameter estimates and their corresponding standard errors. Significance levels: ^ = $p < .10$ / * = $p < .05$ / ** = $p < .01$.

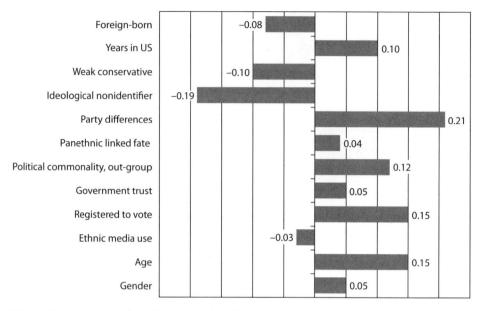

Figure 6.2. Stage one: identifier or nonidentifier (LNS)

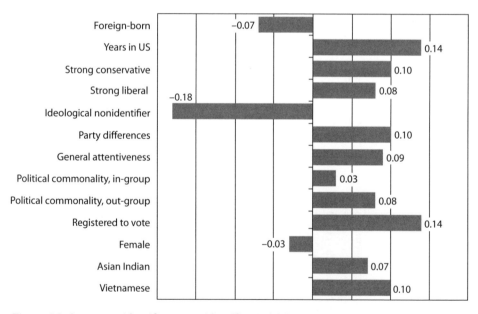

Figure 6.3. Stage one: identifier or nonidentifier (NAAS)

obvious finding is that Latino and Asian American partisan choices are intricately linked to a range of processes related to immigration incorporation. The two tables and figures indicate that in each stage, a myriad of factors measuring different elements of acculturation are strongly and significantly associated with partisan attachments.

This is first manifest in the robust role that the traditional straight-line assimilation model plays in shaping the attachments of both Latinos and Asian Americans. As expected, time lived in the United States takes on a central role—particularly in the initial stage, when respondents choose whether or not to select any form of partisan or nonpartisan attachment. Latinos who were born in the United States are 8 percent less likely than their foreign-born counterparts to remain as nonidentifiers (see figure 6.2).[7] The effect for Asian Americans is very similar at 7 percent (see figure 6.3). Likewise, immigrant Latinos who have lived in the United States for the longest period of time are 10 percent less likely to be uncommitted than immigrant Latinos who have lived in the United States for only a year. For Asian Americans, the magnitude of this effect is somewhat higher at 14 percent. For Latinos, the effect of nativity plays a similar role in the second stage in the choice between remaining Independent and electing to identify with one of the two major parties; foreign-born Latinos are more likely to be nonidentifiers than identifiers, and more likely to be Independents than partisans. For Asian Americans, the effect of nativity is isolated to the first stage.

Findings regarding socioeconomic attainment as a measure of the classic assimilation model were largely absent in the first stage.[8] In the second-stage choice between traditional categories of party identification, these factors had a more pronounced effect. For both Latinos and Asian Americans, higher income levels were significantly associated with greater Republican identification than Democratic identification and greater attachments as Independents than as Democrats. With Latinos, there is the further effect of higher education leading to greater support for the Democratic Party than identifying as either Republican or Independent. For Asian Americans, by contrast, higher educational gains were associated

[7] Predicted probabilities are calculated using the SPost bundle of postestimation commands in Stata (Long and Freese 2006). The command prchange, specifically, calculates the effect of each independent variable on the probabilities of identifying as a Democrat, Republican, or Independent, holding all other specific explanatory variables at their mean values.

[8] In some ways, this conclusion understates the role of class. Further analysis reveals that education and income play an important indirect role for both Latinos and Asian Americans. When we dropped all of the contingent incorporation factors from the model, class gains emerged as significant in the first stage, with members of both groups who had attained higher educational outcomes and higher incomes less likely to remain as nonidentifiers.

with a greater likelihood of identifying as an Independent than either as a Democrat or as a Republican.

The role of incorporation was, importantly, not solely tied to a classic assimilation model. A range of factors relating to more contingent elements of incorporation also played a critical role in shaping Latino and Asian American partisan preferences. To begin with, ideology mattered in both stages of the model. As figures 6.1 and 6.2 show, for both Latinos and Asian Americans, nonplacement on a liberal-conservative scale is among the strongest predictors of nonidentification with a partisan category in the first stage. Latino ideological nonidentifiers were 19 percent more likely than moderates to be partisan nonidentifiers; the parallel figure for Asian American ideological nonidentifiers was 18 percent. In addition, for Asian Americans, a strong ideological identification—whether as liberals or conservatives—led them to ally with Democrats, Republicans, or Independents. For Latinos in this first stage, the only other ideological marker of consequence is identifying as weak conservatives, which is significantly associated with partisan nonidentifiers.

In the second stage of partisanship, the general pattern of self-placement as a liberal associated with Democratic partisanship and self-placement as a conservative aligned with Republican partisanship holds for both groups. With both groups, however, there is a discernible imbalance between the two ideological antipodes: self-identification as a conservative is more forcefully aligned with partisan choices in the second stage than is identification as a liberal. The average impact of strong conservatism on Asian American partisanship, holding all other variables constant at their mean, is 19 percent, and the average impact of strong liberalism is 10 percent; for Latinos, the parallel figures are 16 percent and 6 percent, respectively. While these effects of ideological self-placement may not be that surprising, what is somewhat surprising is that ideological nonidentification continues to have an effect on partisanship even in the second stage. Specifically, Latino nonidentifiers are significantly less likely to identify as Independents than they are as partisans (and also less likely to identify as Democrats than as Republicans); for Asians, this effect holds only between the pairwise choice of identifying as an Independent or a Democrat. These effects, however, are far smaller—the average impact of ideological nonidentification on the three-way partisan choice is 5 percent for Asian Americans and 4 percent for Latinos.

Beyond the ideological self-placement measure we consider here, we would have liked to test for the partisan effects of a range of orthogonal issue concerns that are especially prominent in the Latino and Asian American immigrant communities. Deep-seated concerns such as Puerto Rican statehood and North-South relations in Korea, which are particularly relevant for subgroups of the Latino and Asian American population but that nevertheless are downplayed by the two major parties in America, could affect the strength and extent of partisan attachments. Unfortunately, neither of the surveys we employ allows for a rigorous assessment of these alternative issue dimensions. However, as part of a preliminary investigation into the role played by these kinds of subgroups' concerns, we performed analyses on the 1989 Latino National Politics Survey, which incorporated views on Puerto Rican autonomy, Mexican corruption, and preferences for Latin American immigration—several issue dimensions of distinct relevance to members of the Latino community. Given that the two parties either ignore these issues or stake out moderate and largely indistinguishable positions on them, we expected that strong views on each policy dimension would lead away from attachment to either of the two major parties. That is exactly what we found. In particular, Mexican Americans who believe that economic problems in Mexico are related to governmental corruption, Puerto Ricans who favor independence for the island, and Latinos who believe Latin American immigrants should be given preferential treatment are especially unlikely to identify as Democrats or Republicans (the analysis is not shown). These results imply that Latinos whose views and core concerns do not fit well with either party are unwilling to identify with a partisan option that does little to further their policy interests. Much more work needs to be done on these orthogonal issue concerns, but if these findings are confirmed, it may well be that Democrats and Republicans are losing support by downplaying policy dimensions that core segments of the Latino and Asian American populations care deeply about.

The importance of contingent incorporation was also evident in our measures of information. Here, partisan information cues are especially relevant. The effects are partisan, but in opposite directions. Latinos who can accurately distinguish between the Republican and Democratic parties in Congress are, on average, 11 percent more likely to identify as Republicans and 4 percent less likely to identify as Democrats. For Asian Americans, by contrast, the perception of party differences on an issue of personal salience increases their likelihood of identifying as Democrats by 8 percent and decreases their chances of identifying as Republicans by 3 percent. For Latinos, there is the further effect of being generally attentive to political matters in increasing one's likelihood of identifying as a Republican. Although the data do not allow us to delve more deeply into this result, we speculate that the fact that ideological influences on partisanship are stronger for conservatives and the fact that information cues (at least for Latinos) tip the scales in favor of Republican self-identification signify the degree to which the Republican Party, at least prior to the 2008 election, has been successful in defining the terms of polarized political discourse in recent American history. The fact that information cues work in the opposite direction for Asian Americans may stem from the difference in survey years (2006 for the LNS, 2008 for the NAAS) and and may hint at the relative success of the Democratic Party in framing partisan messages to the electorate in the 2008 election.

The third cluster of variables that we examine as part of our account of contingent incorporation is Latino and Asian American identity. Here there is a stark difference between Latinos and Asian Americans. For Latinos, a panethnic linked-fate orientation is an important factor in party identification, drawing Latinos toward Democratic partisanship by an average effect of 7 percent; for Asian Americans, linked fate does not appear to be significant. What is significant for Asian Americans, by contrast, is perceptions of shared political interests with non-Asian racial/ethnic groups. This sense of political commonality leads Asian Americans to be less likely to identify as Republicans by an average effect of 8 percent. For both groups, the sense of political commonality with other in-group members is significant and leads to a greater likelihood of partisanship (both Democrat and Republican) rather than Independence. The predicted decrease in one's likelihood of being Independent is 8 percent for Asian Americans and 9 percent for Latinos. Finally, for both groups, the personal experience of being discriminated against is also key and pushes both groups away from identifying with the Republican Party. For Asian Americans, this average effect is 8 percent, and for Latinos it is a far more modest 3 percent. These results as a whole show that for *both* Latinos and Asian Americans, racial considerations are significant in their partisan choices. The particular considerations that are brought to bear, however, are in important ways different between the two groups.

We also posited the influence of key institutional markers of contingent incorporation. These factors do turn out to matter, and, perhaps unsurprisingly, the markers of incorporation vis-à-vis formal political institutions are more consistent and strong. What is especially notable here is that the effect of trust in government and voter registration is the same for both groups. Latinos and Asian Americans who are registered to vote are both less likely to identify as Independents and are more likely to identify as Republicans. The average effect of voter registration status on decreasing identification as an Independent is exactly the same for both groups at 7 percent. Similarly, Latinos and Asian Americans who trust government are more likely to identify as Republicans. The average effect for Latinos on identifying as Republicans is 9 percent, and for Asian Americans it is 15 percent.

The effect of the civil society–based institutional measures is somewhat more mixed. For Latinos, ethnic media consumption increases Democratic partisanship by a predicted probability of 5 percent; the effect of membership in nonreligious community organizations is weak and limited to the pairwise choice between identifying as a Republican or an Independent. For Asian Americans, neither ethnic media nor civic participation appears to influence the three-way partisan choice we examine. The influence of ethnic media for Latinos again reinforces our earlier conclusion of the distinctive way in which racial/ethnic status influences partisanship. For both groups, however, religiosity increases the likelihood of identifying as a Republican: for Latinos, the predicted effect is 5 percent, and for Asian Americans, it is 6 percent. Here again—as with our discussion of the asymmetric influence of ideological extremism and of partisan informational cues on Republican partisanship—we speculate that this one-way partisan relationship of religiosity is probably connected to the dominance of the Republican Party in recent years in framing politics in terms of moral and religious considerations.

Of the remaining background controls, there is not much that is surprising. Cubans are the most distinctive Latino group in terms of partisanship and are 29 percent less likely to identify as Democrats than the baseline Latino groups. Vietnamese are similarly most distinctive among Asian American ethnic/national origin groups, being less likely to identify as Democrats by a predicted probability of 34 percent.

Overall, these results serve both to affirm the significance of the incorporation process and to highlight the contingent and multifaceted nature of that process. For immigrant-based groups such as Latinos and Asian Americans, understanding party identification is, in many ways, understanding the nature and shape of incorporation into the American political arena. Moreover, some relationships may strike some readers as nearly tautological. For instance, many states allow or require individuals who register to align with a political party, and partisan campaigns are often the vehicles through which Americans register to vote. Similarly, it is hard to imagine why one would choose to identify as an Independent if one sees a meaningful choice between the two parties. These relationships, nonetheless, are important because (as we noted in chapter 5) political parties and campaigns often view Latinos and Asian Americans as too apathetic toward, unknowledgeable of, or distrustful of politics in the United States to merit voter mobilization efforts.

More generally, the importance of the incorporation process for Asian American and Latino politics may seem simple—perhaps to the point of being too obvious to merit the level of scrutiny we have given it in this chapter. Indeed, we are far from the first scholars to recognize the central nature of immigrant assimilation in the politics of these two communities. Other scholars have already highlighted the relevance of incorporation to the politics of the Latino and Asian American communities (Cain et al. 1991; Jones-Correa 1998; Cho 1999; Lien et al. 2004; Uhlaner and García 2005; Wong 2006). Nevertheless, we believe that this analysis is a significant step forward in that it delineates more clearly the key ingredients of this incorporation process. Our goal is not simply to underscore the role of incorporation but also to identify exactly which aspects of that process are critical. Incorporation and partisanship acquisition do not simply happen after time spent in the United States and the attendant class mobility, which allegedly obtains over time and across generations, according to classic accounts of immigrant assimilation. The analysis in this chapter demonstrates convincingly that there is a crucial informational, ideological, identitarian, and institutional basis to the process of immigrant political incorporation. Whether individual Asian Americans and Latinos choose to join the partisan fray at all and, if they do engage the party structure, which party they choose depends greatly on the extent of their knowledge of, trust in, and familiarity with the political apparatus of the nation, their familiarity with and attachment to the basic ideological divide separating the parties, and the strength of their sense of racial place in the nation.

A Sequential Process

The second major conclusion to be drawn from our arguments and analyses is that Latino and Asian American partisanship follows a multistage, sequential process. The key in this sequential course is the process of coming to identify with the terms of partisan competition in the United States. Nonidentification is a distinctive, yet unexamined aspect of immigrant political incorporation. Given that few studies even acknowledge the existence of nonidentifiers and fewer still incorporate them in their analysis, our first and primary goal is to better understand nonidentifiers and to specify the conditions in which Latinos and Asian Americans come to understand and attach themselves to the conventional partisan categories of Democrat, Republican, and Independent.

So just what are the factors that underlie a reluctance to place oneself on the conventional partisan spectrum? The results suggest that nonidentifiers are distinct along several dimensions. Nonidentifiers tend to be newer Americans—foreign-born and recently arrived immigrants. Nonidentifiers are also political neophytes—they are less apt to hold strong (if any) ideological views, less likely to be informed about partisan differences or to be generally attentive to politics, and, institutionally, less prone to trust government or to have registered to vote. Nonidentifiers are also less disposed to hold a racialized view of their identity and its relation to politics. The differences are often quite substantial. Not being able to place oneself along a liberal-to-conservative ideological continuum, for instance, increases one's chances of being a partisan nonidentifier by 19 percent for Latinos and 18 percent for Asian Americans. Not knowing which party in Congress holds power or perceiving no differences between the parties on key policy issues further increases the odds of being a nonidentifier by 21 percent for Latinos and 10 percent for Asian Americans. Latinos who see no common political ground with non-Latinos are 12 percent more likely to be nonidentifiers than their counterparts. Likewise, for Asian Americans who feel a great deal of commonality with Asian Americans, the probability of being a nonidentifer increases by 8 percent.

These results—and the fact that almost 38 percent of Latinos and 36 percent of Asian Americans can be labeled as nonidentifiers—indicate that for immigrant-based groups, choosing one of the conventional partisan categories that other Americans seem to reflexively associate themselves with is neither effortless nor intuitive. Before Asians and Latinos choose to express their views about the mainstream world of American partisan politics, they have to decide whether they possess enough knowledge of, trust in, and understanding of where the parties stand and where they themselves stand. If not, they are likely to indicate (as large numbers do) no preference or settle on a noncompliant response (refusing to answer or answering "not sure" or "don't know).

Whereas the first stage stands out for almost exclusively reflecting a process of incorporation, the second stage, as the results in tables 6.1 and 6.2 indicate, is more of a hybrid—reflecting both elements of immigrant political incorporation and elements of a more mainstream partisan politics. In the second stage, Independents are partly differentiated by markers of immigrant incorporation—such as the effect of foreign-born status for Latinos or the status of being registered to vote for both groups. But it is also clear that identifying as an Independent is distinct from partisan nonidentification. In the first stage, contra expectations from straight-line assimilation theory, education has no effect on partisan identification. In the second stage, education actually has the opposite effect for Asian Americans from what assimilation theory would predict: Asian Americans who are better educated are *more* likely to identify as Independents, not less.

The differentiation between nonidentifiers and Independents is more pronounced when we consider the relationship between ideology and partisanship. In the first stage, no factor is as decisive in discriminating between identifiers and nonidentifiers as ideological nonidentification, which goes hand in hand with partisan nonidentification. In the second stage, ideological nonidentifiers are actually more likely to be *partisans* than Independents. This opposite and significant relationship suggests a more complex notion of either ideological or partisan identification: it may be that some ideological nonidentifiers are low-information partisans; it may also be that Asian American and Latino Independents are ideologically sophisticated, but that a liberal-conservative continuum does not layer over a Democrat-Republican continuum for these populations as neatly as it does for whites; or it may be that some other aspect of the way in which Asians and Latinos understand ideological terms, including nonrandom measurement error resulting from the way that terms such as "liberal," "moderate," "conservative," and "ideology" are translated into Spanish, Korean, Chinese, Vietnamese, and other non-English languages, affects their partisan choices.

The second stage of partisanship, shown in tables 6.1 and 6.2, also demonstrates well-behaving patterns of party identification among whites. The determinants of the pairwise choice between identifying as a Republican or a Democrat in particular mirror the established findings on the effect of factors such as education, family income, self-placement as a liberal or a conservative, and religiosity. At the same time, there are relationships that are somewhat less expected. The fact that racial considerations are also an influence on partisanship may not be surprising for the two racial minority groups in question, but there are some crucial differences in how identity influences partisanship for Latinos and Asian Americans. For Asian Americans, the effect of identity is rarely found in linked fate and, most crucial, in pairwise choices between identifying as a Democrat or Independent and Republican or Independent. For Latinos, the effect of race on partisanship is more pervasive (including ethnic media consumption), and there is a greater direct effect of linked fate on the pairwise decision between Democrat and Republican. Also, at a superficial level, we might expect such defining democratic elements as registering to vote or system legitimacy (as measured by political trust) to be neutral with respect to the choice between identifying as a Republican or a Democrat. Yet these factors all significantly increase Latinos' and Asian Americans' likelihood of identifying as Republicans. As we noted earlier, however, we think these partisan effects may wellrepresent differences in party control, partisan electoral mobilization, and partisan framing of political messages between the Democratic and Republican parties.

A COMPARISON OF LATINOS AND ASIAN AMERICANS

Our analysis helps us not only to examine the degree to which competing accounts of how immigrants adapt to a new society come to form (or fail to form) a relationship to the party system and to specific political parties in the United States, but also to consider the degree to which Latinos and Asian Americans are alike and different in fashioning their party identification. It is important to note, however, that because we are using separate data sets to test our model of party identification for Latinos and for

Asian Americans, there is not a perfect correspondence in this comparison. The two surveys employ somewhat distinct sample designs (state-level samples in the LNS; geographically weighted list-based samples in the NAAS), were fielded in different years (in an off-election year in the LNS; at the height of the 2008 presidential election in the NAAS), present different question ordering and wording, and so on. With the exception of a difference in our measures of political information, however, the questions that we use to estimate the determinants of party identification for Latinos and Asian Americans are almost identical.

The most striking finding to emerge from our comparison of the two panethnic groups relates to the often remarkable parallels between the partisan decision making of Latinos and Asian Americans. Especially in the first stage of the model, members of both groups rely on an almost identical list of factors. For both groups the choice of whether too remain as nonidentifiers is shaped by time, ideology, information, and identity. Moreover, the critical variables for both groups are almost indistinguishable in this initial stage. Most Latinos and Asian Americans who end up as nonidentifiers are likely to be foreign-born, to have spent fewer years in the United States, to hold no clear liberal-conservative views, to have low levels of partisan knowledge, to be unregistered to vote, and to have a fairly limited sense of racial identity. Parallels are also present in some aspects of the second stage. Voter registration and political trust increase the odds of identifying as a Republican rather than a Democrat for both groups; experiencing discrimination increases the odds of *not* identifying as a Republican for both groups.

It is primarily in the choice between Democratic and Republican identification that the two groups start to diverge. Here, in the terra cognita of competitive party politics, class is a significant marker for Latinos but not for Asian Americans, and racial identity strongly shapes Latino choices but has a less salient effect on Asian American partisanship. Also, we find evidence that information cues have opposite effects for Latinos (drawing them to Republican partisanship) and Asians (beckoning them to Democratic partisanship).

CONCERNS AND REMNANTS

These findings make a strong case that partisanship acquisition is indeed sequential and that multiple dimensions of incorporation shape whether Latinos and Asian Americans think in partisan terms, and if they do so, which partisan categories they identify with. A number of aspects of our analysis remain incomplete, however. Three remnants in particular merit our attention in this concluding section.

First, we noted earlier in this chapter that there are two possibilities in the sequence of partisanship acquisition. One is to think of party identification in two stages, the possibility we have been pursuing thus far. Another is to model partisanship in three stages: one in which a political newcomer sees little meaning, content, or value to the partisan options that are typically offered; a second one in which a rational skeptic comes to see the option of Independent as a reasonable entry point into the partisan world; and a third in which the political actor comes to view the distinction between Democrats and Republicans as meaningful and actively engages in the partisan world. A second remnant is that our central theoretical arguments have been about party acquisition as steps toward immigrant political incorporation. We have chosen to take Latinos and Asian Americans as a group, but we could have proceeded by disaggregating our analysis between foreign-born and U.S.-born Latinos and Asian Americans. Third, as DeSipio (1998), Uhlaner and García (2005), Lien et al. (2004), and others have shown, the political choices that members of different national origin groups make often differ. It may also be that factors that drive partisanship differ across the groups and that we should have disaggregated our analysis by ethnic/national origin. In this last section, we briefly consider each of these three remnants in turn.

Party Identification in Three Stages

One important question that we are uncertain about is where to put Independents and third-party supporters in the sequence of partisan choices. One possibility is to think of Independence as an end station and on par with supporting the Democratic and Republican parties. This leads to party identification in two stages, the model we have been examining thus far. We opt for this model in large measure because the root question in surveys such as the American National Election Studies present the choices of identifying as a Democrat, Republican, and Independent together. We also opt for this route to be consistent with our approach to modeling partisanship in the remaining chapters (using multinomial logit).

As we noted earlier in this chapter, however, another way is to think of nonpartisanship as an interim way station on the road from nonidentification to full-fledged partisanship. This conceptualization leads to a three-stage process—a first stage, in which individuals choose whether to remain outside the party-identification scale altogether; a second stage, where they choose to jump into the fray of partisan politics or remain nonpartisan spectators, and a final stage, where they choose between the two major parties. Although we are convinced of the value of recognizing nonidentifiers and placing them alone in the first stage of the sequence, we are open to the possibility that there might be empirical verisimilitude in modeling partisanship as a three-stage sequence. There is no clear empirical test that can definitively rule in favor of one or the other model.

Nevertheless, it is instructive to consider the results of an alternate three-stage model. Tables 6.A.1 and 6.A.2 in the online appendix (http://press.princeton.edu/titles/9468.html) present that model. To a certain extent, the results indicate that the modeling choice is inconsequential. The two tables show that for both Latinos and Asian Americans there is very little substantive difference between a two-stage model and a three-stage model. One noticeable difference is in the way identity works. Our measures of racial identity are most consequential for Asian Americans in the second stage of identifying as partisans or Independents, with in-group political commonality pushing them toward partisanship and both out-group commonality and the experience of discrimination pushing them toward Independence. For Latinos, identity appears more defining in the end-stage choice between identifying as a Democrat and as a Republican. Another smaller difference is that civic participation now also appears significant in predicting Republican partisanship for Latinos.

Comparing the Foreign-Born with the U.S.-Born

Given the centrality of incorporation in our model of Latino and Asian American partisanship, we also thought it important to repeat our analysis with those who are native-born and foreign-born separately. The results of this analysis are displayed in the online appendix (http://press.princeton.edu/titles/9468.html) in tables 6.A.3–6.A.6. There are a few differences worthy of note. In the first-stage choice between identifiers and nonidentifiers, identity is a significant factor for both foreign-born Latinos and foreign-born Asian Americans, but not for their U.S.-born counterparts. In the choice between Democrat and Republican in the second stage, identity is a significant factor for U.S.-born Latinos, but less so for foreign-born Latinos. There is no parallel effect for Asian Americans.

At the same time, U.S.-born Asian Americans look distinct from foreign-born Asian Americans in several ways in the second stage of partisanship. First, class issues come to the fore: for the U.S.-born, greater family income leads to greater Republican partisanship. Second, voter registration has a differential effect by nativity: for foreign-born Asians, voter registration is associated with Republican partisanship; for U.S.-born Asians, it is associated with Democratic partisanship. Third, religiosity is not significant for U.S.-born Asians, but civic participation does emerge as a significant predictor of a move away from Republican partisanship. While these differences teasingly hint at potential divergences by nativity, it is important to keep in mind that in the NAAS, the sample sizes of the U.S.-born are quite small, and it is difficult to ascertain whether differences are substantively meaningful or simply a function of sample size. For the most part, a comparison of the foreign-born and native-born tells one simple story. The tables indicate that the processes driving partisanship among the native-born are strikingly similar to the processes driving partisanship among the foreign-born.

Comparing across Ethnic Groups

Our final remainder is the potentially distinct partisan experiences of different ethnic/national-origin groups. In lumping together the constituent groups that make up the panethnic categories of "Latino" and "Asian American," we have made our analysis much easier. But these efforts at parsimony create their own concerns. Observers with little more than a modicum of knowledge about these different national-origin groups are well aware that they do not constitute a single, coherent whole. Underneath each panethnic umbrella stands a diverse array of national-origin groups with varying socioeconomic levels, assorted languages and religions, divergent cultural practices, and, perhaps most important, different politics. As such, it is far from clear that the dimensions underlying partisan choices will be identical for members of each national-origin group.

To test this proposition and to see how similar or dissimilar the process of partisanship is for these groups, we repeated the analysis in tables 6.1 and 6.2 separately for twelve identifiable subgroups. The results are found in a series of tables in our online appendix (http://press.princeton .edu/titles/9468.html). The LNS allows subgroup analysis for respondents of Mexican, Puerto Rican, Cuban, Salvadoran, Dominican, and Central American origin. The NAAS allows subgroup analysis for Asian Indians, Filipinos, Japanese, Koreans, Vietnamese, and Chinese. The same caveats regarding smaller sample sizes apply in general for these subgroup regressions, although we note that the number of Mexicans in the LNS, even after taking account of missing data, is almost four thousand.

Although important differences do emerge, the main insight from this analysis is that there is a fairly consistent story. For the most part these rather different groups choose to align themselves with parties in rather similar fashion. This is especially so in the first stage of partisan choice. Where ideology, information, and identity mattered before with the panethnic group as a whole, they continue to matter for each ethnic/ national-origin subgroup. Ideological nonidentifiers are, across the board, less likely to be partisan identifiers; perceived party differences and voter registration, largely across the board, increase one's odds of identifying with a partisan category; where perceived out-group commonality is significant, it always draws Latinos and Asian Americans toward partisan identification. And so on.

In the second stage of partisan choice, we see a similar pattern in the pairwise choice between identifying as a Democrat or as a Republican. Ideological self-placement is a predictable guide to this choice, and much more consistently and strongly so for self-identified conservatives than for self-identified liberals. When family income, trust in government, and religiosity are significant, they pull any ethnic / national-origin group toward Republican partisanship. And so on. This general pattern also holds for the two other pairwise choices (Republican-Independent and Democrat-Independent), but the parallels across subgroups are not as consistent or pronounced.

CONCLUSION

These findings, in toto, present a pretty compelling case that partisan choice among Latinos and Asian Americans is a process of sequential choice: first, whether to think in terms of America's two-party system or not, and second, whether to remain an Independent or align with either the Democratic or the Republican Party. Asians and Latinos first have to decide whether they possess a sufficient feel for the game and adequate knowledge of its rules of engagement to play partisan politics. If not, they are likely to indicate (as many do) no preference or settle on a noncompliant response (refuse to answer or answer "not sure" or "don't know"). Once they gain a toehold in the political realm and have sufficient familiarity with the system, they must choose between the two halves of America's party system or choose to remain an Independent.

These findings also make the case that acculturation in its various forms is a key factor in each stage of this sequential choice. Understanding Latino and Asian American party identification is, in many ways, understanding the nature and shape of Latino and Asian American incorporation into the political arena. Latinos and Asian Americans move along the partisan pathway not only as they spend more time in the United States but also in response to their divergent experiences in the United States and the information they glean from those experiences. As Latinos and Asian Americans learn more about the politics of the nation and begin to trust its institutions, they become much more apt to develop ties to one of the parties. Similarly, when they come to understand their own racial positioning in the terrain of American politics and society, they are apt to develop stronger and more Democratic partisan ties. And all of this is cemented within a mix of formal and informal institutions that Latinos and Asian Americans do or do not encounter. Learning what it means to be an American and learning what it means to be a partisan are deeply interconnected.

As this process of contingent incorporation and partisan learning continues into the future, the potential to affect the partisan balance of power in this nation is enormous. Right now, despite the fact that a large majority of Latinos and Asian Americans, according to exit poll data, appear to favor the Democratic candidate in federal elections, it remains the case that a larger plurality of Latinos and Asian Americans are choosing to remain on the sidelines without attaching their political colors to either party. As a result, both parties stand to gain potentially great electoral support from these immigrant-based populations. To the extent that Latino and Asian American communities continue to become racialized or to the extent that economic inequalities deepen and grow, the prospects for the Republican Party look bleak. To the extent that electoral politics continue to be framed as a debate about patriotism, trust, and moral standing, those prospects turn from bleak to brimming for the Republican Party. Further, either party can reap vast electoral rewards by controlling its ideological self-definition—what it means to be conservative and Republican, what it means to be liberal and Democratic—and communicating that self-definition in ethnically and culturally sensitive and meaningful ways to Latinos and Asian Americans. Either party could, in effect, be the winner in this incorporation process. That is the essence of contingent incorporation. There is not a single clear path and no clear end line of assimilation. Where we go and where the parties end up depend a lot on how they and the rest of America treat these newcomers.

CHAPTER 7

Beyond the Middle: Ambivalence, Extremism, and White Nonpartisans

> I am a man who believes with all fervor and intensity in moderate progress. Too often men who believe in moderation believe in it only moderately and tepidly and leave fervor to the extremists of the two sides.
>
> —Theodore Roosevelt

> The core of America is not racist. It is not hostile to women. It is increasingly offended by gay bashing. Yet it abhors government waste. It believes strongly in fiscal responsibility such as balanced budgets. It is pro-economic growth. It is concerned about the environment. It is intolerant of people on welfare who disdain the notion of work. But it wants poor kids to have school lunches and it wants to spend money to have good schools. In sum, most Americans are sensible, good-hearted, and prudent. The issue, then, is whether there is a political party that can welcome them home.
>
> —Senator Paul Tsongas

IN THE PRECEDING chapters we have shown that conventional accounts of party identification cannot fully explain the partisan choices of racial and ethnic minorities. In this chapter, we focus on the more difficult case of white Americans. Given that conventional accounts have largely been developed to explain white partisan identification, we might expect whites to conform especially well to these traditional models. If any group fits, it should be whites. But in this chapter, we question whether all or even most white partisans' decisions really do conform to these traditional accounts. We contend, instead, that we can learn something about how whites choose parties by applying the lessons we have learned from studying the political decisions of racial and ethnic minorities.

In this chapter, we attempt to show that, as with other groups, the two major parties do not represent the views of all whites. Many white Americans do not fit neatly along a single liberal-conservative partisan divide, and this has important consequences for their partisan choices.

Specifically, we posit two alternate avenues to nonpartisanship: ambivalence and extremism. First, nonpartisanship is likely to be a logical alternative for individuals who hold strong but conflicting views that put them on both sides of the liberal-conservative partisan divide. Second, nonpartisanship is likely to be an appealing option for those who hold extremely liberal or extremely conservative views that distance them from the "middle-of-the-road" policy agendas of both parties. In both cases, individuals who hold far from moderate views end up being nonpartisan by default.

The rest of this chapter proceeds as follows. We begin by proposing an alternate model of white partisan choice that incorporates these two new dimensions of choice. We test this account using data from the General Social Survey and the American National Election Studies. We then focus on the implications of nonpartisanship for whites' voting behavior. We close with a discussion of the implications of this multidimensional model for our understanding of partisan choice and the balance of power between the Democratic and Republican parties.

WHY WHITES MIGHT NOT FIT

Although existing accounts have been designed largely to explain white partisan decision making, there are reasons to suspect that even among the white population, there will be a range of partisan "misfits" who cannot easily place themselves along the linear partisan scale. As we have already noted, we see a fairly sharp disjuncture between a partisan duopoly and a national population that is ideologically diverse.

America's partisan duopoly provides the public with only two options. Moreover, there is a strong incentive for both parties to cluster together around the middle of the liberal-conservative ideological spectrum, close to the median voter (Downs 1957; Black 1948, 1958; Hotelling 1929). The divide between parties has grown in recent years, but compared with those in other countries, the two parties continue to be relatively similar and relatively centrist (Hetherington 2001; Layman and Carsey 2002; Castles and Mair 1984). These two observations about American politics raise questions about the ability of the party system to effectively incorporate the interests of many citizens. Unless individual Americans hold consistently moderate liberal views or consistently moderate conservative views, they are unlikely to have a party that mirrors their views. With a population as large and heterogeneous as white America, it is very likely that at least some segments of the community will hold views that are not well represented by the available partisan options.

ALTERNATE DIMENSIONS OF NONPARTISANSHIP

From these two basic facts about the American political system, we derive expectations about alternate routes to nonpartisanship. We present what we hope is a deeper account of nonpartisanship that focuses on the ideological underpinnings of Independence. Specifically, we suggest that outside of ideological moderation, there are two routes that lead to Independence[1] among white Americans: ambivalence and extremism.[2]

First, we contend that Independence is likely to be an attractive choice for individuals who hold a range of strong but conflicting views. Certainly, some Americans do hold views that are consistently liberal or consistently conservative across the range of issues debated in American politics (Achen 1975). But others do not. Existing studies, in fact, suggest that few Americans hold consistent ideological positions that allow them to be neatly placed on one point of a liberal-conservative continuum (Converse 1964, Campbell et al. 1960). Some of those who hold "inconsistent" views do so because they are confused about the meaning of the questions, have not thought about the issue, or are simply guessing to provide survey researchers with answers (Carpini and Keeter 1996; Zaller 1992). Others with mixed views are, however, likely to hold principled and logical positions that, at different times, put them on different ends of the liberal-conservative spectrum (Layman 2001; Layman and Carsey 2002; Lavine 2001, Alvarez and Brehm 1995). Indeed, it may be perfectly rational to hold conservative views on some policy questions and liberal views on others.[3]

We suspect that these kinds of divergent preferences have two sources. First, a clash of views could come from a reasoned ideological differentiation across issues. For example, one can logically feel that conservative

---

[1] Since so few white Americans are categorized as uncommitted nonpartisans, in this chapter we focus specifically on those respondents who label themselves Independent.

[2] Our work builds on the insights of Dennis (1988b) and Rosenstone et al. (1984), who claim that Americans choose Independence when they dislike or are indifferent to the major American parties. Unfortunately, neither study attempts to explain the sources of indifference and distaste for the parties. We suspect that ambivalence (mixed views) and extremism (strong views) may underlie indifference and dislike toward the parties.

[3] We are by no means the first to identify ambivalence as an important force in American politics. Kaplan (1972) was one of the first to note that responses at the midpoint of a scale might indicate ambivalence (simultaneously having positive and negative feelings) rather than simply holding middle-of-the-road views. More recent work by Feldman and Zaller (1992), Alvarez and Brehm (1995), and others suggests that ambivalence "is a prevalent characteristic of the public political opinions, and that ambivalence has nontrivial implications for political judgment and choice" (Lavine 2001, 915).

fiscal policies are the best avenue to economic growth while simultaneously believing that more liberal stances on moral or religious questions are the best way to maximize human well-being. Alternatively, divergent views could also emerge as a result of a clash of identities. For example, one's primary political orientation as a liberal may clash with one's primary social group identity as white. In this case, generally liberal views would conflict with resentment and conservatism on racial policy.

In either case, these mixed views raise the specter of difficult choices when it comes to identifying with a party (Keele and Wolak 2006).[4] Since the Democratic Party consistently places itself somewhat to the left on the range of issues being debated in American politics and the Republican Party places itself somewhat to the right on the same issues, there is no obvious choice for individuals with mixed views. For individuals who hold strongly liberal views on some issues and strongly conservative views on others, there are strong ideological reasons for supporting both parties and equally strong reasons for opposing them. The ambivalence that results is likely to push this group of Americans toward Independence. This leads to our first hypothesis related to white partisan choices:

Hypothesis 1: Individuals who hold a mix of liberal and conservative views should be more likely to identify as Independents.

Second, we argue that individuals can identify as Independents because they hold strong views on issues that are not well represented by either party. Americans who have deep-seated concerns about a particular issue and who hold views that are strongly liberal or strongly conservative on that issue are unlikely to fit all that well into a two-party system where both parties often maintain fairly centrist policy agendas and sometimes ignore issues that could harm their electoral standing (Castles and Mair 1984; Downs 1957). For these "issue publics" either on the left or on the right, there may be little to draw them to either party. The divide between their views and the approach taken by both parties can be sharp, and they may feel that neither party serves their interests particularly well. Even if one party is marginally closer to their view, that marginal difference may not be enough to persuade an extremist to compromise and support that party. Rather than support a

---

[4] Several researchers have already examined the implications of ambivalence for vote choice and other political evaluations (Basinger and Lavine 2005, S. Greene 2005). The authors of *The American Voter* (1960) were among the first to show that individuals with what they called "conflicted" issue attitudes were less likely to consistently vote for the same party. Keele and Wolak (2006) present some of the first research to look at the implications of competing values on partisanship. Their analysis suggests that ambivalence can lead to instability in partisanship. We extend their analysis to see how ambivalence affects the direction of partisan choice.

party whose agenda conflicts in many ways with their own, these individuals may opt to remain Independent.[5]

Hypothesis 2: Individuals who hold strongly liberal or strongly conservative views should be more likely to identify as Independents.

For both groups, Independence, then, is not the result of ideological moderation but instead the consequence of strong views that do not accord well with either of the two mainstream parties. If true, these two accounts of Independence imply that a linear scale of party identification, with Independents in the middle, is inappropriate. To really understand partisanship and Independence, we need to model partisan choice in a more complex, unordered fashion that takes into account several dimensions of choice.

ASSESSING AMBIVALENCE AND EXTREMISM IN AMERICAN POLITICS

Although interesting and perhaps even logical, our account, up to this point, is largely devoid of any mention of substantive issues or concrete, real-world policies. It might make sense that Americans with mixed views and Americans with extreme views would opt for Independence, but it might also be that there are few Americans with these kinds of views or at least few white Americans who hold these kinds of views on issues that they not only care about but that are also relevant to partisan politics. To test these two alternate routes to Independence, we need to move from theory to empirical reality. Specifically, we need to find a set of plausibly important issues on which white Americans hold either mixed or extreme views.

Mixed Views and Partisan Choice

We begin by searching for issue arenas where mixed views might regularly lead to partisan ambivalence. Logically, for a mix of liberal and conservative views to matter enough to deter white Americans from supporting either major party, two conditions must be met. First, the issues on which the mixed views are held have to be core elements of the main liberal-conservative divide that separates the two parties. If the two parties do not hold different positions on any given issue, then any mix of preferences may not factor into partisan choice. Second, the particular

[5] Downs (1957) hints at a similar phenomenon. In his defining work on partisan competition in democracy, he briefly argues that individuals with extreme views might choose to abstain or support a third party in the hope of encouraging an electorally viable party to move closer to their extreme positions in future elections.

mix of liberal and conservative views has to be commonly held. If too few people have that particular mix of views, then it cannot be a central factor in white partisan choice.

We suspect that only three sets of issue areas have been central enough to the partisan divide to pass the first test. Economic policy, racial policy, and social morality all help to define core elements of the partisan divide. There is ample evidence that each of these three dimensions regularly influences individual political choices in American politics (Carmines and Stimson 1989, Petrocik 1987, Abramowitz 1994, Alvarez and Nagler 1998, Franklin and Jackson 1983).[6] Because these issues define the parties and help many Americans to distinguish between the two major parties, holding liberal views on one dimension and conservative views on another is likely to lead to considerable mental conflict for individual Americans trying to choose a partisan option. Liberal views on one of these issues will push them clearly toward the Democratic Party, but conservative views on a second issue will push them just as clearly toward the Republican Party. With strong reasons for supporting both parties and strong reasons for opposing them, ambivalence and Independence may result.

In recent years, two other policy areas, immigration and security issues related to foreign wars and the war on terrorism, have clearly grown in importance. Evidence as to how strongly views on immigration shape the partisanship of the American public is still limited, but it is clear from exit polls in 2004 and 2008 that terrorism and foreign policy rank very high among the concerns of Americans. It is also clear that the two parties have diverged on matters of national defense. Unfortunately, limited data availability for more recent contests precludes an analysis of mixed views on these two emerging issue arenas.

Mixed views on the three issue arenas that we can examine should matter only to the extent that these views are held by large numbers of individual Americans. Unless large segments of the public hold simultaneously liberal and conservative views on some combination of these

---

[6] The dividing line between the Democratic and Republican parties has traditionally been defined along economic or social policy (Franklin and Jackson 1983). The main questions dividing the policy agendas of the two major parties have been how active the government should be in managing the economy and how generous the government should be in redistributing resources to the less advantaged. But this is clearly not the only dimension of the current liberal-conservative policy divide. Since at least the 1960s, race has provided a second or even primary issue dimension, with racially liberal whites supporting the Democratic Party and racially conservative whites favoring the Republican Party (Carmines and Stimson 1989; Edsall and Edsall 1991; Huckfedlt and Kohfeld 1989; Greenberg 1990). Finally, the two parties have also begun to divide more clearly and more sharply on issues related to social morality. With the Republicans increasingly highlighting their party's positions on issues such as homosexuality and abortion, morality has become more central to partisan decisions (Abramowitz 1995; Nussbaum and Gelbart 2004).

three issues, we can safely ignore mixed views as a major factor in partisanship. Of all the possible combinations of views on the three issues, accounts of American politics often highlight two. Studies of recent presidential campaigns and accounts based on public opinion surveys regularly focus on a group of white Americans that is both racially conservative and generally liberal. Sometimes referred to as Reagan Democrats, this group is composed of individuals who profess to be liberal and who support many elements of a liberal agenda but who at the same time identify strongly as white and resent recent changes to the racial status quo that have diminished whites' status relative to black America (Greenberg 1990; Edsall and Edsall 1992). Another group that gets some attention come election time is fiscal liberals who are conservative on religious or moral questions (Rasmussen 2007). Although this group, sometimes referred to as Main Street Republicans, is not as well publicized as the Reagan Democrats, recent accounts suggest that it has been important in Democrats' failures in recent presidential contests (Nussbaum and Gelbart 2004).[7]

A cursory examination of the ANES and GSS confirms that substantial numbers of white Americans do hold these two particular sets of views. Depending on how we define each group, we find that somewhere between 6 and 13 percent of the public are liberals who are racially conservative,[8] and about 14 percent can be considered fiscal liberals who are morally conservative.[9] In short, significant segments of the American population hold views that conflict with each other on these dimensions.[10]

---

[7] Brady (2003) distinguishes between Main Street Republicans (who are conservative on religious or cultural issues and fiscally liberal) and Wall Street Republicans (who are liberal on religious or cultural issues and fiscally conservative). It is not clear, however, how firmly either of these groups stands behind the Republican Party.

[8] The range occurs because we are forced to use slightly different questions and codings to define those who are ambivalent in the GSS and the ANES. For the ANES, these are respondents who place themselves to the left of center on the basic ideology scale and to the right of center on a seven-point scale asking whether or not "government should make any special effort to help blacks." For the GSS, they are respondents who place themselves to the left of center on the basic ideology scale and who are against more government spending to "improve the conditions of blacks." Full coding details and question wording are included in the online appendix.

[9] For the ANES, these are respondents who place themselves to the left of center on a seven-point question asking about the trade-off between increasing government services and reducing government spending and who take the two more conservative views on a four-point scale that asks under what conditions abortion should be legally allowed. Full coding details and question wording are included in the online appendix. This measure is not available across most years of the GSS.

[10] We could find no other group with conflicting views that were held by equally large shares of the public across the three policy areas of race, economics, and social morality.

Hypotheses 1.1 and 1.2: Liberals who are racially conservative and fiscal liberals who are religious conservatives should be more likely to identify as Independents.

Extreme Views and Partisan Choice

Extreme views are also unlikely to lead to Independence unless two conditions are met. For white Americans to reject both parties in favor of Independence, they must feel that a particular issue is critically important and they must believe that neither party has engaged in or co-opted the issue. If the issue is not that important, then there is little reason to abandon the only two electorally viable partisan options. And if one or both parties have signaled that they care about the issue and have put it on their agenda, then there will be a strong impetus to support that party (or both parties).

To try to identify likely issues, we consider the four major social movements that have emerged on the American scene in the last half century: civil rights, women's rights, environmentalism, and religious fundamentalism.[11] In each movement, large subsets of the population care deeply about the issue, and a large part of their political identity centers on the movement. In other words, there are large issue publics for each movement. The key question in each case is whether either political party has engaged the movement and tried to incorporate its concerns into the party's agenda. We believe that for at least two of these social movements—environmentalism and women's rights—individuals who hold extreme views on the subject may not have a clear partisan advocate. An environmentalist, for example, who advocates extensive animal rights will get little comfort from the positions of either the Democratic or the Republican Party. Similarly, feminists who push for more expansive women's rights often fail to get an enthusiastic response from either party. The Democratic and Republican parties certainly regularly address both issues, but neither party stakes out positions that come close to the preferences of issue advocates. To the extent that neither party stakes out a position in line with the views of members of these issue publics, those who feel strongly about these issues would not be drawn to either party. For the most recent social movement, religious fundamentalism, whether or not a party has engaged or co-opted the views of extremists is less clear. The Republican Party has staked out positions that align neatly with much of the Christian Right, but there are certainly areas where

---

[11] Antiglobalization is a fifth emerging social movement that, we suspect, is beginning to influence partisan identification. We cannot, however, systematically test how strong views on this issue affect partisanship because available political surveys have not addressed this topic in sufficient depth.

those with sharply conservative religious and moral preferences often feel that the Republican Party is unwilling to accede to their demands. Since our expectations are not clear on this latter issue, we include it in our analysis. Finally, in the case of the civil rights movement, it is clear that the two parties have engaged in the issue. Racial policy is now near the heart of the partisan divide, with racial liberalism clearly associated with the Democratic Party and racial conservatism clearly associated with the Republican Party (Carmines and Stimson 1989). This leads to the following three hypotheses:

> *Hypotheses 2.1, 2.2, 2.3: Environmentalists should be more likely to identify as Independents. Feminists should be more likely to identify as Independents. Religious fundamentalists may be more likely to identify as Independents.*

With these concrete policy issues in mind, we can now proceed to empirically test this alternate model of white partisan choice. As we have done throughout the book, we test our multidimensional model of party identification against more traditional accounts of partisan choice. Specifically, we test the Downsian, ideologically based view of party identification by assessing whether those with more moderate views end up in the middle as Independents. To assess childhood socialization and whether Independents are the offspring of Independents—both associated with the Michigan School account of party identification—we measure the link between Independence and parental party identification and political apathy.

RESEARCH DESIGN

To test these hypotheses, we begin with the standard tool of American public opinion research—a pooled sample (1948–2000) of the American National Election Studies (Miller and National Election Studies 2000). The principal advantage of the ANESover other surveys is the fact that in most years it incorporates questions that directly assess conventional models of party choice. The principal disadvantage of the ANES is that it contains only basic questions on policy. This means that it is difficult to identify respondents with extreme views on each of the three issue publics. Thus, we supplement this primary analysis with data from a pooled sample (1972–2002) of the General Social Survey (GSS).[12] The GSS con-

---

[12] The GSS is an annual survey of face-to-face interviews with a multistage area probability sample of the national adult population. Each survey includes roughly two thousand respondents, and the response rate over this period averages close to 75 percent. For more

tains a range of questions that gauge more comprehensively the policy positions of Americans on the environment, feminism, and religion. The principal disadvantage of the GSS is that it asks these policy questions only in certain years. Therefore, a complete model that incorporates all of the key concepts we are concerned with cannot be constructed for any single year of the GSS.

THE DEPENDENT VARIABLE

Our dependent variable of interest is the respondent's self-identification as an Independent. As we noted in chapter 1, there is some debate about exactly who should be characterized as Independent. In this chapter we once again focus primarily on the more inclusive measure, namely all respondents who identify in the first instance as Independents (including those who lean toward one party).[13] However, given the doubts we have about the Independence of those who lean toward one party, we repeat the analysis and include only those who profess no partisan leanings—so-called pure Independents.[14]

THE INDEPENDENT VARIABLES

We include a range of measures to test standard accounts of partisan identification. As we noted earlier, the underlying dimension of the Downsian model of party identification is ideology (Downs 1957; Key 1966; Kramer 1971; Fiorina 1981; Erikson, Mackuen, and Stimson 2002). From this Downsian perspective, one would expect Independents to be found disproportionately in the middle of a conservative-liberal ideological spectrum. To determine if the Independents-as-ideological-moderates view is accurate, we include the basic seven-point scale of political ideol-

---

details on the survey, sampling procedures, and survey methodology, see Davis, Smith, and Marsden (2003).

[13] We do so primarily because the political behavior of pure Independents, Independent leaners, and weak partisan identifiers does—under the right circumstances—differ substantially. In particular, as we will show in chapter 8, the willingness of the three groups to support third-party candidates differs—especially when a viable third-party option emerges. Categorizing Independent leaners as partisan, therefore, is problematic.

[14] Given questions about those who offer more noncompliant responses such as "no preference" or "no answer," we also attempted to single out this group. We suspect that these nonresponses indicate a certain amount of ambivalence or uncertainty about partisan choice. However, it is difficult to test this with white respondents, since the number of non-responses is so small. Among white Americans, this group comprises less than 2 percent of the population.

ogy (from liberal to conservative). Recall that there are two empirical claims folded into this account: first, moderates are the ideological group most likely to identify as Independent; second, the remaining categories of party identification have a linear statistical relationship to the remaining categories of political ideology. To test both claims, we specify our models with dummy variables for each category (from strong liberal to strong conservative).

By contrast, the Michigan School views party identification as an enduring attachment that is acquired through a socialization process in one's youth. To assess socialization and the intergenerational transfer of partisan identification, we included a measure that indicated whether two, one, or neither of the respondent's parents were "generally identified" as Independents. Since the Michigan School also tends to view nonpartisanship as a sign of political apathy, we also attempted to assess this Independence as "apolitical" account. Specifically, we included measures of political information, political efficacy, political trust, political interest, and political participation. Political information was measured as a dummy variable indicating that a respondent could correctly name the majority party in the House of Representatives. Political efficacy was a reversed additive scale of agree/disagree responses to the following two statements: (a) "Public officials don't care much what people like me think" and (b) "People like me don't have any say about what the government does." How regularly respondents felt they could trust "the government in Washington" to do the right thing is employed as a measure of political trust. Responses to a question about one's level of interest in "following the political campaigns (so far) this year" were used to measure political interest. Finally, political participation was based on the number of different types of political acts a respondent had undertaken over the course of the last campaign. Possible acts included attending a meeting, working for a party or candidate, contributing money, displaying a political sign, trying to influence others, and contacting a public official.[15]

To test our own alternate accounts of Independence, we include two additional sets of measures. First in the ANES, to gauge the explanatory power of the Independents-as-extremists hypothesis, we include three measures. To gauge views on women's rights, respondents were asked whether "women should have an equal role with men in running business, industry, and government" or whether "a woman's place is in the home." The answers ranged along a seven-point scale. To assess religious conservatism, we employed a question about abortion. Respondents were

---

[15] In the GSS, the only regularly available measure of political apathy is whether the respondent reported voting in the last presidential election.

asked where their views fit along a four-point continuum ranging from "abortion should never be permitted" to "a woman should always be able to obtain an abortion." A basic measure asking respondents the degree to which they would support increased funding for environmental protection is used to assess attitudes toward environmentalism. These measures are problematic in that they do not allow us to isolate those with truly extremist views. They are, however, the only available policy measures in the ANES.

Since the ANES measures are limited in their depth, we repeat the analysis utilizing the greater range of policy measures included in the GSS. In the GSS, to identify advocates of women's rights, we combine responses from five questions that ask about various aspects of women's equality. The questions probe respondents about the importance of women's staying home to take care of their families, the degree to which women should support their husband's careers, the role of women in running the country, whether women should work if they already have a husband who is working, and whether they would support a female presidential candidate. To gauge support for the Christian Right's social program, we created a scale that included questions on abortion, homosexuality, premarital sex, and how fundamental respondents felt their religious values were. To see if strong proenvironment views are associated with Independence, we created a scale that included questions about the use of animals for medical research, how much we should spend to protect the environment, and the relationship between the environment and human progress.[16] In each case, we tested the robustness of our findings by replacing the scales with dummy variables that isolated those respondents with the most extreme views. These tests generally confirmed the results that we present below.

In all of our measures of extremism, we explicitly focused on issue publics on one end of the political spectrum. If we thought that extremists on either side of an issue were equally prone to identifying as nonpartisan, we would have "folded" answers into each issue around the midpoint to obtain a measure of the intensity of preferences. However, since these three social movements were clearly identified with one side of the political spectrum, we did not do so. Those who cared deeply enough about the environment to vote almost exclusively on the issue are almost all on the left. Likewise, the women's movement emerged from the Left, and the religious Right is obviously located on the other end of the pole.

Finally, to see if individuals with strong but divergent views and identi-

---

[16] The reliability of these three scales is reasonable with Cronbach's alpha of 0.71 for the feminist scale, 0.59 for the religious conservatism scale, and 0.53 for the environmentalism scale.

ties are more likely than others to choose Independence, we focused on the partisan choices of two different groups: (1) racially conservative liberals and (2) religiously conservative fiscal liberals. To isolate those with generally liberal views and racially conservative attitudes in the ANES, we combined the general ideological scale (self-placement as liberal, moderate, or conservative) and views on a single question asking whether special assistance should be provided to improve conditions in the black community. Specifically, we isolated all those who placed themselves to the left of center on the seven-point ideological scale and those who also placed themselves to the right of center on the seven-point assistance-to-blacks scale.[17] For the GSS, we combined the same ideological scale and the question whether enough was being done to improve conditions in the black community. Here we singled out all respondents who placed themselves to the left of center on the seven-point ideology scale and who also did not agree that we should spend more money to "improve the conditions of blacks." To identify religious, conservative fiscal liberals in the ANES, we combined responses to the same abortion question mentioned earlier (asking under what conditions abortion should be legally allowed) with a question that asked where respondents fit on a seven-point scale ranging from "government should provide many fewer services: reduce spending a lot" to "government should provide many more services: increase spending a lot." Here, to identify those with mixed views, we singled out respondents who placed themselves to the left of center on the question of government services / reducing government spending and who also chose one of the two more conservative options on the four-point abortion scale.[18] The exact question wording, coding, and cutoffs for all of these measures, as well as basic descriptive statistics, are included in the online appendix (http://press.princeton.edu/titles/9468.html).

Independents in the Middle?

We begin to test the assumptions underlying conventional accounts of Independence and partisanship by looking at the relationship between liberal-conservative political ideology and partisanship. If basic assumptions about the linearity and ideology of partisanship hold, these two measures should move in unison. And given that we are looking only at whites, the relationship should be especially tight.

---

[17] Six percent of white respondents fit these criteria.

[18] Since similar measures are not available across most years of the GSS, we cannot test this particular mix of views using the GSS.

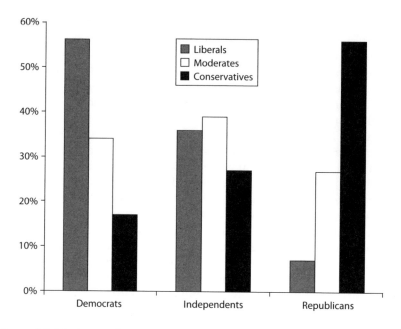

Figure 7.1. Ideology and partisanship

Figure 7.1, which shows the breakdown of partisanship among different ideological groups, leads to several provisional conclusions about the link between ideology and partisanship. First, the figure provides strong support for the conventional notion that partisanship is based at least in part upon a linear liberal-conservative ideological dimension. As the figure shows, those who identify as liberals are also much more apt than other ideological groups to identify as Democrats. Over half of all self-avowed liberals (56 percent) end up as Democrats. By contrast, only 17 percent of conservatives choose to identify as Democrats. Similarly, when we look at Republicans, we see that those who identify themselves as conservative are more apt to be Republican than those with different ideological leanings. Roughly half (49 percent) of those who call themselves conservative choose to be Republican versus only 7 percent of liberals. Partisanship is obviously undergirded by a liberal-conservative ideology.

However, it is also clear from figure 7.1 that the relationship between ideology and partisanship is far from perfect. The correlation between the two measures is only 0.31. This figure is fairly high for a public opinion survey but certainly not an indication that partisanship and ideology are one and the same. This leads to two slightly less obvious but nevertheless important observations about figure 7.1 and ultimately about partisanship. First, as can be seen in the figure, Independents are an extremely ideological diverse population. Very roughly, a third of self-proclaimed liberals, a third of admitted moderates, and a quarter of self-identified strong conservatives end up as Independents. In other words, it is not accurate to view Independents as moderates who hold middle-of-the-road views. Second, there is a hint of an ideological bias to Independence. Whereas 34 percent of all liberals identify themselves as Independents or nonpartisans, only 27 percent of all conservatives choose not to identify with a major party. And as we will see later in this chapter, when we isolate those with extreme views on either pole, the difference is even starker. Fully 44 percent of strong liberals identify as Independent. By contrast, only 26 of strong conservatives do so. This suggests—but certainly does not prove—that those on the far left are more apt to abandon the Democratic Party for Independence than those on the right are to abandon the Republican Party for Independence. Ultimately, figure 7.1 illustrates that while a single ideological dimension does help to place many Americans along a linear scale of partisanship, many white Americans do not seem to fit where they are supposed to.

INDEPENDENTS BEYOND THE MIDDLE

If Independents are not simply ideological moderates, then who are they? In figures 7.2 and 7.3, we begin to look at two other potential dimensions of Independence—extremism and ambiguity. In the two figures, we show how likely it is that different groups of individuals end up identifying as Independent.

In the first figure, we look at the relationship between extremism and Independence. Specifically, we compare the partisanship of those who hold strongly liberal, middle-of-the-road, and strongly conservative views on the environment, feminism, and religious morality. To try to isolate the range of views on each of these subjects, we use the GSS, and as we described earlier, we employ scales that are based on four questions about the environment, five questions on women's rights, and four questions on religious morality (on abortion, homosexuality, premarital sex, and religiosity). Extremists are those who end up in the top 5 percent or the bottom 5 percent of each scale.

If traditional accounts of partisanship hold, we would expect those who hold middle-of-the-road views to be the most likely to identify as Independents. Instead, we find that those who hold more extreme views are more apt to identify as Independents. In particular, as we expected, those who are strongly proenvironment and those who are strongly pro–

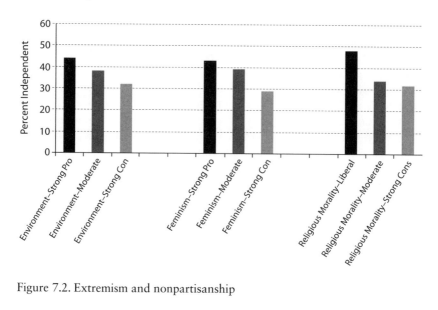

Figure 7.2. Extremism and nonpartisanship

women's rights are significantly more likely than others to end up as Independent[19]—a pattern that suggests that advocates on these issues often do not feel that they have a natural partisan home. On religious morality, the pattern is not what we expected but is nevertheless interesting. Given the relatively recent rise of the religious Right, we might have guessed that members of the religious Right had not yet found a clear partisan home. It is, however, clear, from figure 7.2 that those on the Far Right on religious views are quite partisan—only 32 percent end up as Independents. Presumably, the Republican Party has done enough to incorporate their views. By contrast, fully 48 percent of those who hold strongly liberal views on questions of morality and religion choose to identify as Independents. All told, the figure suggests that a disproportionate number of those on the Far Left on emerging social movements do not choose to identify with a party. Extremism appears to matter, and at least at first glance, it appears to be hurting the Democratic Party on the left.

In figure 7.3, we perform a similar analysis of the relationship between mixed views and Independence. Here we attempt to see whether two groups of individuals are particularly apt to identify as Independent: (1) those who call themselves liberals but espouse racially conservative views and (2) those who hold fiscally liberal and socially conservative

[19] Significant difference in a pairwise T-test at $p < .01$.

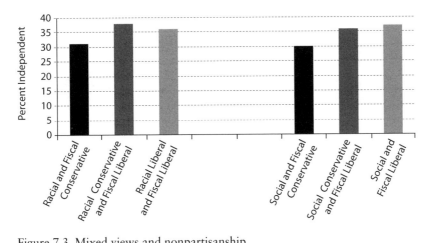

Figure 7.3. Mixed views and nonpartisanship

views. Racially conservative liberals are those who place themselves to the left of center on the basic seven-point liberal-conservative ideology scale and who also place themselves to the right of center on a seven-point assistance-to-blacks scale (e.g., those who identify as liberal and who also indicate that the government does "too much" to improve conditions for African Americans). Fiscally liberal social conservatives are respondents who place themselves to the left of center on a seven-point question asking about the trade-off between increasing government services and reducing government spending and who take the two more conservative views on a four-point scale that asks under what conditions abortion should be legally allowed.

The pattern in figure 7.3 is more mixed than the one in figure 7.2. There are some signs that those who hold conflicting views on race and other policy areas are more likely to choose Independence. In this case, 38 percent of those who hold mixed views identify themselves as nonpartisan. However, the magnitude of the difference between those who hold mixed views and those who hold consistent views on the two issues is not that large. Fully 36 percent of those who hold consistently liberal views and 32 percent of those who hold consistently conservative views also identify as Independent. The findings on divergent views on fiscal and social policy are clearer. Those who hold mixed views on these two policy areas are no more likely than those who hold consistently liberal views to be nonpartisans. Thus, while there is some indication that holding divergent views marginally increases the odds of identifying as Independent in some cases, much more work needs to be done to establish this causal relationship.

In table 7.1 we attempt to offer a more complete account of Independence that incorporates both conventional accounts and our own assertions about extremist Independents and ambiguous Independents. In the table, which focuses on white respondents to the ANES, we control for the two conventional accounts of Independents: (1) the Downsian model—Independents as moderates—and (2) the Michigan School—Independents as the offspring of Independents or as apolitical. We also include measures of ideological extremism and ideological ambiguity. The table shows the results of a single logistic regression modeling Independence. Independence is a simple dummy variable indicating whether or not respondents first identified as Independents or nonpartisans instead of as partisan supporters.

The first and most obvious conclusion to be drawn from table 7.1 is that conventional accounts do work. First, the "Independents as moderates" claim seems to fairly accurately depict the partisan pathways of at least some white Americans. Self-proclaimed ideological moderates and those who view themselves as being only weakly liberal or weakly conservative are significantly more likely to be Independent than those who call themselves conservatives or liberals. The childhood-socialization hypothesis is also borne out for whites. Even after controlling for their ideological views and several other measures of their political orientation, the identification of respondents' parents strongly predicts party choice.[20] The more critical view of Independents as apolitical also finds support here. Those who are less interested, less knowledgeable, less efficacious, less trusting, and less active in politics are significantly more likely to identify as nonpartisan or Independent.

The second and more interesting conclusion is that Independents also tend to be extremists. In two of the three issue publics we examine, the results closely match our expectations. As we predicted, the more liberal their views on the environment and the stronger their support of women's equality, the more likely they are to identify as Independents or nonpartisans.[21] In each case the magnitude of the effect is meaningful if not dramatic. All else being equal, those who are the most supportive of environmental spending are 5 percent more likely to be Independent than those who believe we are already spending too much on the environment.

---

[20] Having two parents who had contrasting party identifications (e.g., one Republican and the other Democrat) also seemed to marginally increase the chances of identifying as Independent. The effect was not quite significant, and the inclusion of this measure had no noticeable effect on any of the other relationships in table 7.1.

[21] If one simply singles out those with the most liberal views on the environment or the most liberal views on women's rights (rather than using the scales in table 7.1), the conclusion is the same. Individuals with strongly liberal views are significantly more likely than all others to be Independents.

TABLE 7.1
The Different Dimensions of Independence (ANES) (Logistic Regression)

	Identify as Independent	
Downsian model		
Independents as moderates		
Weak liberal	.22	(.11)*
Moderate	.72	(.08)**
Weak conservative	.41	(.09)**
Michigan model		
Childhood socialization		
Parents Independent	.74	(.08)**
Independents as apolitical		
Political participation	−.12	(.03)**
Political interest	−.22	(.05)**
Political knowledge	−.24	(.08)**
Government trust	−.01	(.00)**
Political efficacy	−.01	(.00)**
Alternate dimensions		
Independents as extremists		
Environmental spending	.10	(.05)^
Women's equality	.05	(.02)*
Anti-abortion views	−.06	(.04)
Independents as ambiguous		
Racially conservative liberal		
Racial conservatism scale	−.02	(.02)
Racially conservative* liberal	.24	(.13)^
Morally conservative fiscal liberals		
Fiscal liberalism scale	.01	(.03)
Religiously conservative* fiscal liberal	.03	(.13)
Controls		
South	.15	(.07)*
Year	−.01	(.01)
Age	−.01	(.00)**
Education	−.00	(.04)
Income	.08	(.03)*
Constant	22.6	(16.4)
Pseudo R-squared	.07	
N	5,066	

Source: NES Cumulative File.
Significance levels: **$p < .01$ *$p <. 05$ ^$p <. 10$.

Similarly, white Americans who strongly favor efforts to ensure women's rights are 5 percent more likely to identify as Independents or nonpartisans than those who are least in favor of government action on women's equality. On two of the major social movements in America, those who hold strong views on the left are particularly apt to not identify with a major political party. This suggests that if neither party actively endorses an emerging issue, issue publics who care enough about that issue will reject both parties.

In table 7.1 we also looked at how views on religious or moral issues affected partisanship. Since many observers claim that the Republican Party has actively taken up the cause of the Christian Right by opposing gay rights, attempting to ban or limit abortions, and supporting government funding of religious organizations, there are fewer reasons to expect a positive relationship between extremist views on this issue and Independence—and possibly some reasons to expect a negative relationship between moral conservatism and Independence. The results in table 7.1 are informative (if not fully conclusive). What is clear from table 7.1 is that moral conservatism does not lead to greater Independence and nonpartisanship. The negative coefficient for views on abortion indicates that those on the far right on this issue are not more prone to choosing Independence. What is less clear is whether liberals or those on the far left are especially apt to end up not identifying as partisans. The fact that the coefficient is negative and almost significant seems to imply that the more liberal one's views on abortion, the more likely one is to identify as Independent. But any definitive conclusion about moral liberals will have to await an analysis of other, more in-depth measures of moral liberalism.

The third conclusion, as demonstrated in Table 7.1, is that holding ideologically mixed views constitutes yet another route to Independence. The logic here is fairly straightforward. Americans with strong liberal stances on some policy questions and strong conservative preferences on others should, because of their views, have a difficult time fitting in with either party. The results in table 7.1 suggest that this is true for at least one particular set of views. Self-identified liberals who also hold conservative views on racial policy are especially likely to end up as Independents. Importantly, racial views by themselves have no direct effect on Independence in this model. It is only those who are generally liberal but who prefer not to enact special policies to help blacks who are more prone to identifying as Independent. In other words, a clash of liberalism and racial resentment is driving many whites away from the Democratic Party toward Independence. The effects are substantial. Holding other factors constant at their modal value, the probability of identifying as Independent or nonpartisan is 42 percent among white Americans who are both racially conservative and fiscally liberal, compared with only 34 and 33 percent among those who hold either consistently liberal or consistently conservative views across these two areas. Holding both liberal and conservative views simultaneously leads to ambiguity and Independence in this case.

It is worth noting that these ambiguous Independents make up a sizable portion of the Independent population. Almost 7 percent of all Independents hold views that are simultaneously liberal and racially conservative—defined as identifying oneself as liberal on the basic liberal-conservative ideology scale and indicating that the government should not spend more to improve conditions for blacks.[22] The fact that a substantial number of racial conservatives who are otherwise liberal are defecting from the Democratic Party has not gone unnoticed. A number of pollsters and political analysts have noted this trend in presidential voting patterns (Greenberg 1990; Edsall and Edsall 1992; Carmines and Stimson 1989).

It is also important to note that this ambivalent effect is not simply due to a lack of political sophistication. When we reran the analysis to include only those with above-average political knowledge or above-average educational attainment, we found that the relationships we see in table 7.1 were slightly more pronounced. Ideology (even ambivalent ideology) seems to matter more for those with higher levels of political sophistication.

Holding mixed or conflicted views does not, however, always lead to Independence. The same type of effect is not evident when we focus on the clash between fiscal liberalism and religious conservatism. As table 7.1 reveals, those who simultaneously oppose abortion and seek more government spending and services are not especially apt to identify as Independents.[23] We suspect that this may be because both sets of views are not equally important, and a respondent's position on one dimension may dominate. Some social conservatives, for example, may consider themselves conservative and Republican regardless of their fiscal policy views. Other fiscal liberals might see themselves as liberal and identify with the Democratic Party regardless of their social policy views.[24]

---

[22] Obviously, each set of mixed views depends greatly on exactly how the questions are asked and where we institute the cutoff between strong and moderate views on each subject. The questions and cutoffs that we employ in the GSS yield a result of 13.7 percent of the public holding mixed views on these issues.

[23] In alternate tests, we also singled out those who are both socially liberal and fiscally conservative but again found no link to Independence.

[24] There is some concern that the relationship between ideology and party identification is reciprocal and thus that policy positions are in part the result rather than the cause of

To further explore the relationship between mixed views and partisanship, we repeated the analysis with a slightly different measure of mixed views. In these alternative tests, we looked at those who held views that they perceived to be to the left of the Democratic Party on one dimension and to the right of the Republican Party on a second dimension. This may, in fact, be a better test of whether conflicted views lead to Independence. In some ways, what should matter is not where respondents place themselves on an ideological scale but rather where they place themselves relative to the two parties. If respondents believe that they are closer to one party on one key issue and closer to the other party on a second key issue, then there is no clear partisan choice, and Independence becomes a rational alternative. The results of this alternative test closely mirror the findings in table 7.1 (the analysis is not shown). Divergent views on race and other policy areas continued to matter, whereas mixed views on social and fiscal policy continued to have noticeably little effect. Specifically, white Americans who place themselves to the left of the Democratic Party on government spending and to the right of the Democratic Party on racial policy are significantly more likely to identify as Independents or nonpartisans than those who place themselves consistently on the same side of the parties.[25]

Finally, to try to further understand both these ambiguity effects and how extremism leads to Independence, we reran the analysis in table 7.1 using a multinomial logistic regression. This additional analysis allowed us to distinguish between Democrats and Republicans and to see how factors that lead to the choice of Independence over Republican identification differ from the factors that lead to the choice of Independence over Democratic identification. Although there are interesting differences, the bottom line of this analysis is that we continue to see strong evidence of both paths to Independence (the analysis is not shown).

---

party identification. This is certainly true in some cases—although existing research that tests for this reciprocity has generally found that party identification has only a very small effect on most individual policy positions (Franklin 1984; Page and Jones 1979; but see Goren 2005). It is, however, hard to imagine how Independence could lead individuals to hold extreme views on issues such as the environment or to hold a particular mix of views such as liberalism and racial conservatism. For this reason, we believe that endogeneity is likely to be less of a problem when examining Independence as an outcome.

[25] At this point it is also worth noting that these ambivalent Independents are distinct from both self-described ideological moderates and apoliticals. First, individuals who hold mixed views are not significantly more likely than others to consider themselves moderates. Second, individuals who hold mixed views are only marginally less likely to be interested in or informed about politics. Finally, since we control for both ideological moderation and a range of measures of political apathy (including political interest, efficacy, and knowledge), the effects that we see for mixed views are above and beyond these two other factors.

The results presented in this chapter strongly suggest that there are multiple routes to Independence. Using quite basic measures, we have found that those with strong views on issues that neither party is actively addressing and those with divergent views on some core issues often end up identifying as Independents. However, the measures used to test each of these hypotheses in table 7.1 were limited by the fact that the ANES includes only one policy question on each policy domain. With one question and often only three or four response categories, it is difficult to gauge the strength of each respondent's views on the subject and even more difficult to identify those with extreme views. Thus, to try to gauge each of these ideological dimensions more deeply and to test the robustness of our findings, we now turn to an analysis of the General Social Survey. Our results are presented in table 7.2 in the form of a logistic regression modeling Independence. The advantage of the GSS is that it contains an array of measures that help to measure the intensity of preferences and to identify extremists.[26] Again, question wording, coding, and descriptive statistics for these measures are detailed in the online appendix (http://press.princeton.edu/titles/9468.html).

The results from the GSS closely mirror our analysis of the ANES. First, there is a clear link between issue publics and Independence. For all three social movements, those who hold strong views are significantly more likely than others to not identify with one of the two mainstream parties. In particular, as we just saw, those with strong feminist views are much more apt to be Independent. Those who were more supportive of women working outside the home, less concerned about women helping the careers of their husbands, and more willing to support female politicians were 16 percent more likely to be Independent than those who held conservative views on each of these questions. Similarly, table 7.2 reconfirms the tie between environmentalism and Independence. Those who were most concerned about improving and protecting the environment were more than 7 percent more likely to be Independent than those who believed we are already doing too much for the environment.[27]

[26] The principal disadvantage of the GSS, as is visible from the model in table 7.2, is that many of the more mainstream measures of political involvement and parental party identification are not available in most years of the survey. Also, the few questions on fiscal liberalism that are included in the GSS are not asked in the same years as the questions on moral policy. Thus, our model is somewhat incomplete.

[27] Moreover, these effects are robust to changes in the measurement of feminism or environmentalism. For example, for each single question, those who strongly favor animal rights, who oppose genetic modification of food, who believe that humans are bad for the

Table 7.2
The Different Dimensions of Independence (GSS) (Logistic Regression)

	Identify as Independent	
Downsian model		
Independents as moderates		
Weak liberal	.14	(.07)^
Moderate	.40	(.05)**
Weak conservative	.20	(.06)**
Michigan School		
Independents as apolitical		
voters	−.72	(.05)**
Alternate dimensions		
Independents as extremists		
Environmentalist score	.11	(.03)**
Feminist score	.17	(.05)**
Religious conservative score	−.18	(.03)**
Independents as ambiguous		
Racial conservatism scale	.01	(.03)
Racially conservative liberal	.22	(.07)**
Controls		
South	−.17	(.04)**
Year	−.00	(.01)
Age	−.01	(.00)**
Education	.01	(.01)^
Income	−.01	(.01)
Constant	6.0	(6.1)
Pseudo R-squared	.04	
N	11,338	

Source: GSS Cumulative File.
Significance levels: **$p <. 01$ *$p < .05$ ^ $p < .10$.

With the more refined measure of religious fundamentalism that we can create in the GSS, we also see that religious or moral views are now significantly related to partisanship. The direction of the effect is particularly interesting. Those with the most liberal views on religion are the most

environment, or who volunteer to try to protect the environment are more likely than others to identify as Independents. In terms of feminist views, those who think businesses should make special efforts to hire more women, who believe that women are underpaid, who feel that women are discriminated against in employment, and who think the issue of women's rights is important are also significantly more likely than others to choose to identify themselves as Independents.

likely to end up as Independents. The negative and significant coefficient on the religious conservatism score indicates that the more liberal one's views on abortion, homosexuality, and teenage sexual relations, the more likely one is to end up as an Independent. All else being equal, the probability of identifying as an Independent is 40 percent among religious liberals, compared with only 29 percent among religious conservatives.[28] This suggests that the Christian Right has been effectively co-opted by the Republican Party. It is those who are sharply liberal on moral or religious issues who seem to hold a less mainstream partisan allegiance.

When combined, these results point to a clear bias in partisan choice. For all three issue publics, those on the far right of the political spectrum are much less apt to abandon the Republican Party than those on the far left are to abandon the Democratic Party. This has important implications for the Democratic Party and its strategic interests in catering to the Left. We hold off from further elaboration on this point until we test this liberal bias more directly later in the chapter.

Table 7.2 also confirms our second proposed pathway to Independence. Americans who hold strong but conflicted views are particularly prone to being Independent. Once again, we see that those who generally think of themselves as liberal but who also hold racially conservative views are more apt to reject both parties. The key independent variable here is an interaction term that shows that those who place themselves to the left of center on basic ideology and to the right of center on racial concerns are significantly more likely than others to identity as Independent. At least in this one instance, a clash of ideologies or political orientations has a clear effect.

Importantly, the basic conclusions that table 7.2 helps to illustrate garner additional support from a set of alternative analyses that focus on pure Independents. When we grouped Independent leaners with partisans and repeated the analysis in table 7.2, we obtained similar results. The results in the online appendix (http://press.princeton.edu/titles/9468 .html) indicate that extremism and ambivalence play a role in Independence even when Independence is confined to those who profess to have no leaning toward either party.

VARIATION OVER TIME AND ACROSS REGION

One concern with the analysis so far is that it combines surveys across years and regions without considering how parties have changed over time. Since 1960 there has been an important shift in how the parties

---

[28] Alternate tests similarly indicate that Evangelicals and those who identify themselves as religious fundamentalists are especially unlikely to identify as Independents.

have been viewed on matters of race and a resultant shift in partisanship, with many white southern Democrats slowly moving to the Republican side, and many of those who shifted probably identifying as Independent in the middle of that journey (Black and Black 1987, 1973; Valentino and Sears 2005). Also, by at least some accounts, moral and religious questions have become more central to party identification in recent years (Abramowitz 1994; Nussbaum and Gelbart 2004). Given these changes, we attempted to determine how our story of Independents varied across time and region. Our basic method was either to confine the analysis to a particular time period or region or to include in our regression models a range of interaction terms for each of our ideological dimensions with both year and region dummy variables.

Our analysis indicates that there is some variation across region and time. None of the effects we found was particularly strong or particularly robust to different specifications, but there is at least some evidence that the ambivalence of white liberals who hold racially conservative views had a slightly more pronounced effect outside the South. The realignment of southern white racial conservatives undoubtedly contributed to the growth in the number of Independents, but we suspect that the move to Independence among southern whites was not because they held a mix of liberal and conservative views on race and other matters. We believe that much of the ambiguous effect of Independents can be attributed to groups such as Reagan Democrats who were core liberal supporters of the Democratic Party until the issue of race came along (Greenberg 1990). Although the union workers and manufacturing employees that formed the bulk of the Reagan Democrats could be found all around the country, they were certainly more concentrated in the Northeast and Midwest than in the South. The only other significant or nearly significant interactions we could find were with religious views. In both the GSS and the ANES, the religious Right was even less likely to identify as Independent in the South. Similarly, those on the religious Right were somewhat less likely to identify as Independent over time.

But the bigger story is that there is less variation across region and over time than we suspected. Few of the interactions are significant, and the few effects that we noted are marginal in size. Part of this is probably due to data limitations. Although we use the 1948–2000 cumulative file of the ANES, our analysis is restricted to the years in which the ANES asked about the issue dimensions we care about. Since the ANES began asking most of these policy questions only in 1980, our analysis with the ANES is confined to the period between 1980 and 2000.[29] Moreover, when we start to examine the political behavior of extremists and those with mixed

---

[29] Similarly, with the GSS we can go back only to 1972.

views in a particular region or time frame, we note that our sample size gets pretty small. Nevertheless, we do believe that these results are telling us that neither the ambivalence story nor the extremism one is confined to a particular time or place. These two dimensions probably operate with varying intensity, but with a two-party system and an ideologically diverse population, the two dimensions should be relevant in a fairly wide range of circumstances.

The results of this point tell us that party identification is often not linearly related to a liberal-conservative political ideology. Ideological moderates do end up in the "middle" as Independents, but ideological extremists on the left are also very apt to end up as Independents. And for very different reasons, individuals with political orientations on both the Left and the Right also tend to identify as Independents. In both cases, individuals who hold far from moderate views end up as Independents. This tells us that Independents cannot really be placed in the middle of a linear scale of party identification, with Democrats on the left and Republicans on the right. The traditional linear-model party identification used in almost every study of American political behavior should, at least for some purposes, be augmented.

A Liberal Bias among Independents

One important implication of our results concerns a possible ideological bias in partisanship. Whereas individual Americans on the left appear to be abandoning the Democratic Party in large numbers, Americans on the right appear to maintain their allegiances to the Republican Party. In table 7.3 we assess this ideological and partisan bias more systematically. Specifically, we include a range of dummy variables for each category of the seven-point self-identified liberal-conservative ideology scale. The goal is to isolate self-identified strong liberals and strong conservatives to determine if either group is more likely to choose Independence. We present results for both the ANES and the GSS.

The results are fairly clear. Strong liberals are unique. The table demonstrates that in sharp contrast to what we would expect from conventional accounts of party identification, those on the far left of the ideological spectrum are not less likely than ideological moderates to identify as Independents. In the GSS, strong liberals are in fact substantially more likely than moderates to identify as Independents. All else being equal, strong liberals are 5 percent more likely than moderates to end up as Independents.

Importantly, the same pattern is not evident on the far right. In both the GSS and the ANES, strong conservatives, like almost all of the other

TABLE 7.3
The Liberal Bias to Independence (Logistic Regression)

	Identify as Independent			
	GSS		NES	
Downsian model				
Independents as moderates				
Strong liberal	.19	(.10)^	−.06	(15)
Liberal	−.14	(.05)**	−.36	(.07)**
Weak liberal	.01	(.05)	−.17	(.06)**
Moderate (excluded)	—		—	
Weak conservative	−.21	(.04)**	−.25	(.05)**
Conservative	−.56	(.05)**	−.63	(.06)**
Strong conservative	−.57	(.11)**	−.81	(.13)**
Michigan School				
Parental socialization				
Parents Independent	—		.82	(.05)**
Independents as apolitical				
voter/participation	−.77	(.04)	−.16	(.02)**
Political interest	—		−.17	(.03)**
Political knowledge	—		−.26	(.05)**
Government trust	—		−.01	(.00)**
Political efficacy	—		−.01	(.00)**
Controls				
South	−.16	(.03)**	−.01	(.04)
Year	.01	(.00)*	−.01	(.00)^
Age	−.01	(.00)	−.01	(.00)**
Education	.02	(.01)**	.08	(.02)**
Income	−.00	(.01)	.04	(.02)*
Constant	−9.7	(4.2)*	10.9	(5.3)*
Pseudo R-squared	.04		.06	
N	18,810		12,486	

Significance levels: **$p < .01$ * $p < .05$ ^$p < .10$.

ideological groups, are significantly less likely than moderates to identify as Independents. By holding other factors constant, we find that strong conservatives in the GSS are 18 percent less likely than strong liberals to choose Independence. The contrast is equally stark if we simply compare the party identification of strong liberals and strong conservatives without controlling for other factors. Overall, just over 40 percent of strong liberals in the GSS identify as Independents. By contrast, only 27 percent of strong conservatives opt to defect to the Independent option. It is also worth noting that the same pattern is evident if we group Independent leaners with partisans and focus on pure Independents. As the online appendix illustrates, those with views on the far left are not retaining an allegiance to the Democratic Party while choosing to identify themselves as Independent. Strong liberals are especially apt to identify as pure Independents as well. In short, there is a stark imbalance between the degree to which those on the far right and those on the far left abandon mainstream parties to identify as Independents.

There are at least two potential explanations for this liberal bias toward Independence. It could be that the Republican Party caters more to its extremist fringe. Many commentators and academics have argued that the Democratic Party has tended to ignore the interests of "captured" groups such as African Americans, who hold particularly liberal views (Frymer 1999, Walters 1988). Recent events have also suggested that leaders in the Democratic Party are leery of advocating for full rights for gays and lesbians. By contrast, George Bush and the Republican leadership in Congress pushed for a constitutional amendment to prevent same-sex marriage and have put forward fairly conservative positions on a range of moral and religious issues.[30] The lack of partisan defection on the Right could also simply be because there is less ideological distance between the mainstream of the Republican Party and the Far Right and thus less reason to abandon the party. Regardless of how we explain this imbalance, it is clear that liberals are more apt than conservatives and perhaps even ideological moderates to wind up with the Independent label.

One way to obtain further insight into this question is to look at how strong liberals and strong conservatives view the parties. When asked to place the two parties on an ideological continuum, strong liberals place the two parties significantly closer together on a range of basic policy issues than do strong conservatives.[31] Strong liberals also perceive a slightly greater distance between their own views and those of the party closest to them (presumably Democrats) than do strong conservatives who place the closest party (presumably Republicans) near their own views on most basic policy issues.[32] In short, strong liberals are less apt to see large partisan differences and more apt to feel ideologically distant from both

[30] Frymer (1999) argues that this is because the religious Right is particularly politically active and forms one of the largest voting blocs in the Republican coalition. It is, he maintains, also easier to advocate for religious conservative issues because many mainstream Americans are supportive of these kinds of stances. By contrast, when the Democratic Party pushes for expanded rights for blacks or gays and lesbians, it turns away many moderate voters.

[31] Across the five issues that were asked most regularly in the ANES, strong liberals saw an average partisan divide of only 2.7 points on a 7-point scale. That was less than strong conservatives, who perceived an average 3.2-point partisan divide on the same issues.

[32] Across the five issues that were asked most regularly in the ANES, the average distance between the self-perceived positions of strong liberals and their perceived placement of the

parties than are strong conservatives. The ideological bias that we see toward Independence is deeply rooted in perceptions of the ideological positions of the two parties.[33]

In highlighting this liberal bias, we are by no means claiming that the Democratic Party is forever doomed to lose a disproportionate share of its support from its extremist fringe. In fact, we suspect that the nature of any ideological bias toward Independence changes over time as new issues emerge and the two parties choose to engage or ignore more extremist positions on those issues. Our own analysis of change over time regarding this bias leads to mixed results. Using the ANES, we find that this liberal bias is declining over time. Specifically, when we add an interaction term for strong liberal views and the year of the survey to the model in table 7.3, we find that the interaction term is significant and negative, indicating that strong liberals are less and less likely to identify as Independents over time. But a similar analysis of the GSS finds no effects over time and instead indicates that the liberal bias persists to this day.[34] One reason for these mixed results may be that the extent of the liberal bias in recent years has depended in part on the type of candidate who is running a third-party presidential contest. Thus, it is probably not surprising to find that both the GSS and the ANES reveal a slightly weaker link between strong liberal views and Independence in 1992 and 1996, two years in which Ross Perot, a presidential candidate who garnered more support from the Right, ran robust third-party campaigns. Similarly, although the results are far from conclusive, there is at least a hint that strong liberals were particularly likely to identify as Independents in 2000—the year in which Ralph Nader ran a third-party campaign that was focused primarily on left-leaning voters. Ultimately, it is clear that

---

Democratic Party was 1.9 points on a 7-point scale. For strong conservatives and the Republican Party, the average gap was 1.7 points.

[33] All of this is ultimately reflected in how strong liberals and strong conservatives feel toward the two parties. Compared with strong conservatives, strong liberals have, on average, significantly colder feelings toward the parties (49 versus 56 on a 100-point feeling thermometer), significantly more reasons to dislike both parties (2.8 versus 2.3), significantly more negative overall evaluations of the parties (-.61 versus -.34 net affect), and significantly warmer feelings toward Independents (59 versus 48 on a 100-point feeling thermometer). T-tests indicate that all differences are significant at the .05 level.

[34] In the GSS, when an interaction between strong liberal views and the year of the survey is added to the model in table 7.3, it is insignificant. Moreover, an analysis of each year of the GSS survey shows fairly consistent findings over time. In particular, in no year were strong liberal views significantly less likely than moderate views to lead to Independence, and in a range of both more recent and older years, strongly liberal views were significantly more likely than moderate views to lead to Independence. By contrast, in most individual years, strongly conservative views were significantly less likely than moderate views to lead to Independence, and in no year were strongly conservative views associated with greater Independence.

regardless of these year-to-year variations, in recent decades the Democratic Party has had a hard time holding on to the allegiance of individuals whose views place them on the far left of the ideological spectrum. This is something that the Democratic Party will need to think seriously about when it considers the best strategy for trying to win future electoral contests.

DISCUSSION

This research has important implications for our understanding of party identification and partisan politics. First, it suggests that existing accounts of Independence are incomplete. The most common views of Independents—as ideological moderates, as the children of Independents, and as apolitical—fit some Independents, but by no means do they explain the choices of all who end up identifying as Independent. White Americans identify as Independent for a range of reasons that include ideological extremism and mixed or conflicting views.

These different dimensions of Independence strongly imply that party identification should not always be modeled with a single linear dimension ranging from Republicans on one side to Independents in the middle and Democrats on the other side. For many reasons, those who end up in the middle as Independents often hold views that are far from the middle. Thus, to really understand partisanship and Independence, we often need to modify the traditional linear model of party identification that is used in almost every study of American political behavior. The traditional linear scale may work well when predicting the choice between voting for a Democrat and voting for a Republican, but when we trying to predict or understand other dimensions of politics, we may do well to replace the traditional model with a more complex unordered model that takes into account several dimensions of choice.

Our findings should also lead to a different normative view of Independents. Independents should not simply be dismissed as nonideologues prone to apathy and inactivity. Rather, as we indicate, there are multiple routes to Independence, many of which suggest that Independents are anything but apolitical. In turn, this more positive view of Independents leads to a different conclusion about the possibility that Independents will be important political actors. If Independents are seen as apolitical nonideologues, there is little reason to try to mobilize them. Research on political participation suggests that such efforts will be ineffective. However, if we see Independents as being ambivalent or uncertain about parties that they do not fit well into or that do not cater to their interests, then there is every reason to believe that Independents can be integrated and mobilized. The presence of widespread ambivalence and uncertainty also clearly suggests that many Americans are up for grabs politically. We have identified what we think are the most important sources of partisan ambivalence, but issue-based partisan ambivalence could certainly be more extensive than what we have shown here. The authors of *The New American Voter* have shown that even in an age of heightened party polarization and greater issue alignment, only 15 percent of Americans hold consistently liberal or consistently conservative issue positions (Miller and Shanks 1996, 354).[35] If either party is able to reach different segments of the Independent population and present a compelling reason for them to support the party, large numbers of Independents may be swayed and the balance of power between the Democratic and Republican parties could be substantially altered.

[35] Similarly, Rasmussen reports that only 33 percent of Americans claim either to be both fiscally and socially conservative or both fiscally and socially liberal, but the Rasmussen survey asked no specific policy questions (2007).

CHAPTER 8

The Electoral Implications of Nonpartisanship

> The perverse and unorthodox argument of this little book is
> that voters are not fools. To be sure, many individual voters act
> in odd ways indeed; yet in the large the electorate behaves
> about as rationally and responsibly as we should expect, given
> the clarity of the alternatives presented to it and the character
> of the information available to it.
>
> —V. O. Key Jr.

> The inference that the "captive" consumer (or voter) has
> "nowhere else to go" is the epitome of powerlessness.
>
> —Albert O. Hirschman

THROUGHOUT THIS BOOK, we have sought to understand the roots of
nonpartisanship. In this chapter, we shift to its behavioral consequences.
We do so for two reasons. First, in a democratic polity where votes count
and who wins and who loses depend critically on choices in the voting
booth, we are likely to care more about nonpartisanship if it can be linked
to particular patterns of behavior. Identity matters, but actions may matter more. If one of our goals is to assess the significance of nonpartisanship, we need to see how an identity as an Independent or nonpartisan
affects electoral choices across different contexts.

The second reason to focus on behavior is a wide-ranging suspicion
that many, if not most, Independent identifiers are not Independent at all
but are, in fact, closet partisans. In light of this suspicion, it is important
to determine just how regularly nonpartisans remain loyal to one party
and to assess the ways in which nonpartisans might express reservations
about the two major parties.

Over the course of this chapter, we will examine the entire range of
choices that are available to nonpartisans in electoral contests. A key to
understanding the behavioral implications of nonpartisanship, we believe, is not just to look at the degree to which nonpartisans act like partisans by voting for the party that they lean toward but also to focus on
the degree to which nonpartisans seek out alternatives. If, as we have suggested throughout the book, nonpartisans often do not fit neatly into the
partisan divide and are not particularly attracted to either major party,

then logically we would expect many nonpartisans to search for alternative courses of action. To consider these alternatives, we adapt Albert Hirschman's *Exit, Voice, and Loyalty* (1970) to the case of electoral competition in a party duopoly. In our adaptation, nonpartisans have three options. They can exercise an exit option and abstain from becoming involved in a given electoral contest.[1] Nonpartisans can also choose to actively voice opposition to the party they lean toward. There are two possible forms this voice can take. Nonpartisans can vote for a third-party candidate—an action that might be viewed as a sign of dissatisfaction with the party duopoly.[2] Alternatively, nonpartisans can use their voice to support a candidate in a major party that they are not normally associated with—an action that might be attractive to voters who are unhappy with their party's current practices. Finally, nonpartisans can—given some kind of party affiliation—choose to remain loyal by voting down party lines. Only after examining the degree to which nonpartisans choose each of these options will we know the full behavioral implications of not having a party to call one's own.

Showing that nonpartisans, as a group, are more or less apt than partisans to choose exit, voice, or loyalty is, however, only the first step in the process of evaluating the implications of nonpartisanship. As we have tried to show in the previous chapters, nonpartisans come in all kinds of stripes. The road to nonpartisanship is wide and carries a range of travelers. These nonpartisan travelers emerge from different racial and ethnic backgrounds and often have different motivations for choosing nonpartisanship. We believe that these different backgrounds and motivations should not all lead to the same behavioral outcomes. Thus, in this chapter, we break down the nonpartisan population into groups to see how the consequences of nonpartisanship vary within different segments of the population.

We choose to divide the population along three dimensions: (1) self-identified type, (2) context, and (3) race/ethnicity. We choose these three dimensions not merely to complicate the analysis but also because there are logical reasons to expect distinct behavioral patterns to emerge in each case.

To distinguish between different types of nonpartisans, we begin by simply looking at how individuals identify themselves. Typically, in surveys nonpartisans can choose to identify themselves as pure Independents

---

[1] This is likely to be an especially attractive alternative for members of the public who are uncertain about the choices that are available to them and who do not yet trust actors in the political system to represent their interests.

[2] For nonpartisans who are ambivalent about what the parties are offering or who have strong concerns about issues that are not being addressed by either party, this is likely to be an especially appealing option.

who profess no leaning toward either party, as Independent leaners who claim Independence but who later admit a preference for one party, or as unwilling or unable to state a partisan preference. We call these three groups pure Independents, Independent leaners, and nonidentifiers. Assessing the behavioral implications of the first two groups of nonpartisans is particularly important in light of assertions by Keith and his colleagues about the partisan proclivities of Independent leaners. In *The Myth of the Independent Voter* (1992), these authors assert that leaners are really partisans in disguise. If this statement is true, we should be cautious about lumping leaners with pure Independents, who may be much less prone to remain tied to one party.

Isolating and considering the behavior of nonidentifiers may be equally important. We believe that refusing to use the term "Independent" and instead offering responses such as "no preference" or "don't know" may be signs of a unique set of motivations and behaviors. If we are right and nonidentifiers are signaling a lack of trust in the American party system and/or uncertainty about the choices that they have to make, then we have reason to believe that this group of nonpartisans will be especially likely to abstain from voting and particularly unlikely to vote consistently for a single party when they do participate. Although this nonidentifier category has often been ignored in conventional studies of party identification, individuals in this group represent a reasonably large segment of the nonpartisan population and, as such, warrant more attention.

We also expect that the behavioral implications of nonpartisanship will vary considerably across different contexts. How loyal or disloyal a given individual will be to a given party will surely depend on that individual's overall attachment to that party, but it will also just as surely depend on the attractiveness of the candidates in a particular contest and the kinds of options that are available to that individual in that contest. Elections are far from equal in terms of the options that they offer nonpartisans. Most American elections do not, for example, give nonpartisans a chance to voice their grievances by voting for a third party. But that is not always the case. In some contests, a third-party candidate is present, and in more exceptional cases, that third-party candidate is not simply present but also attractive enough to have a real chance of winning. Moreover, it is not just the presence and attractiveness of the third-party option that will vary. The attractiveness of the two major party candidates to different segments of the nonpartisan community will also vary across different electoral contexts.

In all cases, the patterns of exit, voice, and loyalty will depend greatly on the availability and appeal of these alternatives. This means that if we want to understand what nonpartisanship means for citizens' behavior, we have to expand the limited number of contexts that have been examined in past studies and include elections that offer nonpartisans more diverse choices. This also means that authors of works such as *The Myth of the Independent Voter*, which assess the partisan proclivities of nonpartisans by focusing exclusively on electoral contests where the two parties are dominant and where partisan defections are highly unlikely, may reach inaccurate conclusions. Thus, in this chapter, we examine the behavior of nonpartisans and partisans in a wider range of elections and in particular include contests where third-party candidates are present or where the cast of candidates is more diverse than the typical two-party contest.

Race is also a critical variable in all of this. As we have repeatedly noted, the story that has been told of nonpartisans in the past has largely been the story of white Independents. That is also true of the story that has been told of the behavioral implications of Independence. What we know of the actions of Independents is derived almost exclusively from the behavior of white Independents. But if white Independents identify as nonpartisan for reasons that are different from those for nonwhite Americans, we should not expect nonpartisanship to mean the same thing for America's various racial and ethnic groups, and we should not expect America's racial and ethnic groups to make the same choices when faced with the alternatives of exit, voice, and loyalty. If we truly want to understand how nonpartisanship works to effect political behavior, we need to consider and analyze each racial group separately.

As we will see in the rest of this chapter, each of these distinctions is important in the choices citizens make. Not only will we find clear evidence that nonpartisanship matters in terms of behavior, but we will also find ample indication that different kinds of nonpartisans make different choices in different contexts. Further, most of these patterns will vary dramatically across racial and ethnic groups. Thus, the story of nonpartisanship needs to be told not from a single (white) perspective in the context of a single type of election but rather with information that takes into account different partisan categories, different contexts, and different racial and ethnic groups. Only then will we get a complete picture of the significance of choosing not to identify with either major party.

Nonpartisans versus Partisans

We begin this empirical investigation into the consequences of nonpartisanship by looking at the simplest of possible comparisons between the actions of nonpartisans and those of partisans. Our question is, are nonpartisans different? Does failing to identify with either major party signal a detachment from both parties and a willingness to pursue electoral alternatives?

In table 8.1 we look at each of the three options—exit, voice, and loyalty—available to citizens in any electoral contest. Exit in this case represents the proportion of adult citizens who choose not to vote.[3] Voice measures the proportion of voters who favor a third-party candidate.[4] Both measures are based on data from the cumulative file of the ANES, and both focus on behavior in presidential contests. Our measure for loyalty is slightly more complex. To gauge loyalty, we measure support for the same party across several elections. Specifically, to qualify as loyal, an individual has to vote for the same party in three contests during the same election year.[5] We focus on consistent voting across presidential, senatorial, and House elections, since those are the three contests that the ANES regularly queries respondents about.[6]

This differs from work by Keith et al. (1992) and other authors' studies of Independents in which loyalty is typically assessed by focusing on the vote in a single contest. In these works, if in one election a person votes for the party he or she is attached to, that person is considered loyal or partisan. There are, however, real concerns with assessing loyalty by focusing on a single contest. Logically, it seems a stretch to label someone as loyal (or even as partisan) if he or she votes for a particular party once. Rather, an assessment of the consistency with which an individual supports a party over a series of elections seems a much more appropriate gauge of loyalty. Equally important, by focusing on only one electoral contest, there is the danger that any correlation between the vote and partisanship will be spurious. If voters switch their partisanship to match

[3] Most of the voting data reported in this chapter are based on self-reports. There is a fair degree of error or bias in these self-reports. Validated vote tests suggest that roughly 10 percent of the population falsely indicates that it voted in a typical electoral contest (Anderson and Silver 1986). This means that the numbers of voters will generally be inflated in our tables. Moreover, there is evidence that certain groups in the population are more prone to overreport voting. Abramson and Clagget (1984) and Shaw et al. (2000), for example, have shown that racial and ethnic minorities overreport voting more regularly than do whites. But none of this tells us whether the patterns of exit, voice, and loyalty across partisanship would change if we were able to report validated voting records. Sigelman's (1982) research suggests that the substantive factors that drive nonvoting are largely unaffected by the use of the validated vote, but more work needs to be done before we can conclude that overreporting does not affect any of the relative participation rates that we present here.

[4] Another form that voice can take in these elections is voting against one's own party by supporting the other major party. Such crossover voting is not included in table 8.1 because it is impossible to measure for nonpartisans who claim no allegiance to either party.

[5] The loyalty figures in table 8.1 are calculated only for those respondents who vote in all three contests. Thus, any respondents who choose to exit from one of the contests and respondents from states that do not have a senatorial contest in the year of the survey are dropped from the loyalty analysis.

[6] We obtain similar results if we drop senatorial contests or add gubernatorial contests that are asked about in fewer years of the survey.

TABLE 8.1.
The Implications of Nonpartisanship: Exit, Voice, and Loyalty

	Exit Nonvoters	Voice Third-party voters	Loyalty Consistent party voters
Democrats	26%	2%	64%
Nonpartisans	47	7	51
Republicans	19	3	68

their vote in a particular contest, then there may be a close empirical link between partisan leaning and the vote without any causal chain from partisanship to the vote.[7] By looking at loyalty across more than one election, we begin to address this issue of endogenous partisanship.[8]

We divide the population into three groups: Democrats, nonpartisans, and Republicans. As we have done throughout the book, we include Independent leaners within the nonpartisan category. In subsequent analyses, we will look at leaners in isolation, but for now we simply assess the degree to which self-identified nonpartisans as a whole differ from their their partisan neighbors.

The pattern in table 8.1 is clear. Across each alternative, there are large differences between nonpartisans and partisans. In terms of exit, nonpartisans are roughly twice as likely as Democratic and Republican identifiers not to participate in the typical presidential contest.[9] The same pattern would be evident if we were to focus on midterm elections where fully 63 percent of nonpartisans choose to exit compared with only 39 percent of Democrats and 33 percent of Republicans.[10]

---

[7] Moreover, if nonpartisans or subsets of the nonpartisan population are particularly apt to change their partisanship to align with their vote, then comparisons of the loyalty of nonpartisans and partisans will be skewed.

[8] Later we will focus on change over time for the same individual to more fully assess the extent to which nonpartisans switch their partisanship between one election and another and the effect that this may have on assessing loyalty.

[9] How we should interpret this nonparticipation is up for debate. For some, this high rate of exit among nonpartisans is reason enough to label nonpartisans as apolitical and to dismiss them from further analysis. We offer an alternative interpretation. Many nonpartisans may opt out of the election not because they do not care about politics in general but because they do not care much about the alternatives that are offered in the current contest. The evidence for at least some racial groups seems to fit this interpretation. Our analysis of the LNPS indicates that among Latinos, nonpartisans are just as active as partisans across a wide range of political activities that do not involve direct contact with a political party. This includes attending a meeting, protesting, signing a petition, working to solve a problem, and participating in local politics. Generally speaking, Latino nonpartisans are not apolitical.

[10] If we look at the consistency of an individual's participation over time, it once again

Nonpartisans are also more likely than partisans to voice opposition to the two major parties. Although the overall numbers exercising the voice option are small, nonpartisans are two or three times more likely than partisans to support a third-party candidate in presidential elections. Among nonpartisans, 7 percent vote for a third-party candidate on average, compared with 2 percent of Democrats and 3 percent of Republicans. Moreover, these figures may understate the desire of nonpartisans to voice support for an alternative party or candidate. In most of these contests, there is no third-party candidate on the ballot in most states, and in none of these elections does the third-party candidate have a real chance of winning the contest. As we will see, when more viable nonmajor party options are offered, the number of nonpartisans willing to exercise voice surges.

Finally, there is a wide gap between nonpartisans and partisans in terms of loyalty. About two-thirds of partisans (64 percent of Democrats and 68 percent of Republicans) support the same party across presidential, senatorial, and House contests in the same year. By contrast, only about half (51 percent) of all nonpartisans do so. The difference is just as stark if we examine the consistency of an individual's voting patterns over time. Using ANES panel data from the 1950s, 1970s, and 1990s, we found that most partisans remained loyal, and most nonpartisans did not. Across two presidential and two congressional votes over a four-year span, we found that most partisans (61 percent) voted consistently for the same party, whereas most nonpartisans did not (44 percent voted consistently). In short, when loyalty is assessed by measuring support for the same party across more than one election, there is a clear divide between partisans and nonpartisans.

If we ask respondents about their partisan voting histories over a longer time frame, we get even starker differences in the degree to which partisans and nonpartisans remain loyal to one of the major parties. When asked if they have "always voted for the same party for president in the past," nonpartisans generally contend that they are not consistent party supporters.[11] Only 20 percent claim to have always supported the same party. Republicans and Democrats are two and three times more

---

becomes clear that nonpartisans opt to exit much more regularly than partisans. NES panel data indicate that across a four-year period, on average 35 percent of nonpartisans do not vote in any presidential or congressional elections. Only half as many partisans exit in all of these contests (18 percent).

[11] It should be noted that valid concerns have been raised about the accuracy of such retrospective data (see Brody 1991 and Wolfinger et al. 1992). For that reason, we rely primarily on actual voting histories. However, since panel data cover only a four-year period, it is important to at least try to gauge behavior and consistency over a longer time frame.

likely to claim to have been loyal (51 and 63 percent respectively claim to be consistent party supporters). Similarly, when the ANES asked respondents whether or not they had voted a straight party ticket in the most recent state elections, the gap between partisans and nonpartisans was substantial. Some 59 percent of Democrats and 55 percent of Republicans indicated that they had voted along party lines at the state level, whereas only 32 percent of nonpartisans indicated that they had done so. Judged by loyalty over time or across context, the vast majority of nonpartisans are not loyal, whereas the clear majority of partisans are. This is no small divide.

Combined, these three patterns suggest that nonpartisans are behaviorally very different from partisans. It would be hard to label as partisan a group that tends not to vote at all and that when it does vote is especially inclined to vote for third-party candidates and often switches support back and forth between the two parties. Put succinctly, nonpartisanship is not only important when we consider identity but also matters when we consider behavior. The fact that nonpartisans, as a whole, are quite different from partisans is often lost in discussions of how different subsets of the nonpartisan population vote, but it is well worth noting.[12]

DISTINCTIONS AMONG NONPARTISANS

It is clear that nonpartisans are, as a whole, very different from partisans. What we cannot yet tell is whether these overall figures mask important differences between various groups within the nonpartisan population. Given fairly widespread concerns that certain members of the nonpartisan population are not as independent of partisan attachments as they claim to be, an important next step is to break down the nonpartisan population into subpopulations that might be more or less partisan in their behavior. In light of past research, the most important group to assess is Independent leaners—those who profess to be Independent but then admit to favoring one party over the other. If Wolfinger and others are correct, these leaners should behave just like partisans and quite unlike pure Independents. Leaners are not, however, the only subset of nonpartisans that warrants attention. Those respondents who are unwilling or unable to label themselves with any of the conventional categories and who instead submit other difficult-to-code responses such as "other" or "no preference" are, in our view, equally worthy of investigation. If these

[12] This overall pattern is important in light of the fact that Independent leaners, the group who are supposed to act like dyed-in-the-wool partisans, make up the bulk of the nonpartisan population. If leaners really are partisans, the overall differences between nonpartisans and partisans would probably be more limited.

nonidentifiers represent individuals who are uncertain about the partisan environment and who lack the knowledge or the level of trust to place themselves as partisans or even as Independents, we would expect them to be especially prone to exit and particularly unlikely to consistently support the same party when they do vote. As such, they may represent one of the more interesting and impressionable segments of the American population.

Breaking down the nonpartisan population into these three categories leads to one familiar observation and at least one surprise. The familiar observation is that leaners represent the bulk of the nonpartisan population. At least when we aggregate across all racial groups and employ the ANES sample, we find that Independent leaners make up the majority of the nonpartisan population.[13] Of all those who qualify as nonpartisans—that is, everyone who does not immediately admit a preference for either major party—some 57 percent identify themselves as leaners. Leaners are therefore a critically important piece of the nonpartisan story.

But leaners are by no means the entire story. The surprise comes when we consider nonidentifiers, a category that includes respondents who neither claim to identify with a major party nor label themselves as Independents. In spite of the fact that this group has generally been ignored by studies of nonpartisans, its members make up a sizable portion of the nonpartisan population. In the ANES, which for a variety of reasons understates the size of this population, this group still represents 20 percent of all nonpartisans.[14] Since there is reason to suspect that its behavior may be different, we investigate its partisan choices as well.

In table 8.2 we assess the actions of these different segments of the nonpartisan population across the same three alternatives of exit, voice, and loyalty in presidential elections. For comparison purposes, we include the behavior of strong and weak partisans in the table. The measures are identical to those in table 8.1.

---

[13] Since it is impossible to derive the number of nonidentifiers from the questions available in the NES cumulative file, the figures for the proportion of nonpartisans who identify as nonidentifiers, Independent leaners, and pure Independents are based on the total population of three available NES panel surveys from the 1950s, 1970s, and 1990s. Figures describing the behavior of nonidentifiers are based on the same panel data. Data on the behavior of other types of nonpartisans and the two partisan categories that are displayed in subsequent tables, however, are based on data from the entire NES cumulative file.

[14] This figure does not include those who volunteer no answer to the party-identification question—a group of respondents who, we suspect, should be included with nonidentifiers. If this group were to be included, nonidentifiers would probably grow to constitute about a quarter of the nonpartisan population. Those who provide no answer to the party-identification question represent between 1 and 2 percent of the entire respondent population. As we will see, both question wording and the nature of the survey sample greatly affect the proportion of nonpartisans who end up as nonidentifiers.

TABLE 8.2
Exit, Voice, and Loyalty across Different Types of Nonpartisans

	Exit Nonvoters	Voice Third-party voters	Loyalty Consistent party voters
Partisans			
Strong partisans	15	1	81
Weak partisans	27	4	65
Nonpartisans			
Independent leaners	27	7	62
Pure Independents	39	8	51
Nonidentifiers	52	7	40

The first point to note about table 8.2 is that different subsets of non-partisans are far from identical in their behavior. The degree to which different segments of the nonpartisan population choose exit, voice, or loyalty does vary—sometimes dramatically. The gap in terms of exit is the most pronounced. Here the major divide is between leaners and nonidentifiers. While the vast majority of leaners choose to vote (only 27 percent fail to vote in presidential elections), most nonidentifiers opt to exit (52 percent choose not to vote). Nonpartisans also vary substantially in how consistently they support one party. Once again, the biggest gap is between leaners and nonidentifiers. Most nonidentifiers cross partisan lines while voting for president, the Senate, and the House. Only 40 percent remain loyal across the three elections. In contrast, a clear majority of leaners (62 percent) remain loyal and consistently support the same party.[15] Although the behavior of each of these three nonpartisan groups in terms of voice appears, at first glance, to be quite similar, we will see that even for third-party support substantial behavior differences can emerge. The implications of nonpartisanship do vary across different types of nonpartisans.

The other obvious conclusion that emerges from table 8.2 is the unique behavior of nonidentifiers. Despite the limited amount of attention that members of this group have received in the past, their behavior is in many ways remarkable.[16] Nonidentifiers stand out both for their propensity to exit the electoral arena and for their inconsistent voting patterns when

[15] A similarly large divide emerges when respondents are asked about their voting histories. Only 19 percent of pure Independents claim to have loyally supported the same party for president in the past. By contrast, about a third of leaners and nonidentifiers indicate that they have always voted for the same party for president.

[16] Typically, in the ANES coding, nonidentifiers are coded as apolitical (if they do not vote and they show little in interest in politics) or as leaners (if they admit a partisan preference when pushed to do so).

they do enter the electoral arena. Nonidentifiers are, in fact, the only group to exit more often than they vote in presidential contests. No other group comes close.[17] The tendency for nonidentifiers to exit is even more pronounced in midterm elections. Here a whopping 79 percent of this group fail to vote. Nonidentifiers are also the group most likely to exit in local contests. Data from the American Citizen Participation Survey (ACPS) indicate that nonidentifiers are twice as likely as leaners and pure Independents to opt out of local contests (52 percent versus 26 and 25 percent respectively).[18] We do not know if this nonparticipation is due to a lack of interest in politics or to a lack of attraction to the major party options that are on offer in a typical contest, but we do know that for this one subset of the nonpartisan population, by far the most attractive alternative is exit.

Nonidentifiers are also especially unlikely to remain loyal to one party when they do vote. In any given year, only 40 percent of nonidentifiers end up voting for the same party in presidential, congressional and senatorial contests. That contrasts with a 51 percent party-line voting among pure Independents, 62 percent among leaners, 65 percent among weak partisans, and 81 percent among strong partisans. More than any other group, partisan or nonpartisan, the vote of nonidentifiers appears to be more volatile and at least potentially more up for grabs. This fact is well worth noting for parties and candidates interested in acquiring more votes.

These are important patterns to recognize in light of the fact that nonidentifiers constitute 20 percent of the population of nonpartisans. Further, these ANES figures may in some sense underplay the significance of this group. As we will see, among immigrants and nonwhites, nonidentifiers make up a much larger share of the population. Acknowledging the existence of this group and understanding the motivations and choices of its members should be central components of any story of nonpartisanship.

Uncovering Differences between Leaners and Partisans

Table 8.2 allows us to begin to consider one other critical question about the behavior of nonpartisans, namely, are leaners really different from

---

[17] The next least active group, pure Independents, votes, on average, 61 percent of the time in these contests.

[18] The ACPS is a nationally representative sample of about two thousand respondents. These figures reflect answers to a question about voting in the last local election. The same pattern emerges if we instead focus on a question that asked respondents how regularly they vote in local elections.

weak partisans? If Keith and the other authors of *The Myth of the Independent Voter* are correct, we should see leaners behaving like weak partisans. At first glance, the evidence in support of this view is impressive. There is a small and potentially meaningful divide between leaners and weak partisans in terms of third-party support but little else to suggest that leaners are not partisans. Leaners are no more likely than weak partisans to choose to exit the electoral arena.[19] More important, leaners, like partisans, tend to consistently support the same party across elections in the same year. Sixty-two percent of leaners vote for the same party for president, the Senate, and the House in a typical year. The figure for weak partisans is only marginally higher at 65 percent. And if judged by their behavior in a single electoral contest, leaners are often even more partisan than are weak partisans in their preferences. As table 3.3 in chapter 3 demonstrated, a strong majority of leaners typically votes for the candidate of the party that they lean toward. On this measure, leaners are as apt or even more apt to vote along partisan lines than are weak partisans.[20] The bottom line is that relatively few leaners cross over to support the opposition. All of this suggests that the authors of *The Myth of the Independent Voter* are right in concluding: "Leaners are partisans, not neutrals in the contest between parties" (1992, 37).

These signs of partisan loyalty may, however, be somewhat misleading. It may very well be, as several scholars have suggested, that leaners regularly vote for the party they lean toward simply because they change their partisanship whenever their voting preferences change (Shively 1980, Wattenberg 1996, Bartels 2000). If true, consistency between partisan leaning and individual voting may be less a sign of partisan loyalty or partisan attachment than a sign that leaners more regularly alter their partisanship.

To address this kind of concern, we cannot look at only a single election year in isolation as we have largely done up to this point. Instead, we have to assess changes in partisanship and changes in voting patterns *over time*.

---

[19] This is true for presidential contests as shown here or in midterm congressional elections as alternate tests reveal. In midterm contests, 43 percent of leaners choose exit. An almost identical 42 percent of weak partisans choose exit in these contests.

[20] The comparable figures for weak Democrats are 64 in presidential elections and 77 percent in House elections. In certain elections, leaners are also not much more likely than weak partisans to cross over and support the party they lean against. In presidential elections, leaners are slightly less apt to voice opposition by supporting the other major party than are weak partisans. Only 16 percent of leaners choose to cross over, whereas 23 of weak partisans choose to do so. However, for other types of elections the opposite is true. In House elections, for example, the relationship is reversed and the gap is reasonably large. Fully 37 percent of leaners cross over in House contests compared with only 24 percent of weak partisans.

TABLE 8.3
Partisan Change by Partisan Type

	Ever Switched parties	Consistent partisanship in last two years	Switched allegiance in in last two years
Partisans			
Strong partisans	12	65	1
Weak partisans	20	57	12
Nonpartisans			
Independent leaners	34	38	26
Pure Independents	34	46	—

Does the same individual change her partisanship over time? And does that partisan change account for the perceived loyalty of leaners?

To begin to address these questions, in table 8.3 we look at patterns of individual partisan change over time across different types of partisans. The figures in column one are based on a single ANES question asking respondents to retrospectively evaluate whether they have ever changed their partisanship in the past. The second two columns are based on individual change over time that is validated using three sets of ANES panel data—specifically the 1956–60 panel, the 1972–76 panel, and the 1990–92 panel.

The figures here are clear on one point. Leaners regularly change their partisanship. As the first column of table 8.3 shows, 34 percent of leaners admit having changed their partisan allegiance at some point in the past. Since these retrospective evaluations are not always accurate, we also follow patterns of partisan change for a single individual as they occur over time. When we use panel data to look at the same individual over a short period, we see considerable evidence of partisan mobility. As evidenced by the second column of the table, when asked two years later about their partisanship, almost 40 percent of leaners, on average, end up offering a different answer to the standard ANES seven-point scale.[21] And many of those changes are across partisan lines. Only two years later, fully 26 percent of all leaners end up expressing allegiance to the other party or to

[21] Surely some of this is due to measurement error. As Green and his colleagues (1990, 2002) have demonstrated, correcting for that error can reduce partisan instability considerably. However, measurement error cannot explain why certain subsets of the nonpartisan population are more prone to change their partisanship over time. In particular, measurement error cannot explain the fact that leaners are much more apt than weak partisans to switch from one partisan category to another or to altogether switch from one party to another.

neither party.[22] This is not the stable partisan attachment that the authors of *The American Voter* envisioned.

Leaners are not only quite likely to switch their partisanship over time, but also considerably more likely to do so than are weak partisans. Only 20 percent of weak partisans state they have changed their partisan loyalty at some point in the past, whereas among leaners 34 percent admit to doing so. The gap between leaners and weak partisans is just as large if we look at documented changes in partisanship rather than at retrospectively reported change. Most weak partisans (57 percent) place themselves on the same point on the ANES partisan scale two years later. By contrast, a clear majority (62 percent) of leaners are not consistent over that two-year period. Finally, leaners are more than twice as likely as weak partisans to have shifted across partisan lines in the two-year period. All of this suggests that a good portion of the perceived partisan loyalty of leaners revealed in studies of a single election could be spurious.

This suspicion is confirmed when we look at the voting patterns of leaners and nonleaners over time. When we measure partisanship not at the time of a vote but at a point before the vote, we get a substantially modified view of the partisan loyalty of leaners. Recall that in the average presidential contest, fully 69 percent of leaners vote for the party that they lean toward—fairly strong evidence of partisan allegiance. But if we look at loyalty over time using one's party identification measured during the first period in a time series, we find that most leaners do not consistently support the party they originally leaned toward. To assess loyalty over time, we observed whether an individual voted consistently for the same party across four elections—the president and the House in one year and the president and the House four years later. Using the three ANES panel studies, we found that only 43 percent of leaners consistently voted for the party that they originally leaned toward.[23] This figure tells us two things. First, over at least a four-year period, many leaners are strong partisan supporters. For this minority of the leaning population, there is little doubt that the authors of *The Myth of the Independent Voter* got it right. But the same figure also indicates that the majority of leaners switch sides. Over the course of just four years, some 57 percent

[22] We viewed leaners as members of the party that they leaned toward for this measure. Thus, we counted as a partisan switch any movement from leaning toward one party to pure Independnence or leaning toward the other party. If we count only those who move from one party to the other party, the same pattern holds. Three percent of strong partisans, 7 percent of weak partisans, and fully 14 percent of leaners switch party allegiance over a two-year period.

[23] To obtain these figures, we used professed partisanship during the first year of the panel and determined whether individuals subsequently always voted for the party they originally expressed allegiance to.

TABLE 8.4

Leaners vs. Weak Partisans: Lagged vs. Endogenous Party Identification and Party Loyalty

Election Year	Independent leaners	Weak partisans
1960		
Endogenous	1.1 (.14)	.87 (.07)
Lagged	.55 (.12)	.80 (.07)
1976		
Endogenous	.78 (.11)	.68 (.08)
Lagged	.55 (.10)	.71 (.08)
1992		
Endogenous	1.1 (.12)	.95 (.10)
Lagged	.53 (.11)	.76 (.09)

Adapted from Bartels (2000). Probit coefficients with standard errors in parentheses. Regression includes dummies for strong identifiers as well as Republican bias. Analysis includes major-party voters only.

of leaners opted to vote for the party they originally opposed. Not all leaners are unattached Independents who flow back and forth with the current electoral tides, and not all of them are staunch partisans who remain loyal to one side. No longer can we say, as Keith and his colleagues loudly proclaimed, "Leaners are never neutral" (1992, 70).

More formally, we can test the endogeneity of partisanship and the extent to which leaners consistently vote for the same party by comparing estimates of the impact of partisanship on the vote using endogenous or contemporaneous partisanship on one hand and estimates using exogenous or lagged partisanship on the other. When one does this, as Bartels (2000) has, it becomes clear that much of the perceived loyalty of leaners is illusory. The results of Bartels's analysis are displayed in table 8.4. The table presents the results of six separate regressions where the dependent variable is support for the presidential candidate from the party that one identifies with. The data are from the same ANES panel studies that we used in table 8.3. What the table illustrates is that, for leaners, lagged partisanship has a much smaller effect on vote choice than does contemporaneous or endogenous partisanship. Across the three panel studies, Bartels finds that on average a little under half of the presumed partisan consistency of leaners (45 percent) is due to the endogeneity of their partisanship. As Bartels notes, one clear implication of this result is that "work in this area—and especially Keith et al.'s (1992) work on voting loyalty among partisan 'leaners'—may overstate the strength of the relationship between long-term partisan attachments and presidential voting behavior" (2000, 48).

Perhaps just as important, these results indicate that endogeneity is much less of a factor for weak partisans. By Bartels's account, only 8 percent of the presumed partisan consistency of weak partisans is due to party switching. The result, as the lagged rows in table 8.4 indicate, is that after taking into account endogeneity, partisanship has less of an impact on the votes of leaners than it does on the votes of weak partisans. Judged by a single vote at one point in time, leaners are as partisan or even more partisan than weak partisans. But judged by a single vote in the future, leaners are much lesspartisan than many have claimed.

CONTEXT AND THE IMPLICATIONS OF NONPARTISANSHIP

To fully understand the implications of nonpartisanship and in particular the behavior of different types of nonpartisans, we need to look further. The choices that nonpartisans make depend not only on their overall sense of attachment to a particular party but also, just as critically, on the number and type of options that are available in a given electoral context. In American politics, these options vary greatly. Often the choice is severely limited. Voters must choose one of two parties or opt out of the contest altogether. But in some elections, the choices are more varied. In addition to the two major party candidates, there may be a third-party candidate. On rare occasions, that third-party candidate may even represent an electorally viable alternative. Alternatively, as is often the case in local politics, there may be multiple candidates with little or no partisan connection. The availability or unavailability of these options is critical. Especially for those Americans who do not fit squarely within the confines of one of the two major parties, whether or not these additional options are available should strongly shape the choice between exit, voice, and loyalty.

Thus, before we can really judge the behavior and the partisan loyalty of different types of nonpartisans, we need to assess a wider range of electoral contexts where the options available to voters are more varied. Most obviously, we need to consider behavior in contests where a third-party candidate is on the ballot. In table 8.5 we begin to do so by focusing on presidential elections. We make a distinction between presidential elections in which there is a national third-party option—cases where the same candidate appears on more than half of the state ballots—and those where no third-party option is available.

As the table shows, in the typical presidential contest, voice, or at least voice in the form of a vote for third-party candidates, is relatively rare. Partisans and nonpartisans alike are very unlikely to abandon the major parties to support a third-party candidate. But this assessment of third-

TABLE 8.5
The Presidential Vote and the Presence of Third-Party Candidates

| | Vote for the Third-Party Candidate | |
	All elections	Elections with a third-party candidate
Partisans		
Strong partisans	1	4
Weak partisans	4	13
Independents		
Independent leaners	7	19
Pure Independents	8	25

party support ignores the fact that most presidential contests do not offer voters a real third-party option. If we focus our attention on elections where a third-party candidate is present, it is evident that many nonpartisans are eager to voice their opposition to the two-party duopoly. When the option exists, one in four pure Independents and one in five Independent leaners vote for third parties. Given that none of the third-party candidates in any of the presidential elections that are included in the ANES study years had a chance of winning, this level of support among nonpartisans might be viewed as very strong.

Distinguishing between contests with and without a third-party option also makes the difference between weak partisans and Independent leaners somewhat clearer. As one might expect, when voters are given a way to voice their opposition to the two parties, Independent leaners more regularly exercise that option, and the gap in behavior between leaners and weak partisans begins to grow. When a third-party option is available, 19 percent of leaners opt to support the third party compared with only 13 percent of weak partisans.[24] It may be true, as studies have shown, that when Independent leaners vote for one of two main parties, they are very likely to vote for the party that they lean toward. But it is also true that leaners do not always choose to vote for either the Democrats or the Republicans in the first place. When an opportunity presents itself, Independent leaners do vote in reasonably large numbers for Independent candidates. By dropping all of these third-party votes from their analyses, researchers have overlooked some important behavioral differences between nonpartisans and partisans. The comparisons presented here do

[24] The figures for the GSS (which covers a shorter and more recent time frame) are slightly more dramatic. Here, when a third-party candidate is on the ballot, almost a quarter of all Independent leaners (24 percent) opt not to vote for either the Democratic or the Republican candidates. By contrast, only 14 percent of weak partisans follow suit.

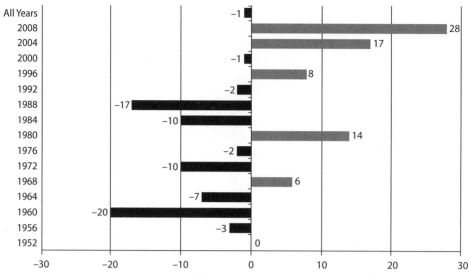

Figure 8.1. Voting against party: Democratic leaners versus weak Democrats

not reveal a dramatic difference between leaners and weak partisans, but they do demonstrate that as the options available to voters become more varied, the tendency of leaners to act like dyed-in-the-wool partisans diminishes.

We can further assess the willingness of leaners to oppose their own party and at the same time gauge the distinction between leaners and weak partisans by looking at individual election years. In figures 8.1 and 8.2, we begin this process by focusing on individual presidential contests over time. In particular, we look at the extent to which Independent leaners and weak partisans choose to voice opposition to their favored party by supporting the other major party or a third-party candidate. Both figures show the difference between the proportion of Independents who lean toward one party and the proportion of weak identifiers of that party who cross over and vote for either the other major party or for a third-party candidate. Gray bars indicate Independent leaners' greater willingness than weak partisans' to exit from their party allegiance; black bars indicate a greater such willingness among weak partisans.

If we simply average across all of the elections as is typically done in studies of nonpartisanship, we find that there is essentially no difference between leaners and weak partisans. In line with the story of Independents as closet partisans, we find that only 28 percent of Democratic leaners vote against their party, a figure that is nearly identical to the 29 percent of weak Democrats who vote against their party. Similarly, on the Republican side, an identical 18 percent of Independent leaners and weak partisans are willing to choose the voice option.

Our point, however, is that this overall assessment hides substantial and meaningful variation that highlights the differences between leaners and weak partisans and that suggests that leaners act like partisans only when they have no real choice. Across the years, the percentage of Independents who express loyalty to their party varies dramatically. For Democratic leaners, the percentage who defect in presidential contests varies from a high of 48 in 1968 to a low of 9 in 1964. For Republican leaners, the range is from a high of 36 in 1992 to a low of 6 in 1956 and 1984.[25]

Importantly, whether leaners are more partisan or less partisan than weak partisans varies across these elections. Among Democrats, leaners are more partisan in their votes than are weak partisans, but in five out of the fourteen cases (the years highlighted in gray bars), leaners are less consistent in their votes than are weak partisans. Further, this variation is meaningfully patterned in two ways. First, Democratic leaners are far more likely to be less partisan than weak Democrats when there is a serious third-party candidate in the race (1968, 1980, and 1996). Second, there is a discernible trend in morerecent elections (1996, 2004, 2008) of Democratic leaners being less partisan than weak Democrats.

The patterning between Republican leaners and weak Republicans, shown in figure 8.2, is similar in some respects and distinct in others. On the whole, the divergences between Republican leaners and weak Republicans is not as great as it is for Democrats. Also, Republican leaners appear to contravene their party ties more often vis-à-vis weak Republicans than do their Democratic counterparts. At the same time, both Republicans and Democrats shared a trend in the last few elections: Republican leaners were more likely than weak Republicans in each of the last four presidential elections to vote against their party allegiance. Moreover, with both Republican and Democratic leaners, the most sizable break from their party leanings was in the 2008 election.

One additional finding of note is that Independent leaners often appear partisan because they may have no attractive alternative. Leaners may vote like partisans more by default than out of loyalty. This suspicion is confirmed when we look at cases where there is a third-party option on

---

[25] If we look at more than one election in each year, we get an equally large variation in partisan loyalty among leaners. Over the same years, we find that the proportion of Democratic leaners who in elections for president, Congress, and the Senate cross over and give most of their votes to the Republican Party varies from a high of 44 percent in 1968 to a low of 6 percent in 1988. Similarly, the proportion of Republican leaners who primarily vote Democratic across the three elections varies from a high of 32 percent in 1992 to a low of 8 percent in 1965. The extent to which leaners are loyal varies dramatically.

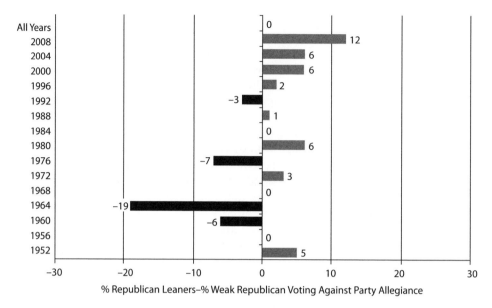

Figure 8.2. Voting against party: Republican leaners versus weak Republicans

the ballot. When a third-party option exists—regardless of whether that option is on the left, right, or middle—leaners are *less* partisan than weak partisans. Overall, when a third party is on the ballot, Democratic leaners are 7 percent less apt to vote Democratic than weak Democrats. Similarly, in these cases, Republican leaners are 3 percent less apt to vote Republican than weak Republicans. By combining the two patterns, we see that when going from elections without a third-party option to elections with a third party, Democratic leaners go from being 9 percent more loyal to being 7 percent less loyal. This 16-point shift is quite large when one considers that the average defection rate for Democrat leaners is 28 percent. Again, none of this means that all leaners are without strong partisan proclivities, but it does suggest that a lot of the supposed partisan tendencies of leaners are due to a paucity of choices.

Importantly, even by focusing on elections with a third-party candidate on the ballot, we are, in many ways, underestimating the willingness of nonpartisans to voice discontent with the two-party duopoly. In addition to considering the *number* of options available to voters, we should consider the *quality* of those options. In all of the presidential contests we looked at, the third-party candidate never had a legitimate shot at winning.[26] The most successful third-party candidate garnered only 18 per-

[26] Even in contests with just two major party candidates, the quality of the candidates and their appeal to different segments of the nonpartisan and partisan populations will

cent of the vote, and the average third-party candidate garnered only 11 percent of the vote. Thus, the quality or viability of all of these third-party options was low. If the extent to which nonpartisans choose exit, voice, or loyalty depends as much or more on the attractiveness of each option than simply on the number of options, we should see even more defections to third-party candidates when those candidates become viable.

When we turn our attention to contests where third-party candidates win or come close to winning, it becomes clear that much larger segments of nonpartisan populations are willing to defect to third-party candidates.[27] Jesse Ventura, for example, in his bid to become the governor of Minnesota in 1998, won more than half of the nonpartisan vote (52 percent). By contrast, he was much less successful among partisan voters, winning only 33 percent of the Democratic vote and 29 percent of the Republican vote (CNN exit poll). More recently, in the 2006 gubernatorial election in Texas, the two Independent candidates, Kinky Friedman and Carole Keeton Strayhorn, combined to take 48 percent of the nonpartisan vote compared with only 22 percent and 23 percent of the Republican and Democratic votes respectively. In the same year, Senators Joe Lieberman of Connecticut and Bernard Sanders of Vermont won the lion's share of the Independent vote (54 percent and 74 percent respectively) when they ran as Independents. Although the number of cases is small and not necessarily representative, these examples do suggest that if there is a quality third-party option, nonpartisans will tend to flock to that option in large numbers and will often do so in larger numbers than partisans.[28] Under the right circumstances, nonpartisanship has real consequences.[29]

---

vary. At times, the party that one leans toward may put forward an agenda and a candidate that are particularly attractive and worth supporting. During such times, loyalty is a perfectly reasonable option. But at other times, one's partisan proclivities may clash with the candidates and issues of the day. On those occasions voice and exit are especially likely.

[27] The attractiveness of the candidates can also have substantial effects on exit. We see, for example, that nonpartisans are less eager to exit in local elections where the options are often more varied and therefore often more attractive to minorities and other groups who are particularly apt to end up as nonpartisans. Using the ACPS, we found that in local elections Independent leaners and pure Independents exit less than weak partisans (26 percent, 25 percent, and 38 percent, respectively). This contrasts sharply with national contests, where pure Independents are twice as likely as leaners to drop out—again suggesting that the options available in these national contests are relatively unattractive to nonpartisans.

[28] Data on third-party voting in local contests are sparse, since the vast majority of local contests are nonpartisan and few have exit polls. Before Chicago shifted to nonpartisan contests, several Independent candidates ran for mayor, generally garnering considerable support from Independent voters. Edward Vrdolyak was perhaps the most successful, winning over some 43 percent of Independent voters in 1987 (CBS News exit poll).

[29] All of this also ignores the message or the content of the third-party candidacy. The degree to which an upstart third party attracts voters from different segments of the nonpartisans should depend on the kinds of campaigns it runs and the closeness of its issue

Nonpartisanship by Race and Ethnicity

The analysis of nonpartisan behavior that we have offered up to this point has, perhaps surprisingly, completely ignored race and the possibility that different patterns of behavior could occur across different racial and ethnic groups. We have deliberately ignored race because we wanted to establish the fact that the behavioral implications of nonpartisanship are important not just when we look at individual racial or ethnic groups in isolation but also when we assess the American population as a whole. Our story is not simply a story of minority, immigrant populations.

Our story is surely also one of race, ethnicity, immigration, and their implications. Since the previous chapters of this book have attempted to demonstrate that the reasons members of different racial and ethnic groups end up identifying as nonpartisan can be varied, we would be surprised to find that the implications of nonpartisanship across America's racial and ethnic groups did not vary in important ways. To that end, we now compare each of the four main racial and ethnic groups on basic indicators of exit, voice, and loyalty and in the following sections examine in more detail questions that are particularly relevant to the voting choices of each particular racial/ethnic group.

Do the implications of nonpartisanship differ across America's main racial and ethnic groups? In table 8.6 we begin to answer that question by looking at the three options of exit, voice, and loyalty that we looked at earlier for the entire population. Only this time we break down results by racial and ethnic groups.[30] The Asian American data from the Pilot National Asian American Political Survey (PNAAPS) of 2001 are not strictly comparable with the data for the other three racial and ethnic groups, which are from the same set of ANES measures. We utilize the PNAAPS data for Asian Americans because it is the only survey with voting behavior and a sufficiently large sample of Asian Americans to confidently estimate patterns within subsets of the Asian American population.[31]

---

positions to those of individual nonpartisans. To really understand the willingness of different members of the nonpartisan population to voice opposition to the two major parties, we would need to find and analyze cases where the third-party messages varied and to determine which segments of the nonpartisan population were defecting.

[30] The one difference is that this time we examine the tendency to support third-party candidates only in elections where there is a candidate on the ballot in more than half of the states. Given the concerns we raised about assessing third-party support in contests without a candidate on the ballot, we believe this is a more accurate portrayal of third-party support.

[31] Since the PNAAPS data have voting preferences for only one election, we were not able to assess loyalty for Asian Americans. The NAAS of 2008 has a broader sample and more recent data but was conducted during the campaign and thus has only voter intentions. The

TABLE 8.6
The Implications of Nonpartisanship across Race/Ethnicity

	Exit—nonvoters				Voice—3rd-party voters				Loyalty—party voters			
	Wh	Bl	La	As	Wh	Bl	La	As	Wh	Bl	La	As
Dems	22%	31%	31%	49%	10%	1%	12%	1%	64%	84%	73%	—
Inds	28	51	47	59	22	1	16	9	58	75	54	—
Reps	15	52	28	65	10	0	10	1	72	17	44	—

Source: ANES Cumulative File and PNAAPS.

A quick glance at table 8.6 indicates that the patterns do indeed differ across race and ethnicity. This is true for all three options of exit, voice, and loyalty, but the differences are starkest for voice and loyalty. In terms of the relationship between nonpartisanship and exit, the divide is between whites, Latinos, and Asian Americans on one hand and African Americans on the other. For the first three groups, nonpartisanship is associated with much lower rates of participation. White Independents are almost twice as likely as white Republicans to exit and a third more likely than white Democrats to choose to sit out. The pattern for Asian Americans and especially for Latinos is similar.[32] For blacks, Republican identifiers are just as likely as nonpartisans to drop out of a presidential contest. This suggests that the Republican Party has high hurdles to overcome with the black community. Not only are African Americans not apt to identify with the Republican Party, but even when they do identify as Republican, they are quite likely to choose exit over active participation.

The implications of nonpartisanship are even more varied when we consider third-party support, or voice. Across the four racial and ethnic groups, nonpartisanship leads either to substantially increased third-party support (whites and Latinos) or to no increase in third-party support (African Americans and Asian Americans). In other words, third-party candidates in presidential elections have been somewhat attractive to nonpartisan whites and Latinos and wholly unattractive to nonpartisan Asian Americans and African Americans. Given that the platform of the typical third-party presidential candidate has been on the right and at times has even been segregationist, the reluctance of black and Asian

---

Asian American sample in the ANES is far too small to present a breakdown within the panethnic group.

[32] The pattern for Latinos in the *Post*/Kaiser poll of 2000 is somewhat different. In that survey, Latino Republicans were more likely than Latino nonpartisans to exit, mirroring the behavior of black Republicans. The exit pattern for the other three racial and ethnic groups in the *Post*/Kaiser poll was similar to what we see in table 8.7.

American Independents to vote for a third-party candidate is hardly surprising.[33] The willingness of Latino Independents to do so is more interesting. It may be that nonpartisans within the Latino population are unhappy enough with the alternatives being offered by either major party that they are willing to support third-party bids that have little chance of succeeding.

Finally, the implications of nonpartisanship for partisan loyalty are equally divergent across the four main racial and ethnic groups.[34] For whites, nonpartisanship leads to much less consistent party-line voting. White nonpartisans are, in fact, almost as likely to cross over as to vote a straight party line in presidential, congressional, and senatorial elections in the same year. For African Americans and Latinos, by contrast, the group least likely to vote loyally is Republicans. Only 17 percent of black Republicans and 44 percent of Latino Republicans consistently favor their party.[35] The other important pattern hidden in these numbers is the partisan imbalance for black nonpartisans. Among African Americans, nonpartisanship does not lead to the abandonment of the Democratic Party in national elections. Three-quarters of black nonpartisans vote a straight party ticket across the three elections, and of these black party-line voters, 71 percent vote a straight Democratic ticket. In short, nonpartisanship for African Americans still means voting Democratic in national elections.[36]

The figures in table 8.6 are telling on several fronts. They demonstrate quite definitively that we cannot fully understand nonpartisanship and its implications without considering race and ethnicity. General conclusions about the electoral choices of nonpartisans will miss an important part of the picture if they do not break down the choices of different racial and ethnic groups.[37]

---

[33] This does not mean that nonpartisan blacks would not vote for an attractive third-party candidate if one were available. Asked if a "black political party is the best strategy," black nonpartisans are especially apt to say yes. Some 51 percent of black nonpartisans agree that forming a black party is an optimal strategy, compared with only 25 percent of Democrats and 39 percent of Republicans.

[34] We see the same divergence in partisan loyalty across race and ethnicity when we examine loyalty in the 2000 elections using the *Washington Post* /Kaiser Foundation data.

[35] The most logical interpretation is that there is no partisan option that is consistently attractive to these nonwhite Republicans.

[36] Among Latinos, both parties benefit from this straight-line voting among Independents. About half of these consistent Independent voters support candidates from the Democratic Party, and half support candidates from the Republican Party.

[37] Given the diversity within each racial and ethnic group, we might seek to further break down the population by immigrant status and national-origin group. When we did this for Asian Americans and Latinos, in particular, we found that the implications of nonpartisanship did not vary dramatically for any subpopulations that we could identify. Nonpartisanship has similar implications for exit, voice, and loyalty for all kinds of communities within the Latino and Asian American populations.

When we do break down choices by racial and ethnic group, we find patterns that hint at the political failings of the Republican Party and at opportunities that are available both to the two major parties and to third-party candidates. Among racial and ethnic minorities, Republican identifiers are especially prone to failing to vote consistently for candidates from their party. The clear implication is that there is no consistently attractive option for minority voters who lean toward the Republican Party. The fact that few nonwhite nonpartisans are drawn to third-party candidates also indicates that there are few attractive electoral alternatives for these nonpartisans. Both patterns suggest that many minority voters in the population have no true home. If properly targeted, this group could shift the balance of power between the two major parties. All of this highlights an important opening for political entrepreneurs.

The Makeup of the Nonpartisan Population by Race/Ethnicity

Perhaps the biggest difference between nonpartisans of the various racial and ethnic groups is not even evident in table 8.6. If we break down nonpartisans by type, we find that black, white, Latino, and Asian American nonpartisans place themselves in very different categories. To illustrate this, table 8.7 breaks down the nonpartisan population of each group by the now familiar categories of Independent leaners, pure Independents, and nonidentifiers. Since no single survey has a sufficient sample size to provide a breakdown of nonpartisans for all four racial and ethnic groups and because nonpartisan figures can be sensitive to question wording—whether the option of "don't know," "other," or "no preference" is explicit or not—we supplement results from the ANES with data from three other surveys. We focus on the *Washington Post* / Kaiser Family Foundation survey of 2000 because it is the only recent survey to explicitly give respondents the option of identifying as something other than Democrat, Republican, or Independent, has large enough numbers of Asian Americans, Latinos, and African Americans to offer estimates for all of these groups, and has questions on voting behavior in multiple contests. However, since the Latino and Asian American samples in the *Post*/Kaiser poll are still small, we also present data from two ethnic-specific surveys—the 2008 NAAS and the Latino National Survey of 2006.[38] Since the ANES includes only citizens, we exclude noncitizens from the other three surveys to ensure comparability across all figures.

[38] We do not focus on the NAAS of 2008 in this chapter because it is a preelection survey and thus has less-reliable data on voting behavior. However, it is worth noting that the breakdown of Asian American nonpartisans in the NAAS is quite similar to the figures presented in table 8.8.

TABLE 8.7
The Makeup of the Nonpartisan Population by Race/Ethnicity

| | Whites | | Blacks | | Latinos | | Asian Americans | |
	NES	Post	NES	Post	Post	LNS	Post	NAAS
Leaners	63%	57%	53%	47%	47%	17%	9%	25%
Pure Independents	32	20	30	23	20	23	18	13
Nonidentifiers	5	23	17	30	32	60	73	61

Put succinctly, when we talk about nonpartisanship, we are talking about very different things for each racial and ethnic group. For white Americans and African Americans, the nonpartisanship story is largely one of Independent leaners. By contrast, for Latinos and Asian Americans, the story is much more about nonidentifiers.[39] The differences are stark. In the ANES some 63 percent of white nonpartisans and 53 percent of African American nonpartisans admit an affinity for one of the two parties. Clearly, if we want to understand the African American and white nonpartisan populations, we need to know what leaners are thinking and doing. Among Latinos and Asian Americans, the proportion of nonpartisans who lean toward one party typically falls to less than one-quarter of the nonpartisan population—depending on which group is the focus and which survey is employed. For these two latter groups, leaners are not the central story and by some measures play only a minor role.

By contrast, if we want to better comprehend Latino and Asian American nonpartisans, we have to focus more on nonidentifiers. The clear majority of Asian Americans and between one-third and two-thirds of the Latino population fit the nonidentifier label.[40] The proportions are even larger if we include noncitizens. This may not be surprising, given the limited knowledge and experience that major segments of the Latino and Asian American populations have with the American party system, but it does set them apart from blacks and whites.[41] Few white Americans

---

[39] We tested the robustness of this basic pattern by looking at the makeup of the nonpartisan population in a range of national public opinion surveys including the General Social Survey cumulative file, the American Citizen Participation Survey of 1990, and the Pew/Kaiser Family Foundation Latino Survey of 2004. The exact numbers for each racial and ethnic group do vary from survey to survey, but the basic pattern persists. The black and white nonpartisan populations are dominated by leaners, whereas among the Latino and Asians American samples, nonidentifiers are a critical—if not the largest—group in the nonpartisan population.

[40] By comparison, in the American Citizen Participation Survey, 48 percent of Latino nonpartisans and 63 percent of Asian American nonpartisans are classified as nonidentifiers.

[41] As expected, there are important differences in the makeup of the nonpartisan popula-

and African Americans fail to place themselves somewhere on the traditional partisan scale. Only 5 percent of whites and 17 percent of blacks in the ANES can be labeled as nonidentifiers.

This divergence in the makeup of the nonpartisan population means that the critical questions that we need to answer to understand the electoral politics of each racial and ethnic group are not the same. If we want to understand white nonpartisans, we need to understand the choices of Independent leaners. As numerous scholars have long realized, the critical question for whites is whether Independent leaners are truly Independent. Fortunately, we have, in the early sections of this chapter, already addressed this question. Although we did not specifically focus on white Independents, the results of our tests certainly apply to the white population. Roughly 90 percent of the voters we looked at in the ANES cumulative file are white, so the conclusions we reached were largely driven by white Americans. Moreover, if we repeat the analysis while dropping all nonwhite respondents, the patterns that emerge are essentially identical to what we saw. When it comes to white Independent leaners, the bottom line is that real differences do emerge between leaners and weak partisans. Although most white Independent leaners do vote with their party in a single election, most of these leaners fail to remain loyal over time, and they often switch their partisan leanings to match their votes. Moreover, when given an attractive third-party option, these leaners regularly abandon their major party attachments. Although many white leaners are quite partisan, we cannot simply lump all leaners with partisans.

To understand black nonpartisanship, as the numbers in table 8.8 suggest, we once again have to focus on leaners. The question for African Americans is, however, slightly different. Although black nonpartisans, like white nonpartisans, tend to be largely made up of leaners, there is a very different partisan balance among the black leaners. White leaners are almost evenly divided between Republican leaners and Democratic leaners (51 percent are Democratic leaners). By contrast, African Americans leaners overwhelmingly gravitate toward the Democratic Party (79 percent are Democratic leaners). Thus, for African Americans, the critical question is more about defections from the Democratic Party than it is about Independence generally. As several researchers such as Dawson

---

tion across generational and national-origin groups for Asian Americans. Among Asian Americans, foreign-born nonpartisans are more likely to be nonidentifiers (61 percent), but the native born are also dominated by nonidentifiers (57 percent). Korean Americans were the group most likely to end up as nonidentifiers (82 percent), and Asian Indians, Chinese, and Vietnamese were the least likely (56, 56, and 59 percent respectively). Differences across generational and national-origin groups among Latinos were much more muted. Cuban Americans were somewhat more likely than other national-origin groups to label themselves leaners (49 percent), and Puerto Ricans were less likely to do so (36 percent).

(1994) and Tate (1994) have noted, for blacks the core question is whether increasing diversity in party identification leads to reduced black support for the Democratic Party in the voting booth. Finally, for the last two groups, Asian Americans and Latinos, we have an entirely different question. Among these racial and ethnic communities, nonidentifiers constitute either the majority of the nonpartisan population or at least a substantial portion of this population. The critical question then relates to these nonidentifiers. We need to know how they react to the opportunities that are presented to them by the American party system and the candidates it puts forward.

For Asian Americans and Latinos, this is largely unchartered territory that we will attempt to fill in with some important but preliminary results. For black nonpartisans, we will seek to shed new light on old questions. Finally, for white nonpartisans, we can add little to what we have already presented.

LATINO AND ASIAN AMERICAN NONIDENTIFIERS

We begin this investigation by focusing on Latinos and Asian Americans, the two least studied and as such most interesting groups. The key partisan type here is the nonidentifier. We now know that a clear majority of Asian American nonpartisans and a large percentage of Latino nonpartisans are nonidentifiers. What we do not know is how this influences the choices that Latino nonpartisans make in the electoral arena. In table 8.8 we begin to outline those choices.

The table presents data on the extent to which Asian Americans and Latinos opt for exit, voice, and loyalty under different circumstances. We are most interested in the behavior of nonidentifiers, but for comparison purposes, we include the choices of other nonpartisans and partisans as well. Since we need relatively large sample sizes and data on voting patterns, we have little choice in terms of the surveys that we analyze. For Latinos, we present data from the only national survey with a sufficiently large Latino sample size and data on voting patterns in more than one electoral contest—the *Washington Post*/Kaiser Family Foundation survey of 2000.[42] For Asian Americans there is no survey with a sufficient number of Asian American respondents that includes questions on voting behavior in multiple elections. Thus, we cannot present figures for Asian

---

[42] As a test of robustness, in alternate analyses we also look at Latino behavioral patterns in the LNS of 2006, Pew 2004, the Latino National Politics Survey (LNPS) of 1990, and the ANES cumulative file and at Asian American political behavior in the NAAS of 2008. Although the data in each case are limited in important ways, the basic patterns are consistent across surveys.

TABLE 8.8
The Implications of Nonpartisanship among Latinos and Asian Americans

	Exit—nonvoters		Voice—3rd-party voters		Loyalty—party voters	
	Latinos	Asian Americans	Latinos	Asian Americans	Latinos	Asians Americans
Partisans						
Strong	43	40	3	0	80	—
Weak	59	52	4	3	66	—
Nonpartisans						
Leaners	72	52	15	8	57	—
Pure Independents	76	66	22	4	58	—
Nonidentifiers	76	64	8	2	53	—

Source: For Latinos, the *Washington Post*/Kaiser Foundation survey of 2000. For Asian Americans, the 2001 PNAAPS.

Americans' loyalty. Instead, for this group we focus on the one survey that has a large sample size and data on voting behavior in at least one general election—the 2001 PNAAPS data.[43]

The exact measures in the table are similar to those we have used before. For both Latinos and Asian Americans, exit is measured as nonvoting in presidential elections. Similarly, for both groups voice is support for a third-party candidate in a presidential contest. For Latinos, loyalty is measured as support for the same party across two presidential and one congressional contest over a four-year period.

Two important aspects of nonidentifiers' behavior stand out. The first is the regularity with which Latino and Asian American nonidentifiers opt to exit electoral contests. Some 76 percent of Latino nonidentifiers chose not to vote in the 1996 presidential election. The Latino National Political Survey (LNPS) shows even higher rates of nonparticipation. It suggests that fully 86 percent of Latino nonidentifiers are inactive in presidential elections. The figures for Asian Americans are not as stark but nevertheless point to widespread exit. Some 64 percent of Asian American nonidentifiers failed to vote in the 2000 presidential contest, according to the PNAAPS survey. Given that these figures include only citizens and are self-reported voting rates, these are remarkably high levels of nonparticipation.

Thus, an important story for both Latinos and Asian Americans is not only that members of both are especially prone to being nonidentifiers

[43] The NAAS of 2008 is obviously more recent and has a more representative sample, but it is a preelection survey.

but also that members of this nonidentifier group have by and large not been attracted enough by the typical electoral contest to get involved. Some might argue that this group of Latinos and Asian Americans is largely apolitical and therefore unlikely to ever get involved in the electoral arena. We contend, however, that two other explanations for this nonparticipation are more plausible. We suspect that large numbers of Latino and Asian American nonidentifiers fail to get involved either because of limited information about the available partisan alternatives or because the available partisan options are not attractive.[44]

When we look at table 8.8, it becomes evident that nonidentifiers from both racial and ethnic groups are not especially apt to voice opposition to the major party system by supporting third-party candidates. Latino nonidentifiers were more likely than Latino partisans to support Perot in 2000, but in the end only 8 percent of Latino nonidentifiers chose this option. Among Asian Americans, uncommitted nonpartisans were not at all likely to support Perot in 2000. Only 2 percent did so. This suggests that in the few contests we have data for, nonidentifiers from these two communities have not been particularly attracted to third-party alternatives. Whether a third-party candidate who appealed more directly to Latinos and Asian Americans would capture a larger share of their votes is an open question.

The last major conclusion to emerge from table 8.8 is that these non-identifiers appear to be particularly unlikely to vote a straight party line. The data for Latinos are limited to three elections during the 1996 and 2000 electoral cycle, and we cannot say anything about Asian American loyalty. Nevertheless, these preliminary figures suggest that when non-identifers do vote, they often switch their support from one party to the other. Only 53 percent of Latino nonidentifiers voted for the same party in all three contests for which we have data (two presidential and one congressional). Partisan voting was, by contrast, much higher among strong and weak partisans and marginally higher among leaners and pure Independents.

The only other finding of note here is the rather large gap in behavior between leaners and weak partisans within the Latino population.[45] Latino leaners are much more likely than weak partisans to choose exit.

---

[44] Data from the LNPS reveal that when asked if there are important differences between the two major parties, 48 percent of nonidentifiers responded that they did not know, compared with only 21 percent of pure Independents and 11 percent of leaners. This suggests that limited information is a significant barrier. There is also evidence to suggest that these nonpartisans are not merely apolitical. As we have already noted, although Latino nonpartisans seldom vote in national contests, they are just as active as partisans across a wide range of political activities that do not involve direct contact with a political party.

[45] We see the same pattern in the LNPS.

Some 72 percent of leaners opt out compared with only 59 percent of weak partisans. Latino leaners are also almost four times more likely than weak partisans to vote for a third party. Whereas only 4 percent of weak partisan Latinos voted for Perot, fully 15 percent of leaners did so. Importantly, on both measures, leaners were much closer to pure Independents in their choices than they were to weak partisans. By contrast, among Asian Americans the behavior of leaners fairly closely paralleled the behavior of weak partisans. What all of this means is that any conclusion we hope to reach about the distinction between leaners and weak partisans has to be specific to race or ethnicity. Broad generalizations based on an analysis of white Independents do not generally apply to minority communities.

Overall, then, the account that emerges from this analysis of the Asian American and Latino nonidentifiers is of a large population of Americans who are up for grabs politically. Large numbers of nonidentifiers feel little attachment to the party system, generally do not vote in that system, and tend to switch their electoral support back and forth between the two parties when they do vote. If these nonidentifiers can be motivated with the right message and a candidate who more directly addresses their interests and concerns, that would be an important pattern for both parties to recognize.

Implications for Black Electoral Politics

The critical question for African Americans, as several observers have noted, is whether increasing diversity in black partisanship translates into less active support for the Democratic Party. As we have seen, African American Independents are growing in number, but most of these nonpartisans are Independent leaners, and the vast majority of these leaners gravitate toward the Democratic Party. If these Democratic leaners continue to support the Democratic Party in the voting booth, the decline in Democratic Party identification may represent only a modest shift in the level of attachment to the Democratic Party and have limited consequences for electoral politics. In this section, we seek to determine if this is really the case.

According to some obvious indicators, there are almost no consequences in the shift in black partisanship that has occurred over the last few decades. Despite some reservations about the Democratic Party and some movement toward Independence, blacks remain fairly steadfast supporters of Democratic candidates in national partisan contests. Data from the ANES indicate that in the last thirty years, in each election an average of 90 percent of black voters supported Democratic candidates at the presidential level, 86 percent in the Senate, and 90 percent in congressional elections.[46] In the 2008 presidential election, a record number of African Americans—95 percent—supported the Democratic nominee. At least in these circumstances, diversity in partisanship does not lead neatly to diversity in voting patterns.[47]

Nevertheless, we suspect that these data are masking important underlying differences of opinion that at least have the possibility of causing defections from the Democratic Party. As Frymer (1999), Walters (1988), and others have argued, black voters may effectively be captured at the national level where there are few attractive alternatives to the Democratic Party. Unity in national contests may be less the result of ongoing agreement over where the country should go and more the result of a lack of viable alternatives for African Americans voters.

To see if African Americans are still largely united and supportive of the Democratic Party, we need to recognize that the national contests we generally focus on are limited in their options—two major-party candidates and no viable alternatives—and we need to examine other contexts where the options may be more varied and more attractive to different segments of the African American population.

We begin this examination by looking at two contexts where the options are not only more varied but also less partisan. The goal here is merely to see if in these different contexts the black vote is less unified. Specifically, we collected data on the black vote in a range of big-city mayoral elections and in a comprehensive set of direct-democracy elections in California.

For the mayoral vote, we collected data on the vote by race/ethnicity for any contested primary or general election that occurred in the nation's twenty largest cities between 1991 and 2002. The data set includes racial voting patterns in forty-five elections.[48] We assess the black vote in direct democracy by examining black preferences on every California statewide proposition that was included in any of the seventeen *Los Angeles Times* exit polls between 1978 and 2000.[49] Neither data set should

[46] Moreover, there was little in the way of an over-time trend on any of these measures.

[47] At the same time, party identification did make some difference, even in these contests. One-quarter of all black Independents voted Republican in these contests, and almost one-half of all black Republicans (60 percent among strong Republican identifiers) supported Republican candidates. By contrast, well under 10 percent of black Democrats supported Republican candidates.

[48] Estimates of the vote by race came largely from exit polls or preelection polls (within a week of the contest), but in some cases, we also used ecological inference or homogeneous precinct analysis (see Hajnal and Trounstine 2005 for more information). Two factors limit the "generalizability" of the findings. First, we were able to obtain estimates of the vote by race for only about half of all elections in these cities. Second, the twenty cities have slightly different racial demographics (fewer whites) than the nation as a whole.

[49] Each survey contains a representative sample of California's voters (average N of

TABLE 8.9
Division in the Black Vote

	Presidency	Congress	Mayoralty	Direct democracy
Blacks opposing the black majority	10%	14%	26%	38%

be viewed as a representative indication of how blacks across the nation generally vote, but the data sets do represent a broad enough set of cases so that the divisions they expose should not be dismissed as anomalies.

As table 8.9 shows, context matters very much to the unity of the black electorate. In urban elections, where the kinds of options available to black voters on the ballot are often much more diverse than they are in partisan contests for president or Congress, we see less unity in the black vote. Across a range of big city mayoral elections, we found that 26 percent of black voters opposed the candidate favored by the black majority in the typical contest.[50] That was still somewhat more cohesive than Latinos (30 percent), whites (34 percent), and Asian Americans (44 percent), but it is a far cry from the near unanimity we see in the black vote in presidential (10 percent) and congressional elections (14 percent).[51]

4,145 in each poll, for a total of 195,019 proposition votes by respondents in the data set). There are, on average, 284 African American respondents in each poll. The demographic characteristics of the black respondents in each poll roughly match the demographic characteristics of the total black population of the state. The exit poll data are very accurate. The actual vote and the estimated vote based on the exit poll data differ by an average of 2.6 percentage points (the standard deviation is 2.3). The statewide black votes on each proposition also closely match the estimates of Voter News Service / CBS News exit polls, as well as estimates derived from an ecological-inference analysis of actual precinct-level returns. The direct democracy data set includes propositions that run the gamut of policy questions, with voters deciding issues as diverse as criminal sentencing, health care policy, immigration policy, affirmative action, school vouchers, Native American gaming, campaign finance reform, tax policy, and nuclear power.

[50] Black voters, as one might expect, tend to be most divided in contests with more than one black candidate. For example, Detroit's 2001 mayoral contest, which pitted Kwame Kilpatrick against Gill Hill, split the black vote by 55 percent to 45 percent. But the black vote can be split in a range of circumstances. Two white candidates can lead to division among the black community, as was the case in San Francisco in 1991 when Art Agnos garnered 62 percent of the black vote in his contest against Frank Jordan. Even a biracial contest between a black candidate and a white candidate can, on rare occasions, divide the black vote. Al Sharpton, for example, is estimated to have received only 60 percent of the black vote in the 1997 Democratic primary in New York City. The rest of the black vote was split between Ruth Messinger (28 percent) and Sal Albanese (12 percent).

[51] Even in these national contests, there are hints that African Americans do not like the choices they are given and would want to consider other options. In the 1996 NBES, 20 percent of black nonvoters indicated they had no preference among the presidential candidates. Among black Independent nonvoters, the figure was 41 percent.

When candidates are taken out of the equation altogether and African Americans vote directly on policy, there are signs of even more diverse preferences among black voters. An analysis of two decades of voting in direct democracy in California indicates that across all propositions, on average, 38 percent of black voters opposed the majority-black position. Even on the topics that African Americans indicated were most important to them, fully 37 percent of black voters voted against the black majority. And on propositions that divided neatly along a liberal-conservative dimension, just over 40 percent of African American voters wound up on the conservative side of the vote (Hajnal 2007). Clearly, there is a range of preferences within the black community that under certain circumstances are expressed in the ballot box.

All of these figures indicate that blacks are more divided in their electoral interests than many have suggested, but they do little to tell us whether African Americans vote against the Democratic Party if offered a viable and attractive option. The data on this question, although limited, strongly suggest that many black voters will go so far as to abandon the Democratic Party if the exit options are appealing enough. When we limited our analysis of mayoral elections to partisan general elections, we found that black unity remained well below what we see in presidential or congressional elections. In these mayoral elections, fully 31 percent of black voters opposed the Democratic Party nominee. In one important but hardly noticed case (this was not in our data set) the percentage of defections was even higher. Specifically, in New York City's recent mayoral contest, roughly half of the black electorate abandoned the Democratic Party and voted for the Republican incumbent, Michael Bloomberg (Roberts 2005). Bloomberg's success among black voters was in no small part driven by his moderate policy positions and his status as the incumbent in a city with a robust economy.[52] But this by no means denies the fact that black partisan ties can be broken. Rather, Bloomberg's success in attracting African American voters seems to suggest that when the Republican Party puts forward moderate candidates, more black voters will defect from the Democratic Party.

Furthermore, Democratic defections in the black vote are not limited to mayoral contests. The recent California recall elections also seem to indicate that when the Democrat candidate is not particularly attractive and the Republican Party offers reasonable alternatives, many blacks will defect. In that contest, 21 percent of black voters voted to recall the in-

[52] Although Bloomberg's support among blacks was quite high, the 2005 election was not the only one in New York in which many black voters defected from the Democratic Party. In the two previous elections, large segments of the black community also abandoned the party. In 2001 the Republican candidate won 25 percent of the black vote, and in 1997 the figure was 20 percent (Roberts 2005).

cumbent Democratic governor, Gray Davis, and in the subsequent election 33 percent opposed the Democratic nominee, Cruz Bustamante.[53] Outside of national contests, defections from the Democratic Party are hardly rare.

African Americans appear to be even more prone to abandoning the Democratic Party if they are offered an Independent black option. Across our three national surveys of the African American population, we found that 38 percent of African Americans said they would support a black political party. Among nonvoters, a group probably disillusioned by the choices offered by the Democratic and Republican parties, fully 48 percent indicated that they felt their interests could best be served by a black party. And it is not just what African Americans say. It is also what they do. In the few cases where African American voters have been given the option of supporting a viable candidate from a black party, black voters have demonstrated a willingness to abandon the Democratic Party in large numbers. Chicago is perhaps the starkest example of this phenomenon. In the last three partisan contests for mayor in Chicago, an average of 85 percent of African Americans voters opposed the Democratic nominee in the general election and supported a third-party alternative from the Harold Washington Party or an Independent closely aligned with the black community (Lewis et al. 1997). When African Americans are offered more diverse and more interesting options in the voting booth, the black community often becomes markedly less Democratic.

It is also apparent that black Independents make up a significant part of this story. Although many of the data on the black vote in the contests that we have already talked about are not broken down along party lines, when we are able to assess the black vote by party, we find that Independents are significantly more apt than Democratic identifiers to oppose the Democratic Party. Data from the ANES indicate that some 15 percent of black Independents voted against the Democratic Party in presidential elections. A further 16 percent did so in congressional elections. Data from Voter News Service exit polls between 1994 and 2002 reveal even higher levels of Democratic Party opposition in other types of electoral contests. According to these exit polls, 36 percent of black Independents abandoned the Democratic Party in gubernatorial elections. In Senate contests the figure was 37 percent.[54] The same pattern is evident in the

[53] Some 26 percent of black voters favored the two Republican candidates. Arnold Schwarzenegger captured 18 percent of the black vote, and the radically conservative candidate Tom McClintock won 8 percent of the black vote. Figures are from the November 2003 *Los Angeles Times* exit poll.

[54] Results from the recent California recall also indicate that defections were high among black Independents. According to the *Los Angeles Times* exit poll, 41 percent of all black Independents voted to oust the Democratic incumbent, and a further 56 percent opposed Bustamante, the Democratic candidate, in the subsequent election.

few partisan mayoral general elections for which we have voting preferences by race and partisanship. For example, in the New York City general election in 2001, 44 percent of black Independents (compared with
33 percent of black Democrats) opposed Mark Green, the Democratic
nominee.[55]

None of this is to say that blacks as a community are sharply divided
or even more divided than other groups. The black community remains
as cohesive or more cohesive in the electoral arena than almost any other
demographic group in society. Even in direct democracy where blacks
showed more signs of division, they are still as cohesive as any other racial or demographic group (Hajnal and Louch 2001).[56] Nevertheless, it
seems that continued support for Democratic candidates is less an indication of continued black unity than a sign that those who would prefer a
different kind of candidate are generally not offered one. When given a
viable alternative to the Democratic Party, blacks will abandon the party
in large numbers. This is something that both the Democratic Party and
potential competitors will have to consider seriously.[57]

---

[55] Unfortunately, it is difficult to discern how much of the Independent opposition to the
Democratic Party comes from black Independents who lean toward the Democratic Party.
In most cases, local surveys do not allow us to distinguish between leaners and pure Independents. Nevertheless, given that Democratic leaners make up well over half of the black
Independent population, the pattern that we see for black Independents as a whole is likely
to reflect voting patterns among Democratic leaners. Moreover, self-reported voting patterns across national elections tend to suggest that Democratic leaners do defect more regularly than other Democrats. Only 57 percent of black Democratic leaners in the NES indicated that they always vote for the same party. That was well below the 75 percent figure
reported for weak black Democrats. This does, however, contrast with the two types of
elections for which we have concrete data on the black leaner vote. According to the NES,
black Democratic leaners are very loyal to the Democratic Party. The defection rate among
black Democratic leaners is only 8 percent in congressional elections and 3 percent in presidential elections. Since none of the voting data at either the city or the state level breaks
down Independents into pure Independents and partisan leaners, it is impossible to know
how this pattern differs across various contexts.

[56] Hajnal (2007) found that on average 37 percent of Latinos, 40 percent of whites, and
40 percent of Asian Americans voted against their group's majority position.

[57] Both political parties should also seriously consider the history of African American
third-party support. Although the black community has generally been reluctant to "waste"
its vote on a candidate or party that has little chance of winning, many blacks have been
willing to turn to third parties when both major parties have clearly ignored their interests.
For example, in the mid-nineteenth century, many blacks championed the antislavery Liberty Party and its successor, the Free Soil Party (Gurin et al. 1989). In the 1890s over a
million blacks joined the Colored Farmer Alliance. Later, during the Great Depression, the
Communist Party won considerable support from the black community for its opposition
to lynching and its advocacy efforts on behalf of the poor (Naison 1983). At the state level,
blacks have also formed their own parties when denied access to the major parties. In the
1960s, blacks in Mississippi and Alabama abandoned the Democratic Party in large num-

Conclusion

In this chapter we have tried to illuminate three broad sentiments about nonpartisanship and its electoral significance. The first is that nonpartisanship matters in the electoral arena. Failing to identify with one of the two major parties can have wide-ranging consequences for the electoral choices that individual Americans make. This is not to say that all nonpartisans are wholly disconnected from the two parties. Many nonpartisans will, despite their self-professed Independence, be closely linked with a political party and, for all intents and purposes, will act like partisans. But many others will not. In the end, whether Americans choose exit, voice, or loyalty depends heavily on their status as partisans or nonpartisans.

We have also tried to show that the choices that nonpartisans make are greatly shaped by the electoral context they face. In America that context is often a two-party duopoly with limited options for the many nonpartisans who do not fit neatly into one of the two parties. But that is not always the case. When these ill-fitting nonpartisans are offered an attractive alternative in the electoral arena—an admittedly rare event in American politics—they tend to respond. Viable candidates and appealing issue platforms can draw in large segments of the nonpartisan population.

Finally, we hope we have convincingly shown that race and ethnicity are critical components in understanding nonpartisanship. Accounts of nonpartisans that rely solely on assessments of the white community are likely to be incomplete, if not totally inaccurate. The meaning and implications of nonpartisanship vary dramatically from one racial and ethnic group to another. To understand nonpartisanship and, perhaps even more important, to try to appeal to nonpartisans, the divergent motivations and actions of nonpartisans from each racial and ethnic group need to be taken into account.

---

bers to support their own third-party alternatives—the Mississippi Freedom Democratic Party and the National Democratic Party of Alabama.

CHAPTER 9

Conclusion

> Anytime you throw your weight behind a political party that
> controls two-thirds of the government and that party can't
> keep the promise it made to you during election time and you
> are dumb enough to walk around continuing to identify
> yourself with that party you are not only a chump but you are a
> traitor to your race. . . . You've been misled, you've been had,
> you've been took.
>
> —Malcolm X

IN THIS, FINAL chapter, we begin with a brief summary of our key findings. We start by returning to the observation that the time is ripe for a
reconsideration of party identification and its place in the American political landscape. Demographic changes in the electorate and changes in
the nature of party competition and partisan ideological polarization
since the first printing of *The American Voter* might tempt some to consider a radical revision of existing conventions on partisanship. We find
no cause to abandon this baby simply because its bathwater is no longer
still. For as long as political scientists have studied the attachments of
mass publics to political parties in America, they have very fruitfully
looked to sources of political socialization and social identity formation,
following a tradition rooted in *The American Voter*, or they have produc-
tively focused on information heuristics, ideological positioning, and rational learning about parties, following a more Downsian approach. In
the pages of this book we have advanced an account of partisanship that
adapts key elements from both the Michigan and the Downsian schools
of thought, both properly modified to match the shifting realities of race
and immigration in the United States in the twenty-first century.

Our proposed adaptations rest on the multiple dimensions of partisanship, coined alliteratively in our book as identity, ideology, and information. The nub of our story here is that the partisan choices of all racial
and ethnic groups in America share the primary social *identities* and the
ideological beliefs that shape their political predispositions and the *information* environments that regulate whether partisan cues come to be accepted as relevant political considerations. Much of the empirical core of
this book has been a demonstration of the distinctive ways in which

group identities, ideological beliefs, and information environments interact to define the relationship that whites, African Americans, Latinos, and Asian Americans have to America's unique system of two-party competition. One key contribution of our book, then, has been the proposal of a general framework of party identification within which to fit the growing diversity of the American electorate.

That said, immigrants, racial minorities, and whites with distinct ideological profiles not attended to by the Democratic and Republican parties and their candidates will be motivated to remain neutral—at least in their self-identification. More generally, when the choices the major parties present to the American public do not match our available stock of political knowledge (information), our deeply held political beliefs (ideology), or how we think of ourselves (identity), nonpartisanship becomes a rationally adaptive strategy. Another key contribution of this book has thus been to highlight the diversity of nonpartisans in the increasingly diverse U.S. electorate. Much of the previous scholarship has focused on white Independents only and with withering scrutiny of one particular aspect of nonpartisanship: whether Independents are truly nonpartisan or whether they reveal their true partisanship preferences in the anonymity of the ballot box. This preoccupation, we submit, results to a significant extent from a very particular approach to the study and measurement of partisanship—using opinion surveys and measuring individuals' self-reported identification with a given set of partisan labels that range from strong Republican at one end of the spectrum to strong Democrat at the other, with "pure Independents" in the middle.

We offer some rejoinders on the matter of whether Independents reveal their underlying partisanship preferences when they vote, but shine a sustained light first on the prior phenomenon of choosing to identify as a nonpartisan. Along the way, we also spotlight a relatively unexamined aspect of partisan choice—namely, the ability to make sense of the conventional three-way choice between identifying as a Democrat, Republican, or Independent. As we have seen, a nontrivial number of Americans indicate no preference when given this three-way choice, and many others simply do not know or refuse to answer the question about their party identification. In recent versions of the ANES's representative sample of adult Americans, almost 9 percent of respondents would be classified as "nonidentifiers." In some subgroups, the prevalence of nonidentifiers is far greater. In the LNS and NAAS data that we use in this book, we find that an identical 36 percent of Latinos and Asian Americans are nonidentifiers. The story of why such large proportions of these newcomers are nonidentifiers, we further submit, is a story about immigrant political incorporation.

In bringing together our claims about the racially group-specific ideological, identitarian, and informational bases of partisanship with our claims about nonpartisanship, we have, along the way, also proposed additional key contributions to our substantive understanding of the ties that African Americans, whites, Latinos, and Asian Americans have to Democrats, Republicans, and Independents. We began in chapter 4 by considering the partisanship of African Americans. African Americans continue to be reasonably well characterized (especially so in the most recent 2008 presidential election) by the joint occurrence of extraordinarily high rates of voting for Democratic candidates and the remarkably crystallized sense of racial group interests and identity. Viewing group identity and political choice as essentially equivalent, however, would confer too much structure and stability to African American partisanship. A century ago, African Americans were similarly homogeneous, but with a strong allegiance to the party of Lincoln and not the party of Jefferson. Even during the span of history covered by American National Election Studies data, African Americans have grown less willing to call themselves Democrats even if they ultimately choose to vote for the Democratic presidential candidate come Election Day. This empirical variation and the observable links between individual circumstances, group interests, and the coordination of collective choice in favor of the Democratic Party are far from automatic. We show, more specifically, that African Americans are especially likely to break with group ranks in identifying as Democrats under three conditions: when the sense of shared group identity is diminished, when ideological beliefs in black autonomy and self-determination become stauncher, and when information-based assessments imply that continued allegiance to the Democratic Party may not be in the best interests of African Americans.

African Americans represent an archetype of sorts for how salient social group identities can intersect with primary political identities qua partisanship in meaningful ways, and Latinos and Asian Americans represent a sharply contrasting archetype of the extent to which both social group identities and political identities can be inchoate and undefined. In chapters 5 and 6, we turned our gaze to these groups and argued that the partisan choices of Latinos and Asian Americans have to be understood in the context of immigrant political incorporation. The consequence of taking the immigration histories of these groups into account is acquiring a view of partisanship as a sequential choice. In the first stage of choice, Latinos and Asian Americans need to feel some connection to the partisan labels "Democrat," "Republican," and "Independent" before they can, in the second stage, make a meaningful selection. In the first stage, factors that capture the uncertainty and ambivalence characteristic of the process of immigrant political socialization are dominant; in the second stage, factors that capture the ideological and identitarian orientation of

Latinos and Asian Americans and their ability to perceive important differences between the two major parties become more important.

Finally, the point of departure—and as we have argued in this book, for most scholars, the entire journey—is the partisanship of white Americans. For this group, the extant body of scholarship continues to explain most of the variation in partisanship, with some notable exceptions defined by nonpartisanship and the link between nonpartisanship and vote choice. Within our theoretical framework, the robust explanatory power of existing models of partisanship is predicted because whites are a more established, predominantly native-born population. Thus, partisanship itself is the primary political identity of relevance, anchored by ideological predispositions set in one's formative (typically) preadult years and set in an environment of information cues that then allow one to situate and update the preferences that derive from these identities and ideologies.

At the same time, we have also seen in these pages that not all white nonpartisans are apolitical beings without well-developed partisanship and ideological beliefs as their primary political predispositions or without access to information cues to situate their own interests and preferences vis-à-vis the stated issue positions of party organizations and candidates. We saw in chapter 7 that many whites arrive at their nonpartisanship through at least two other routes: their strong views on particular policy areas (in effect, being so distinct in their policy profile that identification with neither party is attractive) and their cross-cutting ideological commitments (in effect, having a sufficiently mixed profile of liberalism and conservatism across issue areas so that they are ambivalent about identifying with a party). We further saw in chapter 8 that being a political Independent can—when a viable third-party alternative presents itself—be electorally consequential. Moreover, although it may still be too early to tell, the growing polarization of party competition in the last few election cycles (2000 to 2008) appears to be pushing Independent leaners, as voters, to become increasingly distinct from weak partisans.

THE GROWING IMPORTANCE AND DIVERSITY OF NONPARTISANS

Our attention to America's racial and ethnic diversity and our efforts at building a more inclusive account of the partisan proclivities of the American public have led to a story that highlights the central role that nonpartisans play. This renewed focus on nonpartisans is warranted not only for the reasons we have outlined in this book but also because of the significant growth in nonpartisanship across the nation. That nonpartisanship is an important phenomenon requires no convincing for observers of recent trends in American politics. One of the main developments

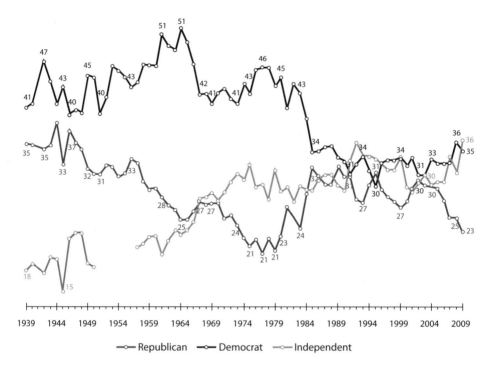

Figure 9.1. The growth of Independence over time

over the nearly seven-decades-long history of survey data on party identification is a real expansion of the nonpartisan population. Figure 9.1
shows this trend from a recent Pew Research Center report, subtitled
"Independents Take Center Stage in Obama Era" (2009). In the earliest
Gallup polls on partisanship, less than 20 percent of respondents self-
identified as Independents; in the most recent polls, this percentage nearly
doubled.[1]

If we instead focus on the ANES version of the party-identification
question, we see that the pattern is essentially the same, with a few refine-

[1] Figure 9.1 further shows the shifts over time in the two-way split in partisanship between the Democratic and Republican parties. Here there is a modest Democratic advantage in the late 1930s and 1940s that then grows to a 20-plus percentage-point margin favoring Democratic partisanship in the 1960s and 1970s. This margin almost completely
vanishes by the 1990s, but in the most recent decade, there is some evidence of a return to
a Democratic advantage.

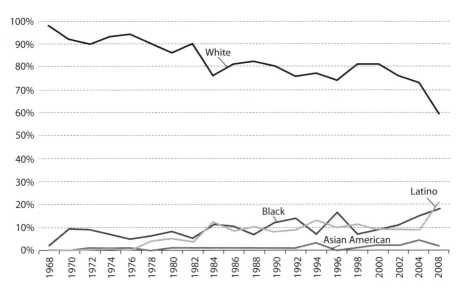

Figure 9.2. The growing diversity of Independence

ments. The percentage of Independents in the ANES also doubles from roughly 20 in the 1950s to almost 40 by 1978. From 1980 onward, the proportion of Independents seesaws and by 2008 returns to historic highs, with just over 38 percent of the public identifying as Independents.

Even Barack Obama's presidential leadership has not appeared to do much to dent the public's aversion to partisan labels. Published Gallup figures indicate that since the end of the 2008 campaign, the proportion of the public that identifies as Independent has grown by roughly 8 percentage points, to a near record high of 38 percent in the fourth quarter of 2009. Although we readily admit that many of these nonpartisans are aligned with either the Democratic or the Republican Party, there is no doubt that there are more than enough uncommitted nonpartisans to sway most of the electoral contests in this nation.

There is also little doubt that race plays a significant role in this story of growing nonpartisanship. Although it was reasonable to argue that Independence was a white phenomenon in the 1950s and 1960s, when the foundational studies of party identification emerged, that is decidedly not the case today. As figure 9.2 demonstrates, in the mid-twentieth century, almost 95 percent of all nonpartisans were white. However, according to the ANES, that figure has dropped consistently over time. In 2008 only 59 percent of all nonpartisan identifiers were white—still a majority, but far from an overwhelming one.[2] As demonstrated here and as we

[2] This 59 percent figure is substantially smaller than the percentage of adults in the nation

have seen throughout this book, there is a salient and growing diversity among nonpartisans, colored by race and contextualized by immigration. To understand and, more important, to try to attract today's nonpartisans, parties and candidates will have to seriously consider the racial dimensions of nonpartisanship.

Lessons for America's Parties

These trends make it eminently clear that neither the Democratic nor the Republican Party can afford to ignore either nonpartisans or the diversifying electorate in the United States. What lessons can we then offer parties and their candidates based on our research? The first and most obvious lesson is that this growing nonpartisan population can be fruitfully targeted by the nation's political operatives. Our analysis suggests that today's nonpartisans can no longer be dismissed as nonideologues disinterested in the game of politics. Within the ranks of the nonpartisan population, there are still many apoliticals who will ignore any range of entreaties from the political sphere and who will remain largely immutable on the sidelines of the country's democracy. But the nonpartisan population is now a compellingly diverse one. In the midst of this diverse nonpartisan population is an array of individuals who would—if properly targeted—become fully engaged in the politics of the nation.

If we recognize that there are multiple routes to nonpartisanship and if we see nonpartisans as being suspicious of parties that they do not know well, ambivalent vis-à-vis parties that they do not neatly fit into, or unsure of parties that do not cater to their interests, then there is reason to believe that the nonpartisan population can be integrated into partisan politics and mobilized in the electoral arena. The environmentalist seeking genuine commitments to scale back greenhouse gases and reverse environmental degradation, the Mexican American looking to either party for direction on amnesty and comprehensive immigration reform, the libertarian longing to be free from the twin scourges of big business and big government, and the Chinese American who seeks a party who will stand up to human rights abuses and unfettered urbanization in her home country are all open to partisan appeals.

Indeed, there is already ample evidence that this kind of recruitment can work. The rapid mobilization of millions of immigrants and their supporters in response to Congress's 2006 efforts at immigration reform testifies to the possibilities. Similarly, the increase in naturalization rates,

---

who are white (69), confirming that racial and ethnic minorities are particularly prone to choosing nonpartisanship.

voter turnout, and Democratic Party identification among Latinos that occurred in California in the aftermath of the Republican Party's efforts to pass Proposition 187—an anti–illegal immigrant initiative—also confirms the potential for engagement (Bowler et al. 2006; Pantoja, Ramírez, and Segura 2001). Field experimental studies showing that contacting individual Asian Americans and Latinos with simple phone calls can increase voter turnout by appreciable numbers highlight the promise of this segment of the electorate (Ramírez and Wong 2006). Finally, there may be no fresher and more forceful a proof point on the efficacy of mobilizing communities of color than the 2008 presidential election. More than 90 percent of the estimated five million new voters in 2008 (compared with the 2004 election), according to the 2008 Current Population Survey, were African American, Latino, and Asian American.

Today's minorities are no different from the minorities of yesterday in one very important sense. They are politically approachable and readily mobilized. In the case of immigrant minorities, at present they may be particularly apt not to participate in American electoral politics, and they may be remarkably ambiguous and uncertain about the nation's partisan landscape, but that is only because the two parties have failed to directly and actively engage them. Or, in the case of African Americans, they may feel taken for granted and boxed in by few exit options beyond racial separatism and ideological conservatism.

The reasons why political parties have not chosen to target these new electorates more directly are numerous. Some of these reasons speak to the shifting organizational capacity of political parties, which have grown weaker locally, more resource dependent, and more candidate centered nationally. Other reasons illuminate the transformed terrain of electoral competition, with the ever-growing ideological polarization of party elites and activists, the strategic impetus to maintain existing party coalitions, and the lingering, if not obsessive, attentiveness to technologies of micromobilization and narrowcasting in battleground districts and among "swing" segments of the electorate. Perhaps the most troubling of reasons, however, is the questionably cynical resort to symbolic (perhaps even culturally inauthentic) overtures toward minority electorates—seemingly aimed more toward reassuring better-established segments of the electorate that a party is not intolerant and hate mongering than toward mobilizing communities of color.

In light of these reasons, how then should parties extricate themselves from these nettles that keep African Americans at bay and Latinos and Asian Americans in check? We hone in on possible strategies or lessons for political parties to draw about nonpartisans. The first is the rationalist logic of racing to the median voter's ideal point. In a diverse electorate, one conventional method has been to target the median voter with a middle-of-the-road approach. We contend, however, that current demographic realities and an array of findings in this book indicate that this method is less sustainable. Given the increasingly multidimensional nature of the American public, it is far from obvious where the median lies and less than clear that if the parties do try to race to that median, whom this strategy will attract.

In a world in which most of the political actors fall neatly along a single spectrum from liberal on the left to conservative on the right, there are compelling reasons to believe in the efficacy of a median voter strategy. But in a political world where multiple factors such as information, ideology, and identity play a role, in which many dimensions impinge on partisan choice, and in which different imperatives dominate the choices of each racial and ethnic group, that strategy is likely to be less profitable. For each of the racial and ethnic groups that we examine in this book, there may not be much of a median to target. African Americans are, as a whole, far from the national median; whites are increasingly definable as issue publics and ideological ambivalents; and an astonishingly high proportion of Latinos and Asian Americans are ideological nonidentifiers. A median position—however that might be defined—is unlikely to be attractive to any of these groups. Quite unsurprisingly, we agree with observers that the decisive turns in the last three presidential elections—especially 2000 and 2004—were not centripetal, toward the median voter, but rather centrifugal efforts to mobilize the base of the Republican Party.

We suggest that to be successful in America's increasingly diverse electorate, candidates and political parties will have to consider a multifaceted and multiracial campaign. This is an approach that the Democrats and Republicans have been reluctant to pursue in the recent past. When racial considerations were incorporated in partisan strategies in the last few decades, it was usually to try to use race to lure whites into a dominant and largely exclusionary majority. The successful efforts of the Republican Party to portray the Democratic Party as the "black party" led, by almost all accounts, to a fairly robust coalition of traditional northern Republicans and racially conservative southern whites (Edsall and Edsall 1992; Frymer 1999; Black and Black 2002). The well-publicized targeting of illegal immigrants in the policy programs of most recent Republican presidential candidates appears to be a replay of this black southern strategy adapted to the fact that Latinos now represent the largest and potentially most threatening racial minority group. For the most part, the response of the Democratic Party has been to try to ignore race altogether. The countermove of "Third Way" Democrats to leave race off the center stage is often epitomized by Bill Clinton's rejection of Sister Souljah but is more broadly an attempt to keep racially contentious issues such as affirmative action out of the electoral equation. The silence of many of today's Democratic leaders on immigration is, in many ways, a continuation of this strategy.

Current demographic realities and the partisan patterns that we have highlighted in this book make both of these approaches increasingly untenable. The white portion of the adult population is at 69 percent and falling. Moreover, a growing proportion of American whites are racial liberals and racial optimists. In the context of the 2008 election, for instance, Michael Tesler and David Sears (2010) powerfully show that their "racial resentment scale"—for decades, wielded by scholars as a probative measure of the lingering residues of racism, refashioned to modern times—now cuts both ways. The relationship of racial resentment to white voters' preferences in the 2008 presidential contest is more telling for those on the low end of the scale (whites who harbor no resentment toward racial progress) than those on the high end of the scale. As a consequence, a whites-only coalition of fiscal, moral, and racial conservatives is sustainable only for short-term and shortsighted fusillades of fear mongering.

The growth, diversity, and increasing activism and empowerment of communities of color also suggest to us that color-blind and postracial approaches will require a great deal more hoe work than the amount that political parties and their candidates seem willing to toil through. African Americans, no matter how electorally "captured" they may be on paper, are clearly not honor bound to accept a continuing role as silent and decidedly junior partners in the managing coalition of the Democratic Party. Latinos and Asian Americans—in the absence of deeper partisan roots—will continue to look to partisan cues that signal their recognition and standing as a group. Even President Obama, for all his historic success in representing the potential transcendence of racial "groupism" in American politics, has on multiple occasions been brought back down to the street-level politics of "wise Latinas," "Beer Summits," and "Tea Baggers."

The alternative that we offer is to communicate multivocally across the spectrum of racial and ethnic segments of the electorate. To borrow a term used to describe Lorenzo de' Medici's grip on power during the Italian Renaissance, this approach is to be a "robust actor" (Padgett and Ansell 1993)—exploiting to great electoral effect the crosscutting identities, ideological ambiguities, and heterogeneous interests that characterize today's American body politic. Thus, a savvy party or politician can, for example, simultaneously appeal to Chinese American interests with a crackdown on China's human rights violations, to white voters with a middle-class tax cut, and to Latino citizens with increased public education funds. The key is to exploit the multidimensional nature of the American public by appealing to each group on areas that are of particular concern to that group. Since the areas of unique concern can often be orthogonal or inconsequential to the core concerns of a second (or third or fourth) group, this multipronged approach can accommodate a fairly diverse array of interests—an accommodation that is a near necessity, given the wide-ranging experiences and disparate issue concerns that now shape the electorate. The basic intuition here is to leverage racial diversity rather than put all one's political chips into one group or ignore race altogether.

This appeal to racial multivocality is not new. Black candidates have, for decades, been walking this electoral tightrope by trying simultaneously to calm white fears by promising racial equanimity and to mobilize black voters by speaking to the core racial concerns of the African American community. Black mayoral candidates such as Tom Bradley often pursued this strategy by consciously using different voices with different audiences. One set of speeches was designed for primarily white spectators, and a noticeably altered script was employed for largely black audiences. Although the contrasting concerns of black and white voters in cities made this electoral equation difficult to navigate, empirical evidence suggests that this biracial strategy has been both widespread and increasingly successful (Hajnal 2007).

A more relevant and probably more convincing exemplar of this approach is the Axelrod-Obama strategy during the 2008 presidential election. President Obama, as we noted in the first pages of this book, did not build his campaign around an appeal to white voters; nor did white voters push him over the top. At the same time, the public face of Obama's campaign as postracial implies too strongly the irrelevance of race on the part of both the candidate and his constituents. Here, we simply note that there has been an unusual degree of identity claims made on Obama's behalf, each taking its own Morrisonian turn.[3] Rabbi Arnold Wolf, head of a synagogue in Obama's own South Side of Chicago, proclaimed, "Obama is from nowhere and everywhere—just like the Jews. He's Black, he's White, he's American, he's Asian, he's African—and so are we."[4] In a similar vein, the *New York Times* reporter Jodi Kantor described the first family's multivocality thus: "The family that produced Barack and Michelle Obama is Black and White and Asian, Christian, Muslim, and Jew-

[3] Toni Morrison famously described Bill Clinton, in a 1998 article in the *New Yorker*, as "our first Black President." In Morrison's terms, "Clinton displays almost every trait of Blackness: single-parent household, born poor, working-class, saxophone-playing, McDonald's-and-junk-food-loving boy from Arkansas."

[4] Rabbi Arnold Wolf, in Tom Hundley, "Barack Obama: The First Jewish President?" *Chicago Tribune*, 12 December 2009. Accessed online on 6 June 2010 at http://articles .chicagotribune.com/2008-12-12/news/0812110155_1_barack-obama-bettylu-saltzman -jewish-vote.

ish. They speak English; Indonesian; French; Cantonese; German; He-
brew; African languages including Swahili, Luo, and Ibgo; and even a few
phrases of Gullah, the Creole dialect of the South Carolina Low country"
(20 January 2009).[5]

Although Obama was uniquely situated to speak multivocally to
America's diverse electorate, we do not believe that the strategy of racial
multivocality need be limited to this one case and the near cult of personality surrounding Obama's candidacy. Requisite to the success of racial
multivocality is a deeper understanding of America's growing diversity
and, to put a finer point on it, the multiple roots of partisanship and nonpartisanship. For a politician with Barack Obama's background, such a
deeper understanding may come more as a felt intuition than as a learned
maneuver. There is always an obvious danger that attention to the needs
of one group will arouse anger and lead to rejection from another. Or,
worse yet, parties and their candidates who blunder through their perhaps earnest appeals to speak multivocally—Gerald Ford's tamale shuck-
ing, John Kerry's attempt to claim the symbolic mantle of the "second
black President of the United States," Mitt Romney's summoning call of
"who let the dogs out," and, yes, Barack Obama's infamous gutterball in
a Pennsylvania bowling alley—may be subject to embarrassment and
notoriety.

Carefully nuanced and artfully executed, this kind of strategy is possible for a range of candidates. A successful racial multivocality entails
knowledge of and attention to the diverse realities of both partisanship
and nonpartisanship. It entails carefully sorting through a political
agenda to hone in on issues of particular concern to one group that are
sufficiently peripheral to other groups so that strong stands on these issues will not repel other groups. For Latinos, that issue might be some
narrow elements of immigration reform. For Asian Americans, access to
higher education might be an area in which to make inroads without
eliciting an equal and opposite reaction. Antidiscrimination efforts might
similarly attract black support without provoking hostility from other
groups. The winnable set may be thin, but the list could go on.

At present, one party—the Democrats—has an inside track on this
strategy. Past opposition by Republican leaders to policies designed to try
to ensure racial equality in the voting booth, in housing, and in many
other aspects of American society and current Republican stands against
immigration and immigrants themselves have, in the minds of many
Americans, marked the Republican Party as the party of white interests.

---

[5] One of us could not resist the opportunity to coauthor an essay cheekily titled "Barack
Like Me," on the extent to which Obama could be claimed as the nation's first Asian American president (Omi and Lee 2009).

By contrast, past support of the civil rights agenda by the Democratic Party and the visible backing of the Democratic Party by large numbers of racial and ethnic minority voters have garnered the Democratic Party a fairly widely held reputation for being prominority. The results of the 2008 presidential election only served to highlight the multiracial nature of the Democratic coalition and the largely white character of Republican Party support. On the Democratic side, Obama garnered a clear majority of the black, Latino, and Asian American vote and some 43 percent of the white vote. On the Republican side, 91 percent of John McCain's votes came from white Americans. Finally, Obama's ongoing presence as the nominal head of the Democratic Party should at least temporarily accentuate this Democratic advantage.

But the partisan consequences of America's increasingly diverse electorate are far from settled. The Democrats may have a clear advantage at present, but as we have repeatedly highlighted in this book, the most dominant forces in this racial equation are ambivalence and uncertainty. The largest segment of the Latino and Asian American population consists of not Democratic identifiers but of nonidentifiers. When combined, nonidentifers and Independents make up the clear majority of both groups. All told, 56 percent of Latinos and 57 percent of Asian Americans identify as Independents or as nonidentifiers.[6] Perhaps even more alarmingly for the Democratic Party, some 41 percent of Latinos see no difference in how the two parties serve their group's interests (Pew Hispanic Center 2007). A nearly identical 42 percent of Asian Americans in the 2008 NAAS see no difference between the two parties on the single issue that they declare to be most important to them. Among blacks, racial considerations are still central, and Democrats are still seen by most as the party that is most sympathetic to black interests. But more and more African Americans are unsure about just how well the Democratic Party serves the black community. Almost 30 percent of blacks feel that the Democratic Party does not work hard for black interests. And even within the white population, there are numerous nonpartisans whose ideological views and issue preferences engender considerable uncertainty about which party to support.

There are also clear opportunities for the Republican Party to exploit. Large segments of the minority population hold relatively conservative ideological views. Some 21 percent of Latinos, 13 percent of Asian Americans, and 15 percent of African Americans label themselves as conservative. For both Latinos and blacks, that is higher than the proportion who

---

[6] Similarly, in terms of ideology, a plurality—roughly 49 percent of Latinos and 34 percent of Asian Americans—expresses uncertainty about where to place itself on the basic liberal-conservative ideological spectrum that divides the two parties.

identify themselves as liberal, and for Asian Americans the conservative figure is only slightly smaller than the liberal segment of the population. Moreover, Republican issue stances on gay marriage, abortion, women's rights, and other key moral issues could appeal to broad segments of the black, Latino, and Asian American communities. Finally, most of the minority population remains outside the electoral arena, with few strong views about either party and no apparent allegiances in the American political sphere. Over 65 percent of the minority adult population did not vote in the last presidential contest. These are individuals who could be mobilized, who could be attracted to a party, and who could sway electoral outcomes.

Thus, the eventual outcome of this battle for the hearts and minds of America's diverse uncommitted population is far from clear. Current Democratic advantages could be translated into a massive and lasting Democratic majority if the bulk of the minority population continues to view Democrats as their party. But if Republicans alter their tactics and appeal more earnestly to this growing minority population, then the huge numbers of nonidentifiers could easily swing victory to the Republican side. What is clear is that the patterns we have detailed are, in some senses, only the tip of the iceberg. If current demographic projections are accurate, racial and ethnic minorities will make up half of the nation's population by the middle part of this century. A party platform that either seeks to use race to unify whites or simply does not incorporate the diverse experiences and interests of the minority population is likely to fail. Politicians and parties ignore these lessons at their peril.

A final observation we offer is that our proposed strategy of racial multivocality is aimed somewhat narrowly as a political gambit between two warring factions, each vying to gain the upper hand. What is clearly at risk when catering to the organizational and electoral self-interests of the Democratic and Republican parties is some notion of a greater collective goal, whether it be the national interest, social welfare maximization, civic republican ideals of virtue, or some other conception of the good. As such, not all normative accounts of partisanship and the web of plural, civic associations they might engender in the service of an idealized democratic politics are sustained by our brass-tacks discussion of racial multivocality. Under a bandwidth of liberalism, however, both individual and group interests are likely to be more crystallized and better pursued if both Republican and Democratic parties can be made to appeal more broadly and deeply to America's increasingly diverse electorate. The prospects for these interests grow even rosier if and when other political parties are able to break the viselike grip of the Republican and Democratic parties on electoral competition in the United States. Until such a time arrives when either or both of these possibilities become an eventuality, we are reminded that the work of forming a more perfect union takes time. Here the central challenge of partisan politics within an ever more diverse democracy is well captured by Charles Merriam's classic text on parties written nearly a century ago:

> It is, of course, inevitable that the formation of a common political consciousness and of a common agreement upon questions of public policy should be more difficult in proportion as the population is more diverse and easier in proportion as it is more homogeneous. Each race brings its own standards, customs, and ideals and these must first be blended before a common understanding in regard to common matters can be reached. In the meantime, appeals to race pride and race prejudice will be made with more or less success by various interests, selfish or unselfish as the case may be, and in this way the day of reaching a common understanding will be so much delayed. This does not involve any reflection upon any particular race, but is merely the statement of the simple fact that it takes time for strangers to reach a common understanding. (1922, 182)

Bibliography

ABC News. 2010. "The President and Race Relations: Fewer See Gains, but Hopes Persevere." http://abcnews.go.com/images/PollingUnit/1100a2RaceRelations.pdf.

Abdelal, Rawi, Yoshiko M. Herrera, Alastair Iain Johnston, and Terry Martin. 2001. Treating Identity as a Variable: Measuring the Content, Intensity, and Contestation of Identity. Unpublished manuscript. Harvard University.

Abrajano, Marisa, and R. Michael Alvarez. 2010. *New Faces, New Voices: The Hispanic Electorate in America*. Princeton: Princeton University Press.

Abramowitz, Alan. 1994. Issue Evolution Reconsidered: Racial Attitudes and Partisanship in the U.S. Electorate. *American Journal of Political Science* 39:1–24.

Abramowitz, Alan, and Kyle L. Saunders. 1998. Ideological Realignment in the U.S. Electorate. *Journal of Politics* 60:634–52.

———. 2004. Rational Hearts and Minds: Social Identity, Ideology, and Party Identification in the American Electorate. Paper presented at the annual meeting of the American Political Science Association, Chicago, IL.

———. 2008. Is Polarization a Myth? *Journal of Politics* 70:542–55.

Abramson, Paul R., John H. Aldrich, Phil Paolino, and David W. Rohde. 1995. Third-Party and Independent Candidates in American Politics: Wallace, Anderson, and Perot. *Public Opinion Quarterly* 110 (3): 349–67.

Abramson, Paul R., and William Claggett. 1984. Race-Related Differences in Self-Reported and Validated Turnout. *Journal of Politics* 46:719–38.

Abramson, Paul R., and Charles W. Ostrom. 1991. Macropartisanship: An Empirical Reassessment. *American Journal of Political Science* 30:562–75.

Achen, Christopher. 1975. Mass Political Attitudes and the Survey Response. *American Political Science Review* 69:1218–31.

———. 1992. Social Psychology, Demographic Variables, and Linear Regression: Breaking the Iron Triangle in Voting Research. *Political Behavior* 14 (3): 195–211.

———. 2001. Parental Socialization and Rational Party Identification. Paper presented at the Parties and Partisanship Conference, October 25–27, Vanderbilt University, Nashville, TN.

Agger, R. E. 1959. Independents and Party Identifiers: Characteristics and Behavior in 1952. In *American Voting Behavior,* ed. E. Burdick and A. J. Brodbeck. New York: Free Press.

Alba, Richard, and Victor Nee. 2003. *Remaking the American Mainstream: Assimilation and Contemporary Immigration*. Cambridge, MA: Harvard University Press.

Aldrich, John H. 1995. *Why Parties? The Origin and Transformation of Political Parties in America*. Chicago: University of Chicago Press.

Aldrich, John, and Forrest Nelson. 1984. *Linear Probability, Logit, and Probit Models*. Newbury Park, CA: Sage.

Allsop, Dee, and Herbert F. Weisberg. 1988. Measuring Change in Party Identification in an Election Campaign. *American Journal of Political Science* 32 (4): 996–1017.

Allswang, John M. 1977. *Bosses, Machines, and Urban Voters*. Baltimore: Johns Hopkins University Press.

Almaguer, Tomás. 1994. *Racial Fault Lines: The Historical Origins of White Supremacy in California*. Berkeley: University of California Press.

Alvarez, R. Michael. 1990. The Puzzle of Party Identification. *American Politics Quarterly* 18:476–91.

Alvarez, R. Michael, and Lisa García Bedolla. 2003. The Foundations of Latino Voter Partisanship: Evidence from the 2000 Election. *Journal of Politics* 65 (1): 31–49.

Alvarez, R. Michael, and John Brehm. 1995. American Ambivalence towards Abortion Policy: Development of a Heteroskedastic Probit Model of Competing Values. *American Journal of Political Science* 39 (4): 1055–82.

Alvarez, R. Michael, and Jonathan Nagler. 1998. Economics, Entitlements and Social Issues: Voter Choice in the 1996 Presidential Election. *American Journal of Political Science* 42:1349–63.

Amemiya, Takeshi. 1975. Qualitative Response Models. *Annals of Economic and Social Measurement* 4:363–72.

———. 1985. *Advanced Econometrics*. Cambridge, MA: Harvard University Press.

American Political Science Association. 1950. Towards More Responsible Two-Party System. *American Political Science Review* 44: Supplement.

Andersen, Kristi. 1979. *The Creation of a Democratic Majority, 1828–1936*. Chicago: University of Chicago Press.

Andersen, Kristi, and Elizabeth Cohen. 2005. Political Institutions and Incorporation of Immigrants. In *The Politics of Democratic Inclusion*, ed. Rodney E. Hero and Christina Wolbrecht. Philadelphia: Temple University Press.

Anderson, Barbara, and Brian D. Silver. 1986. Measurement and Mismeasurement of the Validity of the Self-reported Vote. *American Journal of Political Science* 30 (4): 771–85.

Anderson, Margo. 1988. *The American Census*. New Haven, CT: Yale University Press.

Anderson, Margo, and S. Feinberg. 1999. *Who Counts*. New York: Russell Sage Foundation.

Ansolabehere, Stephen, Jonathan Rodden, and James Snyder. 2006. Purple America. *Journal of Economic Perspectives* 20 (2): 97–118.

Ansolabehere, Stephen, James Snyder, and Charles Stewart. 2001. The Effects of Party and Preferences on Congressional Roll-Call Voting. *Legislative Studies Quarterly* 26:533–72.

Anzaldúa, Gloria E. 1987. *Borderlands/la frontera: The New Mestiza*. San Francisco: Aunt Lute Books.

Archdeacon, Thomas J. 1983. *Becoming Americans: An Ethnic History*. New York: Free Press.

Asian Pacific American Legal Center (APALC). 2007. *Asian Americans at the Ballot Box: The 2006 General Election in Los Angeles County*. Online report

accessed at http://apalc.org/demographics/wp-content/uploads/2007/05/apalc
_ballotbox2006_final.pdf on 3 June 2010.

Austen-Smith, David. 1984. Two-Party Competition with Many Constituencies.
Math. Soc. Sci. 7:177–98.

Bada, Xóchitl , Jonathan Fox, and Andrew Selee, eds. 2006. *Invisible No More:
Mexican Migrant Civic Participation in the United States.* Washington, DC:
Woodrow Wilson International Center for Scholars.

Ball, Terence. 1993. American Political Science in Its Post-war Political Context.
In *Political Science: History and Discipline,* ed. James Farr and Raymond Seidelman. Ann Arbor: University of Michigan Press.

Barreto, Matt, Rodolfo Espino, Adrian Pantoja, and Ricardo Ramírez. 2003. Selective Recruitment or Empowered Communities. Paper presented at the 2003
annual meeting of the American Political Science Association, Philadelphia.

Barreto, Matt, and Nathan Woods. 2005. Latino Voting Behavior in an Anti-
Latino Political Context. In *Diversity in Democracy: Minority Representation
in the United States,* ed. Gary Segura and Shawn Bowler. Charlottesville: University of Virginia Press.

Bartels, Larry M. 2000. Partisanship and Voting Behavior, 1952–1996. *American
Journal of Political Science* 44 (1): 35–50.

Basinger, Scott, and Howard Lavine. 2005. Ambivalence, Information, and Electoral Choice. *American Political Science Review* 99:169–84.

Beck, Paul Allen, and M. Kent Jennings. 1991. Family Traditions, Political Periods, and the Development of Partisan Orientations. *Journal of Politics* 53 (3):
742–63.

Belknap, George, and Angus Campbell. 1952. Political Party Identification and
Attitudes toward Foreign Policy. *Public Opinion Quarterly* 15:601–23.

Berdahl, C. A. 1942. Party Membership in the United States. *American Political
Science Review* 36:16–50 and 241–62.

Berelson, Bernard, Paul F. Lazarsfeld, and William McPhee. 1954. *Voting.* Chicago: University of Chicago Press.

Bertrand, Marianne, and Sendhil Mullainathan. 2004. Are Emily and Greg More
Employable Than Lakisha and Jamal? *American Economic Review* 94 (4):
991–1013.

Bishop, George F., Robert W. Oldendick, and Alfred J. Tuchfarber. 1978. Effects
of Question Wording and Format on Political Attitude Consistency. *Public
Opinion Quarterly* 42:81–92.

Bishop, George F., Alfred J. Tuchfarber, and Robert W. Oldendick. 1978. Change
in the Structure of American Political Attitudes: The Nagging Question of
Question Wording. *American Journal of Political Science* 22:250–69.

Black, Duncan. 1948. On the Rationale of Group Decision Making. *Journal of
Political Economy* 56 (February): 23–34.

———. 1958. *The Theory of Committes and Elections.* Cambridge: Cambridge
University Press.

———. 1959. *The Theory of Committees and Elections.* Cambridge: Cambridge
University Press.

Black, Earl, and Merle Black. 1987. *Politics and Society in the South.* Cambridge,
MA: Harvard University Press.

———. 1992. *The Vital South.* Cambridge, MA: Harvard University Press.

———. 2002. *The Rise of Southern Republicans.* Cambridge, MA: Harvard University Press.

Blank, Rebecca. 2001. An Overview of Trends in Social and Economic Well-Being, by Race. In *America Becoming: Racial Trends and Their Consequences,* ed. Neil J. Smelser, William J. Wilson, and Faith Mitchell. Washington, DC: National Academy Press.

Bobo, Lawrence. 2001. Racial Attitudes and Relations at the Close of the Twentieth Century. In *America Becoming: Racial Trends and Their Consequences,* ed. Neil J. Smelser, William J. Wilson, and Faith Mitchell. Washington, DC: National Academy Press.

Bobo, Lawrence, and Devon Johnson. 2000. Racial Attitudes in a Prismatic Metropolis: Mapping Identity, Stereotypes, Competition, and Views on Affirmative Action. In *Prismatic Metropolis,* ed. Lawrence Bobo, Melvin Oliver, James Johnson Jr., and Abel Valenzuela Jr. New York: Russell Sage Foundation.

Boger, John Charles, and Gary Orfield, eds. 2005. *School Resegregation: Must the South Turn Back?* Chapel Hill: University of North Carolina Press.

Bonilla-Silva, Eduardo. 2003. *Racism without Racists.* Lanham, MD: Rowman and Littlefield.

Borrelli, S., Brad Lockerbie, and Richard G. Niemi. 1987. Why the Democrat-Republican Partisanship Gap Varies from Poll to Poll. *Public Opinion Quarterly* 51:115–19.

Bositis, David. 2000. *Blacks and the 2000 Republican National Convention.* Washington, DC: Joint Center for Political and Economic Studies.

———. 2004. *Blacks and the 2004 Republican National Convention.* Washington, DC: Joint Center for Political and Economic Studies.

Bourdieu, Pierre. 1984. *Distinction: A Social Critique of the Judgment of Taste.* Cambridge, MA: Harvard University Press.

Bowen, H. R. 1943. The Interpretation of Voting in the Allocation of Economic Resources. *Quarterly Journal of Economics* 58:27–48.

Bowler, Shaun, Stephen P. Nicholson, and Gary M. Segura. 2006. Earthquakes and Aftershocks: Tracking the Macropartisan Implications of California's Recent Political Environment. *American Journal of Political Science* 50 (1): 146–59.

Brady, Henry E., and Paul M. Sniderman. 1985. Attitude Attribution: A Group Basis for Political Reasoning. *American Political Science Review* 79:1061–78.

Brehm, John. 1993. *The Phantom Respondents.* Ann Arbor: University of Michigan Press.

Brewer, Marilynn B. 1991. The Social Self: On Being the Same and Different at the Same Time. *Personality and Social Psychology Bulletin* 17:475–82.

———. 2001. The Many Faces of Social Identity. *Political Psychology* 22 (1): 115–23.

Brewer, Marilynn B., and Rupert J. Brown. 1998. Intergroup Relations. In *Handbook of Social Psychology,* ed. Daniel T. Gilbert, Susan T. Fiske, and Gardner Lindzey. 4th ed. Vol. 2. New York: McGraw Hill.

Brimelow, Peter. 1995. *Alien Nation.* New York: Harper Perennial.

Brody, Richard A. 1991. Stability and Change in Party Identification: Presidential to Off-Years. In *Reasoning and Choice,* ed. Paul M. Sniderman, Richard A. Brody, and Philip E. Tetlock. Cambridge: Cambridge University Press.

Brody, Richard A., and Lawrence Rothenberg. 1988. The Instability of Partisanship: An Analysis of the 1980 Presidential Election. *British Journal of Political Science* 18:445–65.

Brown, Craig. 1985. Partisanship, Independence, and No Preference: Another Look at the Measurement of Party Identification. *American Journal of Political Science* 29:274–90.

Brown, Elsa Barkley. 1994. Negotiating and Transforming the Public Sphere: African American Political Life in the Transition from Slavery to Freedom. *Public Culture* 7:107–46.

Brown, Michael K., Martin Carnoy, Elliott Currie, Troy Duster, David B. Oppenheimer, Marjorie Schultz, and David Wellman. 2003. *Whitewashing Race.* Berkeley: University of California Press.

Brown, Robert, and Todd Shaw. 2002. Separate Nations: Two Attitudinal Dimensions of Black Nationalism. *Journal of Politics* 16 (1): 22–44.

Browning, Rufus, Dale Rogers Marshall, and David H. Tabb. 1984. *Protest Is Not Enough: The Struggle of Blacks and Hispanics for Equality in Urban Politics.* Berkeley: University of California Press.

Brubaker, Rogers. 2001. The Return of Assimilation? Changing Perspectives on Immigration and Its Sequels in France, Germany, and the United States. *Ethnic and Racial Studies* 24 (4): 531–48.

Brubaker, Rogers, and Frederick Cooper. 2000. Beyond "Identity." *Theory and Society* 29 (1): 1–47.

Bryce, James. 1888. *The American Commonwealth.* Indianapolis, IN: Liberty Fund, 1995.

Buchanan, James M., and Gordon Tullock. 1962. *The Calculus of Consent: Logical Foundations of Constitutional Democracy.* Ann Arbor: University of Michigan Press.

Buis, Maarten L. 2007. Linking Process to Outcome: The Seqlogit Package. Presentation at the second Nordic and Baltic Stata Users Group meeting, September 7, Stockholm.

Burden, Barry. 2001. The Polarizing Effects of Congressional Primaries. In *Congressional Primaries and the Politics of Representation,* ed. P. F. Galderisi, M. Lyons, and M. Ezra. Lanham, MD: Rowman and Littlefield.

Burgess, John. 1890. *Political Science and Comparative Constitutional Law.* Boston: Ginn and Company.

Cain, Bruce E., and D. Roderick Kiewiet. 1984. Ethnicity and Electoral Choice: Mexican American Voting Behavior in the California 30th Congressional District. *Social Science Quarterly* 65:315–27.

Cain, Bruce E., D. Roderick Kiewiet, and Carole J. Uhlaner. 1991. The Acquisition of Partisanship by Latinos and Asian Americans. *American Journal of Political Science* 35 (2): 390–422.

Calvert, Randall. 1985. Robustness of the Multidimensional Voting Model: Candidate Motivations, Uncertainty, and Convergence. *American Journal of Political Science* 29:69–95.

Campbell, Angus, Philip E. Converse, Warren E. Miller, and Donald E. Stokes. 1960. *The American Voter.* New York: Wiley.

———. 1966. *Elections and the Political Order.* New York: Wiley.

Campbell, Angus, Gerald Gurin, and Warren E Miller. 1954. *The Voter Decides.* Evanston, IL: Row, Peterson.

Campbell, Angus, and Donald E. Stokes. 1959. Partisan Attitudes and the Presidential Vote. In *American Voting Behavior,* ed. E. Burdick and A. J. Brodbeck. Glencoe, IL: Free Press.

Canon, David. 1999. *Race, Redistricting, and Representation: The Unintended Consequences of Black Majority Districts.* Chicago: University of Chicago Press.

Carmichael, Stokely, and Charles V. Hamilton. 1967. *Black Power.* New York: Random House, Vintage Books.

Carmines, Edward G., and James A. Stimson. 1989. *Issue Evolution.* Princeton, NJ: Princeton University Press.

Carpini, Michael X. Delli, and Scott Keeter. 1996. *What Americans Know about Politics and Why It Matters.* New Haven, CT: Yale University Press.

Castles, Francis G., and Peter Mair. 1984. Left-Right Political Scales: Some "Expert" Judgements. *European Journal of Political Research* 12:73–88.

Chhibber, Pradeep, and Ken Kollman. 2004. *The Formation of National Party Systems.* Princeton: Princeton University Press.

Cho, Wendy Tam. 1999. Naturalization, Socialization, Participation: Immigration and (Non)Voting. *Journal of Politics* 61:1140–55.

Chong, Dennis, and Reuel Rogers. 2003. Reviving Group Consciousness. Paper presented at the Nation of Immigrants Conference, Berkeley, California.

Citrin, Jack, and David O. Sears. 2005. *American Identity and the Politics of Multiculturalism.* New York: Cambridge University Press.

Claggett, William. 1981. Partisan Acquisition versus Partisan Intensity: Life-Cycle, Generation, and Period Effects, 1952–1976. *American Journal of Political Science* 25 (2): 193–214.

Clark, Terry N. 1996. Structural Realignments in American City Politics: Less Class, More Race and a New Political Culture. *Urban Affairs Review* 31 (3): 367–403.

Cohen, Cathy J. 1999. *The Boundaries of Blackness: AIDS and the Breakdown of Black Politics.* Chicago: University of Chicago Press.

Cohen, Cathy, and Michael C. Dawson. 1993. Neighborhood Poverty and African American Politics. *American Political Science Review* 87 (2): 286–302.

Cohen, J. Bernard. 1985. *Revolution in Science.* Cambridge, MA: Harvard University Press / Belknap Press.

Cohen, Lizabeth. 1990. *Making a New Deal: Industrial Workers in Chicago, 1919–1939.* New York: Cambridge University Press.

Collet, Christian. 1996. Third Parties and the Two-Party System. *Public Opinion Quarterly* 60 (3): 431–49.

Committee on the American Electorate. 2006. Online report at http://www1.american.edu/ia/cdem/csae/pdfs/csae061102.pdf.

Committee on Political Parties. The American Political Science Association.

1950. Towards a More Responsible Two-Party System. A Report of the Committee on Political Parties. *American Political Science Review* 44: Supplement.

Conover, Pamela Johnston. 1988. The Role of Social Groups in Political Thinking. *British Journal of Political Science* 18:51–76.

Converse, Philip E. 1964. The Nature of Belief Systems in Mass Publics. In *Ideology and Discontent*, ed. David E. Apter. New York: Free Press.

———. 1966. The Concept of a Normal Vote. In *Elections and the Political Order*, ed. Angus Campbell, Philip E. Converse, Warren E. Miller, and Donald E. Stokes. New York: Wiley.

———. 1970. Attitudes and Non-Attitudes: Continuation of a Dialogue. In *The Quantitative Analysis of Social Problems*, ed. Edward R. Tufte. Reading, MA: Addison-Wesley.

Converse, Philip E., and G. B. Markus. 1979. *Plus ca change . . .* : The New CPS election Study Panel. *American Political Science Review* 73:32–49.

Converse, Philip E., and Roy Pierce. 1985. Measuring Partisanship. *Political Methodology* 11:154–66.

Cornell, Stephen, and Douglass Hartmann. 1998. *Ethnicity and Race: Making Identities in a Changing World*. Newbury Park, CA: Pine Forge Press.

Cornwell, Elmer E. 1960. Party Absorption of Ethnic Groups: The Case of Providence, Rhode Island. *Social Forces* 38:205–10.

Cose, Ellis. 1995. *The Rage of a Privileged Class: Why Are Middle-Class Blacks Angry? Why Should America Care?* New York: Harper Perennial.

Craig, Stephen C. 1985. Partisanship, Independence, and No Preference: Another Look at the Measurement of Party Identification. *American Journal of Political Science* 29 (2): 274–90.

Crotty, William. 1984. *American Political Parties in Decline*. 2nd ed. Boston: Little, Brown.

Dahl, Robert A. 1961a. *Who Governs? Democracy and Power in the American City*. New Haven, CT: Yale University Press.

———. 1961b. The Behavioral Approach in Political Science: Epitaph for a Monument to a Successful Protest. *American Political Science Review* 55 (December): 763–72.

David, Paul T. 1992. The APSA Committee on Political Parties: Some Reconsiderations of Its Work and Significance. *Perspectives on Political Science* 21 (2): 70–79.

Davis, Darren. 1997. The Direction of Race of Interviewer Effects among African Americans: Donning the Black Mask. *American Journal of Political Science* 41 (1): 309–22.

Davis, Darren W., and Ronald E. Brown. 2002. The Antipathy of Black Nationalism: Behavioral and Attitudinal Implications of an African American Ideology. *American Journal of Political Science* 46 (2): 239–53.

Davis, James A., Tom W. Smith, and Peter V. Marsden. 2003. *General Social Surveys, 1972–2002* [Computer File]. 2nd ICPSR Version. Chicago: National Opinion Research Center.

Davis, Philip, ed. 1920. *Immigration and Americanization*. Boston: Ginn and Company.

Dawson, Michael C. 1994. *Behind the Mule*. Princeton, NJ: Princeton University Press.

———. 1999. "Dis Beat Disrupts": Rap, Ideology, and Black Political Attitudes. In *The Cultural Territories of Race*, ed. Michele Lamont. Chicago: University of Chicago Press.

———. 2001. *Black Visions*. Chicago: University of Chicago Press.

———. 2006. After the Deluge: Publics and Publicity in Katrina's Wake. *Du Bois Review* 3:239–49.

Dawson, Michael C., and Cathy J. Cohen. 2002. Problems in the Study of the Politics of Race. In *Political Science: The State of the Discipline*, ed. Ira Katznelson and Helen V. Milner. New York: W. W. Norton.

Dawson, Michael C., and Rovana Popoff. 2004. Reparations: Justice and Greed in Black and White. *Du Bois Review* 1 (1): 47–91.

Dawson, Michael C., and Ernest J. Wilson III. 1991. Paradigms and Paradoxes: Political Science and the Study of African American Politics. In *Political Science: Looking to the Future*, ed. William Crotty, vol. 1, 189–234. Evanston, IL: Northwestern University Press.

de la Garza, Rodolfo O. 2004. Latino Politics. *Annual Review of Political Science* 7:91–123.

de la Garza, Rodolfo O., and Louis DeSipio, eds. 1999. *Awash in the Mainstream: Latino Politics in the 1996 Elections*. Boulder, CO: Westview Press.

de la Garza, Rodolfo, Louis DeSipio, F. Chris García, John A. García, and Angelo Falcon. 1992. *Latino Voices*. Boulder, CO: Westview Press.

de la Garza, Rodolfo, Angelo Falcon, and F. Chris García. 1996. Will the Real Americans Please Stand Up: Anglo and Mexican Support of Core American Political Values. *American Journal of Political Science* 40:335–51.

de la Garza, Rodolfo, Angelo Falcon, F. Chris García, and John A. García. 1998. Latino National Political Survey, 1989–1990. Ann Arbor, MI: Interuniversity Consortium for Political and Social Research.

Dennis, Jack. 1988a. Political Independence in America. Part 1: On Being an Independent Partisan Supporter. *British Journal of Political Science* 18:77–109.

———. 1988b. Political Independence in America. Part 2: Towards a Theory. *British Journal of Political Science* 18:197–219.

———. 1992. Political Independence in America. Part 3: In Search of Closet Partisans. *Political Behavior* 14:261–96.

DeSipio, Louis. 1995. *Counting on the Latino Vote: Latinos as a New Electorate*. Charlottesville: University of Virginia Press.

———. 2006a. Do Home-Country Political Ties Limit Latino Immigrant Pursuit of U.S. Civic Engagement and Citizenship? In *Transforming Politics, Transforming America: The Political and Civic Incorporation of Immigrants in the United States*, ed. Taeku Lee, S. Karthick Ramakrishnan, and Ricardo Ramírez. Charlottesville: University of Virginia Press.

———. 2006b. Latino Civic and Political Participation. In *Hispanics and the Future of America*, ed. Marta Tienda and Faith Mitchell. Washington, DC: National Academies Press.

de Tocqueville, Alexis. 1835. *Democracy in America*, trans. George Lawrence, ed. J. P. Mayer. New York: Harper & Row, 1969.

Dionne, E. J., Jr. 1991. *Why Americans Hate Politics*. New York: Simon and Schuster.

Downs, Anthony. 1957. *An Economic Theory of Democracy*. New York: Harper Collins.

Drake, St. Clair, and Horace R. Cayton. 1945. *The Black Metropolis: A Study of Negro Life in a Northern City*. New York: Harcout, Brace.

Dryzek, John. 1986. The Progress of Political Science. *Journal of Politics* 48 (May): 301–20.

———. 2006. Revolutions without Enemies: Key Transformations in Political Science. *American Political Science Review* 100 (4): 487–92.

Duverger, Maurice. 1954. *Political Parties: Their Organization and Activity in the Modern State*. Translated by Barbara and Robert North. New York: Wiley.

Dyson, Michael Eric. 1996. *Making Malcolm: The Myth and Meaning of Malcolm X*. New York: Oxford University Press.

———. 2008. Race, Post Race. *Los Angeles Times*. November 5. Available at http://www.latimes.com/news/opinion/la-oe-dyson5-2008nov05,0,5307282.story. Accessed January 25, 2010.

Edsall, Thomas B., and Mary D. Edsall. 1992. *Chain Reaction*. New York: W. W. Norton.

Eldersveld, Samuel. 1951. Theory and Method in Voting Behavior Research. *Journal of Politics* 13:70–87.

———. 1952. The Independent Vote: Measurement, Characteristics, and Implications for Party Strategy. *American Political Science Review* 46 (3): 732–53.

———. 1964. *Political Parties: A Behavioral Analysis*. Chicago: Rand McNally.

Elliott, Donald. 1980. Recursive Systems Containing Qualitative Endogenous Variables Representing Nonstochastically Dependent Events. *Econometricai* 48 (3): 761–63.

Elms, Laurel. 2001. The Effects of Question Wording and Interview Mode on the Over-Time Measurement of Party Identification: A Comparison of the Roper and Gallup Partisanship Series. Paper presented at the annual meeting of the Midwest Political Science Association, Chicago.

Enelow, James, and Melvin Hinich. 1984. *The Spatial Theory of Voting*. New York: Cambridge University Press.

Epstein, Leon. 1956. British Mass Parties in Comparison with American Parties. *Political Science Quarterly* 71:97–125.

Erie, Stephen. 1990. *Rainbow's End*. Berkeley: University of California Press.

Erikson, Robert S., Michael B. Mackuen, and James A. Stimson. 2002. *The Macro Economy*. New York: Cambridge University Press.

Espiritu, Yen L. 1992. *Asian American Pan-ethnicity*. Philadelphia: Temple University Press.

Evans, Geoffrey, ed. 1999. *The End of Class Politics? Class Voting in Comparative Context*. New York: Oxford University Press.

Farley, Reynolds. 1996. *The New American Reality: Who We Are, How We Got There, Where We Are Going*. New York: Russell Sage Foundation.

Farr, James. 1993. Political Science and the State. In *Discipline and History: Political Science in the United States,* ed. James Farr and Raymond Seidelman. Ann Arbor: University of Michigan Press.

———. 1995. Remembering the Revolution: Behavioralism in American Political Science. In *Political Science and History: Research Programs and Political Traditions,* ed. James Farr, John S. Dryzek, and Stephen T. Leonard. Cambridge: Cambridge University Press.

Farr, James, and Raymond Seidelman, eds. 1993. *Discipline and History: Political Science in the United States.* Ann Arbor: University of Michigan Press.

Feagin, Joe R. 1991. The Continuing Significance of Race: Antiblack Discrimination in Public Places. *American Sociological Review* 56 (February): 101–16.

Feagin, Joe R., and Hernan Vera. 1995. *White Racism.* New York: Routledge.

Ferejohn, John. 1993. The Spatial Model and Elections. In *Information, Participation, and Choice: An Economic Theory of Democracy in Perspective,* ed. Bernard Grofman. Ann Arbor: University of Michigan Press.

Finifter, Ada W., and B. M. Finifter. 1989. Party Identification and Political Adaptation of American Migrants in Australia. *Journal of Politics* 51 (3): 599–630.

Fiorina, Morris. 1977. An Outline for a Model of Party Choice. *American Journal of Political Science* 21:601–26.

———. 1981. *Retrospective Voting in American National Elections.* New Haven, CT: Yale University Press.

Fiorina, Morris, with Samuel Abrams and Jeremy Pope. 2005. *Culture War? The Myth of a Polarized America.* New York: Longman.

Foner, Eric. 1988. *Reconstruction.* New York: Harper & Row.

Foner, Nancy. 2000. *From Ellis Island to JFK: New York's Two Great Waves of Immigration.* New Haven, CT: Yale University Press.

Fraga, Luis, John A. García, Rodney Hero, Michael Jones-Correa, Valerie Martinez-Ebers, and Gary M. Segura. 2006. Latino National Survey: Executive Summary. Paper presented at the Woodrow Wilson Center, Washington, DC, December 7.

Fraga, Luis, and David Leal. 2004. Playing the "Latino Card": Race, Ethnicity, and National Party Politics. *DuBois Review* 1 (2): 297–317.

Franklin, Charles H. 1984. Issue Preferences, Socialization, and the Evolution of Party Identification. *American Journal of Political Science* 28:459–78.

———. 1992. Measurement and the Dynamics of Party Identification. *Political Behavior* 14:297–309.

Franklin, Charles H., and John E. Jackson. 1983. The Dynamics of Party Identification. *American Political Science Review* 77:957–73.

Frazier, E. Franklin. 1957. *Black Bourgeoisie.* New York: Free Press.

Freer, Regina. 1994. The Black-Korean Conflict. In *The Los Angeles Riots: Lessons for the Urban Future,* edited by Mark Baldesarre. Boulder, CO: Westview Press.

Frymer, Paul. 1999. *Uneasy Alliances.* Princeton, NJ: Princeton University Press.

———. 2005. Race, Parties, and Democratic Inclusion. In *The Politics of Democratic Inclusion,* ed. Christina Wolbrecht and Rodney Hero. Philadelphia: Temple University Press.

Frymer, Paul, Dara Z. Strolovitch, and Dorian T. Warren. 2006. New Orleans Is Not the Exception: Re-politicizing the Study of Racial Inequality. *Du Bois Review* 3 (1): 37–57.

Gans, Herbert. 1992. Second Generation Decline: Scenarios for the Economic and Ethnic Futures of the Post-1965 American Immigrants. *Ethnic and Racial Studies* 15 (April): 173–92.

Gans, Judith. 2006. *A Primer on U.S. Immigration in a Global Economy*. Tucson: Udall Center for Studies in Public Policy, University of Arizona.

Garrow, David. 1986. *Bearing the Cross*. New York: Vintage.

Garvey, Gerald. 1966. The Theory of Party Equilibrium. *American Political Science Review* 60 (March): 29–38.

Gay, Claudine. 2004. Putting Race in Context. *American Political Science Review* 98 (4): 547–62.

Gay, Claudine, and Katherine Tate. 1998. Doubly Bound: The Impact of Gender and Race on the Politics of Black Women. *Political Psychology* 19 (1): 169–84.

Gerber, Alan, and Donald Philip Green. 1998. Rational Learning and Partisan Attitudes. *American Journal of Political Science* 42 (3): 794–818.

Gerring, John. 1999. What Makes a Concept Good? An Integrated Framework for Understanding Concept Formation in the Social Sciences. *Polity* 31 (Spring): 357–93.

Gerstle, Gary, and John Mollenkopf, eds. 2001. *E Pluribus Unum? Contemporary and Historical Perspectives on Immigrant Political Incorporation*. New York: Russell Sage Foundation.

Gillespie, J. David. 1993. *Politics at the Periphery: Third Parties in Two-Party America*. Columbia: University of South Carolina Press.

Gilliam, Franklin D. 1986. Black America: Divided by Class? *Public Opinion* 8:53–57.

Gimpel, James G. 2004. Losing Ground or Staying Even? Republicans and the Politics of the Latino Vote. Washington, DC: Center for Immigration Studies.

Gimpel, James G., and Karen Kaufmann. 2001. Impossible Dream or Distant Reality? Republican Efforts to Attract Latino Voters. *Backgrounder* 9-01. Washington, DC: Center for Immigration Studies.

Glazer, Nathan, and Daniel P. Moynihan. 1963. *Beyond the Melting Pot: The Negroes, Puerto Ricans, Jews, Italians, and Irish of New York City*. Cambridge, MA: MIT Press.

Goldman, Ralph. 1951. Party Chairmen and Party Factions, 1789–1900. PhD diss., University of Chicago.

Goldstein, Joshua, and Ann Morning. 2000. The Multiple-Race Population of the United States: Issues and Estimates. *Proceedings of the National Academy of Sciences* 97 (11): 6230–35.

Goodman, Leo. 1953. Ecological Regressions and the Behavior of Individuals. *American Sociological Review* 18:663–69.

Goodman, William. 1956. *The Two-Party System in the United States*. Princeton, NJ: D. Van Nostrand.

Gordon, Milton M. 1964. *Assimilation in American Life*. New York: Oxford University Press.

Goren, Paul. 2005. Party Identification and Core Political Values. *American Journal of Political Science* 49 (4): 881–96.

Grant-Thomas, Andrew. 2000. Representing the Race: The Black Male Crisis and the Politics of Neglect. PhD diss., University of Chicago.

Graves, Scott, and Jongho Lee. 2000. Ethnic Underpinnings of Voting Preference: Latinos and the 1996 US Senate Election in Texas. *Social Science Quarterly* 81:227–36.

Green, Donald P. 1988. On the Dimensionality of Public Sentiment toward Partisan and Ideological Groups. *American Journal of Political Science* 32:758–80.

Green, Donald P., and Alan Gerber. 1998. Using Tracking Polls to Improve Election Forecasts. *Campaigns and Elections* 19 (August): 23–25, 60.

Green, Donald P., Alan S. Gerber, and Suzanna L. de Boef. 1999. Tracking Opinion over Time. *Public Opinion Quarterly* 63:178–92.

Green, Donald P., and Bradley Palmquist. 1990. Of Artifacts and Partisan Instability. *American Journal of Political Science* 34:872–902.

———. 1994. How Stable Is Party Identification? *Political Behavior* 16:437–66.

Green, Donald P., Bradley Palmquist, and Eric Schickler. 1998. Macropartisanship: A Replication and Critique. *American Political Science Review* 92:883–99.

———. 2002. *Partisan Hearts and Minds.* New Haven, CT: Yale University Press.

Green, Donald P., and Eric Schickler. 1993. Multiple-Measure Assessment of Party Identification. *Public Opinion Quarterly* 57:503–35.

Green, John C., and Paul S. Herrnson, eds. 2002. *Responsible Partisanship? The Evolution of American Political Parties since 1950.* Lawrence: University Press of Kansas.

Greenberg, Stanley. 1990. Report on Democratic Defection. Washington, DC: Greenberg-Lake Company.

Greene, Steven. 1999. Understanding Party Identification: A Social Identity Approach. *Political Psychology* 20:393–403.

———. 2000. The Psychological Sources of Partisan-Leaning Independence. *American Politics Quarterly* 28:511–37.

———. 2002. The Social-Psychological Measurement of Partisanships. *Political Behavior* 24:171–97.

———. 2005. The Structure of Partisan Attitudes: Reexamining Partisan Dimensionality and Ambivalence. *Political Psychology* 26 (5): 809–22.

Greene, William H. 1997. *Econometric Analysis.* 3rd ed. New York: Prentice-Hall.

Groves, Robert. 2007. Nonresponse Rates and Nonresponse Bias in Household Surveys. *Public Opinion Quarterly* 70 (5): 646–75.

Groves, Robert, Mick P. Couper, Stanley Presser, Eleanor Singer, Roger Tourangeau, Giorgina Piani Acosta, and Lindsay Nelson. 2007. Experiments in Producing Nonresponse Bias. *Public Opinion Quarterly* 70 (5): 720–36.

Grynaviski, Jeff. 2006. A Bayesian Learning Model with Applications to Party Identification. *Journal of Theoretical Politics* 18 (3): 323–46.

Gunnell, John. 1995. The Declination of the "State" and the Origins of American Pluralism. In *Political Science and Its History: Research Programs and Political Traditions,* ed. John S. Dryzek, James Farr, and Stephen T. Leonard. Cambridge: Cambridge University Press.

———. 2007. Making Democracy Safe for the World: Political Science between the Wars. In *Modern Political Science: Anglo-American Exchanges since 1880,* ed. Robert Adcock, Mark Bevir, and Shannon Stimson. Princeton, NJ: Princeton University Press.

Gurin, Patricia, Shirley J. Hatchett, and James S. Jackson. 1989. *Hope and Independence*. New York: Russell Sage Foundation.

Hajnal, Zoltan L. 2007. Black Exceptionalism: Insights from Direct Democracy on the Race vs Class Debate. *Public Opinion Quarterly* 71 (4): 560–87.

Hajnal, Zoltan L., and Mark Baldassare. 2001. *Finding Common Ground: Racial and Ethnic Attitudes in California*. San Francisco: Public Policy Institute of California.

Hajnal, Zoltan L., Elisabeth R. Gerber, and Hugh Louch. 2002. Minorities and Direct Legislation: Evidence from California Ballot Proposition Elections. *Journal of Politics* 64 (1): 154–77.

Hajnal, Zoltan L., and Hugh Louch. 2001. *Are There Winners and Losers? Race, Ethnicity, and California's Initiative Process*. San Francisco: Public Policy Institute of California.

Hajnal, Zoltan, and Jessica Trounstine. 2005. Where Turnout Matters: The Consequences of Uneven Turnout in City Politics. *Journal of Politics* 67 (2): 515–35.

Hamilton, Charles V. 1982. Measuring Black Conservatism. In *The State of Black America*, ed. J. Williams. New York: National Urban League.

Harris-Lacewell, Melissa Victoria. 2004. *Barbershops, Bibles, and BET: Everday Talk and Black Political Thought*. Princeton: Princeton University Press.

Hattam, Victoria. 2007. *In the Shadow of Race*. Chicago: University of Chicago Press.

Henderson, Errol. 1996. Black Nationalism and Rap Music. *Journal of Black Studies* 26 (3): 308–39.

———. 2000. War, Political Cycles, and the Pendulum Thesis. In *Multicultural Politics in America*, ed. Yvette Alex-Assensoh and Lawrence J. Hanks. New York: NYU Press.

Hero, Rodney. 1992. *Latinos and the US Political System: Two Tiered Pluralism*. Philadelphia: Temple University Press.

Hetherington, Marc J. 2001. Resurgent Mass Partisanship: The Role of Elite Polarization. *American Political Science Review* 95 (3): 619–31.

Himmelfarb, Gertrude. 1999. *One Nation, Two Cultures*. New York: Alfred P. Knopf.

Hinich, Melvin J., and Michael C. Munger. 1994. *Ideology and the Theory of Political Choice*. Ann Arbor: University of Michigan Press.

Hirano, Shigeo, and James Snyder. 2007. The Decline of Third-Party Voting in the United States. *Journal of Politics* 69 (1): 1–16.

Hirschman, Albert O. 1970. *Exit, Voice, and Loyalty: Responses to Decline in Firms, Organizations and States*. Cambridge, MA: Harvard University Press.

Hirschman, Charles, Richard Alba, and Reynolds Farley. 2000. The Meaning and Measurement of Race in the U.S. Census: Glimpses into the Future. *Demography* 37 (3): 381–93.

Hochschild, Jennifer L. 1981. *What's Fair? American Beliefs about Distributive Justice*. Cambridge, MA: Harvard University Press.

———. 1995. *Facing Up to the American Dream: Race, Class, and the Soul of the Nation.* Princeton, NJ: Princeton University Press.

Hochschild, Jennifer L., and Reuel Rogers. 1999. Race Relations in a Diversifying Nation. In *New Directions: African Americans in a Diversifying Nation,* ed. J. Jackson. Washington, DC: National Policy Association.

Hotelling, Harold. 1929. Stability in Competition. *Economic Journal* 39:41–57.

Howell, S. E. 1980. The Behavioral Component of Changing Partisanship. *American Politics Quarterly* 8:279–302.

Huckfeldt, Robert, and Carol Kohfeld. 1989. *Race and the Decline of Class in American Politics.* Urbana: University of Illinois Press.

Huddy, Leonie. 2001. From Social to Political Identity: A Critical Examination of Social Identity Theory. *Political Psychology* 22 (1): 127–56.

Huntington, Samuel. 2004. The Hispanic Challenge. *Foreign Policy* (March/April): 30–45.

Hurtado, Aida. 1994. Does Similarity Breed Respect? Interviewer Evaluations of Mexican-Descent Respondents in a Bilingual Survey. *Public Opinion Quarterly* 58:77–95.

Hutchings, Vincent L., and Nicholas A. Valentino. 2004. The Centrality of Race in American Politics. *Annual Review of Political Science* 7 (May): 383–408.

Hutchinson, Earl Ofari. 1999. Black Politicians Are Getting Hard to Find; California: The Class Division among African Americans Is Partially to Blame for the Drop. *Los Angeles Times,* 8 February, B5.

Hwang, Sean-Shong, Kevin M. Fitzpatrick, and David Helms. 1998. Class Differences in Racial Attitudes: A Divided Black America? *Sociological Perspectives* 41 (2): 367–80.

Ignatiev, Noel. 1995. *How the Irish Became White.* New York: Routledge.

Jackman, Simon, and Lynn Vavreck. 2009. Meaning Beyond Measure? The Role of Obama's Race in the 2008 Election. Unpublished manuscript, UCLA.

Jackson, John E. 1975. Issues, Party Choices, and Presidential Votes. *American Journal of Political Science* 19:161–85.

Jacobson, Matthew Frye. 1998. *Whiteness of a Different Color: European Immigrants and the Alchemy of Race.* Cambridge, MA: Harvard University Press.

Jacoby, William G. 1982. Unfolding the Party Identification Scale. *Political Methodology* 9:33–59.

Jargowsky, Paul. 1997. *Poverty and Place: Ghettos, Barrios, and the American City.* New York: Russell Sage Foundation.

———. 2003. Stunning Progress, Hidden Problems: The Dramatic Decline of Concentrated Poverty in the 1990s. Washington, DC: Brookings Institution.

Jaynes, Gerald David. 1989. *Branches without Roots.* New York: Oxford University Press.

Jaynes, Gerald David, and Robin M. Williams Jr., eds. 1989. *A Common Destiny: Blacks and American Society.* Washington, DC: National Academy Press.

Jennings, M. Kent, and George B. Markus. 1984. Partisan Orientations over the Long Haul: Results from the Three-Wave Political Socialization Panel Study. *American Political Science Review* 78:1000–18.

Jennings, M. Kent, and Richard G. Niemi. 1968. The Transmission of Political Values from Parent to Child. *American Political Science Review* 62:169–84.

———. 1981. *Generations and Politics*. Princeton, NJ: Princeton University Press.

Jiménez, Tomás R. 2008. Mexican-Immigrant Replenishment and the Continuing Significance of Ethnicity and Race. *American Journal of Sociology* 113 (6): 1527–67.

Johnston, Richard. 2006. Party Identification: Unmoved Mover or Sum of Preferences? *Annual Review of Political Science* 9:329–51.

Joint Center for Political Studies (JCPS). 2003. *Black Elected Officials: A National Roster*. Washington, DC: Joint Center for Political Studies.

Jones, Charles. 1987. Testing a Legislative Strategy: The Congressional Black Caucus Action-Alert Communications Network. *Legislative Studies Quarterly* 12 (4): 521–36.

Jones-Correa, Michael. 1998. *Between Two Nations*. Ithaca, NY: Cornell University Press.

———. 2001. *Governing American Cities: Inter-ethnic Coalitions, Competition, and Conflict*. New York: Russell Sage Foundation.

Jones-Correa, Michael, and David Leal. 1996. Becoming "Hispanic": Secondary Pan-ethnic Identification among Latin American–Origin Populations in the United States. *Hispanic Journal of Behavioral Sciences* 18:214–54.

———. 2001. Political Participation: Does Religion Matter? *Political Research Quarterly* 54:751–70.

Joyce, Patrick. 2003. *No Fire Next Time: Black-Korean Conflicts and the Future of America's Cities*. Ithaca, NY: Cornell University Press.

Kahn, L. M., and K. Morimune. 1979. Unions and Employment Stability: A Sequential Logit Approach. *International Economic Review* 20:217–36.

Kamieniecki, Sheldon. 1985. *Party Identification, Political Behavior, and the American Electorate*. Westport, CT: Greenwood Press.

———. 1988. The Dimensionality of Partisan Strength and Political Independence. *Political Behavior* 10:364–76.

Katz, Richard S. 1979. The Dimensionality of Party Identification: Cross-National Perspectives. *Comparative Politics* 11 (1): 147–63.

Keefe, William J., and Marc J. Hetherington. 2003. *Parties, Politics, and Public Policy in America*. 9th ed. Washington, DC: CQ Press.

Keele, Luke, and Jennifer Wolak. 2006. Value Conflict and Volatility in Party Identification. *British Journal of Political Science* 36 (3): 671–90.

Keeter, Scott, Courtney Kennedy, Michael Dimock, Jonathan Best, and Peyton Craighill. 2007. Gauging the Impact of Growing Nonresponse on Estimates from a National RDD Telephone Survey. *Public Opinion Quarterly* 70 (5): 759–79.

Keith, Bruce E., David B. Magleby, Candice J. Nelson, Elizabeth Orr, Mark C. Westlye, and Raymond E. Wolfinger. 1992. *The Myth of the Independent Voter*. Berkeley: University of California Press.

Kelley, Robin. 1994. *Race Rebels*. New York: Free Press.

Kelly, Caroline. 1988. Intergroup Differentiation in a Political Context. *British Journal of Political Science* 27:319–32.

———. 1989. Political Identity and Perceived Intragroup Homogeneity. *British Journal of Social Psychology* 28:239–50.

Kelly, Nathan J., and Jana Morgan Kelly. 2002. Religion and Latino Partisanship in the United States. Paper presented at the annual meeting of the American Political Science Association, Boston, MA.

Kessel, J. H. 1984. *Presidential Primaries.* Homewood, IL: Dorsey.

Key, V. O., Jr. 1964. *Politics, Parties, and Pressure Groups.* 5th ed. New York: Thomas Y. Crowell Company.

———. 1949. *Southern Politics in State and Nation.* New York: Knopf.

———. 1966. *The Responsible Electorate.* New York: Vintage.

Kim, Claire Jean. 2000. *Bitter Fruit: The Politics of Black-Korean Conflict in New York City.* New Haven, CT: Yale University Press.

Kim, Thomas. 2006. *The Racial Logic of Politics.* Philadelphia: Temple University Press.

Kinder, Donald R., and Lynn Sanders. 1996. *Divided by Color.* Chicago: University of Chicago Press.

Kinder, Donald R., and David O. Sears. 1985. Public Opinion and Political Action. In *Handbook of Social Psychology,* ed. Gardner Lindzey and Eliot Aronson. New York: Random House.

Kinder, Donald R., and N. Winter. 2001. Exploring the National Divide: Blacks, Whites, and Opinion on National Policy. *American Journal of Political Science* 45:439–56.

King, Gary. 1997. *A Solution to the Ecological Inference Problem.* Princeton, NJ: Princeton University Press.

King, Gary, Michael Tomz, and Jason Wittenberg. 2000. Making the Most of Statistical Analyses: Improving Interpretation and Presentation. *American Journal of Political Science* 44 (2): 341–55.

Kirkpatrick, Evron. 1971. Toward a more Responsible Two-Party System: Political Science, Policy Science, or Pseudo-Science? *American Political Science Review* 65:965–90.

Kirschenman, Joleen, and Kathryn M. Neckerman. 1991. "We'd Love to Hire Them, But . . .": The Meaning of Race for Employers. In *The Urban Underclass,* ed. Christopher Jenks and Paul E. Peterson. Washington, DC: Brookings Institution Press.

Kosmin, Barry A., and Ariela Keysar. 1995. Party Political Preferences of U.S. Hispanics: The Varying Impact of Demographic Factors. *Ethnic and Racial Studies* 18 (2): 336–47.

Kramer, Gerald. 1971. Short-Term Fluctuations in U.S. Voting Behavior, 1896–1964. *American Political Science Review* 71 (March): 131–43.

Krosnick, Jon A., and Matthew K. Berent. 1993. Comparisons of Party Identification and Policy Preferences: The Impact of Survey Question Format. *American Journal of Political Science* 37 (3): 941–64.

Kuhn, Thomas. 1962. *The Structure of Scientific Revolutions.* Chicago: University of Chicago Press.

Ladd, Everett Carll. 1991. Party Identification: The Idea and Its Measure. *Public Perspective* (May/June): 17.

Laitin, David D. 1995. Disciplining Political Science. *American Political Science Review* 89 (2): 454–56.

Landry, Bart. 1987. *The New Black Middle Class.* Berkeley: University of California Press.

Lavine, Howard. 2001. The Electoral Consequences of Ambivalence toward Presidential Candidates. *American Journal of Political Science* 45:915–29.

Layman, Geoffrey C. 2001. *The Great Divide: Religious and Cultural Conflict in America; Party Politics.* New York: Columbia University Press.

Layman, Geoffrey C., and Edward Carmines. 1997. Cultural Conflict in American Politics: Religious Traditionalism, Postmaterialism, and U.S. Political Behavior. *Journal of Politics.*

Layman, Geoffrey C., and Thomas M. Carsey. 2002. Party Polarization and "Conflict Extension" in the American Electorate. *American Journal of Political Science* 46:786–802.

Lazarsfeld, Paul, Bernard Berelson, and Hazel Gaudet. 1944. *The People's Choice.* New York: Duell, Sloane, and Pierce.

Leal, David L., Matt A. Barreto, Jongho Lee, and Rodolfo O. de la Garza. 2005. The Latino Vote in the 2004 Election. *PS: Political Science and Politics* 38 (1): 41–50.

Lee, Jennifer, and Frank D. Bean. 2004. America's Changing Color Lines: Immigration, Race/Ethnicity, and Multiracial Identification. *Annual Review of Sociology* 30:221–42.

Lee, Taeku. 2000. Racial Attitudes and the Color Line(s) at the Close of the Twentieth Century. In *The State of Asian Pacific Americans: Race Relations*, ed. P. Ong. Los Angeles: LEAP.

———. 2001. Language-of-Interview Effects, Ethnic Identity, and Polling the Opinions of Latinos. Paper presented at the annual meeting of the Midwest Political Science Association, Chicago.

———. 2002. *Mobilizing Public Opinion.* Chicago: University of Chicago Press.

———. 2004. Pan-ethnic Identity, Linked Fate, and the Political Significance of "Asian American." Paper presented at the annual meeting of the American Association of Public Opinion Research, Tucson, AZ.

———. 2005. Social Constructivism, Self-Identification, and the Survey Measurement of "Race." Manuscript under review.

———. 2008. Race, Immigration, and the Identity-to-Politics Link. *Annual Review of Political Science* 11:457–78.

Lehrer, Warren, and Judith Sloan. 2003. *Crossing the Boulevard.* New York: W.W. Norton.

Leighley, Jan E., and Arnold Vedlitz. 1999. Race, Ethnicity, and Political Participation: Competing Models and Contrasting Explanations. *Journal of Politics* 61 (4): 1092–1114.

Lewin, Kurt. 1948. *Resolving Social Conflicts: Selected Papers in Group Dynamics.* New York: Harper and Brothers.

Lewis, James H., D. Garth Taylor, and Paul Kleppner. 1997. *Metro Chicago Political Atlas, 97–98.* Springfield, IL: Institute for Public Affairs.

Liao, Futing Tim. 1994. *Interpreting Probability Models: Logit, Probit, and Other Generalized Linear Models.* Quantitative Applications in the Social Sciences, 07-101. Thousand Oaks, CA: Sage.

Lieber, Francis. [1838] 1911. *Manual of Political Ethics*. 2 vols. Philadelphia: J. B. Lippincott.

Lieberson, Stanley, and Mary Waters. 1993. The Ethnic Responses of Whites: What Causes Their Instability, Simplification, and Inconsistency? *Social Forces* 72:421–50.

Lien, Pei-te. 2000. *The Making of Asian America through Political Participation*. Philadelphia: Temple University Press.

Lien, Pei-te, M. Margaret Conway, Taeku Lee, and Janelle Wong. 2001. The Pilot Asian American Political Survey: Summary Report. In *The National Asian Pacific American Political Almanac, 2001–2002,* ed. James Lai and Don Nakanishi. Los Angeles: UCLA Asian American Studies Center.

Lien, Pei-te, M. Margaret Conway, and Janelle Wong. 2004. *The Politics of Asian Americans*. New York: Routledge.

Lien, Pei-te, Dianne Pinderhughes, Carol Hardy-Fanta, and Christine Sierra. 2007. The Voting Rights Act and the Election of Nonwhite Officials. *PS* (July): 489–94.

Lipset, Seymour Martin. 1960. *Political Man: The Social Bases of Politics*. Baltimore: Johns Hopkins University Press, 1981.

Lipset, Seymour Martin, Paul F. Lazarsfeld, Allen H. Barton, and Juan Linz. 1954. The Psychology of Voting: An Analysis of Political Behavior. In *Handbook of Social Psychology,* ed. Gardner Lindzey. Vol. 2. Cambridge, MA: Addison-Wesley.

Lipsitz, George. 1998. *Possessive Investment in Whiteness*. Philadelphia: Temple University Press.

Lodge, Milton, and Bernard Tursky. 1979. Comparisons between Category and Magnitude Scaling of Political Opinion Employing SRC/CPS Items. *American Political Science Review* 73:50–66.

Long, J. Scott, and Jeremy Freese. 2006. *Regression Models for Categorical Dependent Variables Using Stata*. 2nd ed. College Station, TX: Stata Press.

Lopez, David, and Yen Espiritu. 1990. Panethnicity in the United States: A Theoretical Framework. *Ethnic and Racial Studies* 13 (2): 198–224.

Lowell, A. Lawrence. 1898. Oscillations in Politics. *Annals of the American Academy of Political and Social Science* 12:69–97.

Lowell, James Russell. 1888. *Political Essays*. Boston: Houghton Mifflin.

Lowi, Theodore J. 1985. *The Personal President*. Ithaca, NY: Cornell University Press.

———. 1992. The State in Political Science: How We Become What We Study. *American Political Science Review* 86 (1): 1–7.

Luks, Samantha, and Laurel Elms. 2003. Generational Change and Partisan Shifts among African Americans. Paper presented at the New Perspectives on the Psychology of Race conference, University of Minnesota.

Lupia, Arthur, and Mathew D. McCubbins. 1998. *The Democratic Dilemma: Can Citizens Learn What They Need to Know?* Cambridge: Cambridge University Press.

MacKuen, Michael B., Robert S. Erikson, and James A. Stimson. 1989. Macropartisanship. *American Political Science Review* 83:1125–42.

———. 1992. Question Wording and Macropartisanship. *American Political Science Review* 85:475–81.

Manza, Jeff, and Clem Brooks. 1999. *Social Cleavages and Political Change: Voter Alignments and U.S. Party Coalitions.* New York: Oxford University Press.

Marable, Manning. 1990. *Race, Reform, and Rebellion.* Jackson: University Press of Mississippi.

———. 1991. *Race, Reform, and Rebellion.* Jackson: University Press of Mississippi.

Massey, Douglas S. 1995. The New Immigration and the Meaning of Ethnicity in the United States. *Population and Development Review* 21:631–52.

———. 2000. The Residential Segregation of Blacks, Hispanics, and Asians, 1970–1990. In *Immigration and Race,* ed. Gerald D. Jaynes. New Haven, CT: Yale University Press.

Massey, Douglas S., and Nancy A. Denton. 1993. *American Apartheid.* Cambridge, MA: Harvard University Press.

Mattei, Franco, and Richard G. Niemi. 1991. Unrealized Partisans, Realized Independents, and the Intergenerational Transmission of Partisan Identification. *Journal of Politics* 53:161–74.

Mayhew, David. 1986. *Placing Parties in American Politics.* Princeton, NJ: Princeton University Press.

McAdam, Doug, Sidney Tarrow, and Charles Tilly. 2002. *Dynamics of Contention.* Cambridge: Cambridge University Press.

McCartney, John. 1991. *Black Power Ideologies.* Philadelphia: Temple University Press.

McCarty, Nolan, Keith T. Poole, and Howard Rosenthal. 2006. *Polarized America: The Dance of Ideology and Unequal Riches.* Cambridge, MA: MIT Press.

McCloskey, Herbert. 1958. Conservatism and Personality. *American Political Science Review* 52:27–45.

———. Consensus and Ideology in American Politics. *American Political Science Review* 58:361–82.

McClosky, Herbert, Paul Hoffmann, and Rosemary O'Hara. 1960. Issue Conflict and Consensus among Party Leaders and Followers. *American Political Science Review* 54:406–27.

McCormick, Joseph, and Sekou Franklin. 2000. Expressions of Racial Consciousness in the African American Community: Data from the Million Man March. In *Multicultural Politics in America,* ed. Yvette Alex-Assensoh and Lawrence J. Hanks. New York: NYU Press.

McDonald, M., and S. E. Howell. 1982. Reconsidering the Reconceptualizations of Party Identification. *Political Methodology* 9:73–92.

McKean, Dayton David. 1949. *Party and Pressure Politics.* Boston: Houghton Mifflin.

McKelvey, Richard. 1976. Intransitivities in Multidimensional Voting Models and Implications for Agenda Control. *Journal of Economic Theory* 12:472–82.

McKelvey, Richard, and Peter Ordeshook. 1976. Symmetric Spatial Games without Majority Rule Equilibria. *American Political Science Review* 70:1172–84.

Melucci, Alberto. 1989. *Nomads of the Present*. Philadelphia: Temple University Press.

Merriam, Charles E. 1922. *The American Party System*. New York: Macmillan.

Merriam, Charles E., and Harold F. Gosnell. 1949. *The American Party System*. New York: Macmillan.

Miller, Arthur H., Patricia Gurin, Gerald Gurin, and Oksana Malanchuk. 1981. Group Consciousness and Political Participation. *American Journal of Political Science* 25 (3): 494–511.

Miller, Arthur H., and Martin P. Wattenberg. 1983. Measuring Party Identification: Independent or No Partisan Preference? *American Journal of Political Science* 27 (1): 106–21.

Miller, Arthur H., and Christopher Wlezien. 1993. The Social Group Dynamics of Partisan Evaluations. *Electoral Studies* 12:5–22.

Miller, Jerome. 1996. *Search and Destroy: African-American Males and the Criminal Justice System*. New York: Cambridge University Press.

Miller, Warren E. 1976. The Cross-National Use of Party Identification as a Stimulus to Political Inquiry. In *Party Identification and Beyond*, ed. Ian Budge, Ivor Crewe, and Dennis Farlie. New York: Wiley.

———. 1991. Party Identification, Realignment, and Party Voting: Back to Basics. *American Political Science Review* 85:557–68.

Miller, Warren E., and National Election Studies. 2000. *American National Election Studies Cumulative Data File, 1948–2000*. Ann Arbor: University of Michigan, Center for Political Studies.

Miller, Warren E., and J. Merrill Shanks. 1996. *The New American Voter*. Cambridge, MA: Harvard University Press.

Mills, Charles. 1997. *The Racial Contract*. Ithaca, NY: Cornell University Press.

Mindiola, Tatcho, Yolanda Flores Niemann, and Nestor Rodriguez. 2002. *Black-Brown: Relations and Stereotypes*. Austin: University of Texas Press.

Morrison, Toni, ed. 1992. *Race-ing Justice, En-gendering Power*. New York: Pantheon.

Nagakura, Daisuke, and Masahito Kobayashi. 2007. Testing the Sequential Logit Model against the Nested Logit Model (October). Social Sciences Research Network (SSRN). http://ssrn.com/abstract=957505.

Naison, Mark. 1983. *Communists in Harlem During the Depression*. New York: Grove Press.

Nakanishi, Don, and James Lai, eds. 2003. *2002–2003 National Asian Pacific American Political Almanac*. Los Angeles: UCLA Asian American Studies Center.

NALEO. 2008. *National Roster of Hispanic Elected and Appointed Officials*. Washington, DC: NALEO.

NALEO Education Fund. 2000. *National Director of Latino Elected Officials*. Los Angeles: NALEO Education Fund.

Ngai, Mae M. 2004. *Impossible Subjects: Illegal Aliens and the Making of Modern America*. Princeton, NJ: Princeton University Press.

Nicholson, Stephen P., and Gary M. Segura. 2005. Issue Agendas and the Politics of Latino Partisan Identification. In *Diversity in Democracy: Minority Representation in the United States*, ed. G. M. Segura and S. Bowler. Charlottesville: University of Virginia Press.

Nie, Norman H., Sidney Verba, and John R. Petrocik. 1979. *The Changing American Voter*. Cambridge, MA: Harvard University Press.

Niemi, Richard G., and M. Kent Jennings. 1991. Issues and Inheritance in the Formation of Party Identification. *American Journal of Political Science* 35:970–88.

Niemi, Richard G., David Reed, and Herbert F. Weisberg. 1991. Partisan Commitment. *Political Behavior* 13:213–20.

Nobles, Melissa. 2000. *Shades of Citizenship*. Stanford, CA: Stanford University Press.

Norrander, Barbara. 1997. The Independence Gap and the Gender Gap. *Public Opinion Quarterly* 61:464–76.

Nussbaum, Paul, and Marcia Gelbart. 2004. The Values Vote: For Some, It Became a Matter of Faith. *Philadelphia Inquirer*, November 4, A1.

Oboler, Suzanne. 1995. *Ethnic Labels, Latino Lives*. Minneapolis: University of Minnesota Press.

O'Connor, Edwin. 1956. *The Last Hurrah*. Boston: Little, Brown.

Oestericher, Richard. 1988. Urban Working-Class Political Behavior and Theories of American Electoral Politics, 1870–1940. *Journal of American History* 74 (4): 1257–86.

Olsen, Marvin. 1970. Social and Political Participation of Blacks. *American Sociological Review* 35:682–97.

Omi, Michael, and Taeku Lee. 2009. Barack Like Me: Our First Asian American President. In *Obama Reflections*. Columbus: Kirwan Institute, Ohio State University.

Omi, Michael, and Howard Winant. 1994. *Racial Formation in the United States*. New York: Routledge.

Ong, Paul, and Don T. Nakanishi. 1996. Becoming Citizens, Becoming Voters: The Naturalization and Political Participation of Asian Pacific Immigrants. In *Reframing the Immigration Debate*, ed. Bill Ong Hing and Ronald Lee. Los Angeles: LEAP Asian Pacific American Public Policy Institute and UCLA Asian American Studies Center.

Ophem, Hans van, and Arthur Schram. 1997. Sequential and Multinomial Logit: A Nested Model. *Empirical Economics* 22:131–52.

Pachon, Harry, and Louis DeSipio. 1994. *New Americans by Choice: Political Perspectives of Latino Immigrants*. Boulder, CO: Westview Press.

Padgett, John F., and Christopher K. Ansell. 1993. Robust Action and the Rise of the Medici, 1400–1434. *American Journal of Sociology* 98:1259–1319.

Padilla, Felix M. 1984. *Latino Ethnic Consciousness*. Notre Dame, IN: Notre Dame University Press.

Page, Benjamin I., and Calvin C. Jones. 1979. Reciprocal Effects of Policy Preferences, Party Loyalties, and the Vote. *American Political Science Review* 73:1071–89.

Pager, Devah. 2003. The Mark of a Criminal Record. *American Journal of Sociology* 108 (5): 937–75.

Paine, Albert Bigelow. 1912. *Mark Twain: A Biography; The Personal and Literary Life of Samuel Langhorne Clemens*. New York: Harper and Brothers.

Pantoja, Adrian, Ricardo Ramírez, and Gary M. Segura. 2001. Citizens by Choice, Voters by Necessity: Patterns of Political Mobilization by Naturalized Latinos. *Political Research Quarterly* 54:729–50.

Pardo, Mary. 1998. *Mexican American Women Activists: Identity and Resistance in Two Los Angeles Communities*. Philadelphia: Temple University Press.

Parent, Wayne, and Paul Steckler. 1985. The Political Implications of Economic Stratification in the Black Community. *Western Political Quarterly* (1985): 522–38.

Park, R. E. 1926. The Urban Community as a Spatial Pattern and Moral Order. In *Urban Community*, ed. E. W. Burgess. Chicago: University of Chicago Press.

Parker, Christopher S. 2003. Shades of Patriotism: Group Identity, National Identity, and Democracy. Paper presented at the annual meeting of the American Political Science Association, Philadelphia.

Pasek, Josh, Alexander Tahk, Yphtach Lelkes, Jon A. Krosnick, B. Keith Payne, Omair Akhtar, and Trevor Tompson. 2009. Determinants of Turnout and Candidate Choice in the 2008 U.S. Presidential Election. *Public Opinion Quarterly* 73 (5): 943–94.

Pearlstein, Steven. 2002. U.S. Poverty Rate Rises, Income Drops: Increase in Ranks of Poor Is First in 8 Years. *Washington Post*, September 25, A3.

Pennock, J. Ronald. 1952. Responsiveness, Responsibility, and Majority Rule. *American Political Science Review* 46:790–807.

Perlmann, Joel, and Mary Waters, eds. 2003. *The New Race Question*. New York: Russell Sage Foundation.

Petrocik, John R. 1974. An Analysis of the Intransitivities in the Index of Party Identification. *Political Methodology* 1:31–47.

———. 1987. Realignment: New Party Coalitions and the Nationalization of the South. *Journal of Politics* 49:347–75.

———. 1996. Issue Ownership in Presidential Elections, with a 1980 Case Study. *American Journal of Political Science* 40 (3): 825–50.

Pew Hispanic Center. 2007. Hispanics and the 2008 Election: A Swing Vote? http://pewhispanic.org/reports/report.php?ReportID=83.

Pinderhughes, Dianne. 1986. Political Choices: A Realignment in Partisanship among Black Voters? In *The State of Black America*, ed. J. Williams. New York: National Urban League.

Pomper, Gerald M. 1971. Toward a More Responsible Two-Party System? What? Again? *Journal of Politics* 33:916–40.

Pomper, Gerald, and Marc Weiner. 2002. Toward a More Responsible Two-Party Voter: The Evolving Bases of Partisanship. In *Responsible Partisanship?* ed. John Green and Paul Herrnson. Lawrence: University Press of Kansas.

Poole, Keith T., and Howard Rosenthal. 1984. The Polarization of American Politics. *Journal of Politics* 46 (4): 1061–79.

———. 1997. *Congress: A Political-Economic History of Roll Call Voting*. New York: Oxford University Press.

Popkin, Samuel L. 1991. *The Reasoning Voter*. Chicago: University of Chicago Press.

Portes, Alejandro, ed. 1995. *The Economic Sociology of Immigration*. New York: Russell Sage Foundation.

Portes, Alejandro, and Robert Bach. 1985. *Latin Journey*. Berkeley: University of California Press.

Portes, Alejandro, and Ruben Rumbaut. 1996. 2nd ed. *Immigrant America*. Berkeley: University of California Press.

Portes, Alejandro, and Min Zhou. 1993. The New Second Generation: Segmented Assimilation and Its Variants. *Annals of the American Academy of Political and Social Sciences* 530 (November): 74–96.

Public Papers of the Presidents of the United States: Lyndon B. Johnson, 1965. 1966. Vol. 2, entry 546, pp. 1037–40. Washington, DC: Government Printing Office.

Przeworski, Adam, and John Sprague. 1986. *Paper Stones: A History of Electoral Socialism*. Chicago: University of Chicago Press.

Rabinowitz, G., and S. E. Macdonald. 1989. A Directional Theory of Issue Voting. *American Political Science Review* 83:93–121.

Ramakrishnan, S. Karthick. 2005. *Democracy in Immigrant America*. Stanford, CA: Stanford University Press.

Ramakrishnan, S. Karthick, and Thomas Espenshade. 2001. Immigrant Incorporation and Political Participation in the United States. *International Migration Review* 35:3.

Ramírez, Ricardo. 2002. The Changing Landscape of California Politics, 1990–2000. PhD diss., Stanford University.

Ramírez, Ricardo, and Janelle Wong. 2006. Nonpartisan Latino and Asian American Contactability and Voter Mobilization. In *Transforming Politics, Transforming America: The Political and Civic Incorporation of Immigrants in America*, ed. T. Lee, K. Ramakrishnan, and R. Ramírez. Charlottesville: University of Virginia Press.

Ranney, Austin. 1951. Toward a More Responsible Two-Party System: A Commentary. *American Political Science Review* 45:488–99.

———. 1954. *The Doctrine of Responsible Party Government*. Urbana: University of Illinois Press.

Rasmussen Reports. 2007. 24% Are Both Fiscal and Socially Conservatives, 9% Fiscally and Socially Liberal. http://www.rasmussenreports.com/public_content/politics/general_politics/november_2007/24_are_both_fiscal_and_socially_con servatives_9_fiscally_and_socially_liberal.

Reed, Adolph. 1999. *Stirrings in the Jug: Black Politics in the Post-segregation Era*. Minneapolis: University of Minnesota Press.

Reimers, David. 1992. *Still the Golden Door: The Third World Comes to America*. New York: Columbia University Press.

Reiter, Howard. 2006. The Study of Political Parties, 1906–2005: The View from the Journals. *American Political Science Review* (November): 613–18.

Riker, William H. 1962. *The Theory of Political Coalitions*. New Haven, CT: Yale University Press.

———. 1982. *Liberalism against Populism*. San Francisco: Freeman.

———. 1990. Political Science and Rational Choice. In *Perspectives on Positive*

Political Economy, ed. James Alt and Kenneth Schepsle. Cambridge: Cambridge University Press.

Roberts, Sam. 2005. Mayor Crossed Ethnic Barriers for Big Victory. *New York Times*, November 10, A1.

Robinson, Edgar E. 1924. *The Evolution of American Political Parties*. New York: Harcourt, Brace.

Robinson, W. S. 1950. Ecological Correlations and the Behavior of Individuals. *American Sociological Review* 15:351–57.

Rodriguez, Clara. 2000. *Changing Race*. Philadelphia: Temple University Press.

Roediger, David. 1991. *The Wages of Whiteness: Race and the Making of the American Working Class*. London: Verso.

Rogers, Reuel. 2000. Between Race and Ethnicity: Afro Caribbean Immigrants, African-Americans, and the Politics of Incorporation. PhD diss., Princeton University.

———. 2006. *Afro-Carribean Immigrants and the Politics of Incorporation: Ethnicity, Exception, or Exit*. Cambridge: Cambridge University Press.

Rose, Tricia. 1994. *Black Noise: Rap Music and Black Culture in Contemporary America*. Hanover, NH: Wesleyan University Press.

Rosenstone, Steven J., and John Mark Hansen. 1993. *Mobilization, Participation, and Democracy in America*. New York: Macmillan.

Rosenstone, Steven J., Roy L. Behr, and Edward H. Lazarus. 1984. *Third Parties in America: Citizen Response to Major Party Failure*. Princeton, NJ: Princeton University Press.

Ross, Dorothy. 1979. The Development of the Social Sciences in America, 1860–1920. In *The Organization of Knowledge in Modern America, 1860–1920*, ed. Alexandra Oleson and John Voss. Baltimore: Johns Hopkins University Press.

———. 1991. *The Origins of American Social Science*. Cambridge: Cambridge University Press.

Rossi, Peter H. 1959. Four Landmarks in Voting Research. In *American Voting Behavior*, ed. E. Burdick and A. Brodbeck. New York: Free Press.

Rusbult, C. E., I. M. Zembrodt, and L. K. Gunn. 1982. Exit, Voice, Loyalty, and Neglect: Responses to Dissatisfaction in Romantic Involvements. *Journal of Personality and Social Psychology* 43:1230–42.

Saad, Lydia. 2010. U.S. Waiting for Race Relations to Improve Under Obama: Hope for Long-Term Improvement Still Abounds. http://www.gallup.com/poll/124181/u.s.-waiting-race-relations-improve-obama.aspx.

Sait, Edward McChesney. 1942. 3rd ed. *American Parties and Elections*. New York: D. Appleton-Century.

Saito, Leland. 1998. *Race and Politics*. Bloomington: Indiana University Press.

Santa Ana, Otto. 2002. *Brown Tide Rising*. Austin: University of Texas Press.

Sartori, Giovanni. 1976. *Parties and Party Systems*. Vol. 1. Cambridge: Cambridge University Press.

Sartori, Giovanni, ed. 1984. *Social Science Concepts*. London: Sage Publications.

Sawyer, Mark. 2005. *Racial Politics in Post-revolutionary Cuba*. New York: Cambridge University Press.

Schattschneider, E. E. 1942. *Party Government*. New York: Holt, Rinehart, and Winston.

———. 1948. *The Struggle for Party Government*. College Park: University of Maryland Press.

Schickler, Eric, and Donald P. Green. 1996. Issues and the Dynamics of Party Identification. *Political Analysis* 5:151–81.

———. 1997. The Stability of Party Identification in Western Democracies: Results from Eight Panel Surveys. *Comparative Political Studies* 30:450–83.

Schier, Steven E. 2002. From Melting Pot to Centrifuge: Immigrants and American Politics. *Brookings Review* 20 (1): 16–19.

Schuman, Howard, Charlotte Steeh, Lawrence Bobo, and Maria Krysan. 1997. *Racial Attitudes in America: Trends and Interpretations*. Rev. ed. Cambridge, MA: Harvard University Press.

Sears, David O., Nicholas A. Valentino, and Sharmaine V. Cheleden. 1999. Long-Term Continuities in the Politics of Race. Paper presented at annual meeting of American Political Science Association, Atlanta.

Segal, Adam J. 2006. Total 2004 Spanish-Language TV Spending by Market and Campaign. Hispanic Voter Project, Johns Hopkins University.

Segura, Gary M., Dennis Falcon, and Harry Pachon. 1997. Dynamics of Latino Partisanship in California: Immigration, Issue Salience, and Their Implications. *Harvard Journal of Hispanic Policy* 10:62–80.

Segura, Gary, and Helena Alves Rodrigues. 2006. Comparative Ethnic Politics in the United States: Beyond Black and White. *Annual Review of Political Science* 9:375–95.

Shaw, Daron, Rodolfo O. de la Garza, and Jongho Lee. 2000. Examining Latino Turnout in 1996: A Three-State, Validated Survey Approach. *American Journal of Political Science* 44 (2): 332–40.

Shelby, Tommie. 2005. *We Who Are Dark: The Philosophical Foundations of Black Solidarity*. Cambridge, MA: Harvard University Press.

Shingles, Richard D. 1981. Black Consciousness and Political Participation: The Missing Link. *American Political Science Review* 75:76–91.

Shively, W. Phillips. 1979. The Development of Party Identification among Adults: Exploration of a Functional Model. *American Political Science Review* 73 (4): 1039–54.

———. 1980. The Nature of Party Identification: A Review of Recent Developments. In *The Electorate Reconsidered*, ed. John C. Pierce and John L. Sullivan. Beverly Hills, CA: Sage.

Shoer, Daniel. 2008. Politics Pays off for Spanish TV. *Miami Herald*, October 24, A1.

Sigelman, Lee. 1982. The Nonvoting Voter in Voting Research. *American Journal of Political Science* 26 (1): 47–56.

Sigelman, Lee, Timothy Bledsoe, Susan Welch, and Michael W. Combs. 1996. Making Contact? Black-White Social Interaction in an Urban Setting. *American Journal of Sociology* 101 (5): 1306–32.

Sitkoff, Harvard. 1978. *A New Deal for Blacks*. New York: Oxford University Press.

Smith, Hedrick. 1988. *The Power Game*. New York: Random House.

Smith, Rogers M. 1997. *Civic Ideals*. New Haven, CT: Yale University Press.

———. 1993. Beyond Tocqueville, Myrdal, and Hartz: The Multiple Traditions in America. *American Political Science Review* 87:549–66.

Smithies, Arthur. 1941. Optimum Location in Spatial Competition. *Journal of Political Economy* 49:423–29.

Snipp, C. Matthew. 2003. Racial Measurement in the American Census. *Annual Review of Sociology* 29:563–88.

Snow, David A., and Robert D. Benford. 1992. Master Frames and Cycles of Protest. In *Frontiers in Social Movement*, ed. Aldon D. Morris and Carol McClurg Mueller. New Haven, CT: Yale University Press.

Sorauf, Frank. 1964. *Political Parties in the American System*. Boston: Little, Brown.

Sowell, Thomas. 1981. *Ethnic America: A History*. New York: Basic Books.

Stern, Mark. 1992. *Calculating Visions: Kennedy, Johnson, and Civil Rights*. New Brunswick, NJ: Rutgers University Press.

Sterne, Evelyn Savidge. 2001. Beyond the Boss: Immigration and American Political Culture from 1880 to 1940. In *E Pluribus Unum? Contemporary and Historical Perspectives on Immigrant Political Incorporation*, ed. Gary Gerstle and John Mollenkopf. New York: Russell Sage Foundation.

Stokes, Donald E. 1963. Spatial Models of Party Competition. *American Political Science Review* 57 (2): 368–77.

Stokes, Susan C. 1999. Political Parties and Democracy. *Annual Review of Political Science* 2:243–67.

Sullivan, John L., James E. Piereson, and George E. Markus. 1978. Ideological Constraint in the Mass Public: A Methodological Critique and Some New Findings. *American Journal of Political Science* 22:233–49.

Sundquist, James L. 1983. *Dynamics of the Party System: Alignment and Realignment of Political Parties in the United States*. Washington, DC: Brookings Institution Press.

Suro, Roberto, and Gabriel Escobar. 2006. 2006 National Survey of Latinos. Washington, DC: Pew Hispanic Center.

Suro, Roberto, Richard Fry, and Jeffrey Passel. 2005. Hispanics and the 2004 Election: Population, Electorate and Voters. Washington, DC: Pew Hispanic Center.

Tajfel, Henri. 1978. Social Categorization, Social Identity, and Social Comparisons. In *Differentiation between Social Groups*, ed. Henri Tajfel. London: Academic Press.

———. 1981. *Human Groups and Social Categories: Studies in Social Psychology*. Cambridge: Cambridge University Press.

Tajfel, Henri, C. Flament, M. G. Billig, and R. F. Bundy. 1971. Social Categorization: An Intergroup Phenomenon. *European Journal of Social Psychology* 1:149–77.

Tajfel, Henri, and John C. Turner. 1986. The Social Identity Theory of Intergroup Behavior. In *Psychology of Intergroup Relations*, ed. S. Worchel and W. G. Austin. Chicago: Nelson.

Tate, Katherine. 1994. *From Protest to Politics*. New York: Russell Sage Foundation.

———. 2003. *Black Faces in the Mirror*. Princeton, NJ: Princeton University Press.

Taylor, Robert Joseph, and Karen Lincoln. 1997. The Million Man March: Portraits and Attitudes. *African American Research Perspectives* 3 (1): 62–67.

Telles, Edward E., and Vilma Ortiz. 2008. *Generations of Exclusion: Mexican Americans, Assimilation, and Race*. New York: Russell Sage Foundation.

Tesler, Michael, and David Sears. 2010. *Obama's Race*. Chicago: University of Chicago Press.

Thompson, Dennis. 1976. *John Stuart Mill and Representative Government*. Princeton, NJ: Princeton University Press.

Thernstrom, Stephan, and Abigail Thernstrom. 1997. *America in Black and White: One Nation, Indivisible*. New York: Simon and Schuster.

Tichenor, Daniel. 2002. *Dividing Lines: The Politics of Immigration Control in America*. Princeton, NJ: Princeton University Press.

Tienda, Marta. 2002. Demography and the Social Contract. *Demography* 39 (4): 587–616.

Trounstine, Jessica. 2006. Dominant Regimes and the Demise of Urban Democracy. *Journal of Politics* 68 (4): 878–92.

Tsongas, Paul. 1995. *Journey of Purpose: Reflections on the Presidency, Multiculturalism, and Third Parties*. New Haven, CT: Yale University Press.

Turner, John C., Michael A. Hogg, Penelope J. Oakes, S. Reicher, and M. Wetherell. 1987. *Rediscovering the Social Group: A Self-Categorization Theory*. Oxford: Basic Blackwell.

Turner, Julius. 1951. Responsible Parties: A Dissent from the Floor. *American Political Science Review* 45:143–52.

Uhlaner, Carole Jean, Bruce E. Cain, and D. Roderick Kiewiet. 1989. Political Participation of Ethnic Minorities in the 1980s. *Political Behavior* 11:195–221.

Uhlaner, Carole Jean, and F. Chris García. 2005. *Foundations of Latino Party Identification: Learning, Ethnicity, and Demographic Factors among Mexicans, Puerto Ricans, Cubans, and Anglos in the United States*. Irvine, CA: Center for the Study of Democracy Research Monograph Series.

Uhlaner, Carole Jean, Mark M. Gray, and F. Chris García. 2000. Ideology, Issues, and Partisanship among Latinos. Paper presented at the annual meeting of the Western Political Science Association, San Jose, CA.

U.S. Census Bureau. 2005. Foreign-Born Population Tops 34 Million, Census Bureau Estimates. http://www.census.gov/newsroom/releases/archives/foreign born_population/cb05-22.html.

U.S. Department of Homeland Security. 2006. *2005 Yearbook of Immigration Statistics*. Washington, DC: U.S. Department of Homeland Security, Office of Immigration Statistics.

Valentine, David C., and John R. Van Wingen. 1980. Partisanship, Independence, and the Partisan Identification Question. *American Politics Quarterly* 8:168–86.

Valentino, Nicholas, and David O. Sears. 2005. Old Times There Are Not Forgotten: Race and Partisan Alignment in the Contemporary South. *American Journal of Political Science* 49 (3): 672–88.

van Buren, Martin. 1867. *Inquiry into the Origin and Course of Political Parties in the United States.* New York: Hurd and Houghton.

van Woodward, C. Vann. 1974. *The Strange Career of Jim Crow.* Oxford: Oxford University Press.

Verba, Sidney, and Norman H. Nie. 1972. *Participation in America: Political Democracy and Social Equality.* Chicago: University of Chicago Press.

Verba, Sidney, Kay Lehman Schlozman, Henry Brady, and Norman H. Nie. 1993. Citizen Activity: Who Participates? What do They Say? *American Political Science Review* 87 (2): 303–18.

Verba, Sidney, Kay Lehman Schlozman, and Henry Brady. 1995. *Voice and Equality.* Cambridge, MA: Harvard University Press.

Volpp, Leti. 2001. "Obnoxious to Their Very Nature": Asian Americans and Constitutional Citizenship. *Citizenship Studies* 5 (1): 57–71.

Walters, Ronald W. 1988. *Black Presidential Politics in America: A Strategic Approach.* Albany: State University of New York.

Walton, Hanes. 1972. *Black Political Parties: An Historical and Political Analysis.* New York: Free Press.

Waters, Mary. 1990. *Ethnic Options.* Berkeley: University of California Press.

Wattenberg, Martin. 1996. *The Decline of American Political Parties, 1952–1994.* Cambridge, MA: Harvard University Press.

Weber, Max. 1946. *From Max Weber: Essays in Sociology.* New York: Oxford University Press.

Weisberg, Herbert F. 1980. A Multidimensional Conceptualization of Party Identification. *Political Behavior* 2 (1): 33–60.

———. 1983. A New Scale of Partisanship. *Political Behavior* 5 (4): 363–76.

———. 1993. Political Partisanship. In *Measures of Political Attitudes,* ed. John P. Robinson, Phillip R. Shaver, and Lawrence Wrightsman. San Diego: Academic Press.

———. 2002. The Party in the Electorate as a Basis for More Responsible Parties. In *Responsible Partisanship?* ed. John C. Green and Paul S. Herrnson. Lawrence: University Press of Kansas.

———. 2003. The Political Psychology of Party Identification. In *Electoral Democracy,* ed. Michael B. MacKuen and George Rabinowitz. Ann Arbor: University of Michigan Press.

Weiss, Nancy J. 1983. *Farewell to the Party of Lincoln.* Princeton, NJ: Princeton University Press.

Welch, Susan, and Michael W. Combs. 1985. Intra-racial Differences in Attitudes of Blacks: Class Cleavages or Consensus? *Phylon* 66 (2): 91–97.

Welch, Susan, and Lorn Foster. 1987. Class and Conservatism in the Black Community. *American Politics Quarterly* 15 (4): 445–70.

Welch, Susan, and Lee Sigelman. 1993. The Politics of Hispanic Americans: Insights from National Surveys, 1980–1988. *Social Science Quarterly* 74:76–94.

White, John Kenneth. 1992. Responsible Party Government in America. *Perspectives on Political Science* 21 (2): 80–90.

Wilson, David. 2002. Blacks Making Huge Strides in March to Top Ranks. *Atlanta Journal Constitution,* July 24, 14A.

Wilson, William Julius. 1978. *The Declining Significance of Race*. Chicago: University of Chicago Press.

———. 1987. *The Truly Disadvantaged*. Chicago: University of Chicago Press.

Wittman, Donald. 1977. Candidates with Policy Preferences: A Dynamic Model. *Journal of Economic Theory* 14:180–89.

Wolfe, Alan. *One Nation, After All*. New York: Viking Press.

Wolfinger, Raymond E. 1965. The Development and Persistence of Ethnic Voting. *American Political Science Review* 59 (4): 896–908.

Wong, Janelle S. 2000. The Effects of Age and Political Exposure on the Development of Party Identification among Asian American and Latino Immigrants in the United States. *Political Behavior* 22 (4): 341–71.

———. 2001. *The New Dynamics of Immigrants' Political Incorporation*. PhD diss., Yale University.

———. 2006. *Democracy's Promise: Immigrants and American Civic Institutions*. Ann Arbor: University of Michigan Press.

Wong, Janelle, Karthick Ramakrishnan, Taeku Lee, and Jane Junn. 2009. Race-Based Considerations and the 2008 National Asian American Survey. *Du Bois Review* 6:219–38.

York, Anthony. 1999. Latino Politics. *California Journal* (April).

Zaller, John. 1992. *The Nature and Origins of Mass Opinion*. Cambridge: Cambridge University Press.

Zaller, John, and Stanley Feldman. 1992. A Simple Theory of the Survey Response: Answering Questions versus Revealing Preferences. *American Journal of Political Science* 36 (3): 579–616.

Zhou, Min, and John R. Logan. 1991. In and Out of Chinatown: Residential Mobility and Segregation of New York City's Chinese. *Social Forces* 70 (2): 387–407.

Index